Word 2003

Document Automation with VBA, XML, XSLT, and Smart Documents

Scott Driza

Wordware Publishing, Inc.

Library of Congress Cataloging-in-Publication Data

Driza, Scott.
Word 2003 document automation with VBA, XML, XSLT, and Smart Documents /
by Scott Driza.
p. cm.
Includes index.
ISBN 1-55622-086-3 (pbk.)
1. Microsoft Word--Handbooks, manuals, etc. 2. Microsoft Visual Basic for applications--Handbooks, manuals, etc. 3. XML (Document markup language) -- Handbooks, manuals, etc. 4. XSLT (Computer program language) -- Handbooks, manuals, etc. I. Title.
Z52.5.M52D77 2005
005.52--dc22 2005009717
CIP

2320 Los Rios Boulevard
Plano, Texas 75074

Printed in the United States of America

ISBN 13: 978-1-55622-086-3
ISBN 10: 1-55622-086-3
10 9 8 7 6 5 4 3 2 1
0506

All inquiries for volume purchases of this book should be addressed to Wordware Publishing, Inc., at the above address. Telephone inquiries may be made by calling:

(972) 423-0090

For Debra and Connor

Contents

Acknowledgments

I'd like to thank my beautiful wife, Debra, for being the single most important person in my life! Thanks to my son, Connor, for cheering me up with his little smile. I also need to mention our two dogs, Shani and Peanut (Peanut for growling when appropriate and Shani for giving moral support). Credit also goes to my parents, Steve and Dolores Driza, for overcoming all obstacles and engraining a "can do" attitude in me. In that respect I also owe a great deal to my brother and his wife, Steve and Rene Driza, and my sister and her husband, Sue and Mark Fadden, and finally, my uncle, Mark Driza.

I am indebted to Wes Beckwith, Beth Kohler, and Tim McEvoy from Wordware Publishing, Inc. They are a great group of people and it has been a pleasure working with them. They have helped me tremendously, and everything appearing correctly in this book is the result of their effort; any mistakes are mine and mine alone.

Perhaps the most credit for this material belongs to Melvin Helfand (the father of modern Word programming). His innovative thoughts and our working relationship through the years had a big influence on me.

Special thanks to all of the people who were involved with the cultivation of this material and any growth I've undergone in the information technology arena: Carl Bucaro, Ken Cornell, Tom Finney, Richard Astle, Donovan Plummer, Steven Haynes, Bayard Woodworth, Brigette Kaluzny, Ted Yates, Harry Kimura, Gordon Neuls, Dr. William Sun, Joe Chang, and Binh Li.

Special thanks to some of the finest business people and managers I've had the opportunity to see in action: Scott McNulla, Tim Green, Ed Stevens, Jeff Hallberg, Bill McFarlane, Chris Randazzo, John Lind, Jason Connolly, T.J. Maggliozzo, Brett Schaffer, Ken Muntz, and Carl Sternberg.

Thanks throughout the years to: Bob Rockwell, Thaddeus Murphy, Shannon Farley, Tim Probst, Tom Struble, J.B. Trew, Randy Lee, Bryan Gaston, Mark Strachota, Leo Irakliotis, Art Hogue, Andy Longo, Doug Melton, Brian Howard, Chuck Cornell, Arthur LeFrancois, Mark Shaklette, Craig Grotts, Dann O'Brien, David Lehman, Clare Hallan, Sara Walker, Larry and Geraldine Lusk, John Nix, Richard and Melissa Brown, Tom Barry, Linda and Danny Cannon, Steve Bender and Dawn Brandewie, Nancy and Jerry Brandewie, Alfred Brophy, Lee Cannon, Rodney Cooke and Page Dobson, Robert T. Keel and Martha Kulmacz, Cheyenne Dupree, Donnie Wachtman, Brad Warren, Jude Henry, Keith and Ashleigh Muse,

… and, of course, Dr. Thomas Edward Wyatt.

Introduction

Microsoft Word is more than just a word processing application; Word documents and templates can be programmed to provide a level of functionality previously unavailable. Microsoft Word 2003 has the ability to fundamentally change the way users interact with documents and offers improved data integration via XML and smart documents. With this new functionality, Office developers finally have the ability to create truly interactive documents. The embedded development tools still exist (including Microsoft Visual Basic for Applications, or VBA). In addition, there are two fundamental improvements that change the way we need to think about Word solutions: Word XML and smart documents. Word 2003 uses XML as both a native document format (.doc is still around as well) and the structural foundation upon which smart documents are built. In addition, Visual Studio (either 6 or .NET) can be used to write code behind the documents.

XML in Word 2003

Word documents typically contain more enterprise data than any other source. The problem is that it has been exceedingly difficult to work with this data outside of Microsoft Word. The data was essentially locked away because of the proprietary binary (*.doc) format of Word. Of course, developers, being as creative as they are, began devising all sorts of ways of getting at the Word data. Routines to loop through documents, slow and clumsy as they were, became de rigueur in many organizations. Other organizations chose to save in the RTF format and attempt to parse through the documents looking for keywords. Earlier versions of Word lured developers in by exposing its COM objects, but this method was limited at best and required complicated, error-fraught programming to get at the data.

Word 2003 approaches the data repository aspect of Word by utilizing XML. XML is great for relational data, and, when combined with schemas and XSLT, is also great for data presentation. When that is all rolled together, and you grasp the concept that when users are editing a Word document they are really editing data within an XML document, then you have a whole new approach to solution building. This has tremendous potential for traditional data gathering applications as well as document management systems, data mining, and database-aware Word documents. These new opportunities will definitely impact how developers build solutions based on Word 2003.

XML schemas can be used to define the structure of data that the user enters into a document. The end user has all the capabilities of Word, and can seamlessly enter data in the structure required by the schema. Word allows users to save documents as XML data only, as XML data plus formatting using a predefined WordprocessingML schema, or with an XSLT transformation that modifies the structure of the XML data.

VBA in Word 2003

Word 2003 contains the latest version of VBA. This version is relatively equivalent in functionality to Visual Basic 6. It contains many additional features that were not included in the previous version of VBA, including modeless UserForms and support for many additional controls. VBA allows you to customize and program almost every function available through Word's built-in toolbars and native functions.

Word makes all of its elements available to VBA as objects. Word 2003 has even added new objects to support XML and smart document functionality. In addition, VBA is the language used by all of the other Office applications, including Access and Outlook. Other third-party software developers are also implementing VBA into their applications. The latest versions of Visio and AutoCAD both contain VBA.

VBA is the macro language underlying all of Microsoft's Office applications, including Access 2003. VBA is rapidly gaining acceptance as a macro language that can easily be incorporated into many different programs. This enables you to transfer your VBA knowledge to any application that takes advantage of VBA. This also enables a process called "automation," which allows you to simply reference another VBA application in your program and work with its object model directly. We'll get to this later.

Keep in mind that VBA code is produced when you record a macro in any Office application. Sometimes you can overcome sticking points by simply editing a recorded macro and seeing the relevant code. Of course, VBA enables many functions that a recorded macro will never be able to duplicate.

What Is Document Automation?

The preparation of documents has always been a tedious process, especially when lengthy documents were typed page by page. And remember — the typewriter was a revolutionary instrument. Even though early word processors were a major advance over the typewriter, by today's standards they are both inefficient. Yet despite all of the recent advancements in office workflow solutions, most organizations still prepare documents in an outdated fashion. At best, they may have an off-the-shelf solution. These are notoriously difficult to work with, may not even let an organization use its own documents, and sometimes don't even allow for the file to be exported to a word processor.

VBA Word-based document creation provides a way for the user to not only control the preparation of documents (a major advantage), but also easily include additional functionality that was unheard of just a few years ago. The real power of the Microsoft suite of Office products is lying dormant in most offices. True workflow solutions can easily, cheaply, and quickly be created using these products — but the mindset in many organizations is often more in line with traditional approaches. In the end, many managers find it easier to hire qualified consultants to do work for them that may well be within the reach of their competent business users. Maintaining Office 2003 systems doesn't require a programming genius; all users can make suggestions and, in some cases, even implement the changes.

In all cases an automated template solution will obtain the correct data to enter into the document; this data may be obtained from a database or from a UserForm that queries a user to input relevant information. This data is used either to fill the document or to make decisions and react accordingly. The first usage is simple to illustrate. Imagine having a lengthy contract that requires the names of each party in several places. You can type this into a text box and automatically insert it in appropriate places in the document. The second usage is somewhat more multifaceted. Let's assume that there are different versions of the same document depending on whether a party is a business or an individual. You could have an option button that required the user to choose either a business or individual. If "Individual" were checked, you could put in different requirements, eliminate lengthy signature blocks, and use the correct terminology. If "Business" were checked, the code could ask for a state of incorporation, include lines for titles in the signature block, and include wholly different provisions. This can all be done without ever manually editing the document.

Smart Documents

It has always been possible to create customized Word solutions to walk users through the creation of documents. First there was WordBasic, then (and still) VBA, and now — thanks to the new XML support — we have smart documents. Smart documents are solutions that utilize XSD, XML, and managed code that executes behind Word 2003. The real crux of this solution as compared with the UserForm-driven applications of the past is that it allows context-sensitive interaction with the document. This requires a new approach to interacting with users. Previously, in a UserForm-driven template solution, it was possible to prevent a user from entering certain information if other prerequisite information wasn't entered. Now, the relatively unstructured framework of a Word document (previously, the end document was the result of entering the data in the UserForms) can actually be used as both the entry point of the data and the resultant document.

This custom task pane can be used to guide the user through the application, prompting for data to add to the document, helping the user navigate the solution, and validating both the structure and content of the information. You can build smart document solutions based either on an existing or new Word 2003 document. An XML schema defines the structure and content of the data in the document, just like other XML-based documents. Then you can write code to automate it by implementing the ISmartDocument interface defined in the smart documents type library and creating forms for the custom task pane that guide the user. Your Word solution can leverage the new collaboration features of the Microsoft Office System to route documents to various people, such as to a manager to approve a deal proposal before sending it to a client.

Smart documents also alleviate one of the most common Office solution problems — multiple versions of the same solution floating around the network. There wasn't really a foolproof way to ensure version control with network-available Word templates. This problem became more complicated as an organization grew larger. Smart documents solve this problem utilizing XML expansion packs. These expansion packs reside on the server and contain a list of the solution's required files and its current version. Of course, this introduces other complications, but they are largely networking/procedural complications rather than problems with each individual template. The smart document has information about where to find these files embedded within the solution. Every time the solution is instantiated, it can automatically check for new files and download the appropriate pieces so that the end user has the current version of the solution.

Smart Tags

Office developers have been slow to integrate smart tag functionality, which is greatly expanded in Office 2003. Word 2003 has made smart tags both easier to develop and more intuitive than in Word 2002. Word 2003 also offers two new interfaces: ISmartTagRecognizer2 and ISmartTagAction2. Best of all, the smart tag model transcends all of the applications in the Microsoft Office System. This makes it easier to reuse code and complete tags across the Office applications

Basically, smart tags recognize text in a Word 2003 document and provide a menu of actions that a user can take. These can range from inserting text into a document to launching another application. Smart tags are an integral part of functionality of smart documents, and the underlying structure of smart tags allows Word programmers to utilize context sensitivity. Unfortunately, smart tags exist relatively independent of each other and don't lend themselves to offering a comprehensive, structured solution. You will notice in the later chapters that smart document solutions reference the same type library that smart tags utilize, the Microsoft Smart Tags 2.0 Type Library.

Who Is This Book For?

On that note, it is probably a good time to describe the intended audience for this book. One audience for this book includes advanced Word users who are looking to automate the task of preparing documents. In an effort not to bore these users, an effort has been made to be brief when dealing with relatively simple concepts. Following a similar vein, an effort has been made to distinguish particularly useful concepts or, in some cases, even snippets of code where applicable.

Another audience for this book includes competent programmers who are unfamiliar with document automation and the Word object model. In many ways, document automation may be more difficult for people with years of programming experience. In many cases, these programmers have good skills dealing with relational data; however, their solutions often mimic simple table design structures. While this may be perfectly fine when working in an information gathering environment, the preparation of documents lends itself to establishing a logical flow that guides the user through the preparation of the document. This is one of the two aspects of document automation that is somewhat out of the ordinary for most programmers. The other aspect is that of creating and piecing together complex documents. In a large document automation solution there may be hundreds of alternative paragraphs or even sentences. Further, these may have other textual dependencies throughout the document. Keep this in mind at the outset and obtain the help of someone familiar with the documents right away. This will help you avoid unnecessary headaches.

Example files are available at www.docbuilder.com and www.wordware.com/files/wordvba2.

Happy coding!

Chapter 1

Automation Without Programming

Introduction

Microsoft Word is easy to use, but it is an amazingly complex tool. A novice Windows user can generally create a simple document right out of the box. I've also seen experienced programmers spend countless hours trying to format tables and struggle with the proper application of styles. There are innumerable ways to accomplish many common tasks. In most instances, the "right" method may boil down to a question of preference. Document automation is a prime example of this. There is no "right" way to automate a document.

Most of the topics set forth in this chapter are relatively widely known and covered, at least to some extent, by most Word manuals. However, those manuals rarely cover topics in the context of document automation. Hopefully, this chapter will introduce you to some novel ways of using common Word functionality to make your life (or the lives of your users) easier.

Because of the relative simplicity of each of these topics, even relative Word novices can benefit by implementing one or more of them. In many cases, the simple techniques described here may be all the document automation they need.

Why Templates?

Many, if not most, non-retail businesses require the use of frequently and repetitively prepared documents. Typically, each time a new document is needed, a Word user will open a recent version of the same document, and click File | Save As to save the document under a new name. There is, of course, nothing intrinsically wrong with this approach — as long as you remember to delete from the Save As file any changes made to the basic document that were specific to the last transaction. However, time and again we have seen examples where changes made for a particular transaction or situation were adopted as new standard provisions without much thought being given to the effect of the changes on other transactions or situations. In other cases, metadata specific to a completely separate transaction has been discovered in a document. These unfortunate oversights boil down to a simple misuse of Microsoft Word. If a document is reused with that much frequency, it should be turned into a template.

Fortunately, Word provides a simple way to preserve commonly used documents through its template feature. Templates are essentially the shell of a document in a basic, mostly untouchable form. After a document is saved as a template, new documents can be created that are essentially copies of the templated document. The template (and its accompanying VBA code) stays in the background in its original form. You can, of course, edit the template at any time. However, the use of the template eliminates inadvertent changes to standardized documents.

Templates also open the door to numerous other forms of customization and automation. For example, a custom template can have a different font and different margin sizes than found in your "normal" template — the template Word runs by default. As to automation, you will see how templates are an integral part of most of the projects outlined in this book.

Creating a Template

Creating a template is simple. Just do the following:

1. Create the document you want to save as a template.
2. Click **File | Save As**.
3. From the Save as type drop-down list, choose **Document Template**.

As you can see, creating a template is very easy.

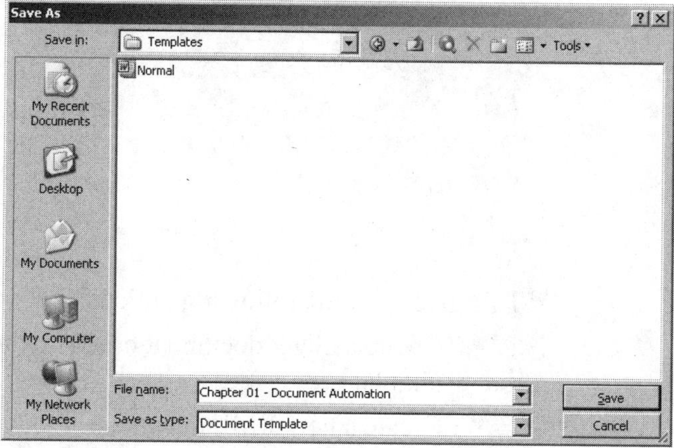

Figure 1-1

Using Templates

Office 2003 has dramatically improved the ability to create documents based on templates. You now have the option to choose templates from many different locations. To create a document based on a template:

1. Click **File | New**.
2. This will open up the New Document task pane shown in Figure 1-2.

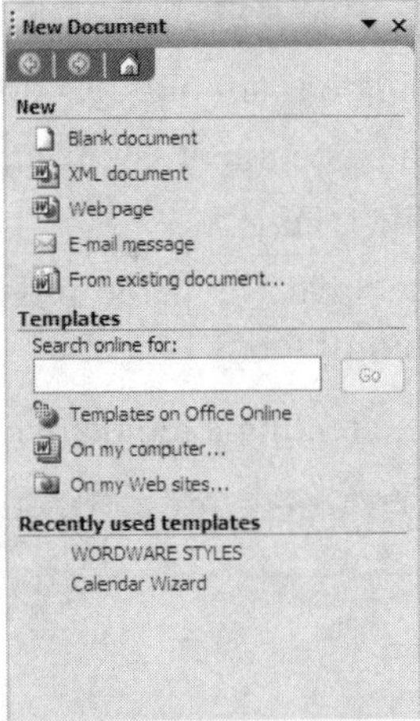

Figure 1-2

This gives you the following options:

- Create a blank document based on the Normal template.
- Create a new XML document.
- Create a new web page (HTML).
- Compose an email message.
- Create a new document based on an existing document.
- Search Office Online for a template.
- Navigate templates on Office Online (opens a browser session).

- Open the traditional File | New dialog box.
- Open a template from a web site location.
- Create a document based on a recently used template.

Workgroup Templates

If more than one person is going to use a template and you have a network, you should consider installing your templates on your network server and accessing them through the workgroup templates feature. This will avoid the necessity of updating each computer every time a template is added or changed.

To allow your PCs to access templates located on a network, each PC must be set up to recognize workgroup templates. Assume that your network location for templates is J:\Wordtemplates. On each PC:

1. Click **Tools | Options | File Locations**.
2. Highlight the line **Workgroup templates** and click **Modify**.

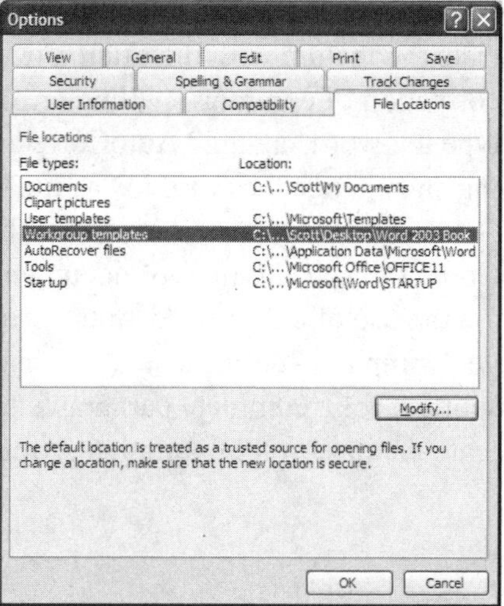

Figure 1-3

3. In the dialog box that opens, go to the network drive (J) and find and highlight the Wordtemplates folder.
4. Click **OK** twice.

Even if you are not networked, you might want to set up a special templates folder on the C drive as a container for workgroup templates (or user templates) — primarily because of the ease of finding and editing those templates relative to the default Word 2003 location. Workgroup templates appear in the same File | New window as user templates.

Note: Although workgroup templates can be used by multiple people at the same time (since each is working with a copy of the template, and not the original), template modifications cannot be saved to the network drive if anyone has a document open that was created with the template.

AutoCorrect

AutoCorrect is another widely known feature whose automation benefit is relatively unknown. Many Word users know about the AutoCorrect feature of Word — they associate the feature with the often unwanted automatic correction of common spelling errors. For example, if you type the word "agian," AutoCorrect will correct the spelling and change the word to "again."

Somewhat less well known is the ability of AutoCorrect to speed typing of documents. This is accomplished via the use of customized AutoCorrect lists. The concept is very simple — define a set combination of characters as a shortcut for a complete paragraph and you can easily automate the insertion of complete clauses.

Using AutoCorrect

Assume, for example, that the name of your company is "North American First Widgets and Capital Formation Company, Incorporated." To avoid having to type that name numerous times:

1. Click **Tools | AutoCorrect Options**.
2. In the box titled Replace, type **nafw** (see Figure 1-4).
3. In the box titled With, type **North American First Widgets and Capital Formation Company, Incorporated**.
4. Click **Add** and **OK**.

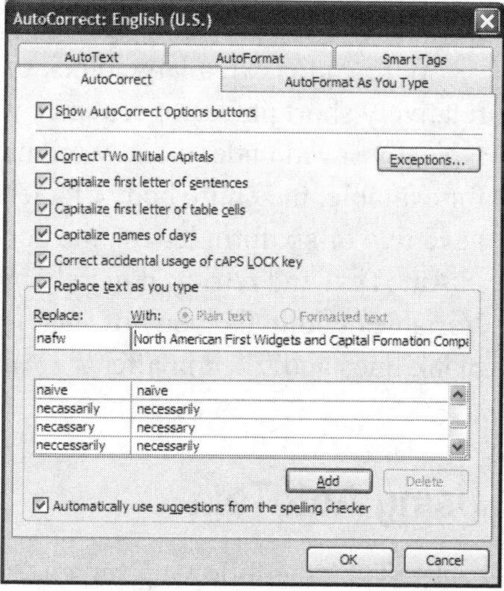

Figure 1-4

Now you can type the name of your company merely by typing the letters "nafw" and hitting the Spacebar or Enter or typing a punctuation mark. Doing so will cause Auto-Correct to expand the entry to the full name.

Caution: AutoCorrect clearly has a place in reducing the amount of typing for many phrases. There is a downside, however; you have to remember the abbreviation you used to trigger AutoCorrect. In common practice, it seems to work really well for a limited number of frequently used entries (8 to 10). After that, we found users spending significant amounts of time trying to remember what letters to type to activate the AutoCorrect. The lack of an easy-to-use interface further complicates this problem.

AutoText

AutoText is essentially an expanded cousin of AutoCorrect. From the perspective of document automation, AutoText is much more versatile and can begin to provide some real and meaningful document automation.

With AutoText, a large block of text (as opposed to the relatively short phrase or sentence with AutoCorrect) is typically saved under a one-word name. That text can be, for example, the entire body of a letter. Accordingly, if you have five or six form letters, the body of each can be saved in AutoText and retrieved merely by typing a single word. Variables within the body of such letters can be stored as blank lines and filled in after the AutoText is inserted.

Using AutoText

1. Type the following sentence: **The quick brown fox jumped over the Land Rover.** (This sentence has been updated to the 21st century.)
2. Select (highlight) the entire sentence and either choose **Edit | Copy** or press **Ctrl + C** (they do the same thing). Include the paragraph mark if you want your AutoText to be a separate paragraph and/or contain the formatting in which it was originally typed.
3. Click **Insert | AutoText | AutoText** (twice) | **New**.

4. In the AutoText entry area, type **brownfox** as the name for your AutoText and click **OK**.

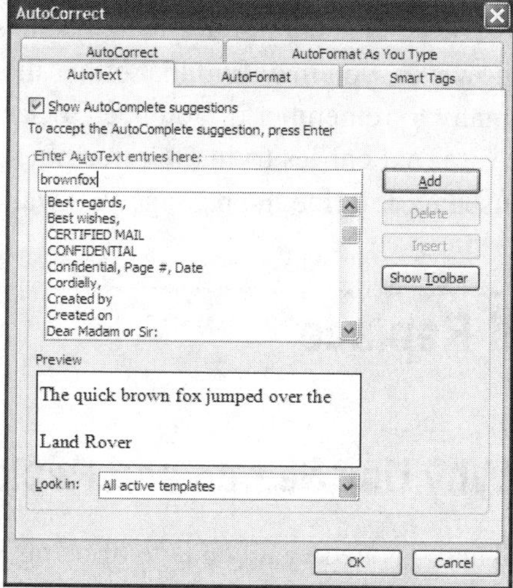

Figure 1-5

Retrieving Your AutoText

To retrieve the AutoText you just created, begin by typing "brownfox" and the pop-up box displayed in Figure 1-6 will appear. Once this pop-up is displayed, you only need hit Enter for the text to appear.

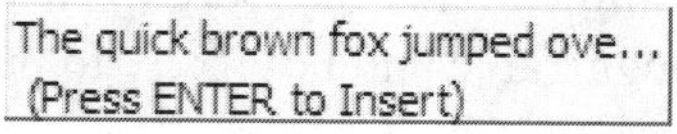

The quick brown fox jumped ove...
(Press ENTER to Insert)

Figure 1-6

Alternatively, you can use the following routine:

1. Place your cursor at the point you want to insert your AutoText.
2. Click **Insert | AutoText | AutoText** (twice).
3. In the dialog box that appears, click once on the name of the AutoText you want to insert (in this example, "brownfox") and then click **Insert**.

Practical Limitations

In practice AutoText works great for about 20 to 30 entries — more than enough for most businesses. Beyond that, however, you may find that either there are simply too many to remember or you need to scroll through the list of AutoText entries trying to remember which keyword you used to describe the passage you want.

Search and Replace

Why Use Search and Replace?

There is one key advantage of using Word's Search and Replace functions to update either a template created document (as we recommend) or even the last used version of your form letter. The advantage occurs if the same piece of variable information is used more than once. If that is the case, then Search and Replace will eliminate the duplicate typing.

The first key to keep in mind is to use easily recognized words as your "search" words. If you set up a form as a template and you want to use Search and Replace to update it, then we recommend that the words you use should be both easily recognizable and not likely to be confused with intended words.

Tip: You may even want to enclose the words in some sort of bracket {}, [], () or pipes ||.

Our recommendation is that you use all capital letters for the words to be replaced, and that those words prompt you to make the change. In any event, it is important that the words to be replaced not mislead the user into overlooking the replacement.

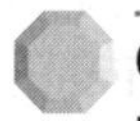

Caution: Make sure your words are unique and will not occur naturally elsewhere in the letter. Consider using [LASTNAME] instead of "last" — you may replace something inadvertently, such as "send in your payment prior to the *last* day of the month."

Consider the following letter as a simple example:

[PREFIXNAME] [FIRSTNAME] [LASTNAME]
[CUSTOMERADDRESS]
[CITYSTATEZIP]

Dear [PREFIXNAME] [LASTNAME],

We are pleased to enclose the Widgets you ordered from us. [PREFIXNAME] [LASTNAME], we know that you have a choice of Widget suppliers, and appreciate your choosing us.

If you have any questions or need any help with your Widgets, please do not hesitate to call your personal sales rep, Joe Smith.

Sincerely yours,

Here, the key benefit of the Search and Replace comes from being able to avoid typing [PREFIXNAME] [LASTNAME] more than once.

Using Search and Replace

Using Search and Replace is one of the more common Word actions known to most users. Nevertheless, for completeness, here are the instructions:

1. Click **Edit | Replace** or (our preference) press **Ctrl + H**.
2. In the "Find what" section of the dialog box that appears, type **[PREFIXNAME]**. (Note that if prior to opening the Search and Replace dialog box you selected this word, it would have automatically been copied into the "Find what" section.)

3. In the "Replace with" section of the dialog box, type **Mr.**
4. Click **Replace All**.

Repeat this process for each word you want replaced.

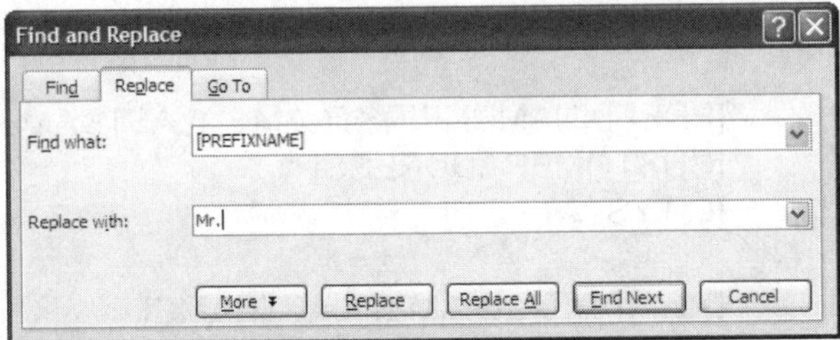

Figure 1-7

Assuring Replacement

You can assure that every word required to be replaced is actually replaced by typing a list of the words to be replaced at the beginning of the document or template. Follow this list with either a page break (Ctrl + Enter or Insert | Break | Page Break) or a section break (see the following section). When you are done with the word replacement, delete the page and/or section containing the list.

Section Breaks

It's easy to use section breaks to bundle multiple documents. Frequently, more than one document is sent to a customer at the same time. So, for example, a sales order is likely to be accompanied by a thank you letter, and a sales proposal is likely to have a brief cover letter. If you prepare legal documents, chances are that each document is part of a package of documents.

If you bundle each of the related documents into a single document, using section breaks between each document, then, assuming that you use Search and Replace or one of the other methods of updating variable information described in this book, you will be able to type all of the documents at once, and never have to retype the same information. So, for example, if you use Search and Replace to insert a customer's name, it will appear in each of the bundled documents.

Why Use Section Breaks?

As mentioned previously, you can use page breaks to separate multiple documents. Why then do we recommend the use of section breaks? Because section breaks are much more flexible than mere page breaks in that they can be used to vary formatting, allow different margins on the same page, mix columns and text on the same page, and have different headers and footers on different pages of the same document. Most important, however, from the context of document automation and assembly, is the relative ease with which each document can be given its own page numbers (see below).

Inserting a Section Break

To insert a section break:

1. Click **Insert | Break**.
2. In the Break dialog, under Section break types, choose **Next Page**.

Note that Next Page as opposed to Continuous is the appropriate choice for bundling multiple documents. If, on the other hand, you want to perform one of the other tasks enabled by section breaks (such as mixing columns and text on the same page) choose a Continuous section break. The other types of section breaks allowed by the dialog box, Even Page and Odd Page, are probably most suitable for separating the chapters of a book or long paper where it is desired that all chapters start on the same side.

Page Numbers

No discussion of section breaks would be complete without a reference to page numbers. As set forth above, page numbers are one of the principal reasons for using section breaks to bundle multiple related documents. Page numbers also cause the most problems for those who attempt such bundling. The reason is the tendency of Word to continue page numbers from one document to the next notwithstanding the section break between documents. Word does, however, provide an easy way around this problem. The following steps describe the most commonly used method to insert page numbers.

1. Start on the first page of your bundled document.
2. Click **Insert | Page Numbers**.
3. In the dialog box that appears, click the Alignment drop-down box to change the alignment to Center. (You can, of course, place the page numbers anywhere else in the document, as allowed by both the Position and Alignment drop-down boxes. We believe, however, that most people prefer page numbers centered in the footer.)

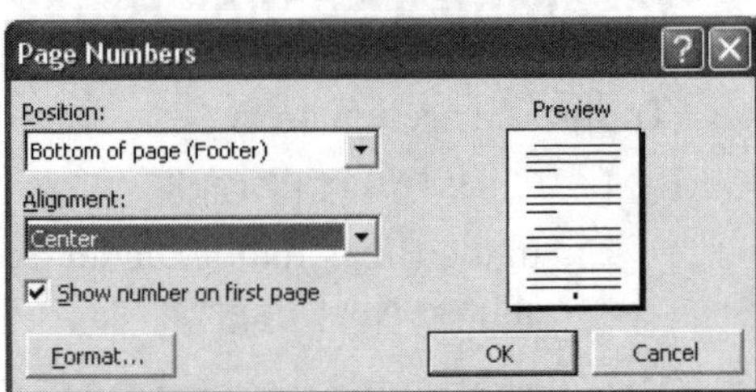

Figure 1-8

4. If you don't want a page number on the first page of a document (we almost never do), then uncheck the box titled Show number on first page.
5. With the dialog box open, click **Format**. If you want to change the number type, do so at this point.

6. In the Page Numbering section of the dialog box, much sure that **Start at 1** is checked.
7. Click **OK** twice.
8. Go to the first page of the next document and repeat each of the previous steps (and in particular step 6).

Listing the steps makes this sound more complicated than it really is. When you actually try it, you will see that it is easy to do. We suggest that you try it by first actually bundling two or more documents that don't have page numbers (using Section Break | Next Page between documents), and then inserting page numbers following the method described above.

Provision Banks

A *provision bank* is our term for a single document that holds a number of different provisions or bodies of language. Assume, for example, that your business has 50 different form letters, with most of them used only once or twice a year. You could set up a template for each of the form letters and/or store them in AutoText. But a provision bank may be an easier solution, particularly for those letters that are infrequently used.

Storing infrequently used provisions (or even those you use every day) in a single document gives you the assurance that you will always be able to find the provision you need. Provision banks are particularly recommended for attorneys as a method of storing specially drafted contract or other document provisions.

Organizing a Provision Bank

If you only have a few provisions in your provision bank, you won't have to worry about how it is organized. If, on the other hand, your provision bank is extensive, then organization becomes necessary. We recommend that each provision be given a meaningful descriptive title, and that the provisions then be organized in alphabetical order.

Saving as a Template

In order to be assured that your provision bank is not inadvertently changed, make sure that you save it as a template.

Adding a Hyperlinked Index

If you accumulate a large provision bank, it may be helpful to add a hyperlinked index at the beginning of the provision bank. This will enable you to immediately move to any hyperlinked provision.

To add a hyperlink:

1. First, insert a bookmark (using **Insert | Bookmark**) at the spot where you want to go — typically, the start of a particular provision. The name of the bookmark must be a single word.
2. Scroll back up to the beginning of the provision bank document (or better yet, press **Ctrl + Home**).
3. Click **Insert | Hyperlink** (or press **Ctrl + K**).
4. In the Insert Hyperlink dialog box that appears, click on the **Bookmarks** button.
5. In the Select Place in Document dialog box that opens, click on the name of your new bookmark, and then click **OK** (this closes the Select Place in Document dialog box and takes you back to the Insert Hyperlink dialog box).

6. In the Text to display text box, enter a descriptive title for the hyperlinked provision.
7. In the text box titled Type the File or web page name, you should see a "#" followed by the name of your bookmark.
8. Click **OK**. You should now see your hyperlink at the beginning of the provision bank document.

Field Basics

What Is a Field?

Word fields are hidden codes that store variable information. You have seen fields in operation every time you inserted page numbers using the technique described earlier. Although you seem to see a page number, you are in fact seeing a PAGE field that changes the page number as and when necessary due to the addition or deletion of text.

You have also seen a field if you used the INSERT DATE command and checked the box titled Update automatically. In that case, a Word field acts in the background to "magically" change the date to the current date every time you reopen the document. There are in fact over 80 types of fields embedded within Word. The Word Help files are very comprehensive regarding the use of fields; please consult them for the individual details of the field you wish to use. However, for the purpose of this introductory chapter, only a handful are relevant.

How Do You View a Field?

Although Word fields are normally hidden, you can view them at any time by selecting the text containing the field and pressing Alt + F9. In the following steps you insert a DATE field code and then view it.

1. From the Insert menu, click **Date and Time**.
2. From the list of available formats, click on the one that formats a date like this: January 1, 2005.
3. Check the box titled **Update automatically**.
4. Click **OK**. This has the effect of inserting a date field with the current date.
5. Select the entire date you just inserted.
6. Press **Alt + F9**.

You should now see the field code, which should look like this:

{ DATE \@ "MMMM d, yyyy" }

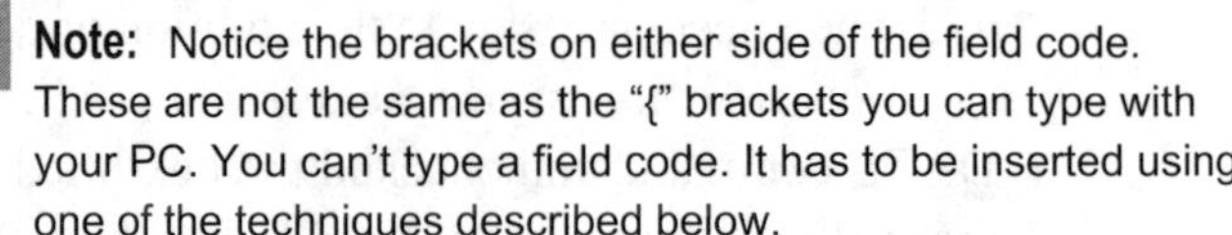

Note: Notice the brackets on either side of the field code. These are not the same as the "{" brackets you can type with your PC. You can't type a field code. It has to be inserted using one of the techniques described below.

The first word in the field code is the field type — in this case DATE. It is followed by a formatting switch that sets the format of the date as the full name of the month, the day as a number, and the full year as a number.

You can view some of the other date formatting switches by choosing a different available format when inserting the date. Alt + F9 acts as a toggle switch. So, if you want to turn the field code back into text, select the text and press Alt + F9.

Note that there is a TIME field that also inserts a date. The difference between the TIME and DATE fields is that the TIME field will insert both dates and times, as well as combinations.

Inserting Field Codes

Since we cannot directly type the brackets surrounding a field code, you have to find another way to insert a Word field. Actually, we are going to show you two ways. The first is the one most people use and was probably intended by Microsoft as the primary method. The other is one we find both quicker and easier. Either method is acceptable.

The first method uses Insert | Field.

1. Click on **Insert | Field**.
2. In the dialog box that appears, click **User Information**.
3. In the right portion of the dialog box, click on **UserName**.
4. Click **OK**.
5. You should see the following field: {USERNAME *MERGEFORMAT}.

You can toggle the field code display by selecting the field and pressing **Alt + F9** (or right-clicking the field and choosing **Toggle Field Codes**). This should change the field to your name — or the name of the registered Windows user whose session is active. (If it doesn't, go to **Tools | Options | User Information**, type in your name, and click **OK**. Then try selecting the field and pressing **Alt + F9** again.)

As with the TIME field, the first word in the field, USERNAME, is the field type, and the part after the * is a formatting switch that formats the name in the same manner as the Word document.

Word includes the Mergeformat switch if you select the Preserve formatting during updates check box while using Insert | Field. Our experience with the Mergeformat switch has been less than positive (sometimes the results have surprised us). We prefer the Charformat switch described below for its greater reliability and control in inserting field characters.

Although the Insert | Field procedure described above may be helpful for people not familiar with Word fields, we prefer the greater control and, for us, speed of the manual process as follows:

1. Press **Ctrl + F9** (most manipulation of fields involves the use of F9).

   This has the effect of inserting field brackets that look like this: { }. It also has the effect of toggling the View Field Codes command (Alt + F9) so that all field codes are visible.
2. Place your cursor between the two brackets of the field code you have inserted and type **UserName *charformat**.
3. Underline the first letter of the field name (i.e., the "U" in UserName).
4. Select the field and press **Alt + F9**. This should toggle the field to your name as above.

Note: The Charformat switch has formatted your name with the same formatting as the first letter of the field name — in this case, your name is underlined.

Commonly Used Fields

In this first chapter, we introduce some of the available Word 2003 fields that can have a big impact with relatively little effort. Before we explore the options of combining Word fields with VBA code, we'll explore these easy-to-use ways to use Word fields and include them in a real-world application.

One of the key considerations when designing templates is to make sure users will enter data in the right place. The reason templates are so popular is that difficult document creation can be simplified so that, in some cases, even entry-level clerks can complete large, complex documents.

The MacroButton

This has long been a pet peeve of mine, but I am finally giving in and admitting the usefulness of this “creative” way of using the MacroButton. Strictly speaking, the MacroButton can be used to run code (macros) when a user clicks on a certain place in the document. However, it can also be used as a placeholder to allow the entry of text (which is how we will explore it here). The MacroButton field code lets you create place markers in your template that users can click on to enter text. You can include prompts that essentially tell the end user exactly what is expected in the field he or she is editing. When a user clicks the MacroButton, the appropriate prompt is highlighted. Once the text has been entered, the prompt and the field code disappear and are replaced by the actual text that the user typed. A good example of this technique can be found by exploring the Word fax and letter templates.

To insert a MacroButton, follow these steps:

1. Position your cursor where the text should appear and choose **Insert | Field**.
2. From the Categories list, choose **Document Automation**, and from the Field names list, choose **MacroButton**.
3. Enter a prompt in the Display text box. This is the text the end user will see. In Figure 1-9 we used “TypeNameHere” for the Display text.

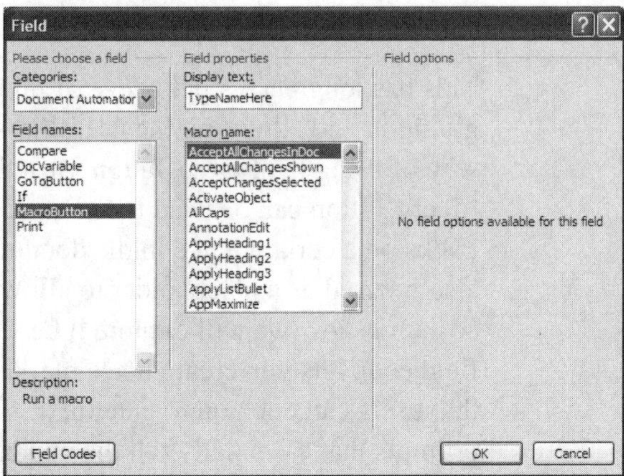

Figure 1-9

4. Now, notice the macros in the Macro name list. The MacroButton, by default, wants to run a macro when the user clicks it. In order to avoid unwanted behavior, you must "clear out" the macro that is specified by Word. Do this by clicking the **Field Codes** button. Simply replace the default macro (AcceptAllChangesInDoc) with two double quotes and you are ready to use the MacroButton.

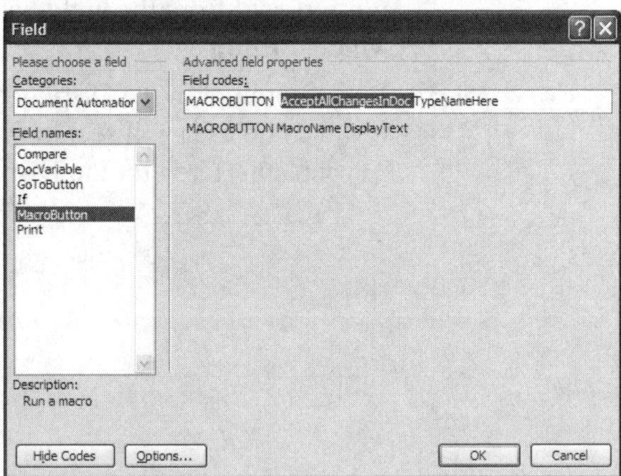

Figure 1-10

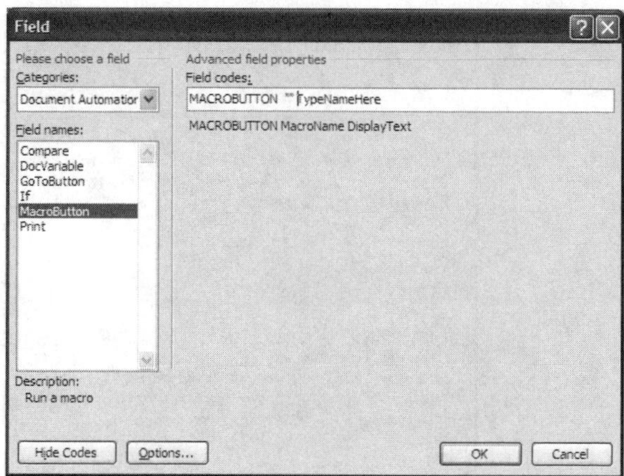

Figure 1-11

5. Click **OK** to finish and you'll see the words appear in the document. If you see the field code {MACROBUTTON TypeNameHere}, press **Alt + F9** to toggle the display of field codes. Save your template and test the result.

Caution: Make sure you use the double quotes. If you inadvertently have a macro with the name you used as the display text, you may wind up running that instead.

You can have multiple MacroButton fields in a given template; just be sure to keep them properly differentiated. You can also surround the text with specific symbols or characters to provide the user with a visual cue that the field is one that requires editing. Another tip to ensure that fields are not glossed over is to save the document with field code shading turned on for all fields. Choose Tools | Options, select the View tab, and choose When selected or Always from the Field shading drop-down list as shown in Figure 1-12 to make your field codes stand out even more.

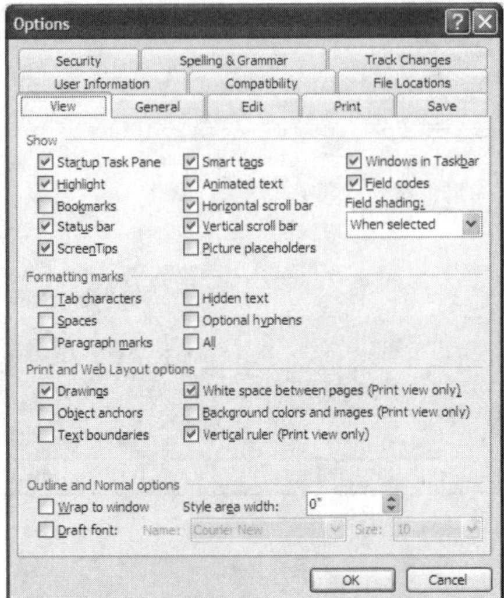

Figure 1-12

The AutoTextList Field

The AutoTextList field code lets you create a drop-down list of AutoText entries. Users select an item from the list to insert the item into the document. Follow these steps to create AutoText entries and an AutoTextList field:

1. Type the entries you want for your drop-down list (single lines or even paragraphs) in a new document.
2. Select them all, and create a new named style for them by typing a name in the Style box on the Formatting toolbar. We'll assume you've typed a list of companies and given it the style name **CompanyList**.
3. One at a time, select each entry and set it as an AutoText entry by choosing **Insert | AutoText | New**. Type the name that will identify this entry in the list and click **OK**. When you're done, you can delete the entries or discard the document. When you select words or phrases as entries, don't include the trailing paragraph marker.
4. To create the AutoTextList to display your entries, choose **Insert | Field**. From the Categories list,

choose **Links and References**, and from the Field names list, choose **AutoTextList**.

5. Click the **Field Codes** button in Word 2003. Complete the text area so it looks like this:

```
AUTOTEXTLIST "Company list" \s "CompanyList" \t
"Right-click to select a company"
```

The first part of the command is the text that will appear in the document. The part after the \s switch is the name of the style you created. The part after the \t switch is ToolTip text that appears when you hold your mouse over the field code.

Note that once you type the first few letters of a designated AutoText item, the full text will pop up in a floating tip. Pressing Enter will fill in the whole thing.

6. Click **OK** to continue and save the document before testing it.
7. Test the ToolTip text by holding your mouse pointer over the words "Company list," then right-clicking the field code and choosing an entry from the list.

There are a couple of issues to watch out for, however. First, any feature that displays a right-click menu will override this list, so, for example, make sure Track Changes is turned off before you insert Company List. Second, right-clicking the inserted name to access the AutoTextList won't work for a name marked as a spelling error. Right-clicking this word will display the spelling menu.

You can use this AutoTextList field code for selectable lists in document templates, too. Create your list separately, then save the AutoTextList field code itself as an AutoText entry. You can insert the text anywhere you need it.

Fill-in Fields

There are two Word field codes that can be used to prompt a user for data entry in a more formal manner than the MacroButton field. These fields are the Ask and Fill-in field codes. These field codes create prompt dialogs for text entry. The resultant dialogs are small and unprofessional looking, similar to InputBoxes. The main difference between the two is that Fill-in responses appear in one position in the document, and Ask data can be used in multiple places in the document. They're both useful for creating forms and legal contracts.

Creating a Fill-in field is easy.

1. Simply click where you want the data to appear and choose **Insert | Field**. From the Categories list, choose **Mail Merge**, and from the Field names list, choose **Fill-in**.

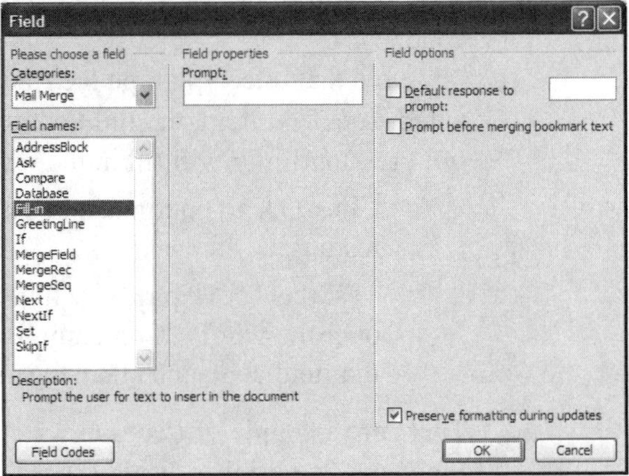

Figure 1-13

2. Fill in the Prompt and Default response to prompt boxes.

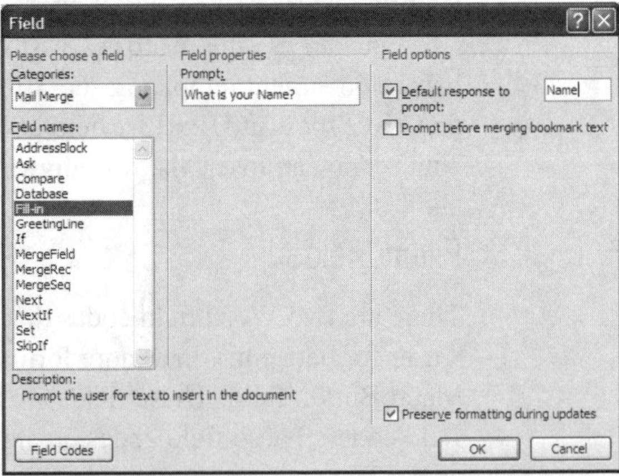

Figure 1-14

3. Once you've entered the prompt and default text, click the **Field Codes** button. This provides a useful method to review the exact syntax of the field code. Once you've reviewed the field code text for accuracy (you can edit here as well), click **OK**. When you see the prompt dialog box appear, click **OK** to accept it. For each entry you expect, create one Fill-in field in the place that the data will appear.

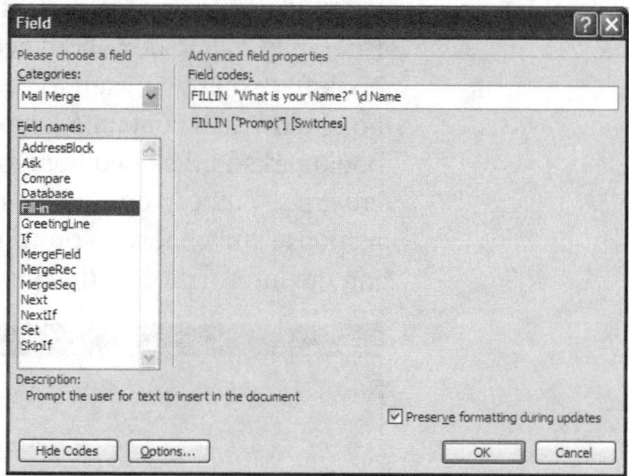

Figure 1-15

4. When you're done, save the document as a template using **File | Save As**, and from the Save as type list, choose **Document Template (*.dot)**. Close the document. Whenever you create a document based on this template, you'll be prompted to enter the data. Once you enter the data, click **OK** to move to the next input dialog.

Ask Fields

Like the Fill-in field, the Ask field lets you prompt the user and then place the resultant data in one or more places in the document. Unlike Fill-in fields, however, Ask fields aren't automatically updated when you create a document based on a template that contains them. Instead, you must update the fields manually, as we'll discuss later. When you create an Ask field, you specify a bookmark name under which to store the data, and then you create references to the bookmark text wherever that data should appear in the document.

Here's how to create an Ask field and place the resulting text in two places in a document:

1. Begin by choosing **Insert | Field**. From the Field names list, choose **Ask**. Next, fill in the Prompt text box with the prompt you want the user to see. The Bookmark name box should contain the name of the bookmark that you want to be populated. The list box below will contain a list of all the available bookmarks in the document or template that you are creating. You can optionally specify a default response and choose to prompt the user before merging the information to the bookmark.

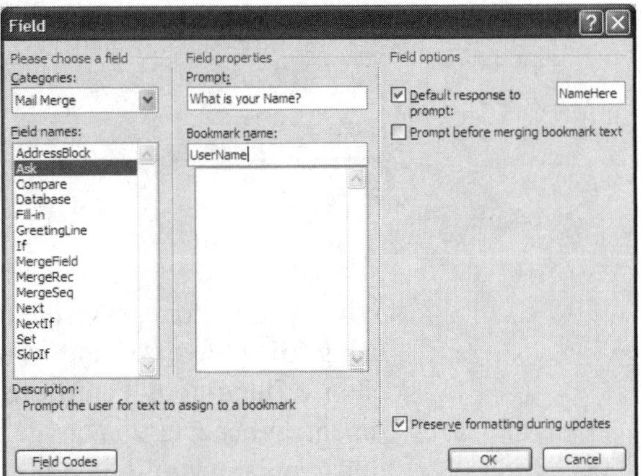

Figure 1-16

2. Click **OK**. A prompt dialog will open; click **OK** to accept it.

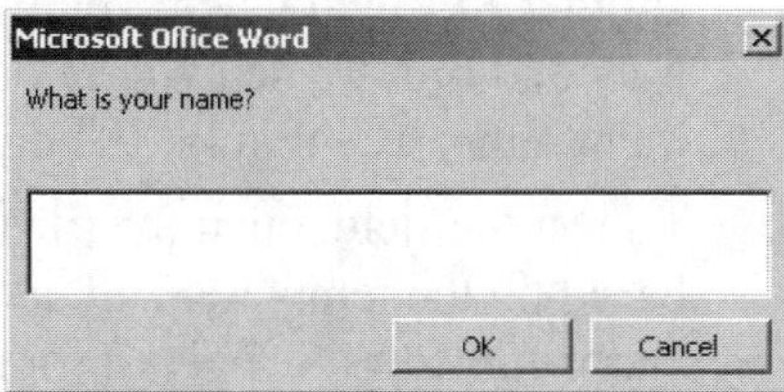

Figure 1-17

3. To create the fields for displaying the text, click in the first position that the name should appear. Choose **Insert | Field**. From the Categories list, choose **Links and References**, and from the Field names list, choose **Ref**. Complete the text area like so: **REF UserName**. This creates a cross-reference to the bookmark called UserName, which is the bookmark name you created in the Ask field.

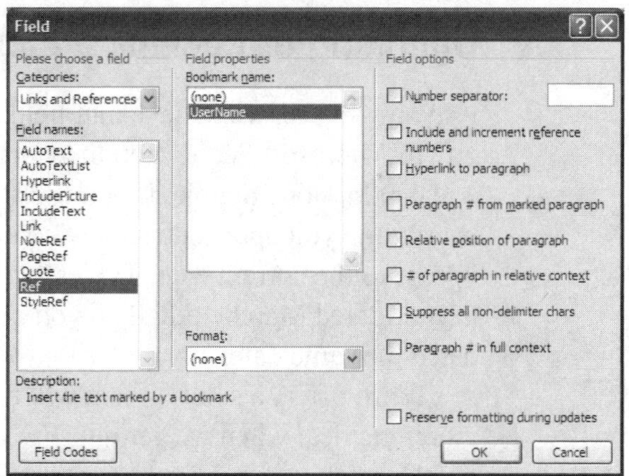

Figure 1-18

4. In the document, you'll see your name appear where you placed the Ref field. Repeat this process to add another Ref field where you want the data to appear a second time. When you're done, save the document either as a regular file or as a template.
5. To test the field, open the file (or create a document based on the template) and update the field codes by choosing **Edit | Select All** (or pressing **Ctrl** + **A**), then press **F9**. You'll be prompted for your name, and it will then appear in both places in the document.

You can request multiple pieces of text by creating a different Ask field code for each and allocating a different bookmark name to each. You can also automate field code updating by recording these steps as a macro stored in the file. If you name the macro AutoOpen, it will run whenever the file is opened.

Unlinking or Locking a Field

As you will see, we believe that fields are an exciting feature of Microsoft Word. Yet, there are times when they are a real pain. For example, if you use a TIME or DATE field, every time you open a document containing that field it will update to the current date. Typically, however, if you send a letter dated March 15th, then you always want that letter dated the same date.

Word offers a solution that will become somewhat more practical when we get into VBA. That solution involves "unlinking" fields, as follows:

1. Choose **Edit** + **Select All** or, better yet, use the keyboard shortcut, **Ctrl** + **A**. Either method has the effect of selecting the entire document.
2. Press **Ctrl** + **Shift** + **F9**.
3. Click anywhere on the document to deselect the text.

This procedure has the effect of turning the field codes into regular text. The field codes disappear. As an alternative, you can lock the fields — i.e., prevent them from being updated or changed — by selecting all of the text as above and pressing Ctrl + F11. Once locked, they can be unlocked by selecting the text and pressing Ctrl + Shift + F11.

Locking is the better alternative if you expect to want to use the fields to update a document after it has been prepared. We, on the other hand, have generally used the unlinking process. You decide which is easier.

Updating Fields

Updating is the process of making sure the value of a field is its current value. To update a field on a document, select the text containing the field and press F9. If, on the other hand, you open a new document under a template, it will (at least since Word 97) automatically update all fields in the same manner as if you selected the text and pressed F9. Prior to Word 97 it was necessary to use a specialized program called an AutoNew macro to update fields.

Although such a macro is no longer necessary to update fields, we will use one when we get to VBA. Certain fields, specifically the DATE and TIME fields (and possibly others), automatically update every time a document is opened, whether or not it is a new document. PAGE fields, used to insert page numbers, automatically update each time text is added or deleted to the extent that a page number is changed.

More on Switches

You have already seen the date switch — a backslash and "@" sign followed by the date format in quotes with "MMMM" representing the month fully written out, "d" representing the day of the month, and "yyyy" representing the year as four digits.

You have also seen the \Charformat switch, which formats the field result's font and font size, and whether the field result is bold, italic, and/or underlined — all based upon the first letter in the field. \Mergeformat formats the field result in the same manner as the rest of the paragraph in which it is located. This switch does not, for example, allow the field result to be bold unless the entire paragraph is bold.

However, Word will on occasion automatically insert the Mergeformat switch by itself — which is why we generally add the Charformat switch to every field. The Charformat switch does not affect the case of the field result. To do that you have to add *Upper, *Lower, *Caps, or *FirstCap to the field, generally after the Charformat switch.

Number Switches

Numbers are formatted using a backslash followed by a "#" and then the format in quotes. If you want to format a number with two decimal places, you would use \# "0.00". On the other hand, if you are looking for a whole number without a decimal point, you can probably do without a number switch. Lawyers frequently use both words and figures to describe a number. The *CardText switch will write out as text all numbers up to 999,999.99.

By way of an example, we will use the NumPages field, which counts the number of pages in a document. If a document has 35 pages, the following field:

```
{NumPages \*CardText} ({NumPages})
```

should update to "thirty-five (35)".

The other number switches we use often are the *Ordinal and *OrdText switches. *Ordinal returns an ordinal number such as "1st" or "2nd". *OrdText converts an ordinal number to text. Accordingly, {Page * OrdText } ({Page * Ordinal }), where the page number is "5" should update to "fifth (5th)."

Dollar Switches

Somewhat more important (at least for us) has been dollar switches. For our example here, we will use a REF field — one that refers to a bookmark. So, {REF loanamount \#$,0.00}, where loanamount is One Thousand Dollars will return "$1,000.00." If the loan amount were Five Million Three Hundred Thousand Five Hundred and Forty Dollars and Fifteen Cents, the field result would appear as "$5,300,540.15."

*DollarText will convert numerical dollars into text up to $999,999.99. Continuing with our first example, {REF loanamount *DollarText (REF loanamount) \#$,0.00}, where loanamount is again $1,000, will return "One Thousand Dollars ($1,000.00)."

Conclusion

As you've seen, Microsoft Word is easy to use, but it is an amazingly complex tool. Although novice Windows users can generally create a simple document right out of the box, there are many advanced features that even experienced programmers spend countless hours trying to perfect. Remember, there is no "right" way to automate a document. You need to make a careful assessment of what you are trying to accomplish and then use the most efficient route to get to the end result.

Chapter 2

Introduction to VBA

Introduction

This chapter introduces you to the programming language behind Microsoft Word 2003 and the entire suite of Office 2003 applications. This language is called Visual Basic for Applications (VBA). Microsoft has been using VBA in Word since version 97, so there is already a wealth of information available. If you are already familiar with VBA, you may want to skim this chapter as a refresher. If you are new to VBA, please read this chapter thoroughly and be sure to acquaint yourself with the Visual Basic Editor (VBE) and work through the sample exercises. Also, pay special attention to the Tips, Notes, and Cautions. These flags have helpful information and, in many cases, may help you avoid pitfalls. Remember, this chapter is meant only as an introduction. The following chapters are meant to give you a deeper understanding of the VBA programming language.

A Quick Introduction to the Visual Basic Editor (VBE)

VBA has an easy-to-use interface called the Visual Basic Editor that you can access in Word by choosing Tools | Macro | Visual Basic Editor (or by pressing Alt + F11). If you've only been a Word user up until now, the first thing you will notice in Figure 2-1 is that the VBE doesn't resemble anything close to a document. The VBE is a very powerful development environment.

The application window is divided into three subwindows when you first enter the VBE. On the left are the Project Explorer and Properties windows. The main window is the Module window. This is where you'll be writing the majority of your code. You can add other debugging windows to monitor variable values while you step through code. These debugging windows will be covered later.

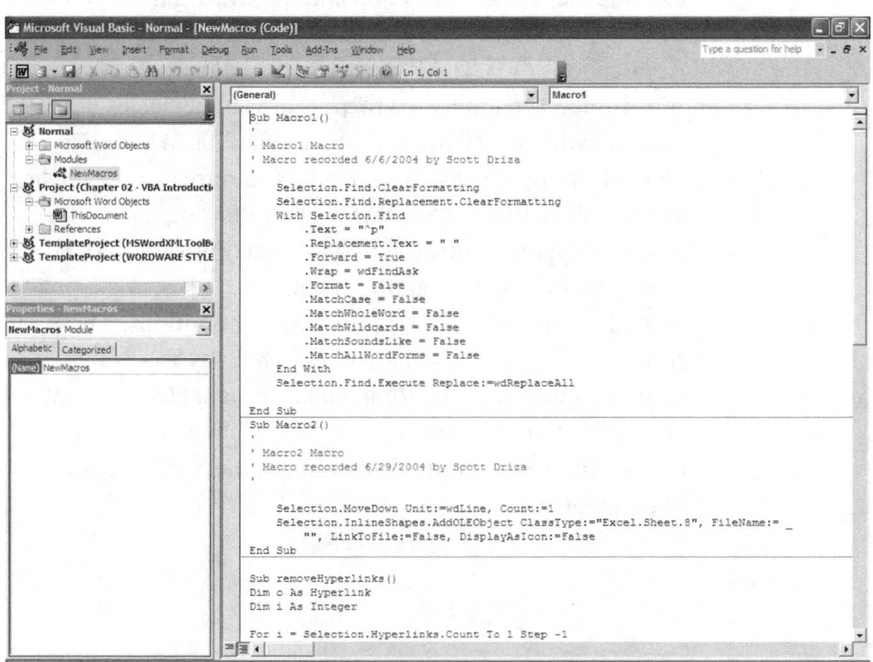

Figure 2-1

VBE Component Basics

The Visual Basic Editor contains a number of development tools that were once found only in advanced development environments. Each of these components appears in a different window and each window may be resized, moved, or docked (double-click the left mouse button on the title bar or choose Tools | Options | Docking). If you need to view Help for an individual window within VBE, position your cursor within the window and press F1. Each of these windows is described below.

Module Window

The main window that occupies the majority of the screen is the Module window, shown in Figure 2-1. This is where you enter the VBA code that lies behind a Word template or document. The Module window displays the VBA code that is associated with the selected object. If you are viewing an object, you can display the Module window by double-clicking the object. For example, add a UserForm, then double-click the UserForm to display the Module window. (The process of double-clicking will also automatically create a subroutine for the UserForm_DoubleClick event.)

Object List and Procedure List

At the top of the Module window are two drop-down menus. The drop-down menu on the left is called the Object List. It contains a list of all objects in the active module. For instance, when the active module is a UserForm, all of the controls on the UserForm will appear in the drop-down. Finally, most modules also contain a General section. The General section is a place where general declarations can be typed. We'll cover general declarations later, but basically these include any option statements, such as Option Explicit (to force variable declaration) or Option Compare Text (to compare text rather than ASCII character values). The drop-down list on the right is the Procedure and Event List. This will contain all of the available events for the current object.

Project Explorer

In the upper-left corner is the Project Explorer window, shown in Figure 2-2. In Word, this window has a tree structure representing all open documents and templates. These documents and templates are projects as far as VBA is concerned. A project is basically a warehouse for objects and the code behind them. You can click on any of the small plus signs to expand the branch; this will expose any of the five possible nodes: ThisDocument, UserForms, Modules, Class Modules, and References. In addition, there are two small buttons toward the top of the window that can be used to switch between viewing a form and its accompanying code.

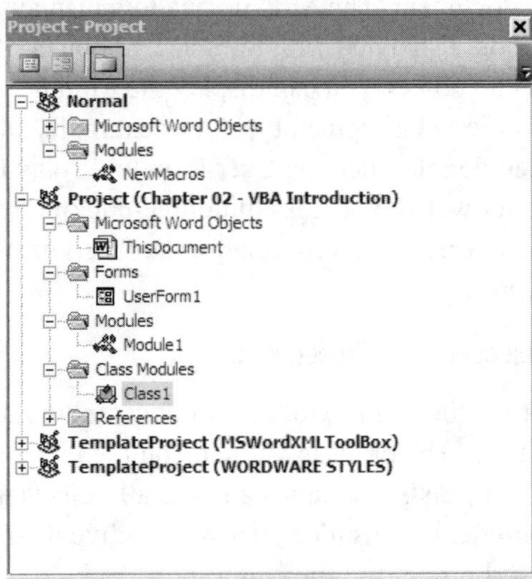

Figure 2-2

UserForms

The UserForms branch will contain any customized UserForms attached to the document or template. The term UserForm is often used interchangeably with dialog box.

(Generally, in the VBA vernacular, a UserForm is one that is custom created, and a dialog box is one that is built into the program.) It may help to think of a UserForm as a blank object that can be turned into a dialog box through the use of controls and code. Controls facilitate certain tasks by executing the code behind the control's events. The actual UserForm is manipulated by changing its properties or adding controls from the toolbox (Edit | Toolbox). Properties will be discussed at the end of this chapter. See Figure 2-3.

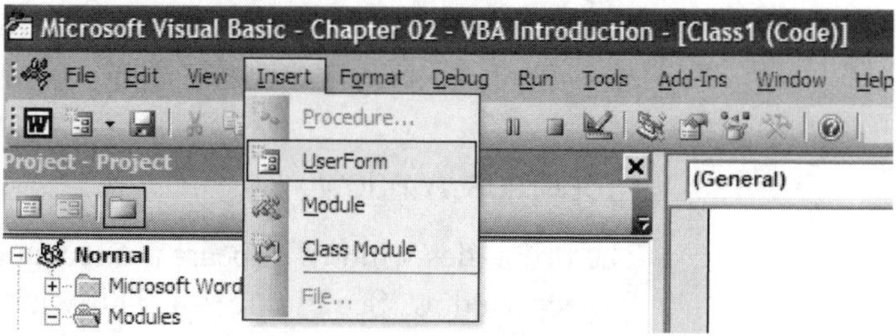

Figure 2-3

Modules

Modules are basically storage areas for procedures (functions and subroutines). Variables may also be declared outside of procedures in the Modules section.

Class Modules

Class modules are a specialized form of a module that allow for the creation of an object. Class modules can be used in creative ways to capture events for many intrinsic objects that are dynamically created or accessed.

References

The References section here allows for one project (usually a document) to call procedures in another project (usually the template used to create that document). You will see that references are invaluable for using Office automation. In Word, all documents will contain a reference to the template that was used to create them.

Tip: Do not confuse a reference displayed in the Project Explorer with one that shows up in the Tools | References section. References in Word's Project Explorer are generally other templates. References in the Tools | References section refer to the object libraries available to the project (usually DLL files).

ThisDocument

The ThisDocument section contains the properties of the actual document or template. This section operates in a very similar manner to a standard code module. If you are familiar with any of the recent Word macro viruses, you probably have seen how they use this section to propagate.

Properties Window

The Properties window appears immediately below the Project window. See Figure 2-4. This window displays the design-time properties for the object that has the focus.

Tip: The object may have other properties that do not show in the Properties window. Several objects have properties that are only available at run time.

As a general rule, you can think of properties as the adjectives of an object. They determine an object's characteristics. Common properties include height, width, background color, and font. In addition to these simple properties, all controls have advanced properties that allow greater manipulation to achieve desired results.

Note: Some properties may be changed only at run time and thus will not show up in the Properties window, while others are read-only and do not allow the alteration of their values.

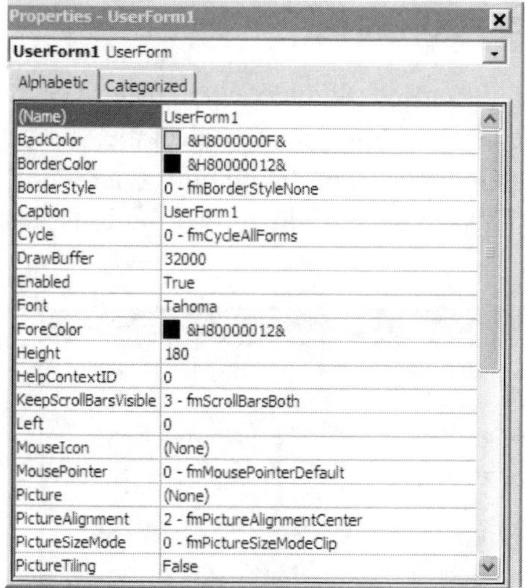

Figure 2-4

VBE Top-Level Menu

Like all Microsoft products, there is a top-level menu bar that provides access to all of the application's features. The VBE is no different. Figure 2-5 shows the top-level menus associated with the VBE. This menu bar provides access to many of the same top-level menus you will find in Word. Most Windows users are familiar with all of the commands that are typically contained in the File submenu. Typically, this provides access to opening, closing, and saving files.

Figure 2-5

VBE Toolbars

Toolbar buttons can be clicked once to carry out the appropriate action. You can also select the Show ToolTips option in the General tab of the Options dialog box to display ToolTips for each of the toolbar buttons as shown in Figure 2-6.

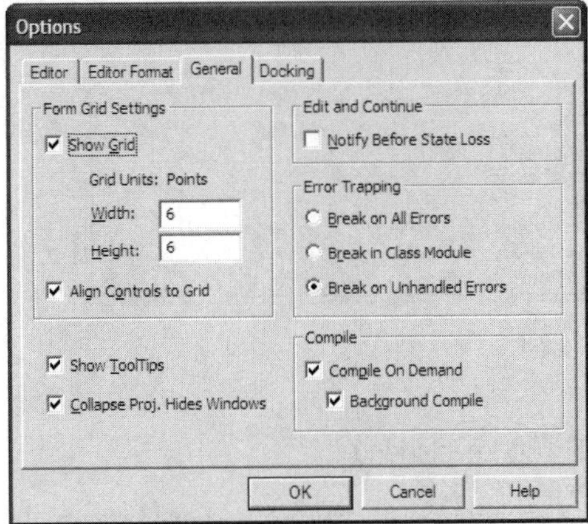

Figure 2-6

Edit Toolbar

Figure 2-7 shows the Edit toolbar. This toolbar contains buttons that access some commonly used menu items for editing code. You should make an attempt to become very familiar with this toolbar. Even many experienced programmers waste valuable time searching for information that is available at the click of a button. The Edit toolbar is broken up into four sections: Shortcuts, Indents, Comments, and Bookmarks. The toolbar has vertical bars to divide the sections. Following is a brief description of what each of these buttons does.

Figure 2-7

The List Properties/Methods button displays a box in the Module window that indicates the available properties and methods for the object preceding the period (.).

The List Constants button opens a box in the Module window listing the valid constants for the property preceding the equal sign (=).

The Quick Info button illustrates the proper syntax for a variable, function, method, or procedure based on the location of the cursor within the name of the function, method, or procedure.

The Parameter Info button displays information about the parameters of the function in which the cursor is located.

The Complete Word button will automatically complete the word you are typing with the characters that Visual Basic inputs through Microsoft's IntelliType feature.

The Indent button shifts all lines in the selection to the next tab stop.

The Outdent button shifts all lines in the selection to the previous tab stop.

The Toggle Breakpoint button sets or removes a breakpoint at the current line. A breakpoint is equivalent to the Stop command. See Figure 2-8. A red indicator will appear to the left of the code (the margin indicator bar) and the line of code will be red with inverted text.

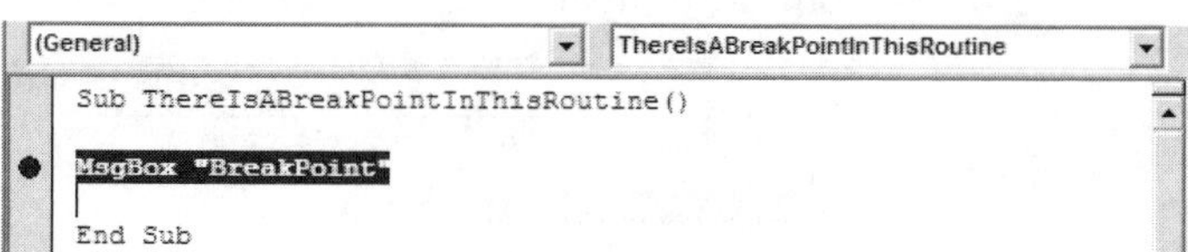

Figure 2-8

Note: Breakpoints cause normally executing code to enter break mode and display the VBE at the line where the breakpoint occurs. Then you can use the buttons on the Debug toolbar to step through the code.

The Comment Block button adds the comment character (') to the beginning of each line of a selected block of text.

Note: Comments allow you to communicate with future programmers (including yourself!). You can store any type of information in a comment, but it is usually best to include the purpose of the procedure and the name of the creator. Also, comments often include the date the procedure was created. This may come in handy if you are searching for a procedure based on a specific version.

The Uncomment Block button removes the comment character from each line of a selected block of text.

Bookmark Buttons

Bookmarks provide a convenient medium for navigating through a VBA project. The VBE will add a blue, rounded rectangle next to the code in the margin indicator bar (see Figure 2-9). Bookmarks may be added in a few different ways in VBA. One is to select Edit | Bookmarks | Toggle Bookmark. You can also right-click the margin indicator bar next to the appropriate statement and select Toggle Bookmark. Of course, the easiest method is to use a button from the toolbar.

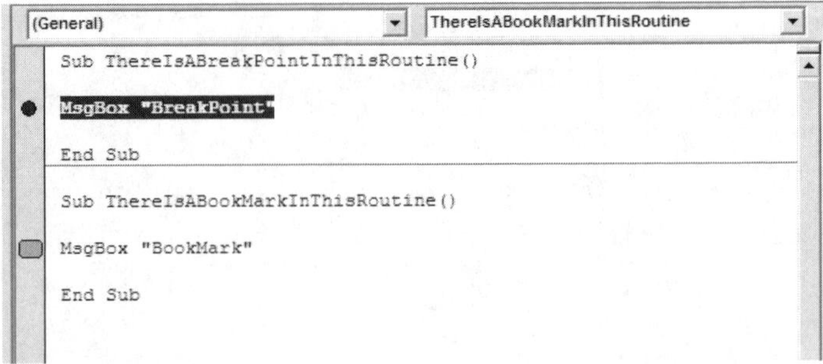

Figure 2-9

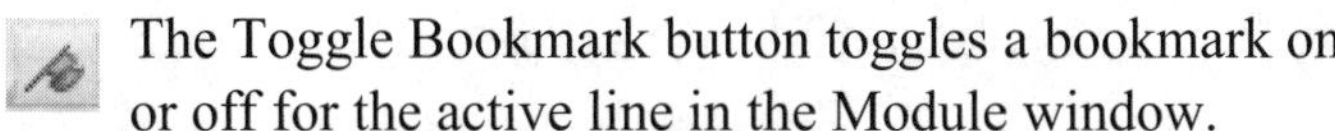

The Toggle Bookmark button toggles a bookmark on or off for the active line in the Module window.

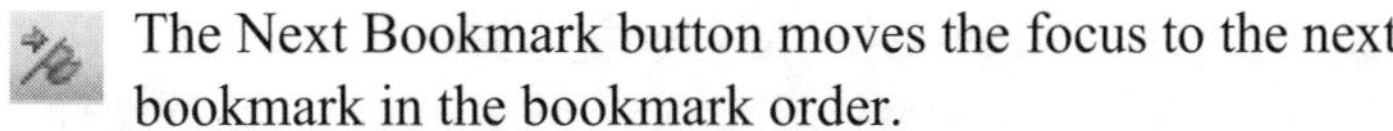

The Next Bookmark button moves the focus to the next bookmark in the bookmark order.

The Previous Bookmark button moves the focus to the previous bookmark in the bookmark order.

The Clear All Bookmarks button removes all bookmarks.

Debug Toolbar

The Debug toolbar is shown in Figure 2-10. This toolbar contains buttons for some commonly used debugging features.

Figure 2-10

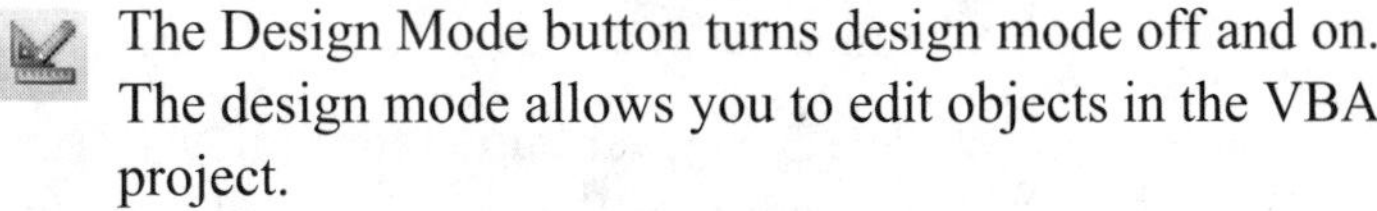

The Design Mode button turns design mode off and on. The design mode allows you to edit objects in the VBA project.

The Run button runs the current selection. This may be a procedure if the cursor is in a procedure, a UserForm if the UserForm is the currently active selection, or a macro.

The Break button stops execution of a program while it is running and switches to break mode.

The Reset button resets the project. All variables will lose their values and control will return to the user.

The Toggle Breakpoint button operates similarly to the Toggle Bookmark button in that it sets or removes a breakpoint at the current line.

Stepping Through a Project

The Debug toolbar provides access to some of the most powerful debugging techniques available. Stepping through a project allows you to monitor variable values, loops, and program flow. Each button also has a corresponding keystroke combination. The next line to be executed will be highlighted in yellow, with a yellow arrow displayed in the margin indicator bar, as shown in Figure 2-11.

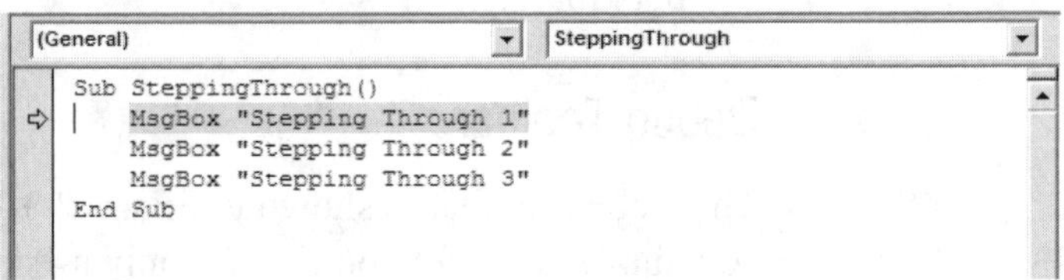
(General)
SteppingThrough
Sub SteppingThrough()
MsgBox "Stepping Through 1"
MsgBox "Stepping Through 2"
MsgBox "Stepping Through 3"
End Sub

Figure 2-11

Tip: You can monitor variables using one of the windows discussed below, or you can simply position your cursor atop the variable to display the value via control tip text.

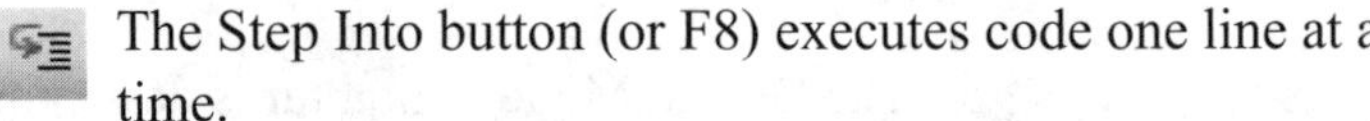

The Step Into button (or F8) executes code one line at a time.

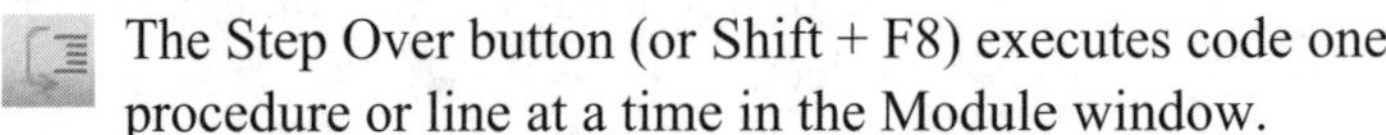

The Step Over button (or Shift + F8) executes code one procedure or line at a time in the Module window.

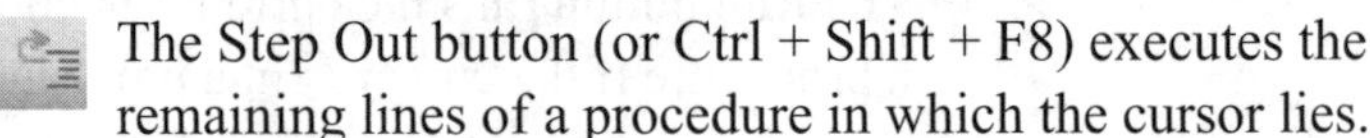

The Step Out button (or Ctrl + Shift + F8) executes the remaining lines of a procedure in which the cursor lies.

Monitoring Project Values

Oftentimes, your program may run without encountering an error, but the end result will be incorrect in some way. This is most likely due to a flaw in your logic. Keeping track of a variable's value and stepping through a project will show you where the flaw occurs. VBA is especially robust when it comes to monitoring values. This section discusses the options available through the Debug toolbar.

The Locals Window button displays the Locals window, shown in Figure 2-12. The Locals window allows you to monitor all variables in any procedure. In break mode, the Locals window will display each variable in the current procedure on a separate line. The top line is the name of the module. If you expand the variable, you will see a list of the global variables.

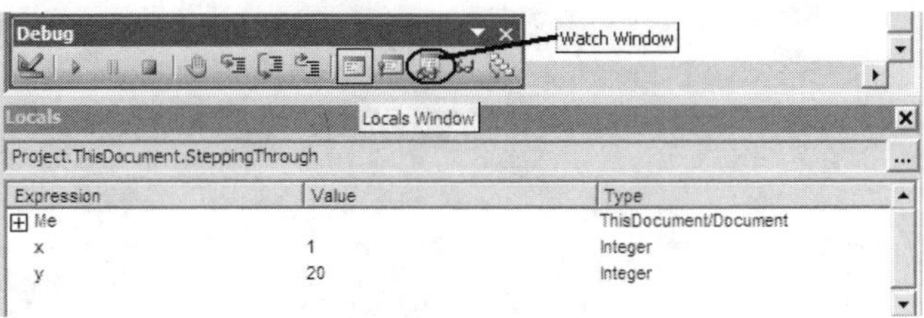

Figure 2-12

The Watch Window button displays the Watches window, as shown in Figure 2-13. Sometimes you will want to watch more than just the values of a variable. The Watches window allows you to monitor the result of any expression or the value of an object's property. You will need to set up watch expressions in order to monitor either of these through the Watches window.

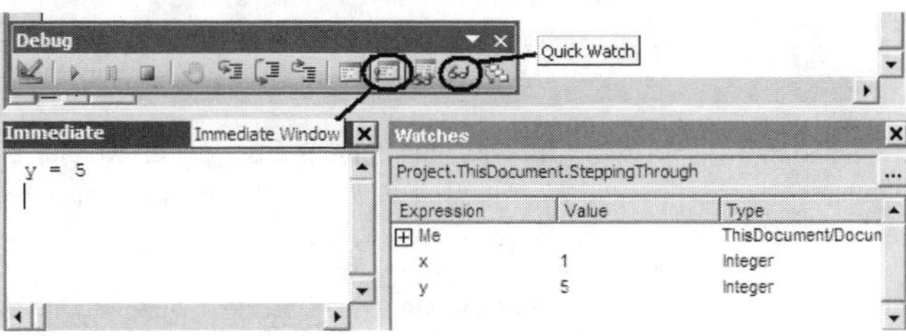

Figure 2-13

In order to set up a watch, you need to perform the following procedure:

1. Select the expression by placing the cursor inside the word for single-word expressions or highlighting the entire expression.
2. Select **Debug | Add Watch** to display the Add Watch dialog box, as shown in Figure 2-14.

3. If the expression isn't shown in the Expression text box, enter the expression manually. The value you enter can be any valid variable name, a property, a user-defined function name, or a valid VBA expression.
4. Use the Context section to specify where the variable is used, including the procedure and module.
5. Set the type of watch to specify how VBA will react.

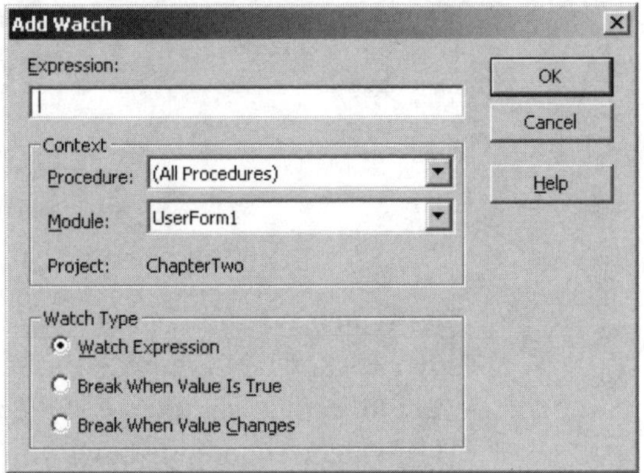

Figure 2-14

Watch Type	Explanation
Watch Expression	The expression will be displayed in the windows in break mode.
Break When Value Is True	VBA will stop executing and enter break mode when the expression value becomes True.
Break When Value Changes	VBA will stop executing and enter break mode when the expression value changes.

6. Click **OK**.

The Immediate Window button displays the Immediate window, which is shown in Figure 2-13. The Watches window allows you to view the values of a given expression, but doesn't allow you to manipulate that value. If you need to manipulate a value, you can use the Immediate window. The Immediate window can be used to test experimental statements to see how they affect a procedure, to change the value of a variable or property, or to run other procedures. You can type lines of code in the Immediate window just as you would in the Modules section.

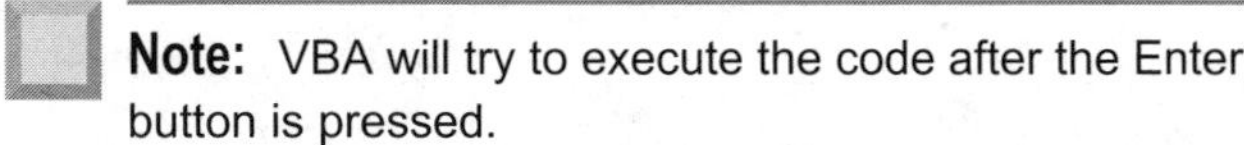

Note: VBA will try to execute the code after the Enter button is pressed.

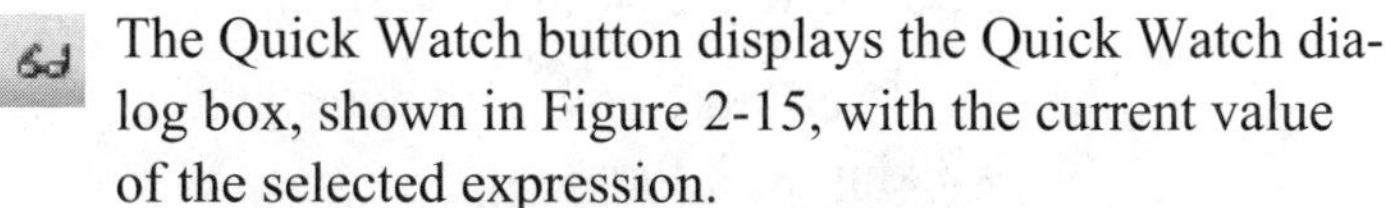

The Quick Watch button displays the Quick Watch dialog box, shown in Figure 2-15, with the current value of the selected expression.

Figure 2-15

The Call Stack button displays the Call Stack dialog box, which lists the currently active procedure calls (procedures in the project that have started but are not completed).

Tip: Understanding the call stack can often prevent problems in advance. In a large project you may show and hide several UserForms. Remember that the procedure that shows a UserForm doesn't finish executing.

Standard Toolbar

The Standard toolbar, shown in Figure 2-16, provides access to the most common functionality in a project. You can execute many standard Windows commands such as Save, Insert, Cut, Copy, Paste, Find, Redo, Undo, and Help. The Standard toolbar also has some buttons contained on the Edit toolbar — Run, Reset, Break, and Design View. It also has shortcut buttons to display the Properties window, Project Explorer, Form Toolbox, and Object Browser.

Figure 2-16

UserForm Toolbar

The UserForm toolbar contains buttons that are useful for working with forms.

Figure 2-17

Note: The UserForm toolbar is used to manipulate an existing form. To add a UserForm, either use the Insert button on the Standard toolbar or select Insert | UserForm.

 The Bring To Front button moves the selected controls to the front of all other controls on a form.

 The Send To Back button moves the selected control behind all other controls on a form.

 The Group button is used to create a group of controls. Draw a box around the controls that you wish to group together and click this button to form a group.

 The Ungroup button ungroups the controls that were previously grouped.

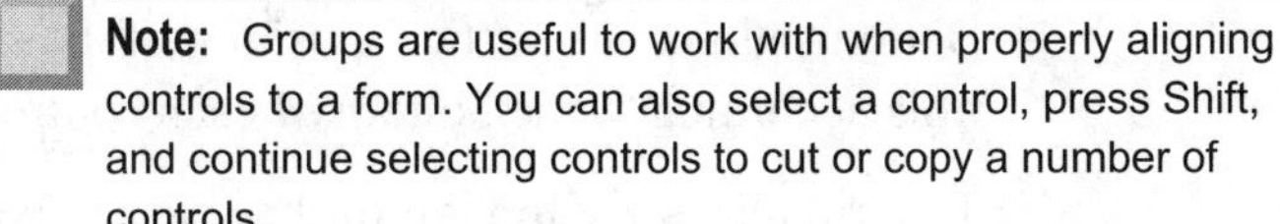

Note: Groups are useful to work with when properly aligning controls to a form. You can also select a control, press Shift, and continue selecting controls to cut or copy a number of controls.

Alignment

The Alignment buttons are shown in Figure 2-18. In order for any application to be successful, the user must easily understand it. One of the most frequent mistakes programmers make is to design an unfriendly interface. Jagged edges, unaligned controls, poor color choices, and inconsistency all lead to design disaster. Fortunately, Microsoft provides many tools to make sure you get your design *right*! Following are the alignment choices available from the UserForm toolbar:

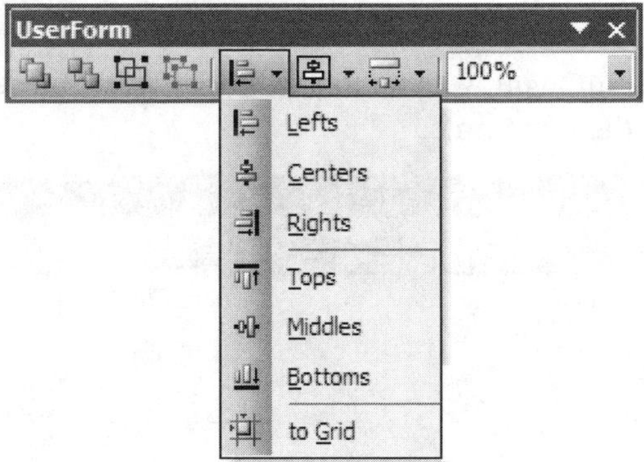

Figure 2-18

- Lefts aligns the horizontal position of the selected controls according to the leftmost edges.
- Centers aligns the horizontal position of the selected controls according to the centers of each control.
- Rights aligns the horizontal position of the selected controls according to the rightmost edges.
- Tops aligns the vertical position of the selected controls according to the top of each control.
- Middles aligns the vertical position of the selected controls according to the middle of each control.

Bottoms aligns the vertical position of the selected controls according to the bottom of each control.

To Grid aligns the top left of the selected controls to the closest grid.

The Centering button is shown in Figure 2-19. This button allows you to center controls on the form either horizontally or vertically.

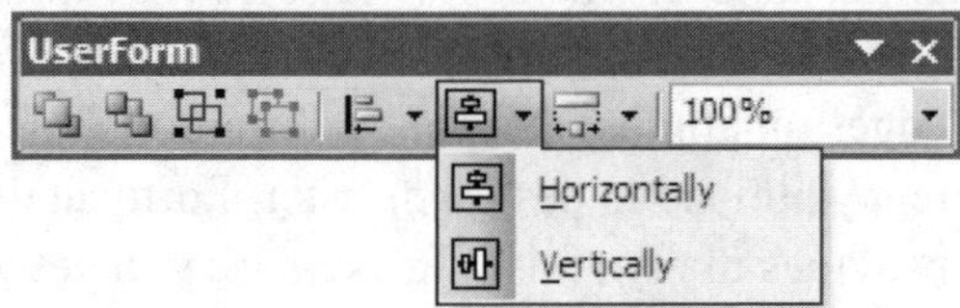

Figure 2-19

The Make Same Size button is shown in Figure 2-20. This button allows you to adjust the width, the height, or both at the same time.

Figure 2-20

The Zoom button is shown in Figure 2-21. This reduces or enlarges the display of all controls on the UserForm. You can set any magnification from 10 to 200 percent.

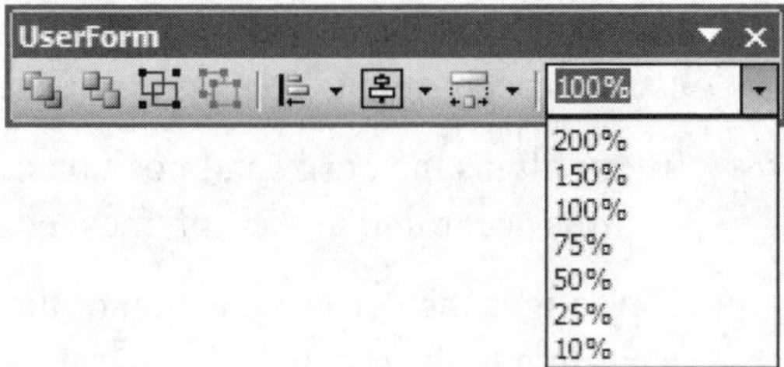

Figure 2-21

Object Browser

Figure 2-22 displays the Object Browser. The Object Browser is used to browse through all available objects in your project. It displays each object's properties, methods, and events. You can also see the procedures and constants available from the different object libraries in your project. The Object Browser is capable of viewing all objects, including objects you create as well as objects from other applications.

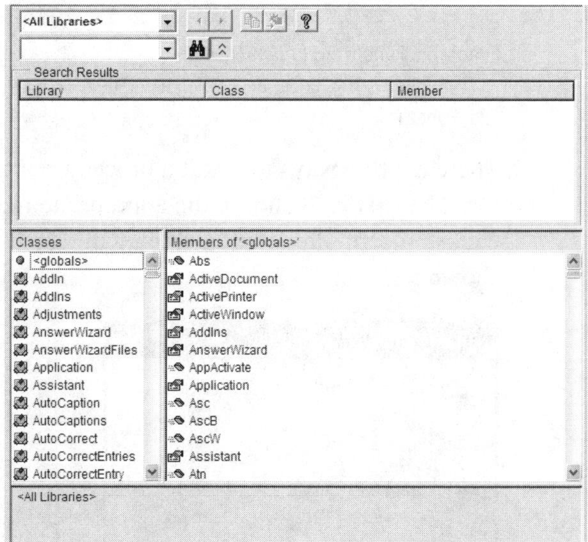

Figure 2-22

The Object Browser becomes especially useful when you add a reference to an external object. In the upper-left corner of the Object Browser is a drop-down that allows you to select a single library for viewing. This allows you to determine exactly what properties, methods, and events pertain to the newly referenced object.

The Visual Basic Environment

Procedures

Procedures encompass both functions and subroutines. These can be distinguished by the syntax in which they appear:

```
Sub Subroutine1()
      'Underlying Code
End Sub
Function Function1() As Integer
      'Underlying code and return value
End Function
```

There are two ways to insert a procedure into a code module. The first is to choose the appropriate module and then choose Insert | Procedure, which will display the dialog box shown in Figure 2-23.

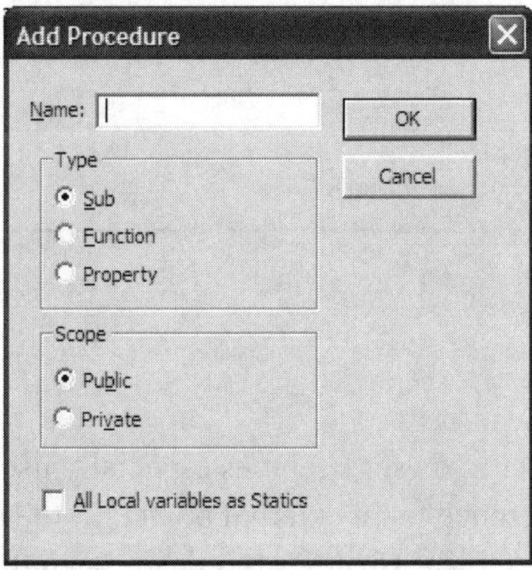

Figure 2-23

The second, easier method is just to type either "Sub" or "Function" followed by the appropriate name in the Module window. When you click Enter, the VBE will automatically create an "End Sub" and position the cursor on the proceeding line. Now you can simply start typing your code.

Think of procedures as all of the different actions that your program can execute. You can manipulate your code to trigger different procedures depending on different events. Generally, you want your procedures to perform only one specific event so that you can reuse procedures to accomplish the same tasks with different code. For example, you may have a project that has multiple UserForms, all of which have a button that will determine the number of loaded UserForms at any one time and give the name of the active UserForm. Rather than writing procedures behind each command button, you could have publicly declared procedures in a module that would be available to all of the UserForms. This also makes it easier to add additional UserForms. The ability to reuse portions of your code in different areas is referred to as the *modularity* of your code. Following is a brief description of both subroutines and functions.

Functions

Functions can be either private or public. This is referred to as *scope* and is relevant with all procedures and applies in a very similar manner to variables. The best programming practice is to declare them private, which means they will be locally available, unless you are going to access them from other modules. Scope refers to the visibility of functions, subs, or variables to other modules. The Visual Basic Editor doesn't make it necessary to declare the function as private or public, but it is good programming practice to declare everything explicitly from the outset so others can distinguish your intent. By default, functions are private unless declared otherwise.

The main difference between functions and subroutines is that functions can return a value to the calling procedure while subroutines cannot. To return a value from a function, we must assign a variable that returns the value. See the following example:

```
Private Sub ShowMsg()
    MsgBox "The number is " & NumReturn(4)
End Sub
Private Function NumReturn(iNumber As Integer) As Integer
    NumReturn = iNumber * 5
End Function
```

In the above example, the subroutine ShowMsg calls a message box (a built-in VBA feature) and displays the result of the NumReturn function when the number 4 is passed as an argument. The function multiplies the integer 4 by the number 5 and returns an integer, 20, that will be displayed in the message box. Also, notice the ampersand (&) is used to tie together the text and the number. This sign can be used to tie together different information. This is known as *concatenation* and will be discussed periodically throughout this book.

Subroutines

Subroutines are identical to functions concerning scope. Subroutines may be declared either public or private. The main difference is that subroutines do not return values. However, you can call subroutines from other subroutines. There will be instances where you call subroutines to manipulate either module-level or public variables that might be used by other functions or subroutines. While this is not good programming practice, it is important to take note if you will be trying to interpret the code of others. Please look closely at the following examples:

```
Option Explicit
Public iNumber As Integer
Private Sub ShowMsg()
    iNumber = 4
    NumChange
    MsgBox "The number is " & iNumber
End Sub
Private Sub NumChange()
    iNumber = (iNumber * 5)
End Sub
```

Running ShowMsg accomplishes the same result as the above function — a message box with the number 20 displayed. Here, the number 4 is also multiplied by 5, but we are using a subroutine to modify a public variable. We dimension (declare) the variable Public at the module level so it will be available to both procedures. The ShowMsg subroutine sets the variable iNumber equal to 4, then runs the embedded subroutine NumChange, which multiplies the variable by 5. ShowMsg finishes by displaying the message box with the number 20. Notice, however, that if the variable were declared within the ShowMsg subroutine, a compile error (variable not defined) would result because NumChange would not be able to "see" the variable. Its scope would then be limited to only the procedure in which it is declared.

Parameters and Arguments

Anything following either a sub or a function that is enclosed in brackets is a parameter of that procedure. The value of a parameter is called its argument. If you begin typing in a predefined VBA function that requires arguments (i.e., has parameters), you'll notice that some of the arguments are included in brackets while others are not. See Figure 2-24.

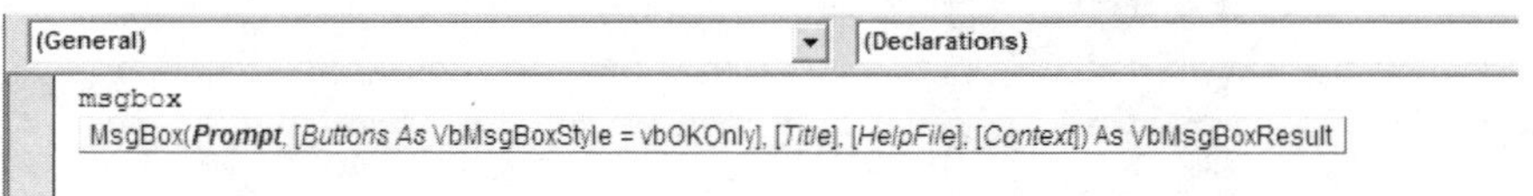

Figure 2-24

Anything that is not enclosed in the brackets is a required parameter. If an argument is not assigned to such a parameter, the procedure will fail. It almost goes without saying that if a parameter is optional (included in brackets), then it is not necessary to assign an argument to it.

When declaring a function, you will want to assign a variable type for the return value as well as define any parameters that will be used in the function. See the example in Figure 2-25 for declaring parameters.

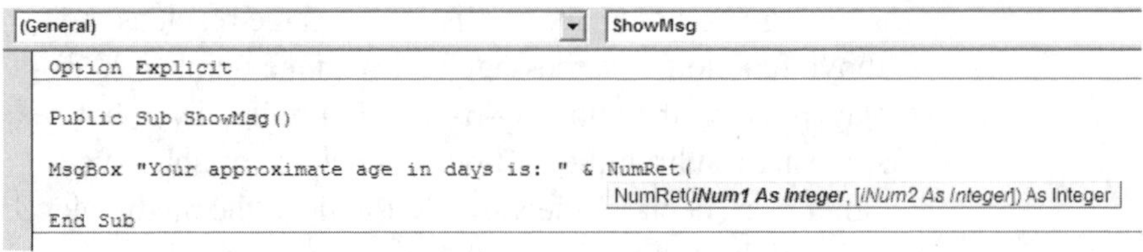

Figure 2-25

Notice that we have added the optional parameter iNum2 to our previous function. Now the IntelliType feature shows both parameters with the optional parameter in brackets as illustrated above.

UserForms

UserForms are the medium through which you will interact with users. Think of these as your own customizable dialog boxes. Broadly defined, they are objects. They have properties and methods that allow you to change the way they look and act. (We'll discuss properties and methods next.) To create a UserForm, simply choose Insert | UserForm as shown in Figure 2-26.

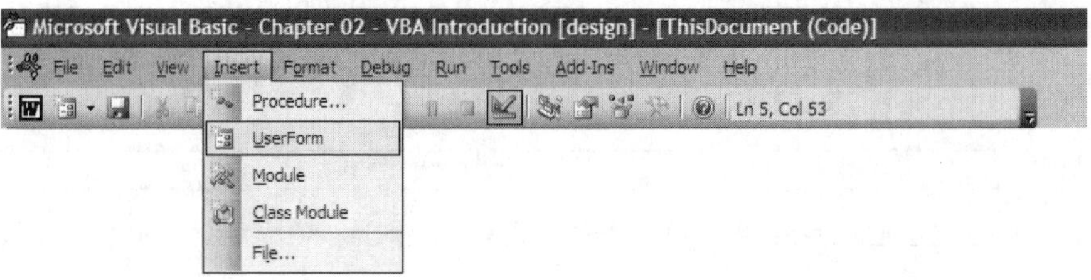

Figure 2-26

The first thing you should always do after inserting a UserForm is give it a distinct name. If you have a project with multiple UserForms, you don't want to get confused by having UserForm1, UserForm2, and so on. Because they are objects, a simple naming convention is to have the first three letters be "frm." The importance of standard naming conventions cannot be overstated. There will be instances where you will need to create collections. One of the easiest ways is to loop through certain variables, controls, etc., and add those with a certain prefix.

VBA Toolbox

A UserForm by itself is capable of doing basically nothing. In order to make a UserForm useful it is necessary to bring out the VBA Toolbox (View | Toolbox) to insert any of the various controls that can be found in the toolbox. The VBA Toolbox is shown in Figure 2-27.

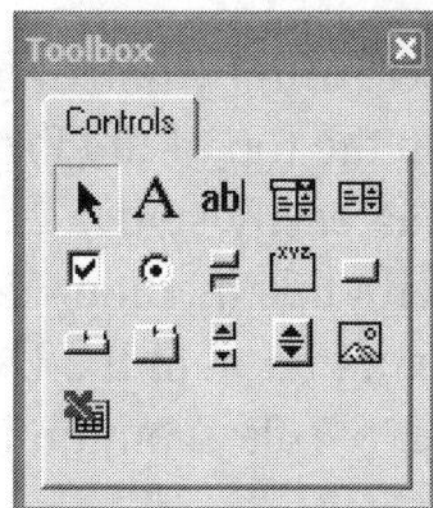

Figure 2-27

It's a good idea to become familiar with the sizing, shaping, and removal of controls. Notice that when you click on a control, the Properties window will show the properties of the control rather than the properties of the UserForm. You can change any of these before the program is run (design time) or you can include code that will change any of these properties while the program is running (run time).

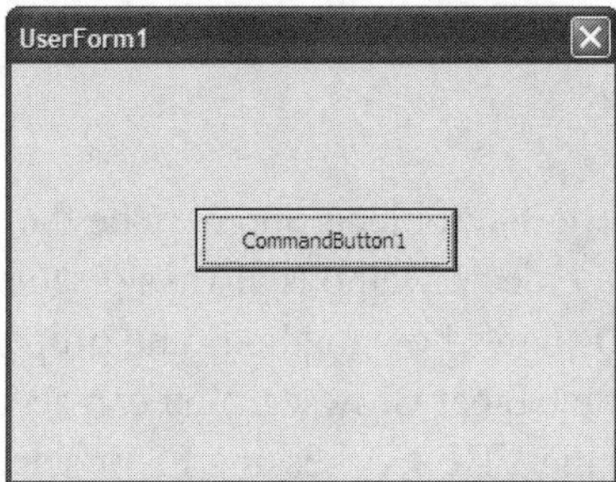

Figure 2-28

To see how a UserForm can be changed at run time, try the following example. Insert a UserForm, shown in Figure 2-28, and put a CommandButton near the top. In the design environment, double-click on the CommandButton; this should take you to the Module window behind the UserForm. Insert the following subroutine for the CommandButton1_Click event:

```
Private Sub CommandButton1_Click()
    Me.Height = Me.Height - 5
End Sub
```

You can return to the UserForm by clicking the small image of the UserForm in the top of the Project Explorer window. Note that you can easily switch between a UserForm and its code with this method. Now, run the UserForm either by pressing F5 with the UserForm highlighted or by pressing the ▶ (play) button in the toolbar.

Figure 2-29

Notice that every time you click the button, the event fires and the UserForm's height is decreased. At design time you could decrease the UserForm's height by changing its property in the Properties window.

Methods

Methods pertain to objects and may be thought of as the verbs of the object. Methods always perform some action. Figure 2-30 shows how methods and properties are displayed in the Object Browser. You can access the Object Browser in the VBE by pressing F2 or selecting View | Object Browser.

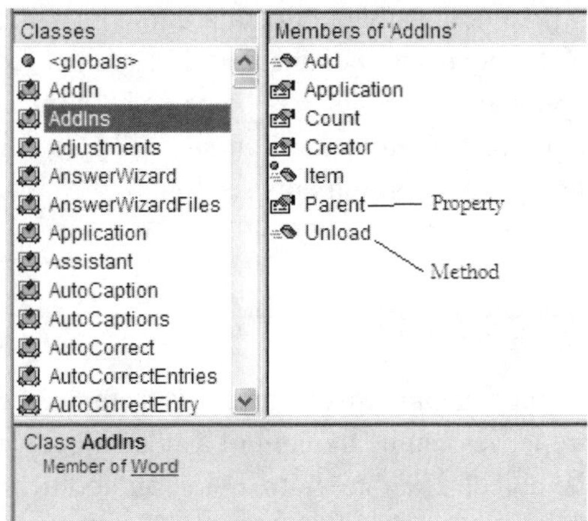

Figure 2-30

A simple illustration is the ActiveDocument object, which represents the document with the focus in a Word session. Its methods are comprised of the same things you might manually do when interacting with a document: Save, SaveAs, Close, etc. Methods often involve the use of arguments, many of which may not be required for the method to execute. The Close method uses the following syntax:

```
ActiveDocument.Close(SaveChanges, [OriginalFormat],
[RouteDocument])
```

In the above example, the only required argument is SaveChanges. If you try to execute the Close method without passing a valid argument, an error will be generated. There are two valid ways of passing arguments. One is by separating the arguments by commas. The better alternative, however, is to use named arguments. Using named arguments will make your code much easier to read because a future programmer can see what arguments are being used. Another advantage is that named arguments may be declared in any order. Named arguments use the name of the argument followed by a specific operator (:=) and the value for the argument. For example:

```
ActiveDocument.Close SaveChanges:=wdDoNotSaveChanges
```

A final note is that optional arguments will always show up in [] brackets to indicate that they are not required. Optional arguments may be passed the same as required arguments. Optional arguments will also always appear at the end of the arguments section.

Properties

While you can think of methods as the verbs of the object, properties can be thought of as the adjectives that describe the object. Height, width, color, and border style are all general examples of properties. They have much the same syntax as methods in that they appear immediately following a period after an object's name. For example:

```
ActiveDocument.Name
```

Properties entail two additional dimensions that methods do not. Properties can be either read-only or both read and write. The above example is a read-only property. This means that it can only return the value of the Name property as it exists in the active document already.

However, there are some objects where the Name property is both read and write. The Font object is an example of an object with a read/write Name property. You can use Font.Name to return the value of the current font, or you could use Font.Name=Arial to set the current font. All properties may be set using the "=" operator.

What perplexes most beginners is that some properties may do double duty as objects. Again, Font is a good example. Font is a property of the ActiveDocument object in addition to being its own object. In other words, it represents a property of the ActiveDocument, and it is an object with its own individual properties such as Bold.

Modules

Modules are the areas where the code is stored. This makes modules the storage house for your code. It is important to note that modules take a few different shapes. For example, a module may be inserted from the Insert menu. This is what is normally referred to as a module. It can be referenced globally throughout the project.

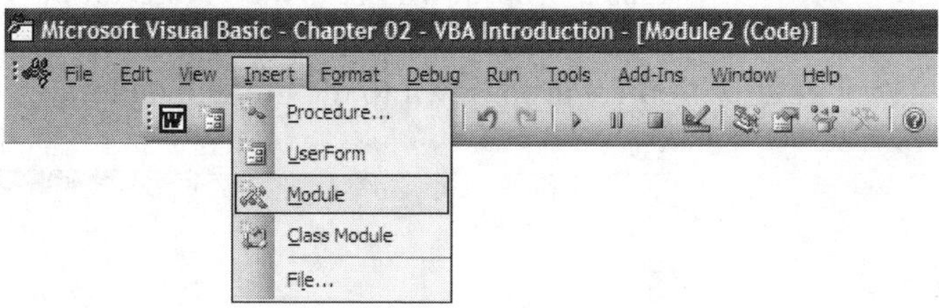

Figure 2-31

Another example of a module is the code that exists behind a form. This is often referred to as a form module. The form is just the graphical representation of all the properties that make up the form. These properties are given a default value so there is something to initialize (and it saves you the trouble of building one from scratch!).

Every document and template will contain a ThisDocument module that contains the code underlying the actual document. It also contains properties that can be manipulated in the Properties window or by code. ThisDocument is also an object in Word.

Lastly, there are class modules that may be inserted using the Insert menu. For now, you can think of them as special-duty modules that enable you to create your own objects.

Modules may be imported or exported through the used of the File menu in the Visual Basic Editor. This allows for you to reuse code that you create in other projects. The same is true of UserForms and class modules. Modules that are exported will have the file extension .bas.

Events

The most important thing to know about VBA programming is that it is event driven. All of your code will be triggered by predefined things that the user can do. Clicking on a button, scrolling on a page, and expanding a drop-down list are all examples of events. The upper right-hand corner of the Module window in the VBE contains a drop-down list that contains all the events that correspond to whatever object is in the accompanying object drop-down to the immediate left.

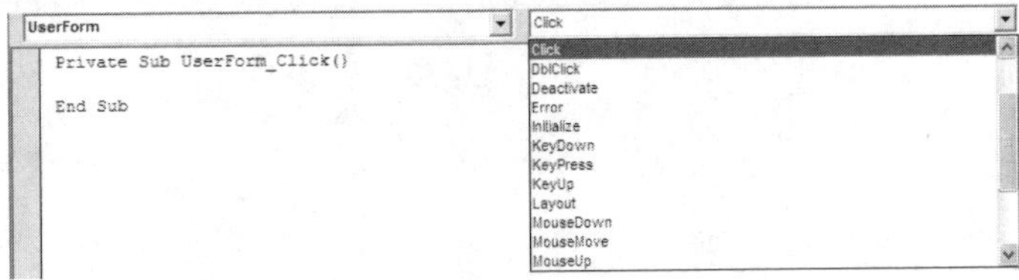

Figure 2-32

Events are triggered by certain user actions. Some are intuitive, such as clicking, but for others you will have to resort to the Microsoft Help files. When programming, always make sure that you capture the action that you intend the user to follow.

In addition, Word provides some automatic events that come in handy when creating a template system. You can trigger code to execute whenever a document is opened, closed, or chosen as File | New. We will go over the specific applications of these events in the following chapters.

Class Modules

Class modules give programmers the ability to create and manipulate their own classes of objects. Class modules are extremely powerful and extremely useful. One of the main benefits of class modules is that they lend themselves to modularity. That is, once you've created your own custom object replete with properties and methods, you'll find that you can probably reuse it in another project.

Another advantage of modules is that they embody the idea of encapsulation. In other words, you can control the manipulation of the data that your object represents. Rather than manipulating the raw data, you will be using the properties and methods of your object to control the process.

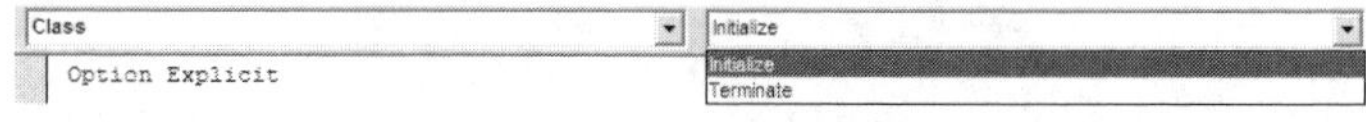

Figure 2-33

Although class modules define the properties and methods of the object, those properties and methods do not manipulate the object by themselves. To actually manipulate the data, you will be instantiating the object and calling its methods and setting its properties. Although class modules can be difficult, it's easy to think of them as an intermediate part of programming. Class modules are simply a means to create your own objects. You can then use those objects in your project as you would use any of the built-in objects.

Conclusion

This chapter introduced you to Visual Basic for Applications, the programming language behind the Microsoft Office 2003 programs. If you are new to VBA, you should refer to this chapter often, as it can serve as a refresher. Although the examples were very basic, they will help you build your confidence as you proceed through the book. This chapter also covered the Visual Basic Editor and many of its components in addition to touching on the elements of VBA programming, including events, modules, functions, and subroutines. Now that you've gotten your feet wet, please read the following chapters closely.

Chapter 3

Word 2003 and VBA

Introduction

This chapter takes a look at many of Word's features that will be important in the development of automated Word solutions. This chapter introduces these key features. Throughout this book, we will discuss the means necessary to integrate all of these features together through VBA, XML, and smart documents. We cover the Word 2003 object model in the next chapter. Now it's time to see how it interacts with VBA. Word 2003 has the most extensive set of customization options of all Office applications. To see a large portion of the possibilities, take a look at the Options dialog (Tools | Options) displayed in Figure 3-1.

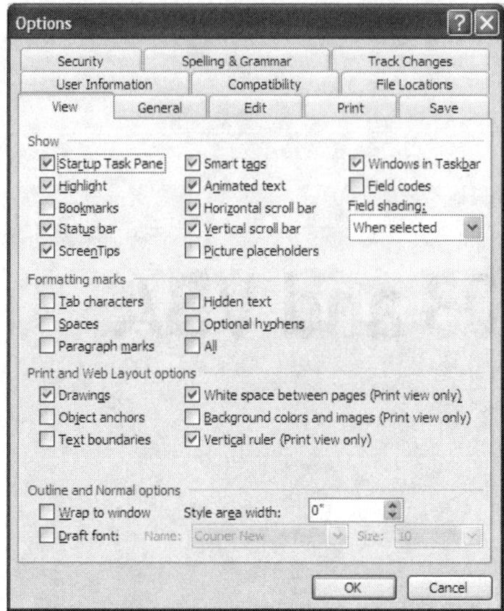

Figure 3-1

You will need to understand these options for the automated documents that you create. Almost anything that can be done normally in Word can be controlled programmatically. Remember that the goal of document automation is to create documents quickly and to ensure that the finished document is free of errors.

Word Macros

Macros are small chunks of VBA code that programmatically perform various tasks. Macros give the everyday user the power to automate routine tasks at the touch of a button. Each of Word's built-in functions is controlled by its own macro(s) (more on this later). In the past, many programs utilized proprietary macro languages that were difficult to learn. Microsoft implemented VBA, which is syntactically identical to Visual Basic, so that users could learn a language that could be used across applications.

How Macros Work

We've already noted that macros are basically just small chunks of code. Every time a macro is recorded, Word stores the resulting VBA code in the appropriate template. Each macro is stored as a separate subroutine. You can also attach your custom macros to buttons or keystrokes, or you can tie the macro to predefined events. Once a macro is recorded, you can manipulate the code in the VBE. This means the macro can be modified to call other macros, open dialog boxes, return values (turned into a function), or even open and work with other applications.

To perform any of these tasks, you must understand VBA. Using both VBA and the Word object model, you will be able to dive deep down into Word and control some of the most advanced Word functions programmatically. VBA also includes functions, statements, and access to type libraries that will enable you to perform various file manipulations, store data, etc. If VBA doesn't provide the functionality that you require, you may need to investigate the newly introduced smart document features.

Recording a Macro

The easiest way to create a macro is to use the Macro Recorder (Tools | Macro | Record New Macro). Once you have clicked Start on the Macro Recorder, you simply carry out your task as you normally would. When you are finished, click Stop. The Macro Recorder will record each step you perform and translate the step into VBA code. You can then view and modify the procedure in the Visual Basic Editor.

Tip: Keep in mind that there are limitations on what you can record. For instance, the Macro Recorder is not able to track your tasks as you switch between applications. However, just because the Macro Recorder isn't capable of recording such a task, please don't think that it's impossible for VBA to complete such a task. As you will see, VBA is capable of doing almost anything you can do manually.

Planning Macros

Before recording any macro, it is advisable to plan out the steps necessary to accomplish exactly what you want. The Macro Recorder will often record much more than just the bare minimum code. If you record a macro and perform trial and error until you get it right, your recorded code will be a bloated mess. Of course, you can always edit the macro, but it's better to start with a plan.

Make sure that you assign an appropriate name to the macro. Word will automatically assign a generic name, such as "Macro1." The best convention is to enter a short descriptive name so that in the future you will know exactly why the macro was created. If the OK button is not enabled, you have probably entered an invalid name. Macro names must begin with a letter and cannot have any spaces.

The default location to store a macro is in the Normal template. This will make the macro available to all documents because the Normal template is a global template. Every time you open Word the macro will be available. If you store the macro in a different document, it will only be available when that document is active. If you store the macro in a different template, it will be available when a document based on that template is open. Although macros usually reside in a standard module named NewMacros, it is possible to put macros into the ThisDocument module of a document.

The Description text box allows for the entry of a description of the macro. This text will appear in the VBA code that the Macro Recorder creates, and will be commented out so the compiler doesn't generate an error when it comes across the text. Commented code is always preceded by an apostrophe. Finally, you will notice in Figure 3-2 that you can assign the macro either to a toolbar or to the keyboard.

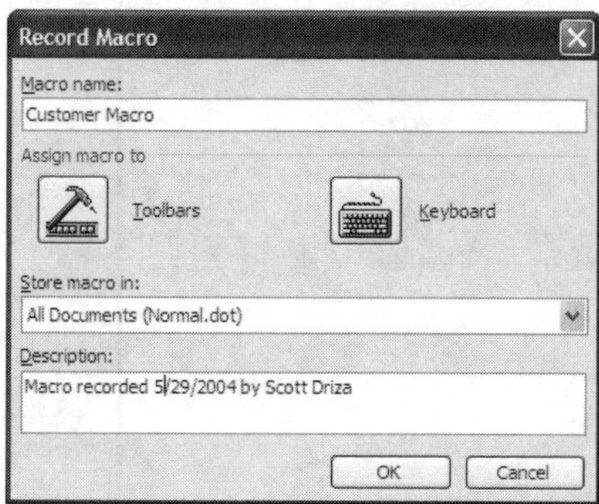

Figure 3-2

Shortcut Keys

Shortcut keys provide a convenient way to make your macros available to a user. The downside is that there is no graphical representation of the macro (a button). Many users remember the days when everything was handled by shortcut keys. Word processing applications were notorious for having confusing key combinations. WYSIWYG interfaces alleviated the need to have the cardboard key indicator sitting above the function keys. These functions are mostly still available through the key combinations, but most users prefer mouse-driven applications.

With all this in mind, there will still be times when you want to have keystroke-driven macros. The Word toolbars can seem pretty cluttered without having custom macros on them. If you start adding your own toolbars and buttons, you may overwhelm users. Save the toolbar buttons for the most frequently used macros. If users hunt around to learn the keystroke combination for a macro once or twice, they will remember it.

Assigning a keystroke combination is very easy. Figure 3-3 shows the dialog box that will be displayed when you choose to assign the macro to the keyboard (Tools | Customize | Commands | Keyboard).

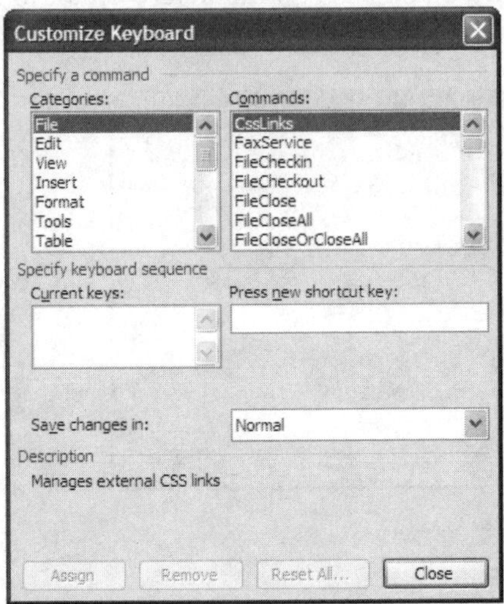

Figure 3-3

The Save changes in drop-down lists the available documents and templates where the key assignment may be saved. Save your changes in a global template if you want to make the change universally available. Again, it is best to save these types of customizations in the Normal template.

The Current keys section displays the current key assignment for the highlighted macro. This section is updated once a key combination is entered in the Press new shortcut key section and the Assign button is clicked. You can use the Remove button to remove individual keystroke settings. Also, you can use Reset All to remove all of the custom keyboard combinations. Finally, make sure not to overwrite any existing keystroke combinations. Combinations that are already assigned will appear directly below the Press new shortcut key text box.

Tip: Remember that you can always remove toolbars, buttons, or keystroke combinations that you don't want.

Tip: You can easily print a list of shortcut keys. Select Tools | Macro | Macros and select Word commands from the Macros in drop-down list. Then, in the Macro name box, click ListCommands | Run. In the List Commands dialog box, click Current menu and keyboard settings. Finally, on the File menu, click Print.

Note: The shortcut keys mentioned in the Help files all refer to a standard U.S. keyboard layout. Foreign keyboards may not match the keys on a U.S. keyboard and may require adjustments when using shortcut keys.

Custom Toolbar Buttons

One of the best ways to make your macros available to the end user is to create toolbar buttons for them. Users in a Windows environment are comfortable clicking on buttons to accomplish a given task. You can also delete certain buttons if the users do not need them. Deleting buttons is not advised, but in a cluttered environment it may become necessary.

The first step in adding your macro to a custom button on a specific toolbar is to make sure that the toolbar you want is visible. You will be dragging your macro directly onto the toolbar. Clicking the Assign Macro to Toolbars button on the Record Macro dialog will bring up the Customize dialog box. Checking any of the toolbars on the Toolbars tab will display that toolbar. Alternatively, you can select View | Toolbars and select the appropriate toolbar.

The second step is to choose the Commands tab of the Customize dialog box. You will then need to choose the appropriate category, which will be macros for your custom designed template. The Commands window to the right will display all of the currently available macros. Drag the macro for which you want to create the button to the appropriate toolbar.

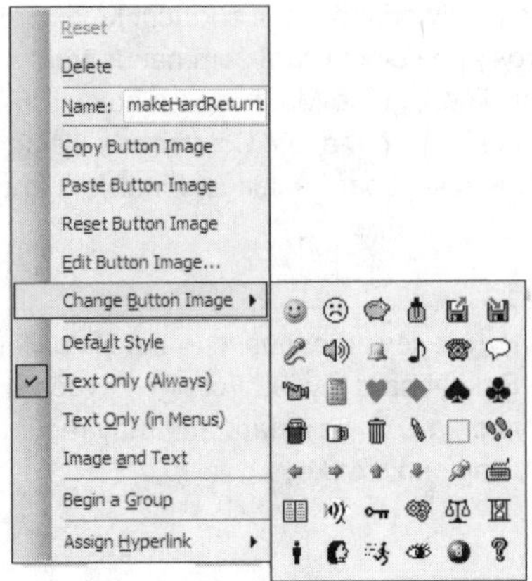

Figure 3-4

As you can see in Figure 3-4, you can customize the actual button in several ways. In addition to choosing from Word's predefined button pictures, you can create your own button with the Button Editor shown in Figure 3-5. Using the Button Editor is very easy. You navigate through the cells with the Move buttons and you can choose colors from the palette to the right. While it may be easy to use, it is not easy to design a button that looks like much of anything. With a little practice you may develop a knack for it.

Figure 3-5

Tip: Be sure to shorten the name. Otherwise, Word will assign the complete name of the macro to the button. This will result in the button being unnecessarily wide.

Viewing Available Macros

The Macros dialog box displays all macros that are currently available. These macros can reside in the Normal template, an active document, or a global template. You can change the option in the Macros in drop-down list to make only certain documents' macros available.

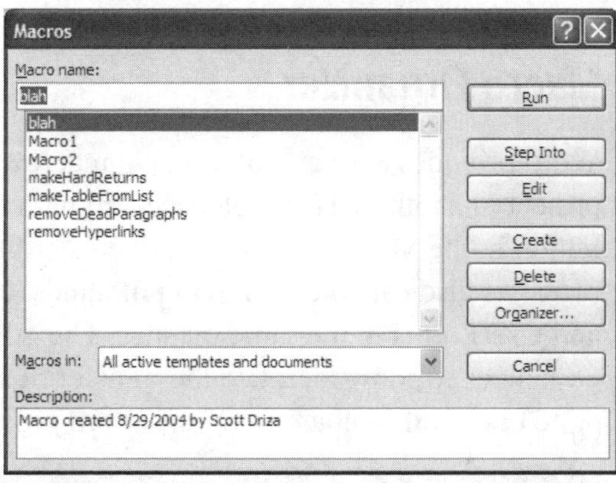

Figure 3-6

Choosing a macro and pressing the Edit button opens the Visual Basic Editor and displays the code behind the chosen macro. Notice that the code contains the commented text that was automatically created by the Macro Recorder. You are free to edit this code and alter the macro in any way you choose. Frequently, Office programmers find themselves stuck trying to write complex routines only to remember that they can use the Macro Recorder to provide the necessary code.

Macro Errors

Your recorded macro may not run correctly in every situation. Word will generate an error if the macro is unable to run. There may be certain options or settings that have changed since the macro was recorded. For example, a macro that searches for hidden text won't run properly if hidden text isn't displayed.

Note: Always write the error number down. You can then search for that specific error message in the Help files.

Macro Organizer

Word provides a great tool to move macros from one Word project to another. This tool, accessed with the Organizer button in the Macros dialog box (Tools | Macros | Organizer), is also capable of moving modules, class modules, and UserForms in the same manner. The other tabs of the Organizer window facilitate the transfer of styles, AutoText, and toolbars from one Word project to another.

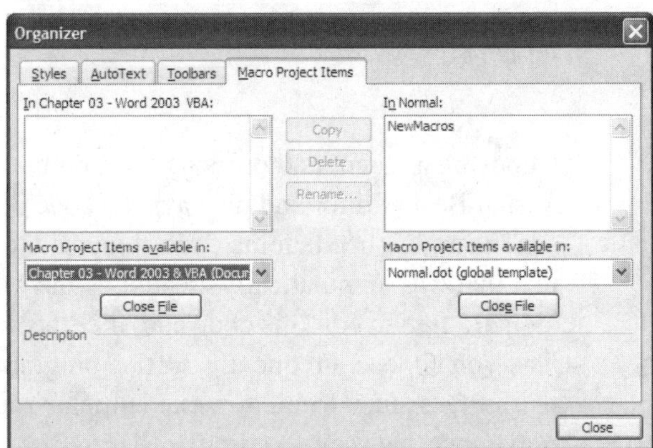

Figure 3-7

Each document or template represents a single project. The Organizer allows you to move parts of these projects. If you have some very useful macros in one template, you can use the Organizer to transfer them to a new project. This is much easier than cutting and pasting large blocks of text in the VBE.

Macro Security

A common obstacle to successful Word programming is the security level of a user's machine. Inexperienced users may not even understand what a macro is, much less what a security level is. If properly administered, Microsoft's new security settings can make your life as a developer much easier.

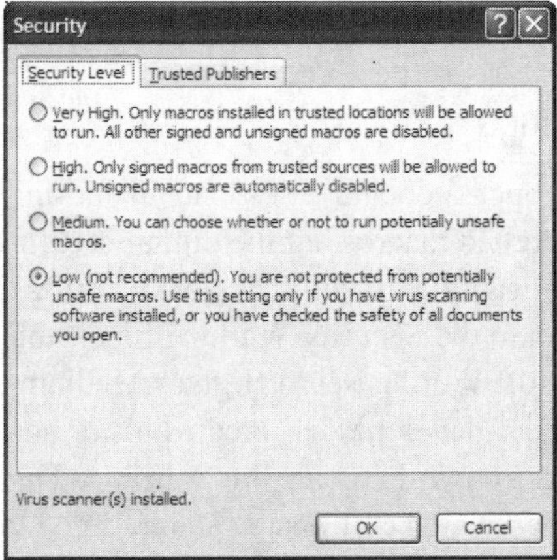

Figure 3-8

If you don't see a warning when opening a document that contains macros, the security level for Word is probably set to Low. Setting the security level to Medium will warn you that a document or add-in contains macros.

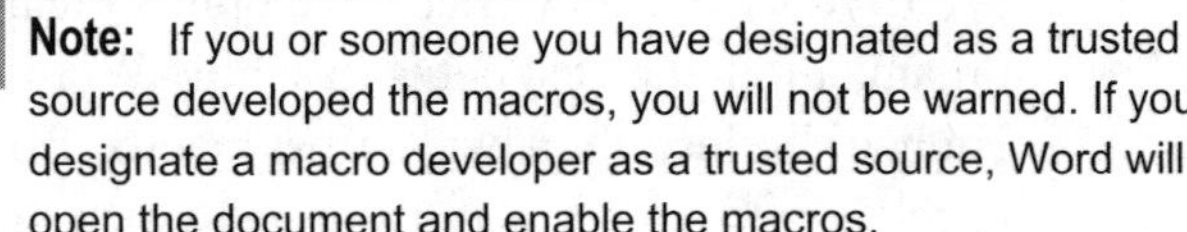

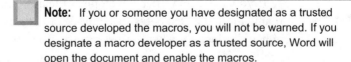

Note: If you or someone you have designated as a trusted source developed the macros, you will not be warned. If you designate a macro developer as a trusted source, Word will open the document and enable the macros.

You can easily remove someone from the trusted source list. If you have no one listed in the list of trusted sources, Word will prompt you every time you open a document or load an add-in that contains macros.

In unfamiliar documents, you should confirm that the macros were signed and check the source of the document. In the VBE, simply click Digital Signature on the Tools menu.

Caution: Documents stored in the folder where a user's templates reside will not trigger a warning. You can set a default location for user templates on the File Locations tab in the Options dialog box. By default, this location is implicitly trusted. You won't see a warning when you open documents or templates that contain macros from this location.

Warnings

If you open a document or load an add-in that contains digitally signed macros but the digital certificate has not been authenticated, you will receive a warning. This warning appears in the Security Warning box if the security level for Microsoft Word is set to High or Medium. For example, if the macro developer has created his or her own digital certificate, you will receive this warning. This type of unauthenticated certificate can be forged to falsify the identity of the certificate's source. For example, a malicious user might create a certificate named "Microsoft Corporation." The only warning you have that the certificate is false is this specific warning. As a general rule, professional software developers should always use authenticated certificates. You should only accept unauthenticated certificates from individual coworkers or friends. Don't accept one from a source you don't know!

If you are in an Office development team for a large organization, the best bet is to set the Word security level to High and select the Always trust macros from this source check box to enable your macros. Remember, even a setting of Medium will not require you to add the macro developer to the list of trusted sources if it is digitally signed. Word macro viruses are extremely prevalent; if you do not know who authored a macro, do not enable the macros. Do not even open the document until you have verified the source is safe.

Word's AutoMacros

Word contains many macros that run automatically. Although these are often referred to as "AutoMacros," they are simply events that can drive the execution of VBA code. Following are Word's most frequently used AutoMacros.

AutoExit

The AutoExit macro runs whenever you exit the Word application. An AutoExit macro should be stored in either the Normal template or any other globally available template. Remember that a macro is only available if the document or template to which it is attached is available. The Normal and global templates are available at all times.

AutoClose

AutoClose is the appropriate macro to run when closing an individual template or document instead of the entire application. When this macro is stored in a template, it will run any time a document based on that template is closed.

AutoNew

The AutoNew macro runs when a new document is created based on the template that contains the macro.

AutoOpen

The AutoOpen macro runs anytime a template or document is opened.

Differentiating Word's Document Events

The names AutoClose, AutoNew, and AutoOpen have been kept the same in Word 2003 for compatibility with versions of Word all the way back to Word 97. You can also use events to control macro execution under the same circumstances. The Document_New event corresponds to the AutoNew macro. The Document_Open event corresponds to the AutoOpen macro. Finally, the Document_Close macro corresponds to the AutoClose macro. As you will see, these events and macros can act differently depending on where they are placed.

You write procedures to respond to these events in the ThisDocument module or in a standard code module, such as NewMacros. Use the following steps to create an event procedure.

1. In the VBE, open the Project Explorer window, choose a project, and double-click **ThisDocument**. ThisDocument is located in the Microsoft Word Objects folder.
2. Select **Document** from the Object drop-down list box and select an event from the Procedure drop-down list box. This will add an empty subroutine to the ThisDocument module.
3. You can then add whatever VBA code you want to control the triggering of that event. The code below uses the MsgBox function to display information to the user. The following example, when placed in the Normal project, will run when a new document based on the Normal template is created:

```
Private Sub Document_New()
    MsgBox "A new document has been created."
End Sub
```

Event procedures in the Normal template do not have a global scope. More precisely, event procedures residing in the Normal template will only be fired if the document is attached to the Normal template. This difference in functionality can be very important when choosing which way to automate your documents.

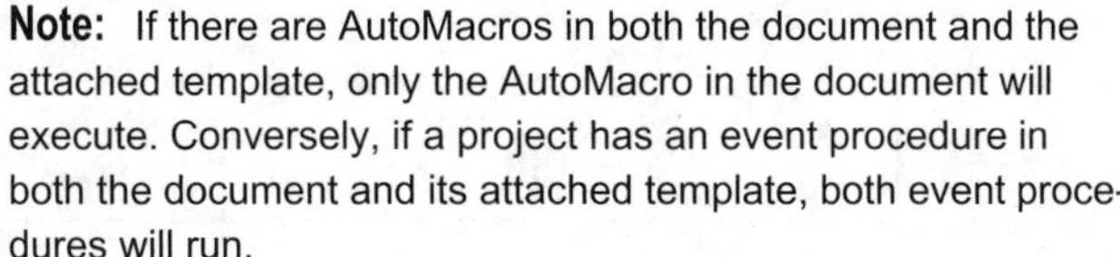

Note: If there are AutoMacros in both the document and the attached template, only the AutoMacro in the document will execute. Conversely, if a project has an event procedure in both the document and its attached template, both event procedures will run.

Changing Word's Built-in Macros

The Macros dialog box also displays the names of all Word commands. A subroutine with that name will replace Word's automatic commands. This can be extremely useful when developing a customized documentation system. You can tweak Word so that it can only be used for specific purposes or so that only specific templates are available to users.

The following code illustrates how Word's built-in macros can be manipulated:

```
Private Sub FileNew()
    MsgBox "Sorry, you do not have permission to create a
            new document"
End Sub
```

The preceding example shows how you can programmatically control Word's built-in functions. Figure 3-9 shows the Macros dialog and some Word commands that can be overwritten. The appendix contains a complete listing of all Word commands.

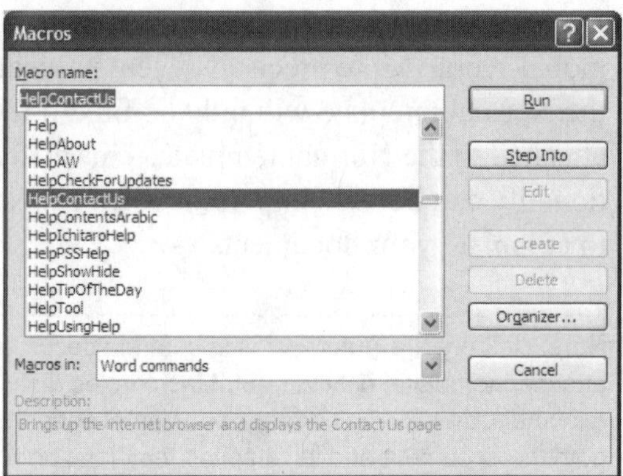

Figure 3-9

Note: Use the same syntax that appears in the Macros dialog box. For example:

```
Sub FileCloseOrCloseAll ( )
```

Templates

All Word documents are based on a template. In the VBE, every Word document will have a reference to the template that created it. The template is basically the storage facility for all the document settings such as UserForms, modules, class modules, AutoText, styles, fonts, menus, page settings, and formatting.

There are two basic types of templates: global templates and document templates. Global templates are available to all documents. The most common global template is the Normal template. This is the default template from which all blank documents are created. Templates contain settings that are available only to documents attached to that template. A document created from a template can use the settings from both the template and the settings in any global template. Word provides numerous document templates. You can also create your own template.

Global Templates

A document can only access settings stored in the template attached to the document or in the Normal template. In order to use settings from another template, you must either load the other template as a global template or attach a reference to the other template. If a template is loaded as a global template, items stored in that template are available to all documents.

Document Templates

There are two areas where templates can reside in order to appear in the File | New menu. The User templates and Workgroup templates directories appear in Word under Tools | Options | File Locations. These directories, and any subdirectories containing templates, will appear in Word's File | New menu. This is where any organization templates should reside. It is important to note that the Templates dialog will display templates appearing in both locations. The General tab will house templates residing in either directory. Subfolders of these directories will appear as tabs on the dialog (provided they contain *.dot files).

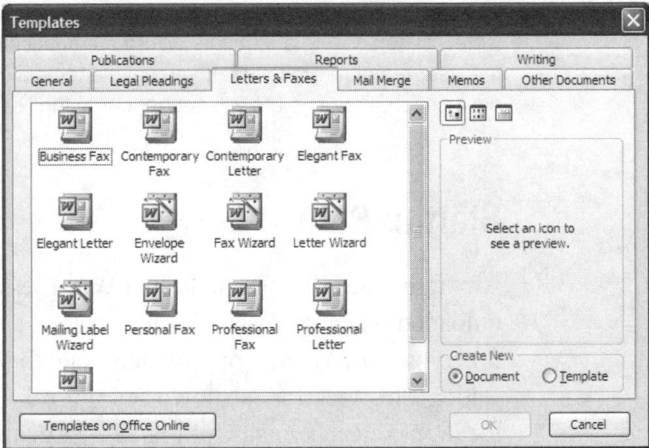

Figure 3-10

Tip: Be careful to avoid cluttering things up with numerous tabs. It's best to have just one tab if possible. If there is a specialized area that has its own set of templates, it may be appropriate to have another tab for them. Otherwise, make templates available to all users.

The Workgroup templates directory should be on a shared network drive. This way the templates can be centrally maintained and administered. You also want to make sure that users do not inadvertently alter the templates.

Tip: Your network files should be read-only. You should also have the systems administrator deny access to anyone without the appropriate permissions.

The User templates folder is where individual users can maintain custom templates. Templates stored in this folder will appear on the General tab. This directory is usually mapped to a user's C: drive. There may be instances when you want to take advantage of this location. This may be a convenient location to install templates in an organization that has remote users.

Caution: Any document (.doc) file that you save in the Templates folder also acts as a template.

Note: When saving a template, Word automatically switches to the User templates location. If you save a template in a different location, the template will not appear in the New dialog box.

Startup Path

Any templates that you load in a Word session are unloaded when you close Word. To load a template each time you start Word, copy the template to the Startup folder. This location is shown in Figure 3-11. To find that location, select Tools | Options | File Locations.

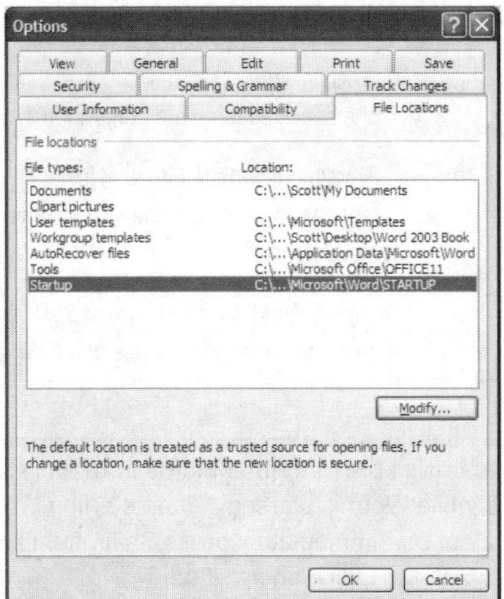

Figure 3-11

Tip: This path is usually C:\Windows\Application Data\Microsoft\Word\STARTUP.

Command-Line Parameters

You can also specify command-line options when starting Word to control how users open and create documents.

The following table lists the command-line parameters that apply to Word.

Parameter	Description
/a	This parameter prevents add-ins and global templates (including the Normal template) from being loaded.
/l addinpath	This parameter loads a specific Word add-in.
/m	This parameter prevents any AutoExec (automatically executing) macros from running.
/m macroname	This parameter runs a specific macro and prevents Word from running any AutoExec macros.
/n	This parameter prevents Word from opening a document when Word is started.

Parameter	Description
/t templatename	This parameter starts Word with a new document based on the specified template rather than the Normal template.
/w	Documents opened in each instance of Word will not appear as choices in the Window menu of the other documents.
(no switch)	A new Word window is opened with a blank document using the existing instance of the Word application.

Tip: You can also prevent AutoMacros from running by holding down Shift while Word is starting. When starting Word from the Office shortcut bar, immediately press Shift after clicking the Word button on the Office shortcut bar.

Add-Ins

Add-ins are supplemental programs that you install to extend the capabilities of Word by adding custom commands and specialized features. When you load an add-in, it remains loaded for the current Word session only. If you quit and then restart Word, the add-in is not automatically reloaded. Like templates, you must store the add-in in your Startup folder to have it available when Word is restarted. The following figures show the tabs in the Templates and Add-ins window.

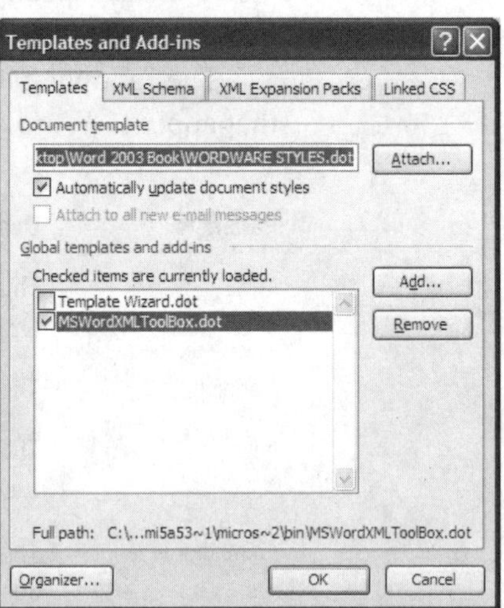

Figure 3-12

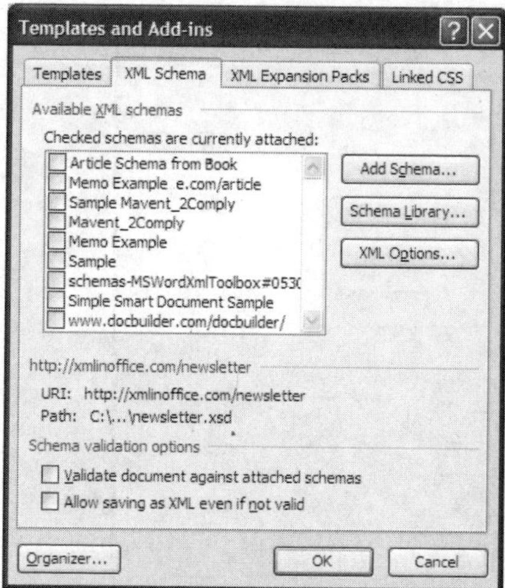

Figure 3-13

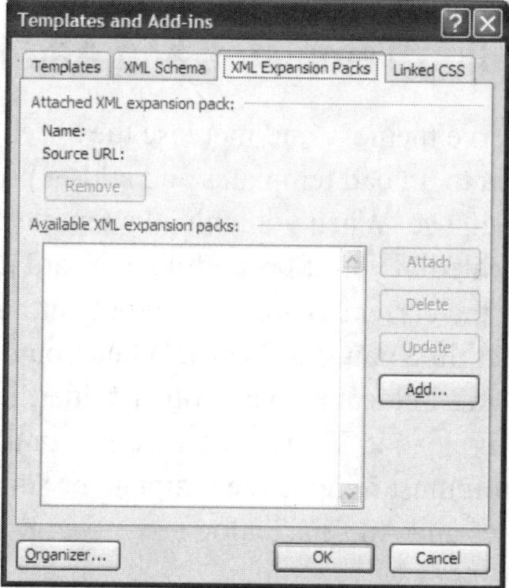

Figure 3-14

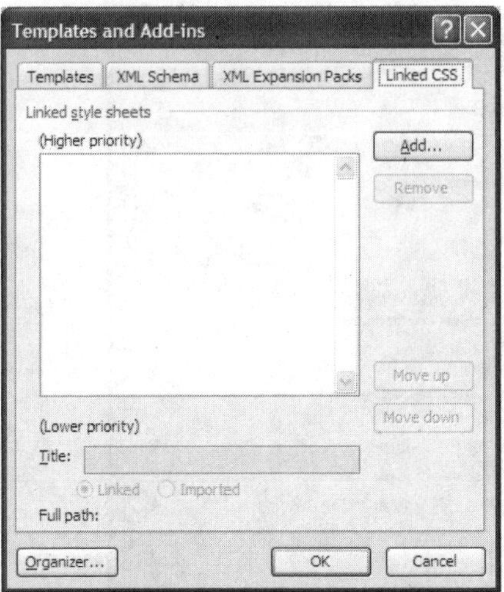

Figure 3-15

Unloading Templates and Add-ins

To conserve memory and increase the speed of Word, it's a good idea to unload templates and add-in programs you don't often use. When you unload a template or add-in that's located in your Startup folder, Word unloads the template for the current Word session but automatically reloads it the next time you start Word. When you unload a template or add-in located in any other folder, it is unavailable until you reload it. To delete a template or add-in from Word, you must remove the template or add-in from the Templates and Add-ins dialog box.

Fields

Fields are used as placeholders for data that might change in a document and for creating form letters and labels in mail-merge documents. Some of the most common fields are the PAGE field, which is inserted when you add page numbers, and the Date field, which is inserted when you click Date and Time on the Insert menu and then select the

Update automatically check box. There is a more thorough description of Word's fields in Chapter 1.

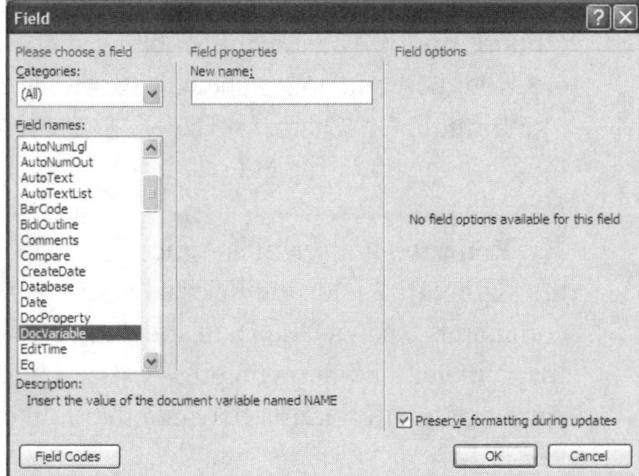

Figure 3-16

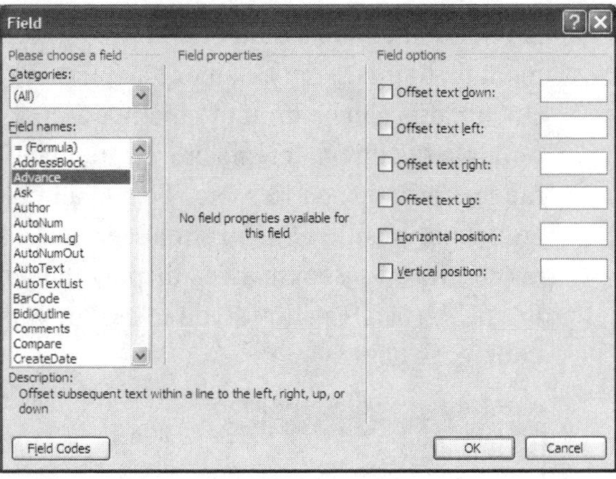

Figure 3-17

Fields are inserted automatically when you create an index or table of contents by choosing the Index and Tables command on the Insert menu. You can also use fields to automatically insert document information (such as the author or filename), to perform calculations, to create links and references to other documents or items, and to perform other special tasks.

Field codes appear between curly brackets, or braces ({ }). To display the results of field codes, such as the results of calculations, hide the field codes by clicking Options on the Tools menu, clicking the View tab, and then clearing the Field codes check box. Fields are somewhat like formulas in Microsoft Excel — the field code is like the formula, and the field result is like the value that the formula produces.

You cannot insert field braces by typing characters on the keyboard. Fields are inserted when you use particular commands, such as the Date and Time command on the Insert menu, or when you press Ctrl + F9 and type the appropriate information between the field braces.

Bookmarks

A bookmark can be either an item or a location in a document that you assign a name to for future reference. Bookmarks can be used to quickly jump to a specific location in a document, create cross-references, mark page ranges for index entries, etc. To add a bookmark, just select an item or position the cursor at a specific location and choose Insert | Bookmark to display the window shown in Figure 3-18. This allows you to assign your selection a bookmark name.

Figure 3-18

Normally, bookmarks aren't visible in your document. If you want to display bookmarks when you're working in a document, you will need to turn them on just as you would to use Word's fields (Tools | Options | View). After turning on the visible characteristic of bookmarks, you'll notice that Word uses brackets to represent bookmarks around an item or an I-beam to represent a bookmark at a location.

Note: Unlike field codes, you cannot print bookmarks.

Bookmarks are quite frequently used in document automation as placeholders for various reasons. Sometimes bookmarks are used as entry points for specific information. Other times, bookmarks are used to mark areas where text will be pasted. As you will see throughout this book, I prefer to use Word's fields when applicable. Fields allow you to see and print a visual aspect that contains both the formatting and information that will be inserted into the document. When you are working with complex documents, it is often easier to insert text using Docvariable fields than bookmarks. However, I've used bookmark examples throughout the book as well. This way, you will be exposed to the different ways in which text can be inserted and documents can be automated.

Word VBA Tips

Before we get to the substance of actually writing code in the following chapters, there are a couple items to note. These will come in handy as you progress in your VBA development. The rest of the chapter discusses the topics of locking your VBA code, preventing unauthorized interference with your code, and distributing your code to users via templates.

Locking Your VBA Code

In many instances, you will want to prevent unauthorized users from accessing your VBA code. The process of locking your VBA code is very straightforward:

1. Open the VBA editor. This is accomplished either by pressing **Alt + F11** or choosing **Tools | Macro | Visual Basic Editor**.
2. Once in the VBE, right-click on the project name in the project window on the left, and select **Template Project properties** from the pop-up menu to open the Project Properties dialog. (You can also access this dialog via Tools | Project Properties.)

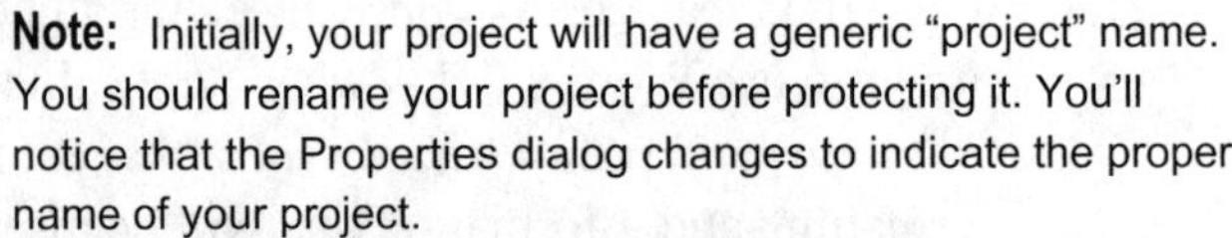

Note: Initially, your project will have a generic "project" name. You should rename your project before protecting it. You'll notice that the Properties dialog changes to indicate the proper name of your project.

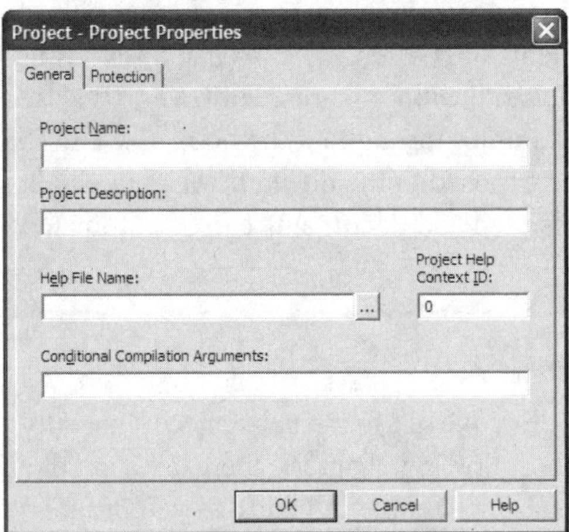

Figure 3-19

There are several options available on the General tab of the Project Properties dialog. You can include a brief project description, specify a help file, and specify the context ID for the help file if you would like to be directed to a specific topic within the help file. VBA also supports conditional compilation. You can use conditional compilation to run blocks of code selectively, for example, debugging statements comparing the speed of different approaches to the same programming task, or localizing an application for different languages. Conditional compiler constants are set in code with the #Const directive. This directive is used to mark blocks of code to be conditionally compiled with the #If...Then...#Else directive.

3. In order to protect your project, you select the Protection tab and select the **Lock Project for viewing** check box. You will then enter a password twice, in the two boxes available. Once you've entered your passwords, simply click **OK** and you are ready to go.

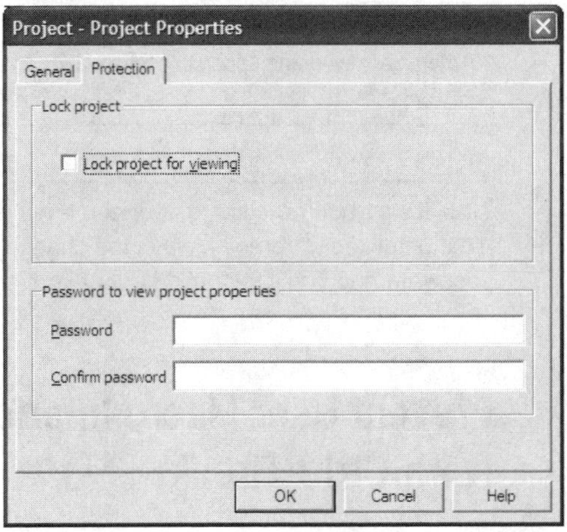

Figure 3-20

Please keep in mind that it is fairly easy to create (or otherwise obtain) a brute force password cracking program. Brute force programs simply continue creating different passwords and trying to crack the password. If you've gone through the trouble of setting up a password, make sure to use one of sufficient length and complexity. The following table lists the amount of time a brute force program (running on a P4 2000 machine) will take to crack a Word VBA password.

4-character lower- or uppercase letters	a few seconds
4-character lower- and uppercase letters	a few seconds
4-character lower- and uppercase letters and numbers	a few seconds
5-character lower- or uppercase letters (e.g., passb)	under 60 seconds
5-character lower- and uppercase letters (e.g., passB)	approx 6 minutes
5-character lower- and uppercase and numbers (e.g., Pasb1)	approx 15 minutes
8-character lower- or uppercase password	approx 58 hours
8-character lower- and uppercase password	approx 21 months
8-character lower- and uppercase letters and numbers password	approx 7 years
10-character lower- or uppercase password	approx 5 years
10-character lower- and uppercase password	approx 4,648 years
10-character lower- and uppercase letters and numbers password	approx 26,984 years

Tip: It's a good practice to keep the original copy of the template unlocked. There is always the chance that you'll forget the password and you'll be locked out of your own project.

Prevent User Macro Interference (with Ctrl + Break)

One common problem with Word projects is that savvy users will figure out how to force a hard stop with the Ctrl + Break key combination. This is easily thwarted by inserting the following code into the appropriate procedures. One note of caution: It is best to insert this code once the routines have been thoroughly tested. If you're accustomed to stopping your infinite loops with Ctrl + Break, these few lines will cause you headaches and reboots.

```
Sub SomeRoutine()
Application.EnableCancelKey = wdCancelDisabled
'code here
Application.EnableCancelKey = wdCancelInterrupt
End Sub
```

Distributing VBA Macros

Distributing macros is a fairly common scenario. A user (perhaps you) creates a couple of specific macros that have a high degree of value to other users in his or her organization. This presents the problem of distributing these macros so that they run properly on other people's machines.

By default, Word stores macros in the Normal template unless you specify a different location. In many cases, an organization may have a default, or shared, Normal template. In other cases, users have created their own macros and saved them in their Normal template. The Normal template also includes extra menu items or toolbars, keyboard shortcuts, AutoText entries, etc. This is why it is almost never an option to simply replace someone's Normal template.

Generally, macros fall into two categories: macros that are specific to a certain document or set of documents, and generic macros that usually pertain to certain formatting or general business use situations.

The rest of this book is largely dedicated to the first type of macro. These macros become part of the template and are distributed as part and parcel of the template. This is usually accomplished by distributing that template to the users by putting it in the Workgroup templates folder or the User templates folder.

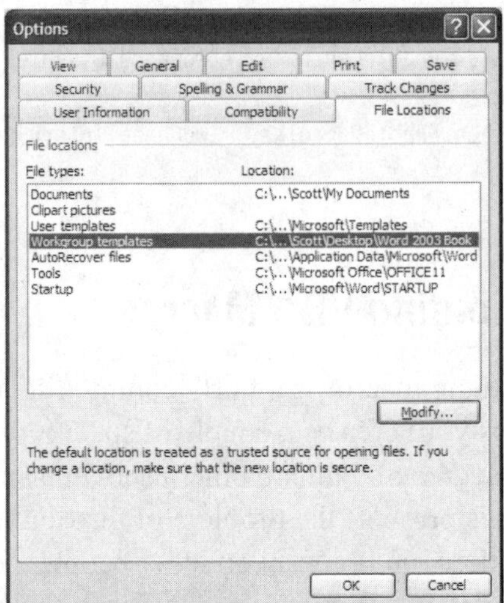

Figure 3-21

If you have a template full of generic macros, you can make them available to your users by propagating the template to the user's Word\Startup folder. Keep in mind that this will allow you to distribute all items specific to the template including any additional menu items, toolbars, and keyboard shortcuts that you want to set up to make it easier to access the macros. This folder can be identified by going to Tools | Options | File Locations, and checking the Startup folder. The template will be available once it is copied to this folder. The template is considered an add-in and will be loaded automatically upon startup. You can see the list of your add-ins by viewing Tools | Templates and Add-ins.

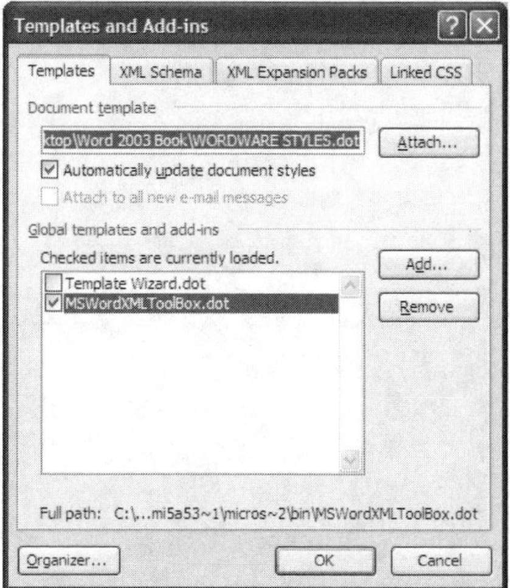

Figure 3-22

Tip Because each situation is different, you may discover that it is easier to point your users' Workgroup Template path and their Startup path to a location on the server (easily done using user profiles).

Conclusion

This chapter introduced many of Word's features that are important in the proper development of a Word document automation system. Throughout this book, we will continue to discuss the means necessary to integrate all of these features together through VBA. There is no way to touch on every possible use of Word because Word 2003 has the most extensive set of customization options of all Office applications. Chapter 4 covers the Word 2003 object model in depth.

Chapter 4

The Word 2003 Object Model

Introduction

Document automation requires that you be well versed in the Word 2003 object model. There are many exciting additions to the object model as a result of the newly introduced XML support. Use this chapter to familiarize yourself with some of the most commonly used Word objects. This chapter does not have a project component. Instead, there are several code snippets in the chapter that are frequently encountered when working with Word documents. The Word 2003 object model is the largest object model of all the Office applications.

The Application Object

As you've already seen, an object is something that is characterized by its properties and methods. Following is a complete listing of the properties, methods, and events for the Word.Application object. Don't let this list intimidate you; the majority of your work will be with a much smaller subset of this list. As you will see, some of these are also top-level objects themselves. Instead of covering each of these in detail, I will discuss the most commonly used objects.

Additions to the Application Object

There have been a couple notable additions to the Application object in Word 2003. First, the XMLNamespaces property provides a mechanism to programmatically access the application's XMLNamespaces collection. This new feature is obviously important when working with XML.

On the event side, Microsoft has added an XMLSelectionChange event that allows you to trigger code whenever changes occur in the immediate parent element of the current Selection object.

Finally, you can capture validation errors (think "help the end user") via the newly added XMLValidationError event whenever a validation error occurs in the document.

Properties of the Application Object

ActiveDocument	ActivePrinter
ActiveWindow	AddIns
AnswerWizard	Application
ArbitraryXMLSupportAvailable	Assistant
AutoCaptions	AutoCorrect
AutoCorrectEmail	AutomationSecurity
BackgroundPrintingStatus	BackgroundSavingStatus
BrowseExtraFileTypes	Browser
Build	CapsLock
Caption	CaptionLabels
CheckLanguage	COMAddIns
CommandBars	Creator
CustomDictionaries	CustomizationContext
DefaultLegalBlackline	DefaultSaveFormat

DefaultTableSeparator
Dialogs
DisplayAlerts
DisplayAutoCompleteTips
DisplayRecentFiles
DisplayScreenTips
DisplayScrollBars
DisplayStatusBar
Documents
EmailOptions
EmailTemplate
EnableCancelKey
FeatureInstall
FileConverters
FileDialog
FileSearch
FindKey
FocusInMailHeader
FontNames
HangulHanjaDictionaries
Height
International
IsObjectValid
KeyBindings
KeysBoundTo
LandscapeFontNames
Language
Languages
LanguageSettings
Left
ListGalleries
MacroContainer
MailingLabel
MailMessage
MailSystem
MAPIAvailable
MathCoprocessorAvailable
MouseAvailable
Name
NewDocument
NormalTemplate
NumLock
Options
Parent
Path
PathSeparator
PortraitFontNames
PrintPreview
RecentFiles
ScreenUpdating
Selection
ShowStartupDialog
ShowVisualBasicEditor
ShowWindowsInTaskbar
SmartTagRecognizers
SmartTagTypes
SpecialMode
StartupPath
StatusBar
SynonymInfo
System
TaskPanes
Tasks
Templates

Top	UsableHeight
UsableWidth	UserAddress
UserControl	UserInitials
UserName	VBE
Version	Visible
Width	Windows
WindowState	WordBasic
XMLNamespaces	

Methods of the Application Object

Activate	AddAddress
AutomaticChange	BuildKeyCode
CentimetersToPoints	ChangeFileOpenDirectory
CheckGrammar	CheckSpelling
CleanString	DDEExecute
DDEInitiate	DDEPoke
DDERequest	DDETerminate
DDETerminateAll	DefaultWebOptions
GetAddress	GetDefaultTheme
GetSpellingSuggestions	GettingHelp
GettingHelponMacintoshKeywords	GoBack
GoForward	Help
HelpTool	InchesToPoints
Keyboard	KeyboardBidi
KeyboardLatin	KeyString
LinesToPoints	ListCommands
LookupNameProperties	MillimetersToPoints
Move	NewWindow
OnTime	OrganizerCopy

OrganizerDelete
OrganizerRename
PicasToPoints
PixelsToPoints
PointsToCentimeters
PointsToInches
PointsToLines
PointsToMillimeters
PointsToPicas
PointsToPixels
PrintOut
ProductCode
PutFocusInMailHeader
Quit
Repeat
ResetIgnoreAll
Resize
Run
ScreenRefresh
SendFax
SetDefaultTheme
ShowClipboard
ShowMe
SubstituteFont
ToggleKeyboard

Events of the Application Object

DocumentBeforeClose
DocumentBeforePrint
DocumentBeforeSave
DocumentChange
DocumentOpen
DocumentSync
EPostageInsert
EPostageInsertEx
EPostagePropertyDialog
MailMergeAfterMerge
MailMergeAfterRecordMerge
MailMergeBeforeMerge
MailMergeBeforeRecordMerge
MailMergeDataSourceLoad
MailMergeDataSourceValidate
MailMergeWizardSendToCustom
MailMergeWizardStateChange
NewDocument
Quit
WindowActivate
WindowBeforeDoubleClick
WindowBeforeRightClick
WindowDeactivate
WindowSelectionChange
WindowSize
XMLSelectionChange
XMLValidationError

Using Events with the Application Object

Each time Word is started, an instance of the Application object is created. This is the top-level object in Microsoft Word (as in most other Office applications). This object exposes properties and methods that manipulate the entire Word environment, including the appearance of the application window. You can either work with the Word application model directly or you can set an object variable equal to the Word Application object. When working with Word, either directly or through automation, use the Application object only to manipulate the properties and methods that pertain directly to Word. In most instances, you will be working with a subobject such as a document.

```
Application.WindowState = wdWindowStateMaximize
```

Tip: When using automation, you should use an early bound object variable to instantiate the Word object model.

As previously discussed, sometimes properties actually return lower-level objects. These objects are called *accessors*. If these accessors are global, you can work with the object directly and do not need to include the "Application" qualifier. You can use the Object Browser to see what objects are globally available (click <globals> in the Classes drop-down), or you can press Ctrl + J to display an IntelliSense window that will list the globally available properties and functions. Each of the following examples returns the same Name property:

```
MsgBox Application.ActiveDocument.Name
MsgBox ActiveDocument.Name
MsgBox Application.NormalTemplate.Name
MsgBox NormalTemplate.Name
```

Figure 4-1 shows the IntelliSense pop-up window accessed by pressing Ctrl + J in the Visual Basic Editor:

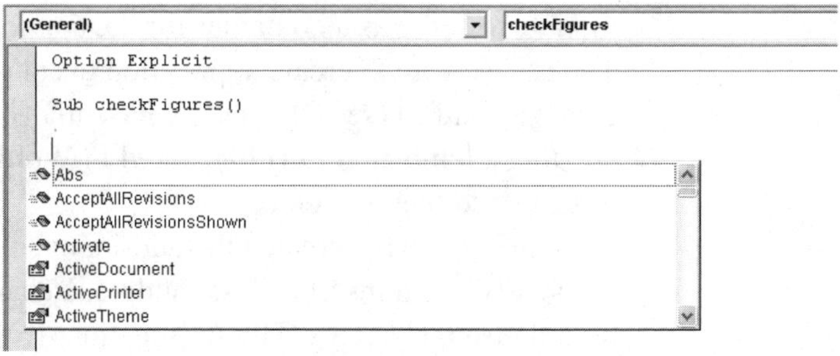

Figure 4-1

Intercepting Application Events

You can respond to certain application-level events using AutoMacros as discussed in the previous chapter. However, there may be times when you need to respond to other application events outside of the context of a particular document or template. In this case, it will be necessary to use the Application object model. This involves creating an Application type object declared "WithEvents." The WithEvents keyword declaration allows the object to respond to the exposed events via a class module.

Responding to Application Events

If you open a template, press Alt + F11, and in the Project window of the VBA environment, double-click on Microsoft Word Objects, you'll see a built-in class module called ThisDocument. If you open this, you can use the list boxes on the toolbar to help you create document event procedures.

So it would make sense for there to be another built-in class module called ThisApplication; unfortunately, this does not exist. In essence, though, a class is simply a container object that allows you to create properties, which are objects in their own right, and then create properties and methods for those objects.

From a high-level viewpoint there are two essential elements: There must be an application variable (declared with WithEvents) to receive the events, and there must be a class module to serve as a container for the application variable. The easiest way to create application event procedures is to create an add-in (see Chapter 3). Essentially, this means creating a template (.dot) file stored in Word's Startup directory so that it is global.

Once you have created the add-in, open it in Word, go to the VBE, and insert a class module. Rename the class module from Class1 to ThisApplication. I've chosen to use "ThisApplication" because it shows that it is similar to the built-in "ThisDocument" class module. But note that the ThisApplication object is simply a container. It doesn't actually represent an application. It represents all the properties of the class object, and we are free to define those properties however we choose.

Insert the following code in the class module:

```
Option Explicit

Public WithEvents oApp As Word.Application
```

Using the WithEvents keyword indicates that the oApp object variable will respond to the events triggered by the Word.Application object. In essence, we are merely mirroring the Word application by creating another object that refers to its instantiation. Because oApp is declared publicly, it is a property of the class object ThisApplication. Keep in mind that we haven't yet assigned oApp to an instance of the Word application (we'll do that in a minute). The WithEvents keyword can only be used in class modules and can only refer to OLE-compliant objects. All we've done is declare the variable of which the type is a Word Application object, and used the WithEvents keyword to declare that the variable will respond to events. As far as memory is concerned, we're still not concerned because the oApp object doesn't actually exist yet.

It is now time to insert a normal code module by selecting Insert | Module. In the module, insert the following code:

```
Option Explicit
Dim oAppClass As New ThisApplication
```

where "ThisApplication" is the name of the class module. The statement creates an object variable oAppClass that references (it is actually a pointer to) the class object ThisApplication you created earlier. The "New" keyword in the declaration creates a new instance of the class object and makes it available via early binding. This means that the object is created real time versus compile time and that an instance of the class is loaded into memory. Now add the following code in the same module:

```
Public Sub AutoExec()
    Set oAppClass.oApp = Word.Application
End Sub
```

The oApp object is available via IntelliSense because it is a property of the class object oAppClass. It was declared as a public variable when we inserted it into the class module. The above code creates an instance of the oApp object and loads it into memory. At this point, the variable actually refers to an instance of the live Word.Application object. Essentially, the creation and allocation of this variable is what makes the oApp object exist in the first place. Keep in mind the subtle nuance: Now there is an actual Word Application instance, whereas previously there was only a declaration of a variable of a specific type.

If you insert an AutoExec procedure you can respond every time Word is loaded. When Word is launched it also launches its accompanying add-ins and they are automatically loaded into memory. When it loads the add-in with the Application variable and accompanying events, those events will be triggered and, in turn, the AutoExec macro will be fired.

You can go back to the ThisApplication class module. The class module contains two list boxes on the toolbar. If you pull down the one on the left and change it from "(General)" to "oApp," a procedure called oApp_Quit() will be created. The list box on the right contains several other application events that can be utilized.

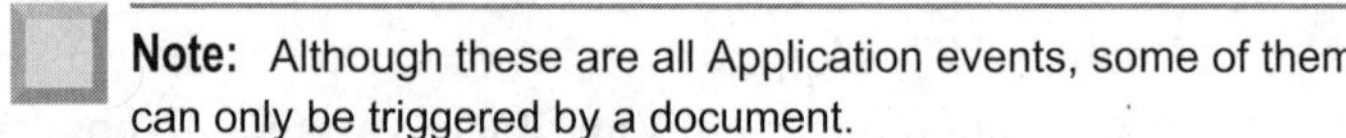

Note: Although these are all Application events, some of them can only be triggered by a document.

The Documents Collection

The Documents collection is a collection of all open documents in the active instance of Word. You can use the Documents collection to reference a specific instance of a document using the Documents(index) syntax, where "index" is either the document's name or its index number. Keep in mind that it is often best to use the actual name of a document instead of the numerical index property; as documents are opened and closed, the index values of the Documents collection change.

Word 2003 Additions to the Document Object

Microsoft has made changes to the Word 2003 Document object. These changes give control over the task pane that appears on the right-hand side of the screen.

Specifically, the XMLHideNamespaces property allows you to programmatically show and hide the namespace aliases in the XML Structure task pane.

Now that Word has XML support, they've added an XMLNodes property. This property returns a collection of all of the document's XML elements. These elements appear in linear order and can be looped through to get at the specific nodes.

The Document object also exposes an XMLSaveDataOnly property. This property specifies whether the document will be saved with all of the corresponding WordprocessingML information or as data only. "Data only" will result in the structure of the data being saved. It is important to note that when a "data-only" document is reopened, all of the previous formatting will be lost.

The Document object allows you to specify the path for an XSLT Transform via the XMLSaveThroughXSLT property. The specified transform will be applied when the document is saved as XML (True).

Note that the XMLUseXSLTWhenSaving property must also be set to True.

You can also programmatically control the attached schemas. Word provides access to the document's XMLSchemaReferences collection via the XMLSchemaReferences property. In addition, if you have errors when validating according to a schema, the XMLSchemaViolations property returns a collection of elements. The elements returned via the XMLSchemaViolations property all have errors associated with them.

If you need more control over your Document object, you can use the XMLShowAdvancedErrors property to display more advanced validation error messages. These messages show up in the Word user interface when the mouse pointer rests on visual validation error cues (such as the zigzag purple underline or the strikeout symbols in the XML Structure task pane).

Note: The advanced validation errors come directly from the MSXML parser 5.0 and require that the object be properly installed on your client machine.

Another property you may frequently work with when using XML is the XMLUseXSLTWhenSaving property. This property indicates whether a transform will be applied to a document saved as XML. In addition, you can use the TransformDocument method to specify the transform that will occur when the document is reopened.

Finally, there are two new XML-driven events that give you additional control. You can use the XMLAfterInsert event to capture the addition/insertion of XML elements when they occur anywhere in the document. If you need to capture deletions from the XML, you can trap the XMLBeforeDelete event. This event fires before an XML element is deleted from the document.

Following is a complete listing of the properties, methods, and events that pertain to the Documents collection.

Properties of the Documents Collection

ActiveTheme	ActiveThemeDisplayName
ActiveWindow	ActiveWritingStyle
Application	AttachedTemplate
AutoFormatOverride	AutoHyphenation
Background	Bookmarks
BuiltInDocumentProperties	Characters
ChildNodeSuggestions	ClickAndTypeParagraphStyle
CodeName	CommandBars
Comments	Compatibility
ConsecutiveHyphensLimit	Container
Content	Count
Creator	CustomDocumentProperties
DefaultTableStyle	DefaultTabStop
DefaultTargetFrame	DisableFeatures
DisableFeaturesIntroducedAfter	DocumentLibraryVersions
DoNotEmbedSystemFonts	Email
EmbedLinguisticData	EmbedSmartTags
EmbedTrueTypeFonts	Endnotes
EnforceStyle	Envelope
FarEastLineBreakLanguage	FarEastLineBreakLevel
Fields	Footnotes
FormattingShowClear	FormattingShowFilter
FormattingShowFont	FormattingShowNumbering
FormattingShowParagraph	FormFields
FormsDesign	Frames
Frameset	FullName

GettingHelponMacintoshKeywords	GrammarChecked
GrammaticalErrors	GridDistanceHorizontal
GridDistanceVertical	GridOriginFromMargin
GridOriginHorizontal	GridOriginVertical
GridSpaceBetweenHorizontalLines	GridSpaceBetweenVerticalLines
HasPassword	HasRoutingSlip
HTMLDivisions	HTMLProject
Hyperlinks	HyphenateCaps
HyphenationZone	Indexes
InlineShapes	IsMasterDocument
IsSubdocument	JustificationMode
KerningByAlgorithm	Kind
LanguageDetected	ListParagraphs
Lists	ListTemplates
MailEnvelope	MailMerge
Name	NoLineBreakAfter
NoLineBreakBefore	OpenEncoding
OptimizeForWord97	PageSetup
Paragraphs	Parent
Password	PasswordEncryptionAlgorithm
PasswordEncryptionFileProperties	PasswordEncryptionKeyLength
PasswordEncryptionProvider	Path
Permission	PrintFormsData
PrintFractionalWidths	PrintPostScriptOverText
PrintRevisions	ProtectionType
ReadabilityStatistics	ReadingLayoutFrozen
ReadingLayoutSizeX	ReadingLayoutSizeY
ReadOnly	ReadOnlyRecommended
RemoveDateAndTime	RemovePersonalInformation
Revisions	Routed

RoutingSlip	Saved
SaveEncoding	SaveFormat
SaveFormsData	SaveSubsetFonts
Scripts	Sections
Sentences	Shapes
SharedWorkspace	ShowGrammaticalErrors
ShowRevisions	ShowSpellingErrors
ShowSummary	Signatures
SmartDocument	SmartTags
SmartTagsAsXMLProps	SnapToGrid
SnapToShapes	SpellingChecked
SpellingErrors	StoryRanges
Styles	StyleSheets
Subdocuments	SummaryLength
SummaryViewMode	Sync
Tables	TablesOfAuthorities
TablesOfAuthoritiesCategories	TablesOfContents
TablesOfFigures	TextEncoding
TextLineEnding	TrackRevisions
Type	UpdateStylesOnOpen
UserControl	Variables
VBASigned	VBProject
Versions	WebOptions
Windows	Words
WritePassword	WriteReserved
XMLHideNamespaces	XMLNodes
XMLSaveDataOnly	XMLSaveThroughXSLT
XMLSchemaReferences	XMLSchemaViolations
XMLShowAdvancedErrors	XMLUseXSLTWhenSaving

Methods of the Documents Collection

AcceptAllRevisions
AcceptAllRevisionsShown
Activate
AddToFavorites
ApplyTheme
AutoFormat
AutoSummarize
CanCheckin
CheckConsistency
CheckGrammar
CheckIn
CheckNewSmartTags
CheckSpelling
Close
ClosePrintPreview
Compare
ComputeStatistics
ConvertNumbersToText
ConvertVietDoc
CopyStylesFromTemplate
CountNumberedItems
CreateLetterContent
DataForm
DeleteAllComments
DeleteAllCommentsShown
DeleteAllEditableRanges
DeleteAllInkAnnotations
DetectLanguage
EndReview
FitToPages
FollowHyperlink
GetCrossReferenceItems
GetLetterContent
GettingHelponMacintoshKeywords
GoTo
MakeCompatibilityDefault
ManualHyphenation
Merge
Post
PresentIt
PrintOut
PrintPreview
Protect
Range
RecheckSmartTags
Redo
RejectAllRevisions
RejectAllRevisionsShown
Reload
ReloadAs
RemoveLockedStyles
RemoveNumbers
RemoveSmartTags
RemoveTheme
Repaginate
Reply
ReplyAll
ReplyWithChanges
ResetFormFields
Route
RunAutoMacro
RunLetterWizard

Save	SaveAs
Select	SelectAllEditableRanges
SelectNodes	SelectSingleNode
SendFax	SendFaxOverInternet
SendForReview	SendMail
SetDefaultTableStyle	SetLetterContent
SetPasswordEncryptionOptions	ToggleFormsDesign
TransformDocument	Undo
UndoClear	UnProtect
UpdateStyles	UpdateSummaryProperties
ViewCode	ViewPropertyBrowser
WebPagePreview	

Events of the Documents Collection

Close	New
Open	Sync
XMLAfterInsert	XMLBeforeDelete

Using Properties and Methods

In addition to the Document object, the ActiveDocument property of the Application object is used to return an individual Document object that represents the document with the focus. The ActiveDocument property is read-only, so it cannot be used to give the focus to a particular document (use the Activate method). If there are no documents open, an error will occur if this property is referenced. You can avoid this error by checking to see that a document is actually open by using the Count property of the Documents collection. For example:

```
If Documents.Count > 0 then
    MsgBox ActiveDocument.Name
Else
    MsgBox "There are no documents open!"
End If
```

You will find that working with the Documents collection is usually the starting point for your Word programming. Therefore, we will spend a few pages covering how to work with the most common properties and methods of the Documents collection.

Opening Documents

You can open existing Word documents using the Open method of the Documents collection.

```
Documents.Open(FileName, ConfirmConversions, ReadOnly,
AddToRecentFiles, PasswordDocument, PasswordTemplate, Revert,
WritePasswordDocument, WritePasswordTemplate, Format)
```

The parameters of the Open method are as follows:

FileName: The name of the document to be opened (paths are accepted).

ConfirmConversions: Set this to True if you want to display the Convert File dialog box (non-Word format files only).

ReadOnly: Set this to True to open the document as read-only.

AddToRecentFiles: Set this to True to add the filename to the list of recently used files at the bottom of the File menu.

PasswordDocument: This allows you to enter the password for opening the document.

PasswordTemplate: This allows you to enter the password for opening the template.

Revert: This parameter is used to control what happens if the file is already open. Set it to True to discard any unsaved changes to the open document and reopen the file. A value of False will activate the open document.

WritePasswordDocument: This allows you to enter a password for saving changes to the document.

WritePasswordTemplate: This allows you to enter a password for saving changes to the template.

Format: This indicates which type of file converter to use when opening the document:
wdOpenFormatAuto (default)
wdOpenFormatDocument
wdOpenFormatRTF
wdOpenFormatTemplate
wdOpenFormatText
wdOpenFormatUnicodeText

Here is a brief code snippet that shows the two different ways you can use the Open method to work with documents. The first line is how you would normally open a document if you were working in a macro. The second and third lines show how you would work with the same document if you were using automation. In this case, you would set a variable equal to the document and work directly with the variable.

```
Documents.Open("C:\Wordware\Sample.doc")
Dim oDoc as Document
Set oDoc = Documents.Open("C:\Wordware\Sample.doc")
```

Programmatically Creating New Documents

Use the Add method to create a new empty document and add it to the Documents collection. By default, the Add method bases newly created documents on the Normal template. Several different collection objects use the Add method to add another member to their collection. The syntax is:

```
Documents.Add(Template, NewTemplate)
```

The Template argument refers to the name of the template to be used for the new document. The default for this argument is the Normal template. If NewTemplate is True,

Word will create the new document as a template. The default value of the NewTemplate argument is False.

The following example creates a new document based on the Normal template:

```
Documents.Add
```

You can also set an object variable equal to a document using the Add method:

```
Dim oDoc as Document
Set oDoc = Documents.Add("C:\Wordware\MyTemplate.dot")
```

Saving Documents

If you've worked with any Windows application, you are familiar with saving files. Using VBA code to save documents is no different than manually saving them from the File menu. The first time you save a document, you'll be using the SaveAs method. This method allows you to specify all of the things you do when you choose to save your document for the first time manually. You can enter a filename, choose a directory, choose a file type, etc.

Once a document has been saved, you can use the Save method. This operates in an identical manner to clicking Save on the File menu. The user will not be prompted and the file will save under the same format with which it was opened. If you use the Save method when working with a file that has never been saved, the Save As dialog box will appear and prompt the user for a name.

You can immediately save a newly created document using the following syntax:

```
Documents.Add.SaveAs FileName:="C:\Wordware\SaveTheDoc.doc"
```

You can also save all open documents (without looping through the Documents collection) by using the Save method with the Documents collection.

```
Documents.Save NoPrompt:=True
```

Closing Documents

Closing a document is accomplished by executing the Close method of the appropriate Documents collection. Programmatically using the Close method is no different than closing documents manually. The syntax is:

```
Documents.Close(SaveChanges, OriginalFormat, RouteDocument)
```

The parameters of the Close method are as follows:

SaveChanges: This argument specifies the save action for the document. Use one of the following wdSave-Options constants:

wdDoNotSaveChanges
wdPromptToSaveChanges
wdSaveChanges

OriginalFormat: This specifies the save format for the document. Use one of the following wdOriginalFormat constants:

wdOriginalDocumentFormat
wdPromptUser
wdWordDocument

RouteDocument: Set this argument to True to route the document to the next recipient. If the document doesn't have a routing slip attached, this argument is ignored.

If there have been changes to the document, Word will prompt the user with a message box inquiring whether the user wants to save changes. See Figure 4-2 below.

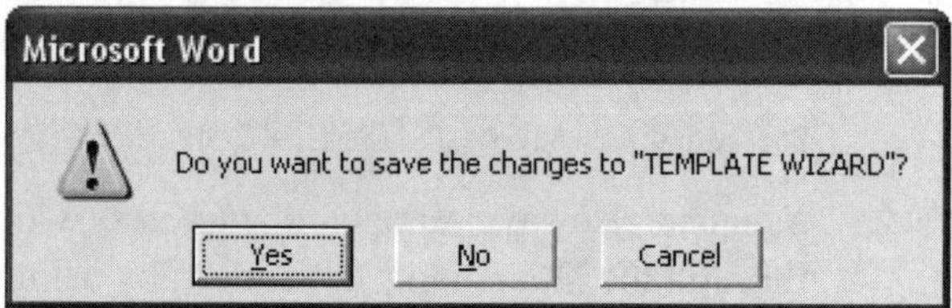

Figure 4-2

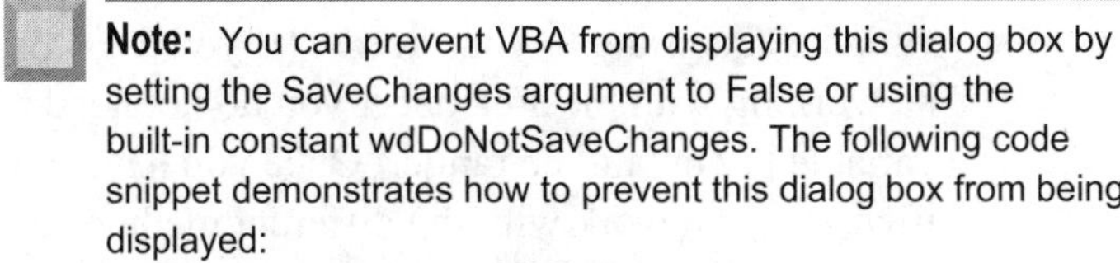

Note: You can prevent VBA from displaying this dialog box by setting the SaveChanges argument to False or using the built-in constant wdDoNotSaveChanges. The following code snippet demonstrates how to prevent this dialog box from being displayed:

```
Documents("SaveTheDoc.doc").Close
SaveChanges:=wdDoNotSaveChanges
```

Caution: Watch out when using the Close method of the ActiveDocument object. If your template works with other documents, this code may operate correctly during normal execution. But if it runs when you are testing your project, your template may close and you will lose your changes.

The following example enumerates the Documents collection to determine whether the document named ShaniDog.doc is open. If this document is contained in the Documents collection, the document is activated; otherwise, it's opened.

```
For Each doc In Documents
    If doc.Name = "ShaniDog.doc" Then found = True
Next doc
If found <> True Then
    Documents.Open FileName:="C:\Wordware\ShaniDog.doc"
Else
    Documents("ShaniDog.doc").Activate
End If
```

The Range Object

A common undertaking when working with Microsoft Word is to programmatically select a specific area within a document and do something with that area. These areas may be tables, sections, paragraphs, or even words. The Range object provides a convenient way to work with these different areas of a document.

Working with ranges generally involves these three steps: (1) Declare a variable as a Range object, (2) set that variable equal to a specific range within the document (this involves returning a range), and (3) manipulate the Range variable according to your needs. (If you are only going to be working with the area once, you do not need to create a variable to contain the range.) Once you have a range specified, you can work with the different methods and properties of the Range object to control how the document will look, respond, etc.

Note: Range objects are contiguous areas within a document defined by a starting and an ending position.

Word 2003 Additions to the Range Object

Word 2003 adds three new properties and one new method to the Range and Selection objects. As with the changes to the Application and Document objects, these changes revolve primarily around XML support.

Perhaps the most used of the new Range object properties is the XML property. This property returns the Word XML representation of the Range or Selection object. It will include any customer-defined XML as well. The return result will be a string that contains a complete, well-formed Word XML document. The root node of this document will be the w:WordDocument element. In addition, the w:body element will contain only the Word XML representation of the Range or Selection object.

The remaining properties and methods are relatively straightforward. You can access all of the XML elements within a Range or Selection object with the XMLNodes property. The immediate parent element of the current Selection or Range object can be accessed via the XMLParentNode property. Finally, the InsertXML method provides a way for you to replace the content of the Selection or Range object. It takes a String value as a parameter. The String must contain text marked up as well-formed XML data.

Properties of the Range Object

Application	Bold
BoldBi	BookmarkID
Bookmarks	Borders
Case	Cells
Characters	CharacterWidth
Columns	CombineCharacters
Comments	Creator
DisableCharacterSpaceGrid	Document
Duplicate	Editors
EmphasisMark	End
EndnoteOptions	Endnotes
EnhMetaFileBits	Fields
Find	FitTextWidth
Font	FootnoteOptions
Footnotes	FormattedText
FormFields	Frames
GrammarChecked	GrammaticalErrors
HighlightColorIndex	HorizontalInVertical
HTMLDivisions	Hyperlinks
ID	Information
InlineShapes	IsEndOfRowMark
Italic	ItalicBi
Kana	LanguageDetected
LanguageID	LanguageIDFarEast
LanguageIDOther	ListFormat
ListParagraphs	NextStoryRange
NoProofing	Orientation
PageSetup	ParagraphFormat
Paragraphs	Parent

PreviousBookmarkID
ReadabilityStatistics
Revisions
Rows
Scripts
Sections
Sentences
Shading
ShapeRange
ShowAll
SmartTags
SpellingChecked
SpellingErrors
Start
StoryLength
StoryType
Style
Subdocuments
SynonymInfo
Tables
Text
TextRetrievalMode
TopLevelTables
TwoLinesInOne
Underline
Words
XML
XMLNodes
XMLParentNode

Methods of the Range Object

AutoFormat
Calculate
CheckGrammar
CheckSpelling
CheckSynonyms
Collapse
ComputeStatistics
ConvertHangulAndHanja
ConvertToTable
Copy
CopyAsPicture
Cut
Delete
DetectLanguage
EndOf
Expand
GetSpellingSuggestions
Getting Help
GettingHelponMacintoshKeywords
GoTo
GoToEditableRange
GoToNext
GoToPrevious
InRange
InsertAfter
InsertAutoText

InsertBefore
InsertBreak
InsertCaption
InsertCrossReference
InsertDatabase
InsertDateTime
InsertFile
InsertParagraph
InsertParagraphAfter
InsertParagraphBefore
InsertSymbol
InsertXML
InStory
IsEqual
LookupNameProperties
ModifyEnclosure
Move
MoveEnd
MoveEndUntil
MoveEndWhile
MoveStart
MoveStartUntil
MoveStartWhile
MoveUntil
MoveWhile
Next
NextSubdocument
Paste
PasteAndFormat
PasteAppendTable
PasteAsNestedTable
PasteExcelTable
PasteSpecial
PhoneticGuide
Previous
PreviousSubdocument
Relocate
Select
SetRange
Sort
SortAscending
SortDescending
StartOf
TCSCConverter
WholeStory

Utilizing the Range Object

Returning Ranges

Before working with a Range variable, you obviously have to return a Range object. The following section describes some simple ways to access the Range object. Usually, you will be setting an object variable equal to the newly declared range; this way you can work with the Range object throughout the lifetime of the variable.

Range Method

One way to create a Range object in a document is to use the Range method (available from the Documents collection). The Range method requires both a starting and an ending position. Following is the syntax of the Range method:

```
Documents(1).Range(Start, End)
```

Start is the starting character position and End is the ending character position.

The Start and End arguments require character position values. These values begin with 0 (zero), corresponding to the very beginning of a document. Every character in the document will be counted, including nonprinting characters.

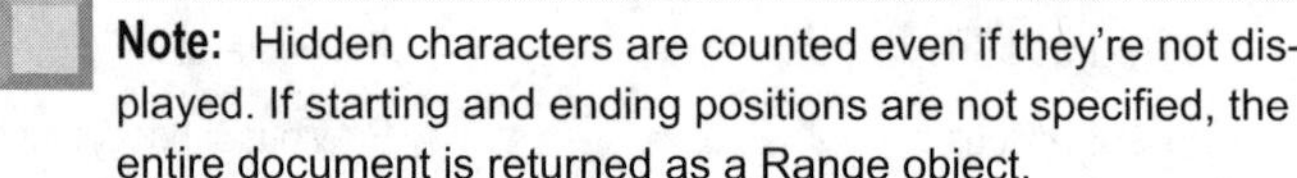

Note: Hidden characters are counted even if they're not displayed. If starting and ending positions are not specified, the entire document is returned as a Range object.

Range Property

Another way to create a Range object is to use the Range property of an object in the document. This property returns a Range object that represents the portion of a document that's contained in the specified object. The Range property is read-only.

The Selection Object

Another useful object, very similar to the Range object, is the Selection object. The Selection object has one key difference: There can only be one Selection object per pane in a document window, and only one Selection object can be active at any given time. You will find the Selection object especially useful when you are interacting with users. You can then use the Selection object to refer to any text that the user may highlight in a document. This enables you to create intelligent macros that apply certain properties to areas that the user selects. Following are the properties and methods of the Selection object.

Word 2003 Additions to the Selection Object

The new additions to the Selection object were outlined in the Range object section.

Following is a list of the properties of the Selection object. Keep in mind that the Selection object follows the highlighted text on the screen.

Properties of the Selection Object

Active	Application
BookmarkID	Bookmarks
Borders	Cells
Characters	ChildShapeRange
Columns	ColumnSelectMode
Comments	Creator
Document	Editors
End	EndnoteOptions
Endnotes	EnhMetaFileBits
ExtendMode	Fields
Find	FitTextWidth
Flags	Font
FootnoteOptions	Footnotes
FormattedText	FormFields
Frames	HasChildShapeRange

HeaderFooter	HTMLDivisions
Hyperlinks	Information
InlineShapes	IPAtEndOfLine
IsEndOfRowMark	LanguageDetected
LanguageID	LanguageIDFarEast
LanguageIDOther	NoProofing
Orientation	PageSetup
ParagraphFormat	Paragraphs
Parent	PreviousBookmarkID
Range	Rows
Sections	Sentences
Shading	ShapeRange
SmartTags	Start
StartIsActive	StoryLength
StoryType	Style
Tables	Text
TopLevelTables	Type
Words	XML
XMLNodes	XMLParentNode

Methods of the Selection Object

BoldRun	Calculate
ClearFormatting	Collapse
ConvertToTable	Copy
CopyAsPicture	CopyFormat
CreateAutoTextEntry	CreateTextbox
Cut	Delete
DetectLanguage	EndKey
EndOf	EscapeKey

Expand	Extend
GoTo	GoToEditableRange
GoToNext	GoToPrevious
HomeKey	InRange
InsertAfter	InsertBefore
InsertBreak	InsertCaption
InsertCells	InsertColumns
InsertColumnsRight	InsertCrossReference
InsertDateTime	InsertFile
InsertFormula	InsertParagraph
InsertParagraphAfter	InsertParagraphBefore
InsertRows	InsertRowsAbove
InsertRowsBelow	InsertStyleSeparator
InsertSymbol	InsertXML
InStory	IsEqual
ItalicRun	LtrPara
LtrRun	Move
MoveDown	MoveEnd
MoveEndUntil	MoveEndWhile
MoveLeft	MoveRight
MoveStart	MoveStartUntil
MoveStartWhile	MoveUntil
MoveUp	MoveWhile
Next	NextField
NextRevision	NextSubdocument
Paste	PasteAndFormat
PasteAppendTable	PasteAsNestedTable
PasteExcelTable	PasteFormat
PasteSpecial	Previous
PreviousField	PreviousRevision

PreviousSubdocument	RtlPara
RtlRun	Select
SelectCell	SelectColumn
SelectCurrentAlignment	SelectCurrentColor
SelectCurrentFont	SelectCurrentIndent
SelectCurrentSpacing	SelectCurrentTabs
SelectRow	SetRange
Shrink	ShrinkDiscontiguousSelection
Sort	SortAscending
SortDescending	SplitTableStartOf
ToggleCharacterCode	TypeBackspace
TypeParagraph	TypeText
WholeStory	

Working with the Selection Object

Returning Selections

There are generally two methods you will use to return a Selection object. The first is to use the Selection property of an object to return the Selection object. If no characters are selected, the Selection property will represent the cursor location when used with the Application object. The following example selects the entire first paragraph of the active document, collapses the selection to the first line, and moves the insertion point to the end of that line.

```
Paragraphs(1).Range.Select
Selection.EndKey Unit:=wdLine, Extend:=wdMove
```

The second way you can create a Selection object is to use the Select method of an object. The Selection property only applies to the Application object, the Pane object, and the Window object. The Select method can be used with many different types of objects. This versatility makes it the preferred way of returning a Selection object.

Working with Selections

In general, the Selection object corresponds to the highlighted section of the currently active Word document. The following example selects the ActiveDocument object, which is a member of the Documents collection, and displays the name of the first bookmark in that document.

```
ActiveDocument.Select
MsgBox Selection.Bookmarks(1).Name
```

When you are working with Selection objects, you can use the Type property to return the selection type. This is very convenient if you only want to work with certain types of selections. You can also use the Information property to return information about the selection. Keep in mind that you can use the Range property to return a Range object from the Selection object. The Selection object also includes numerous methods to expand, collapse, and move around within the selection.

Note: There can be only one Selection object per window pane; however, you can have multiple Range objects. Many Word programmers prefer working with Range objects for that reason.

New XML Objects

Word 2003 introduces five new objects and five new collections. These additions were necessary so that there would be programmatic support for the newly added XML features of Word 2003.

XMLChildNodeSuggestion Object

The XMLChildNodeSuggestion object and the XMLChildNodesSuggestions collection are used to access the possible children of the currently selected element. This collection provides the ability to iterate through the child nodes of a particular element.

Properties

Application	BaseName
Creator	NamespaceURI
Parent	XMLSchemaReference

Methods

Insert

XMLNamespace Object

Namespace support is provided via the XMLNamespace object and the XMLNamespaces collection. These additions represent one or more namespace URIs in the user's Word 2003 schema library. Again, the XMLNamespaces collection can be navigated using an ordinal index number.

Properties

Alias	Application
Creator	DefaultTransform
Location	Parent
URI	XSLTransforms

Methods

AttachToDocument	Delete

XMLNode Object

When working with XML, you'll frequently be working with individual node objects. Support for this is provided via the XMLNode object and the XMLNodes collection. These provide a way for you to programmatically access one or more elements in an XML document or range. The XMLNodes collection may be navigated via the ordinal index number only.

Properties

Application	Attributes
BaseName	ChildNodes
ChildNodeSuggestions	Creator
FirstChild	HasChildNodes
LastChild	Level
NamespaceURI	NextSibling
NodeType	NodeValue
OwnerDocument	Parent
ParentNode	PlaceholderText
PreviousSibling	Range
SmartTag	Text
ValidationErrorText	ValidationStatus
XML	

Methods

Copy	Cut
Delete	RemoveChild
SelectNodes	SelectSingleNode
SetValidationError	Validate

XMLSchemaReference Object

Managing schemas programmatically is easy when using the built-in XMLSchemaReference object and the XMLSchemaReferences collection. These objects allow you to represent one or more schemas for each unique namespace. You can then iterate through the schemas using the XMLSchemaReferences collection using an index number or a namespace URI.

Properties

Application	Creator
Location	NamespaceURI
Parent	

Methods

Delete	Reload

XSLTransform Object

Lastly, there needs to be a way to programmatically access the new XSLT transform functionality via code. This is provided via the XSLTransform object and the XSLTransforms collection. These objects expose the transforms registered for Word only. The XSLTransforms collection supports both an index number and an alias.

Properties

Alias	Application
Creator	Location
Parent	

Methods

Delete

The Find and Replace Objects

You can use either the Selection or the Range object to return Find and Replace objects. There is a slight difference depending on whether you return the Find object from the Selection or the Range object. The Find method returns True if the find operation is successful. These differences will be discussed below. First, let's take a look at the syntax of working with the Find method.

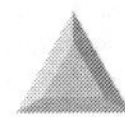

Tip: There are many parameters to FindObject. The best way to find the parameter you need is to use the Macro Recorder and perform a search manually. After you've completed your search, you can view the code and obtain the proper syntax for your code.

The syntax is:

```
FindObject.(Range or Selection).Execute(FindText, MatchCase,
MatchWholeWord, MatchWildcards, MatchSoundsLike,
MatchAllWordForms, Forward, Wrap, Format, ReplaceWith, Replace)
```

FindText: Obviously, this is the text for which you will be searching. If you are searching for formatting only, use an empty string ("").You can find a list in Word of the special characters you can use.

MatchCase: Set this to True to specify that the find text is case sensitive.

MatchWholeWord: Set this to True to force the find operation to locate only entire words and not text that's part of a larger word.

MatchWildcards: When MatchWildcards is True, you can specify wildcard characters and other advanced search criteria. For more information on performing advanced searches, look at the expanded Find and Replace dialog box.

MatchSoundsLike: A True setting will make the find operation locate words that sound similar to the find text.

MatchAllWordForms: Set this to True to have the find operation locate all forms of the find text.

Forward: A True setting will search forward.

Wrap: This controls what happens if the search begins at a point other than the beginning of the document and the end of the document is reached, or if there's a selection or range and the search text isn't found in the selection or range.

Format: Set this to True to have the find operation locate formatting along with the find text (or instead of the find text).

ReplaceWith: This is the replacement text. Again, for more information, the best place is the Find and Replace dialog box.

Replace: This argument lets you specify how many replacements are to be made: one, all, or none.

The Dialogs Object

The Dialogs object represents all of the built-in dialog boxes in Word. A good understanding of the Dialogs object will enable you to intercept Word's built-in commands and add functionality. You can display a built-in dialog box to get user input or to control Word by using Visual Basic. You'll see that you can control every aspect of the Dialogs object that you may need. There are almost 200 built-in dialog boxes to which the Word object model gives you access.

Show Method

If you simply need to display a particular dialog box to the user and do not want to add any functionality, you can use the Show method of the Dialogs object. This will display the dialog according to the wdWordDialog constant that you use. It will also automatically execute the user's selection — as opposed to "Display," which allows you to trap the user's choice. The following example displays the SaveAs dialog box wdDialogFileSaveAs:

```
Dialogs(wdDialogFileSaveAs).Show
```

Once the Show method executes, the SaveAs dialog box will be displayed. If the user enters a new name and clicks OK, the file will be saved. If you need to display a particular tab to the user, you can set the Default Tab property. You can also rely on IntelliSense to display a rather lengthy list of the available options tabs. For example, if you wanted to display the General tab of the Options dialog box (Tools | Options), you could use the following code:

```
With Dialogs(wdDialogToolsOptions)
     .DefaultTab = wdDialogToolsOptionsTabGeneral
     .Show
End With
```

Note: The Show method also has an optional TimeOut parameter. This parameter takes a long variable type and represents the length of time the dialog box will remain displayed (in milliseconds).

Display Method

You can use the Display method to display a dialog box without enabling the actions that are built into the dialog box. This means that any changes entered by the user will not be applied unless we use the Execute method of the dialog box. The Display method can be useful if you need to prompt the user with a built-in dialog box and return the settings. This is also the method you will be using to intercept a user's commands and carry out your own execution. For example, the following code will display the File Open dialog box and return a message box to the user with the name of the file he selected. Remember, although the File Open dialog box is being used, the file will not actually be opened when the Display method is used.

```
With Dialogs(wdDialogFileOpen)
    .Display
    MsgBox .Name
End With
```

If you wanted to actually open the file after displaying the message box in the previous example, you can use the Execute method. The following example displays the File Open dialog box, displays a message box with the chosen file's name, and opens the file (as long as the name is not an empty string).

```
With Dialogs(wdDialogFileOpen)
    .Display
    MsgBox .Name
    If .Name <> "" Then .Execute
End With
```

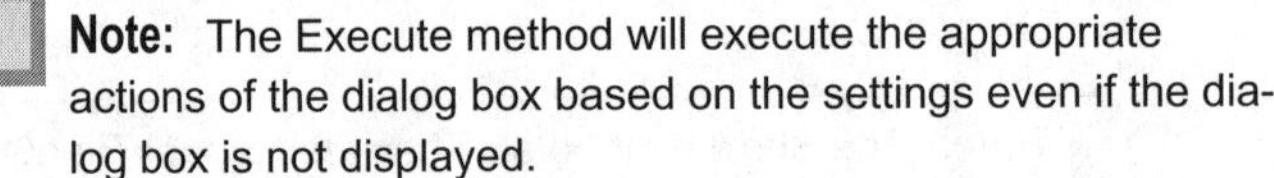

Note: The Execute method will execute the appropriate actions of the dialog box based on the settings even if the dialog box is not displayed.

Dialog Box Arguments

Before we go any further in our discussion of dialog boxes, it is worthwhile to discuss arguments. You may have noticed that ".Name" did not appear in your IntelliSense options. If you rely heavily on IntelliSense, working with dialog boxes can be especially frustrating unless you become accustomed to checking Help and finding the arguments for a specific dialog box. The actual Help topic is "Built-in dialog box argument lists," and if you start Help by clicking F1 with Dialogs selected, it's no less than four layers of Help away. This can be annoying if you're in the middle of a project and you need to find a particular argument. Figure 4-3 shows the Help dialog box with the arguments for the File New and File Open dialog boxes.

Microsoft Visual Basic Help

	LayoutMode, CharsLine, LinesPage, CharPitch, LinePitch, DocFontName, DocFontSize, PageColumns, TextFlow, FirstPageOnLeft, SectionType, RTLAlignment
wdDialogFileFind	*SearchName, SearchPath, Name, SubDir, Title, Author, Keywords, Subject, Options, MatchCase, Text, PatternMatch, DateSavedFrom, DateSavedTo, SavedBy, DateCreatedFrom, DateCreatedTo, View, SortBy, ListBy, SelectedFile, Add, Delete, ShowFolders, MatchByte*
wdDialogFileMacPageSetup	(For information about this constant, consult the language reference Help included with Microsoft Office Macintosh Edition.)
wdDialogFileNew	*Template, NewTemplate, DocumentType, Visible*
wdDialogFileOpen	*Name, ConfirmConversions, ReadOnly, LinkToSource, AddToMru, PasswordDoc, PasswordDot, Revert, WritePasswordDoc, WritePasswordDot, Connection, SQLStatement, SQLStatement1, Format, Encoding, Visible, OpenExclusive, OpenAndRepair, SubType, DocumentDirection, NoEncodingDialog, XMLTransform*
wdDialogFilePageSetup	*Tab, PaperSize, TopMargin, BottomMargin, LeftMargin, RightMargin, Gutter, PageWidth, PageHeight, Orientation, FirstPage, OtherPages, VertAlign, ApplyPropsTo, Default, FacingPages, HeaderDistance, FooterDistance, SectionStart, OddAndEvenPages, DifferentFirstPage, Endnotes, LineNum, StartingNum, FromText, CountBy,*

Figure 4-3

You can use arguments to set options in the dialog box once you are working with the appropriate Dialogs object. In most cases the name of the argument will correspond closely to one of the options on the actual Word dialog box. Checking these dialog boxes can eliminate the headaches of trying to guess the right argument in your code. You control dialog box settings in a very similar manner to the way you return them. The following example sets the .Name argument of the File Open dialog box instead of returning it:

```
With Dialogs(wdDialogFileOpen)
     .Name = "Sonny Ridgeback"
     .Display
End With
```

Note: Do not use a Dialogs object to change a value that you can set with a property or method.

Dialog Box Return Values

Every time a user clicks one of the buttons on a dialog box, a return value is generated. This value indicates which button was clicked to close the dialog box. Once again, the following example displays the File Open dialog box, and then displays a message box indicating which button was clicked:

```
Dim x As Integer
x = Dialogs(wdDialogFileOpen).Display
Select Case x
Case -1
    MsgBox "Open"
Case 0
    MsgBox "Cancel"
End Select
```

Return Value	Description
–2	The Close button
–1	The OK button
0 (zero)	The Cancel button
> 0 (zero)	A command button: 1 is the first button, 2 is the second button, and so on

Other Useful Objects

The objects discussed above will probably cover 80 percent of your Word programming requirements. The following objects will hopefully ratchet that number up another 10 percent. Keep in mind that there are several other objects you can use. If you need any further help, check the Object Browser in VBA. Following is a brief description of some other commonly used objects.

ActivePrinter Object

The ActivePrinter object can be used to either set or return the active printer. VBA has a few limitations in this regard, however. If you are used to programming in VB, you are aware that there is a Printers collection. This is especially helpful in an enterprise organization where there may be several printers installed on a machine. VBA does not provide this functionality.

CommandBar Object

In some instances you may need to work with the CommandBar object. The CommandBar object is a member of the CommandBars collection. You can access an individual CommandBar object using CommandBars (index), where index is the name or index number of a command bar. The following example steps through the collection of command bars to find the command bar named "Drawing." When the command bar named "Drawing" is encountered, the Visible property is set to True so that the command bar is made visible.

```
Dim oCmdBar As CommandBar
For Each oCmdBar In ActiveDocument.CommandBars
    If oCmdBar.Name = "Drawing" Then
        oCmdBar.Visible = True
    End If
Next oCmdBar
```

When working with the CommandBars collection, you can use a name or index number to specify a menu bar or toolbar in the list of the application's menu bars and toolbars. You will need to use the appropriate name when identifying a menu, shortcut menu, or submenu. If two or more custom menus or submenus have the same name, CommandBars(index) can be used to return the appropriate one using the correct index value.

Command Bar Pop-Up Menu Project

When you right-click in a window, the resultant pop-up menu is also just a command bar. You can access it in the same way you access other command bars. Following is the code that will produce the pop-up menu in Figure 4-4. Use the OnAction property to set the procedure to execute when the button is chosen. For a description on how to intercept the right-click event, see the section on events in Chapter 2.

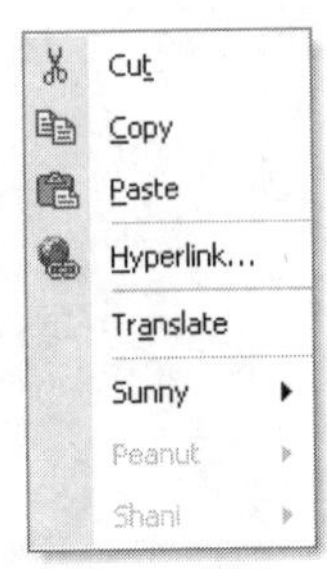

Figure 4-4

```
Public Sub AddPop-upMenu()
Dim Pop-upMenu As CommandBar
Dim myTools(1 To 3) As CommandBarPop-up
     Set Pop-upMenu = CommandBars("Text")
     Pop-upMenu.Reset
With Pop-upMenu
     .Controls.Item("Font...").Delete
     .Controls.Item("Paragraph...").Delete
     .Controls.Item("Bullets and numbering...").Delete
     .Controls.Item("Synonyms").Delete
End With
Set myTools(1) = Pop-upMenu.Controls.Add(Type:=
                 msoControlPop-up)
     With myTools(1)
          .BeginGroup = True
          .Caption = "Sunny"
          .OnAction = "YourCode"
     End With
Set myTools(2) = Pop-upMenu.Controls.Add(Type:=
                 msoControlPop-up)
     With myTools(2)
          .Caption = "Peanut"
          .Enabled = False
     End With
Set myTools(3) = Pop-upMenu.Controls.Add(Type:=
                 msoControlPop-up)
     With myTools(3)
          .Caption = "Shani"
          .Enabled = False
     End With
End Sub
```

```
Sub YourCode()
     MsgBox "This is where you would write your code",
            vbInformation, "Pop-up"
End Sub
```

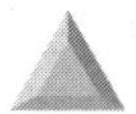

Tip: These settings will be applied to your environment. If you want to change your toolbar back to its original construction, use the Reset method.

HeaderFooter Object

The HeaderFooter object represents either a single header or a footer. It is a member of the HeaderFooters collection. Almost all of the typical properties that pertain to collections also pertain to the HeaderFooters collection, which contains all headers and footers within a section of the document.

Both the header and the footer use the same predefined index constants. You will use this index to return a single HeaderFooter object. The only other way of returning a HeaderFooter object is by using the HeaderFooter property with a Selection object. The proper syntax when working directly with either headers or footers is:

```
Headers(index) or Footers(index)
wdHeaderFooterEvenPages
wdHeaderFooterFirstPage
wdHeaderFooterPrimary
```

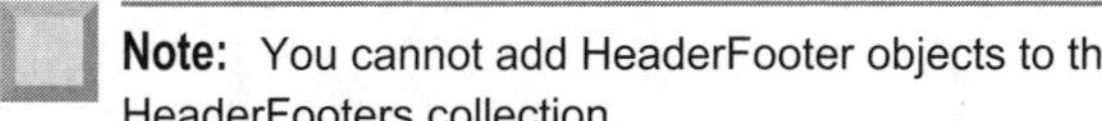

Note: You cannot add HeaderFooter objects to the HeaderFooters collection.

Caution: You might encounter a problem when working with either headers or footers in conjunction with Word's fields.

When you are updating fields in your document you will probably use something similar to the following code:

```
ThisDocument.Fields.Update
```

The above code will not update the fields in either a footer or a header. The only way to update the fields in this case is to update the fields that pertain to that specific section's header objects. For instance, if you were to put a DOC-VARIABLE field in a header in the first section of the document, the following code demonstrates how to update it:

```
ThisDocument.Variables("Test").Value = "Levi Kills Dog Toys!"
ThisDocument.Sections(1).Headers(wdHeaderFooterPrimary).Range
         .Fields
```

Header/Footer Update

If you frequently work with Word fields and headers or footers, you will probably want to write a procedure that will update all of the fields at once. This will allow you to make a central call anytime you need to update the fields in a document. Keep in mind that you will need to enumerate through each section of the document with which you are working. This is best accomplished using a For…Each loop using the Sections collection of the document. Here is a brief example of the necessary loop using headers (you'd want to include footers also):

```
Dim oSec As Section
For Each oSec in ThisDocument.Sections
    With oSec
    If .Headers(index).Exists Then
        .Headers(index).Range.Fields.Update
    End If
    End With
Next oSec
```

You've already seen a brief demonstration of how sections work in the above example. Use the Sections property to return the Sections collection. Most frequently you'll be using either the Add method or the InsertBreak method to add a new section to a document.

Conclusion

Before jumping into document automation, it is probably a good idea to become acquainted with the Word 2003 object model. This chapter will serve as an important reference as you continue programming in Word. Document automation requires a good understanding of what Word objects you will need to use to accomplish a given task.

Chapter 5

The VBA Programming Language

Introduction

This chapter provides an overview of some commonly used VBA programming tools including message boxes, input boxes, arrays, collections, string functions, and string statements. Variables are an integral part of programming in any language. An emphasis on interacting with the user is maintained throughout the chapter. Use this chapter, along with Chapters 4 and 6, as reference sources while programming.

Variables

Variables are a basic element of almost every programming language. In its simplest form, a *variable* is simply a memory address where information is stored. In VBA, variables are created by dimensioning them. Dimensioning a variable is done in several different ways, but the main thing to keep in mind is that the process of dimensioning a variable tells the computer how large of a memory chunk to allocate for a specific variable.

Note: This brings up the first point of good VBA programming. Your programs should always require explicit variable declaration. This book assumes you are using the Option Explicit statement. By contrast, implicit variable declaration simply requires that you type the name of the variable, and when the code is compiled the variable will be assigned to a variant data type. The variant data type is the largest type of VBA variable and consumes the most memory. Another downfall of implicit variable declaration is that your variable names are not checked. In other words, if you use "Name" as a variable in one spot and later misspell it as "neme," the computer thinks this is a new variable and assigns it its own memory address.

Variable Declaration

Explicit variable declaration requires that you specify both the type and scope of the variable. We have already mentioned that variables can be assigned different amounts of space in memory, but a variable can also be available at different times during the execution of a program (scope). In other words, you can limit or expand the procedures that may utilize a specific variable. Let's look at the syntax for some variable declarations.

Local Variable Declaration

A locally declared variable is available only to the procedure in which it is called. In the following example, iLocal is dimensioned locally and would not be available to another procedure. This is helpful when you want to use the same name in different procedures (not a good idea). Also notice that the variable was assigned to the integer data type. (Variable types will be discussed later.)

```
Sub Test()
Private iLocal As Integer
End Sub
```

Module Level Variable Declaration

The next scope option is the module level private scope. As we saw in Chapter 2, modules are where the code is stored and may be behind UserForms, standard modules, or even class modules. A privately declared variable outside of a procedure is available only to the procedures and functions in that specific module.

Global Level Variable Declaration

The final scope of a variable is that of a public variable. The Public keyword indicates that the variable is available to all procedures and functions within the project. These must be declared in a module. This is useful when you want a variable to be utilized throughout the executing life of the project.

Static Variables

Another concern with variables is when they should be extinguished. When a procedure or function quits running, typically any local variables are extinguished. In other words, they lose their value and no longer occupy a memory address. However, a local variable may be declared with the Static keyword. This enables a variable that would normally be extinguished to maintain its value even if no code is executing.

You may be wondering, "Why not use a public variable?" A public variable loses its value when all of the code in the project finishes executing. You can run a complex macro in a document, but once that macro finishes, all variables are extinguished except for static ones. A static variable allows your code to remember values from the execution of one procedure to the next.

In some cases, a public variable can accomplish exactly what a static variable can, but good programming dictates that you use the most restrictive scope available. The following code demonstrates the differences:

```
'at the module level
Public iState As Integer
Sub PublicVariable()
     iState = iState + 1
     MsgBox iState
End Sub
Sub StaticVariable()
     Static iVar As Integer
iVar + 1
     MsgBox iVar
End Sub
```

Note: Make sure you follow consistent variable naming conventions. The most common convention calls for the first one to three characters to describe the type of variable, followed by a meaningful variable name. Some programmers go even further and use a character to indicate the scope of the variable.

Types of Variables

There are a number of types of variables that can be used in VBA. They are discussed further in this section.

Byte

Bytes are stored as single, unsigned, 8-bit (8 bits = 1 byte) numbers. Bytes range in value from 0 to 255. The byte data type best represents binary data. Although they are infrequently used, bytes are the smallest of all VBA data types.

Note: Trying to assign a byte a value of more than 255 results in an overflow error as shown in this figure.

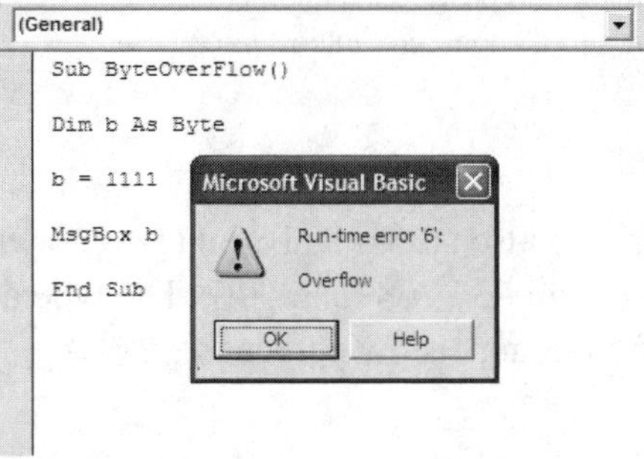

Figure 5-1

Boolean

Booleans are stored as 16-bit (2-byte) numbers. However, Booleans can only be True or False. Numeric values correlate to Boolean values as follows: 0 becomes False and all other values, whether positive or negative, become True (see Figure 5-2). A Boolean False becomes 0, and a Boolean True becomes –1 when Booleans are converted to numeric types.

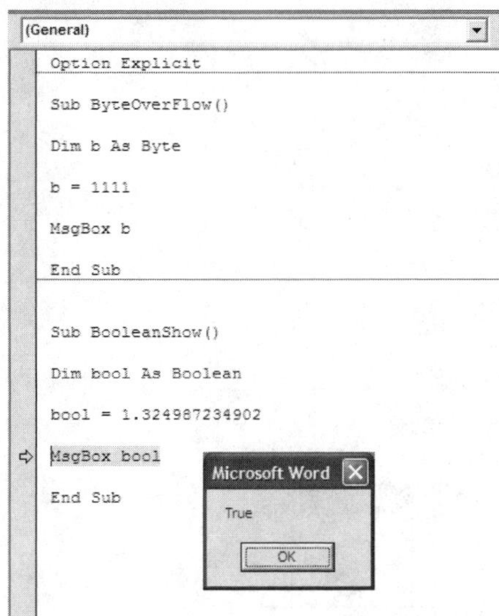

Figure 5-2

Note: Use either True or False to assign a value to Boolean variables. Programmers sometimes use Yes/No, On/Off, X/O combinations. In previous versions of Basic, 0 was recognized as False and all non-zero values were True.

Integer

Integers are also stored as 16-bit (2-byte) whole numbers ranging from –32,768 to 32,767. The type declaration character for integers is the percent sign (%).

Long

Longs are stored as 32-bit (4-byte) whole numbers ranging in value from –2,147,483,648 to 2,147,483,647. The type declaration character for the long is the ampersand character (&).

Note: Keep in mind that integers and longs require whole numbers. Many beginning programmers encounter unexpected errors using these data types for values that require fractional precision. Figure 5-3 shows that assigning an integer a fractional value doesn't generate an error, but rather results in the number being rounded to a whole number.

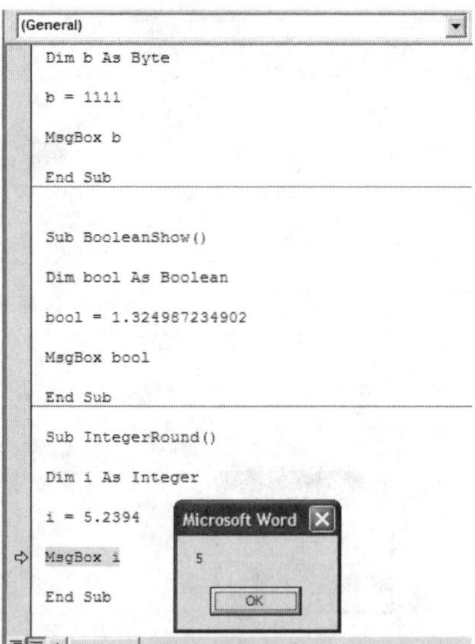

Figure 5-3

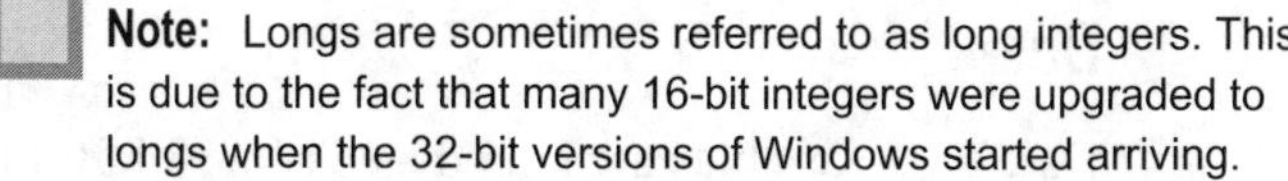

Note: Longs are sometimes referred to as long integers. This is due to the fact that many 16-bit integers were upgraded to longs when the 32-bit versions of Windows started arriving.

Single

Singles are stored as 32-bit (4-byte) floating-point numbers ranging in value from –3.402823E38 to –1.401298E–45 for negative values and from 1.401298E–45 to 3.402823E38 for positive values. The type declaration character for single variables is the exclamation point (!).

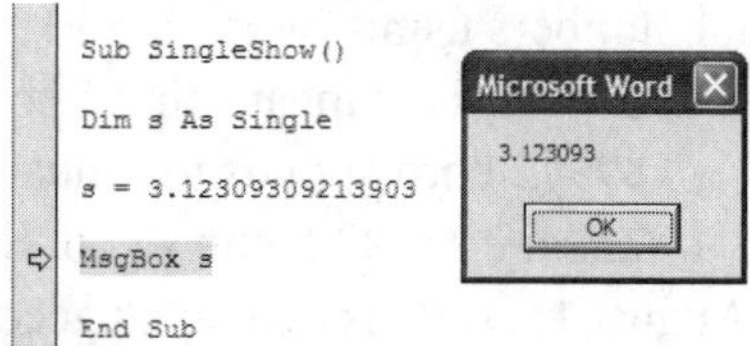
Sub SingleShow()
Dim s As Single
s = 3.12309309213903
MsgBox s
End Sub
Microsoft Word
3.123093
OK

Figure 5-4

Double

Doubles are stored as 64-bit (8-byte) floating-point numbers ranging in value from –1.79769313486231E308 to –4.94065645841247E–324 for negative values and from 4.94065645841247E–324 to 1.79769313486232E308 for positive values. The type declaration character for the double variable type is the number sign (#).

Currency

Variables of the currency type are stored as 64-bit (8-byte) numbers in an integer format, scaled by 10,000 to give a fixed-point number with 15 digits to the left of the decimal point and 4 digits to the right. This representation provides a range of –922,337,203,685,477.5808 to 922,337,203,685,477.5807. The type declaration character for currency is the "at" sign (@).

Note: If you are using calculations involving money, you should be using the currency data type.

Date

Date type variables are stored as 64-bit (8-byte) floating-point numbers that represent dates ranging from 1 January 100 to 31 December 9999 and times from 0:00:00 to 23:59:59. Any recognizable literal date values can be assigned to date variables. Date literals must be enclosed within number signs (#), for example, #January 1, 1993# or #1 Jan 93#.

Date variables display dates according to the short date format recognized by your computer. VBA works with dates as serial numbers using December 31, 1899, as an arbitrary starting point. This means that 1 corresponds to December 31, 1899; 2 corresponds to January 1, 1900; 3 corresponds to January 2, 1900, and so on. See Figure 5-5 to see how August 1, 2004, is displayed according to an absolute numeric value. Times display according to the time format (either 12-hour or 24-hour) recognized by your computer.

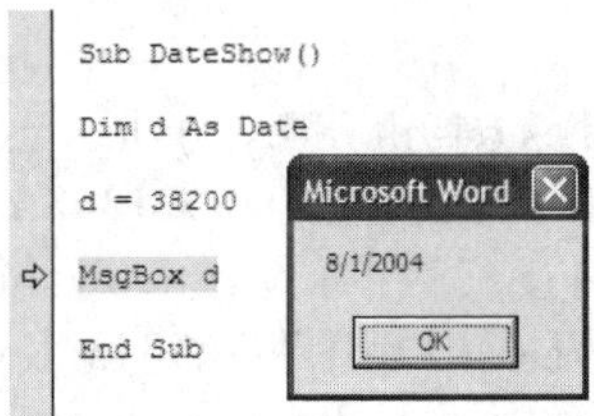

Figure 5-5

Note: When other data types are converted to date, values to the left of the decimal represent date information while values to the right of the decimal represent time. Midnight is 0 and midday is 0.5. Negative whole numbers represent dates before December 31, 1899.

Object

Object variables are stored as 32-bit (4-byte) addresses that refer to objects. Using the Set statement, a variable declared as an object can have any object reference assigned to it.

Note: Although a variable declared with the object type is flexible enough to contain a reference to any object, binding to the object referenced by that variable is always late binding and IntelliSense will not be available. To force early binding, assign the object reference to a variable declared with a specific object variable type.

String

The most common type of variable in Word programming is probably the string data type. A string contains a combination of characters. These may be text characters or specially recognized VBA constants that indicate certain controls such as Tab or Return. Strings can contain a bunch of blank spaces, each representing a character. The important thing about strings is that they must always be enclosed in quotation marks. Strings can be either fixed length or variable length. To define a string as a fixed length, the VBA multiplication sign is used and the corresponding number indicates the length of the string. A fixed-length string can contain 1 to approximately 64K (2^{16}) characters. A variable-length string can contain up to approximately 2 billion (2^{31}) characters.

Note: A public fixed-length string can't be used in a class module.

The codes for string characters range from 0 to 255. The first 128 characters (0 to 127) of the character set correspond to the letters and symbols on a standard U.S. keyboard. These first 128 characters are the same as those defined by the ASCII character set. The second 128 characters (128 to 255) represent special characters, such as letters in international alphabets, accent marks, currency symbols, and fractions. The type declaration character for the string variable type is the dollar sign ($).

See Figure 5-6 for an example using a fixed-length string. Notice that the message box only displays "7 Chars" even though the variable was set equal to a longer string. The second line of the message box contains the length of the string. Due to its declaration, the string is still actually 15 characters wide and occupies the same amount of memory.

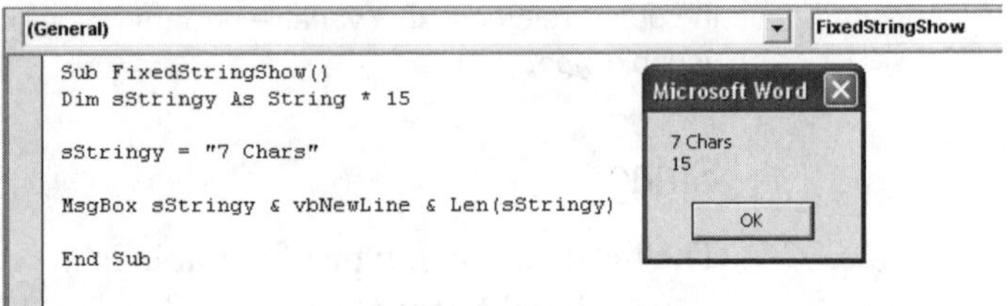

Figure 5-6

Variant

The variant data type is the default data type for all variables that are not explicitly declared as some other type. There is no type declaration character for the variant data type. Variant is a special data type that can contain any kind of data except a fixed-length string. It is important to note that variants can even support user-defined data types. In addition, variants can also contain the special values Empty, Error, Nothing, and Null.

Note: You can determine what type of data is being stored in a variant by using the VarType or TypeName functions.

Variants can hold numeric data including integers or real numbers with values ranging from –1.797693134862315E308 to –4.94066E–324 for negative values and from 4.94066E–324 to 1.797693134862315E308 for positive values. Generally, numeric variant data is maintained in its original data type within the variant. For example, if you assign the numerical value "2584" to a variant, subsequent operations will treat the variant as an integer. However, if an arithmetic operation causes a variant containing a byte, an integer, a long, or a single to exceed the normal range for the original data type, the result is promoted within the variant to the next larger data type. Therefore, a byte is promoted to an integer, an integer is promoted to a long, and longs and singles are promoted to doubles. An error will be generated when variant variables containing currency, decimal, and double values exceed their respective ranges.

Note: Although it is not encouraged, you can use the variant data types to work with data in a more flexible way. If a variant variable contains digits, they may be either the string representation of the digits or their actual value, depending on the context. For example:

```
Dim varVar As Variant
varVar = 90210
```

In the example in the above note, varVar contains a numeric representation — the actual value 90210. This can be used as a string if inserted into another string. The following message box will use varVar as a string:

```
MsgBox "Beverly Hills " & varVar
```

Arithmetic operators also work as expected on variant variables that contain numeric values or string data that can be interpreted as numbers. If you use the + operator to add varVar to a variable of a numeric type, the result is an arithmetic sum.

Other Variant Values

The value Empty indicates a variant that hasn't been initialized (assigned an initial value). A variant containing Empty is 0 if it is used in a numeric context and a zero-length string ("") if it is used in a string context.

Caution: Don't confuse Empty with Null; Null indicates that the variant variable is intentionally absent of value.

In a variant, Error is a special value used to indicate that an error condition has occurred in a procedure. However, unlike for other kinds of errors, normal application-level error handling does not occur. This allows you, or the application itself, to take some alternative action based on the error value. Error values are created by converting real numbers to error values using the CVErr function.

User-Defined Variable Types

User-defined variable types are declared at the module level using the Type statement. This statement is used to define a user-defined data type containing one or more elements. User-defined variables are frequently used when working with external procedures (DLL functions). It is important to understand how to set up your own variable types. Following is the syntax for the Type statement:

```
[Private | Public] Type varname
    elementname [([subscripts])] As type
    [elementname [([subscripts])] As type]
    ...
End Type
```

The Type statement has these parts:

Private: This is an optional part used to declare user-defined types that are available only within the module where the declaration is made.

Public: This is an optional part used to declare user-defined types that are available to all procedures in all modules in all projects.

varname: This required argument contains the name of the user-defined type. It follows standard variable naming conventions.

elementname: This is required and contains the name of an element of the user-defined type. Element names also follow standard variable naming conventions, except that keywords can be used.

subscripts: When not explicitly stated in lower, the lower bound of an array is controlled by the Option Base statement. The lower bound is 0 if no Option Base statement is present.

type: The data type is a required element and may be byte, Boolean, integer, long, currency, single, double, date, string (for variable-length strings), string * length (for fixed-length strings), object, variant, another user-defined type, or an object type.

Once you have declared a user-defined type using the Type statement, you can declare a variable of that type anywhere within the scope of the declaration. Use Dim, Private, Public, ReDim, or Static to declare a variable of a user-defined type. In standard modules and class modules, user-defined types are public by default. This visibility can be changed using the Private keyword. Line numbers and line labels aren't allowed in Type...End Type blocks. User-defined types are often used with data records, which frequently consist of a number of related elements of different data types.

The following example shows a user-defined type:

```
Type PuppyData
     PuppyCode As Integer
     KennelName As String
End Type
Dim Shani As PuppyData
Shani.PuppyCode = 10
Shani.Name = "Wyndrunhr"
```

Constants

If you are going to use frequently occurring values in a particular project, or you need to depend on certain values that are difficult to remember or have no obvious meaning, your code will benefit from using constants. Constants also make your code easier to read and maintain. You can use constants, represented by meaningful names, to take the place of a number or string that doesn't change throughout a project. There are two types of constants — intrinsic and user defined.

Note: You cannot assign new values to constants.

Intrinsic Constants

Intrinsic constants (system-defined constants) are provided by applications and controls. Other applications that provide object libraries, such as Microsoft Access, Microsoft Excel, and Microsoft Word, also provide intrinsic constants. The Object Browser is usually the best place to get a list of the constants provided by individual object libraries. Visual Basic constants are listed in the Visual Basic for Applications type library.

Note: Visual Basic continues to recognize constants created in earlier versions of Visual Basic or Visual Basic for Applications. You can upgrade your constants to those listed in the Object Browser. Constants listed in the Object Browser don't have to be declared in your application.

User-Defined Constants

User-defined constants are declared using the Const statement. By declaring a constant, you can assign a meaningful name to a value and use it consistently throughout your code. You use the Const statement to declare a constant and set its value. After a constant is declared, it cannot be modified or assigned a new value.

You can declare a constant within a procedure or at the top of a module in the Declarations section. Module-level constants are private by default. To declare a public module-level constant, precede the Const statement with the Public keyword. You can explicitly declare a private constant by preceding the Const statement with the Private keyword to make it easier to read and interpret your code. The following example declares the Public constant conAge as an integer and assigns it the value 34:

```
Public Const conAge As Integer = 34
```

Constants can be declared as one of the following data types: Boolean, byte, integer, long, currency, single, double, date, string, or variant. Because you already know the value of a constant, you can specify the data type in a Const statement. You can declare several constants in one statement. To specify a data type, you must include the data type for each constant.

Note: In earlier versions of Visual Basic, constant names were usually capitalized and included underscores. For example:

```
NUMBER_EMPLOYEES
```

Intrinsic constants are now qualified to avoid the confusion when constants with the same name exist in more than one object library, and which may have different values assigned to them. There are two ways to qualify constant names: by prefix and by library reference.

The intrinsic constants supplied by all objects appear in a mixed-case format, with a two-character prefix indicating the object library that defines the constant. Constants from the Visual Basic for Applications object library are prefaced with "vb" and constants from the Microsoft Excel object library are prefaced with "xl." The following examples illustrate how prefixes for custom controls vary, depending on the type library:

vbTileHorizontal
xlDialogBorder

You can also qualify the reference to a constant by using the following syntax:

```
[libname.] [modulename.]constname
```

Collections

A Collection object is an ordered set of items that can be referred to as a unit. It provides a convenient way to refer to a related group of items as a single object. The items, or members, in a collection need only be related by the fact that they exist in the collection. Members of a collection don't have to share the same data type.

A collection can be created the same way as other objects. For example:

```
Dim X As New Collection
```

Once a collection is created, members can be added using the Add method and removed using the Remove method. Specific members can be returned from the collection using the Item method, while the entire collection can be iterated using the For Each...Next statement.

Arrays

Arrays are helpful for obvious reasons: It is easier to declare lFinCharge(1-10) than to declare 10 different variables for the interest charge on each of 10 years. There will be situations when you do not know how many items you will need in the index. VBA allows you to create a dynamic array that can contain any number of values. Further, you can use the ReDim statement to change the number of its contents. The ReDim statement will destroy all existing data unless it is used in conjunction with the Preserve statement.

```
ReDim Preserve JoeArray(100)
```

By default, the subscripts of arrays start with 0. In other words, the lower bound of the array is 0 and the number specified in the Dim statement determines the upper bound. You can change the lower bound for your arrays using the Option Base statement. The following line of code will make all of your arrays start with 1:

```
Option Base 1
```

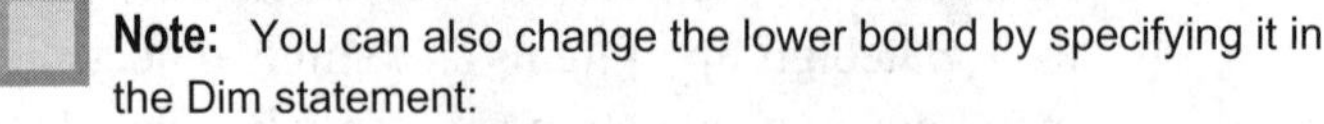

Note: You can also change the lower bound by specifying it in the Dim statement:

```
Dim JoeArray(5 to 500) as String
```

Multidimensional Arrays

VBA also supports the capability to create multidimensional arrays. You can create arrays with one or more dimensions (the maximum is 60). It is easiest to think of two-dimensional arrays in terms of rows and columns (three-dimensional arrays are like a cube, and so on). These rows and columns make up the array's matrix. The syntax for the Dim statement is basically the same, except for the inclusion of the extra dimensions. See Figure 5-7 for a graphical explanation.

```
(General)
Sub MultiDimensionalArray()

Dim Dogs(2, 1)

Dogs(0, 0) = "Shani"
Dogs(0, 1) = "Ridgeback"

Dogs(1, 0) = "Peanut"
Dogs(1, 1) = "Rottweiler"

Dogs(2, 0) = "Sasha"
Dogs(2, 1) = "Doberman"

End Sub
```

Figure 5-7

The code in Figure 5-7 sets up an array that can be represented by the following table:

Dog's Name	Dog Type
Shani	Ridgeback
Peanut	Rottweiler
Sasha	Doberman

Displaying Information to the User

The previous figures utilized a few techniques to display the values of the variables. One of the best ways to interact with users (as well as visually see what your code is doing without stepping through the code) is through message boxes and input boxes. Message boxes are a great way to display errors, tips, and other information.

Message Boxes

The MsgBox function displays a message in the form of a dialog box, waits for the user to click a button, and returns an integer indicating which button the user clicked. Following is the syntax for the MsgBox function:

```
MsgBox(prompt[, buttons] [, title] [, helpfile, context])
```

The MsgBox function syntax has these named arguments:

prompt: This parameter is required. This text will be displayed as the message in the dialog box (maximum length of ~1024 characters).You can make the prompt appear on separate lines by using a carriage return character (Chr(13)), a linefeed character (Chr(10)), or carriage return/linefeed character combination (Chr(13) and Chr(10)) between each line.

buttons: This parameter is optional. It is either a constant or numeric expression that specifies buttons to display, the icon style to use, the identity of the default button, and the modality of the message box.

title: This parameter is optional. This text will be displayed in the title bar of the dialog box. If you omit title, the application name is placed in the title bar.

helpfile: This parameter is also optional. This string expression identifies the Help file to use to provide context-sensitive help for the dialog box. Note: If helpfile is provided, context must also be provided.

context: This is used in conjunction with the helpfile parameter. It is a numeric expression that represents the Help context number assigned to the appropriate Help topic. Note: If context is provided, helpfile must also be provided.

Button Settings

As you will see in many examples throughout this book, using the appropriate button combination is important when interacting with users. Pay careful attention to the standard Microsoft conventions.

In the following table, Group1 describes the number and type of buttons displayed in the dialog box; Group2 describes the icon style; Group3 determines which button is the default; and Group4 determines the modality of the message box. When adding numbers to create a final value for the buttons argument, use only one number from each group. This table also displays the possible buttons argument settings.

	Constant	Value	Description
Group1	vbOKOnly	0	An OK button is displayed.
	vbOKCancel	1	OK and Cancel buttons are displayed.
	vbAbortRetryIgnore	2	Abort, Retry, and Ignore buttons are displayed.
	vbYesNoCancel	3	Yes, No, and Cancel buttons are displayed.
	vbYesNo	4	Yes and No buttons are displayed.
	vbRetryCancel	5	Retry and Cancel buttons are displayed.
Group2	vbCritical	16	A Critical Message icon is displayed.
	vbQuestion	32	A Warning Query icon is displayed.
	vbExclamation	48	A Warning Message icon is displayed.
	vbInformation	64	An Information Message icon is displayed.
Group3	vbDefaultButton1	0	The first button is default.
	vbDefaultButton2	256	The second button is default.
	vbDefaultButton3	512	The third button is default.

	Constant	Value	Description
	vbDefaultButton4	768	The fourth button is default.
Group4	vbApplicationModal	0	Application modal forces the user to respond before continuing in the current application.
	vbSystemModal	4096	System modal suspends all applications until the user responds to the message box.
	vbMsgBoxHelpButton	16384	This adds a Help button to the message box.
	VbMsgBoxSetForeground	65536	Specifies the message box window as the foreground window.
	vbMsgBoxRight	524288	Makes all text right aligned.
	vbMsgBoxRtlReading	1048576	Specifies that the text should appear as right-to-left reading on Hebrew and Arabic systems.

Note: These button constants are specified by the VBA programming language. This means that you can use the constants in place of the actual values.

Return Values

If you are using message boxes to get information from the user, you must obtain a return value and react accordingly. The following example shows you how to concatenate the above button constants and work with the return value. Return values are also constants, so you can use either the numeric value or the built-in VBA constant.

```
Sub MessageBox()
Dim sPrompt As String, sTitle As String
Dim iButtons As Integer, iResponse As Integer
sPrompt = "Eating Lunch Today?" & Chr(13) & "(It's Chicken!)"
iButtons = vbYesNo + vbInformation + vbDefaultButton1
sTitle = "Cafeteria"
iResponse = MsgBox(sPrompt, iButtons, sTitle)
If iResponse = vbYes Then
    MsgBox "See you there!", vbOKOnly, "Tasty"
Else
    MsgBox "Your loss!", vbOKOnly, "Dummy"
```

```
End If
End Sub
```

The following table describes the available return values in VBA:

Constant	Value	Description
vbOK	1	OK
vbCancel	2	Cancel
vbAbort	3	Abort
vbRetry	4	Retry
vbIgnore	5	Ignore
vbYes	6	Yes
vbNo	7	No

When both helpfile and context are provided, the user can press F1 to view the Help topic corresponding to the context. Some host applications, for example, Microsoft Excel, also automatically add a Help button to the dialog box. If the dialog box displays a Cancel button, pressing the Esc key has the same effect as clicking Cancel. If the dialog box contains a Help button, context-sensitive Help is provided for the dialog box; however, no value is returned until one of the other buttons is clicked.

Note: To specify more than the first named argument, you must use MsgBox in an expression. To omit some positional arguments, you must include the corresponding comma delimiter.

Input Boxes

Message boxes provide a great deal of functionality and allow you to get feedback from the end user. Sometimes you will want to obtain more from a user than just the numeric value of the button selected. In this case, you will probably want to work with an input box. Input boxes display a prompt in a dialog box, wait for the user to input text or click a button, and return a string containing the contents of the text box. The syntax is:

```
InputBox(prompt[, title] [, default] [, xpos] [, ypos]
           [, helpfile, context])
```

The InputBox function has these named arguments:

prompt: This parameter is required. This text will be displayed as the message in the dialog box (maximum length of ~1024 characters). You can make the prompt appear on separate lines by using a carriage return character (Chr(13)), a linefeed character (Chr(10)), or carriage return/linefeed character combination (Chr(13) and Chr(10)) between each line.

title: This parameter is optional. This text will be displayed in the title bar of the dialog box. If you omit title, the application name is placed in the title bar.

default: This optional parameter represents the text that will be displayed by default in the text box. If you omit default, the text box is displayed empty.

xpos: This optional numeric parameter specifies, in twips, the horizontal distance of the left edge of the dialog box from the left edge of the screen. If xpos is omitted, the dialog box is horizontally centered.

ypos: This optional numeric parameter specifies, in twips, the vertical distance of the upper edge of the dialog box from the top of the screen. If ypos is omitted, the dialog box is vertically positioned approximately one-third of the way down the screen.

helpfile: This parameter is also optional. This string expression identifies the Help file to use to provide context-sensitive help for the dialog box. Note: If helpfile is provided, context must also be provided.

context: This is used in conjunction with the helpfile parameter. It is a numeric expression that represents the Help context number assigned to the appropriate Help topic. Note: If context is provided, helpfile must also be provided.

If both helpfile and context are provided, the user can press F1 to view the Help topic corresponding to the context. Some host applications, for example, Microsoft Excel, also automatically add a Help button to the dialog box. If the user clicks OK or presses Enter, the InputBox function returns whatever is in the text box. If the user clicks Cancel, the function returns a zero-length string ("").

The following example displays the InputBox shown in Figure 5-8. If the user enters the correct password, a message box is displayed, indicating "You're right!"; if an incorrect value is entered, a "Nope!" message box is displayed.

```
Sub InputboxShow()
Dim sPassword As String
sName = InputBox("What is the secret password?", "Example",
                 "Hint - leaps buildings in a single leap")
If sName = "Superman" Then
    MsgBox "You're right!", vbOKOnly, "Example"
Else
    MsgBox "Nope!", vbOKOnly, "Example"
End If
End Sub
```

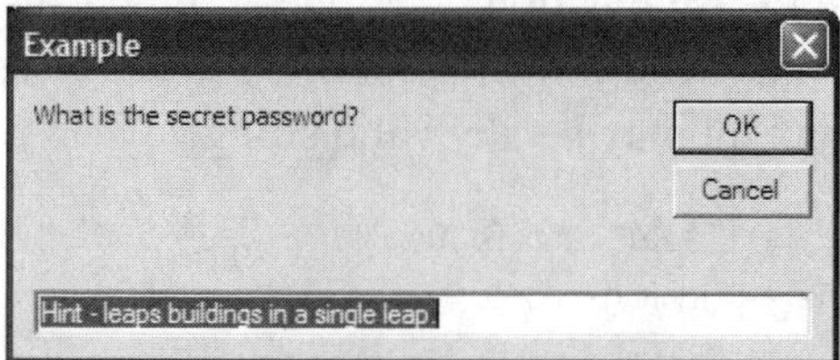

Figure 5-8

Note: If you want to specify more than just the first named argument, you must use the InputBox statement in an expression. If you want to omit one or more of the positional arguments, you must include a comma delimiter and a space.

String Functions

The most frequently used variable type when working with documents is the string. Oftentimes, strings must be manipulated prior to being inserted into a document. For instance, you may want to trim trailing or leading spaces from a name, or you may want to extract information contained in a list. VBA provides many string functions to accomplish your desired goals.

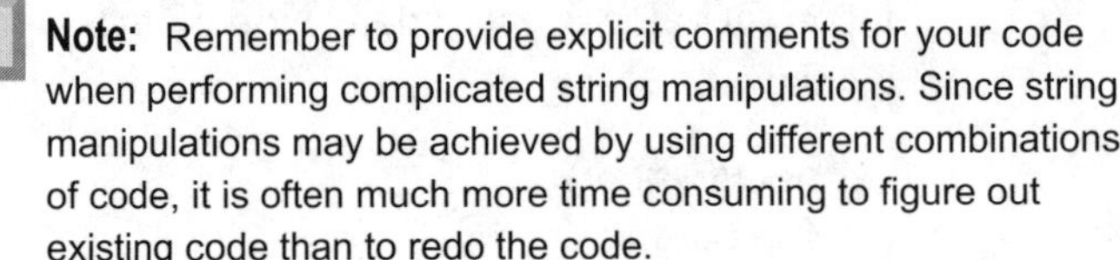

Note: Remember to provide explicit comments for your code when performing complicated string manipulations. Since string manipulations may be achieved by using different combinations of code, it is often much more time consuming to figure out existing code than to redo the code.

The following are some commonly used VBA string functions.

LCase(string)

The LCase function takes one argument and returns a string that has been converted entirely to lowercase. The string argument may be any valid string.

```
SName = LCase("John G. Doe")
SName = "john g. doe"
```

UCase(string)

The UCase function takes one argument and returns a string that has been converted entirely to uppercase. The string argument may be any valid string.

```
SName = UCase("John G. Doe")
SName = "JOHN G. DOE"
```

StrConv(string, conversion)

The StrConv function takes two arguments and changes a string's character set or case. The string argument may be any valid string. The conversion argument may be either an integer value or a constant. See the following table.

Argument	Value	Description
vbUpperCase	1	Converts all characters to uppercase.
vbLowerCase	2	Converts all characters to lowercase.
vbProperCase	3	Converts the first character of every word in the string to uppercase and every other character to lowercase.
vbWide	4	Converts narrow characters to wide characters (Far East versions only).
vbNarrow	8	Converts wide characters to narrow characters (Far East versions only).
vbKatakana	16	Converts Hiragana characters to Katakana characters (Japanese versions only).
vbHiragana	16	Converts Katakana characters to Hiragana characters (Japanese versions only).
vbUnicode	64	Converts the string to Unicode using the default code page of the system.
vbFromUnicode	128	Converts the string from Unicode to the default code page of the system.

The following example sets sSentence to "John Is A Nice Guy":

```
sSentence = StrConv("joHn iS a nIcE guY", vbProperCase)
```

StrComp(string1, string2, [compare])

The StrComp function compares two strings on either a binary or text basis. The string arguments may be any valid string. The optional third argument is a constant that controls the basis for the comparison. If this argument is omitted, the function uses Option Compare. Please refer to the table in the InStr section later in this chapter for the constants.

Comparison	Return Value
string1 = string2	0
string1 < string2 (alphabetically)	–1
string1 > string2 (alphabetically)	1
either string1 or string2 is Null	Null

```
iNum1 = StrComp("john", "JOHN", vbBinaryCompare)
iNum2 = StrComp("john", "JOHN", vbTextCompare)
```

Returns:

```
iNum1 = 1, iNum2 = 0
```

String(number, character)

The String function returns a string filled with the specified number of characters. The number argument is any valid numeric expression (long) that indicates the length of the string. The character argument is the ANSI character code of the string to repeat or a one-character string.

```
sString1 = String(5, "d")
sString2 = String(5, 33)
```

Returns:

```
sString1 = "ddddd", sString2 = "!!!!!"
```

Space(number)

The Space function returns a string full of the specified number of spaces. The number argument may be any valid long data type.

```
sString = Space(5)
```

Returns:

```
sString = "   "
```

Len(string)

The Len function returns a long representing the number of characters in a string. The argument is any valid string.

```
lNum = Len("Billy")
```

Returns:

```
lNum = 5
```

InStr([start], string1, string2, [compare])

The InStr function returns a long representing the position of string2 as it appears in string1. The optional start argument may be any valid numeric expression that determines where in string1 the function will start searching for string2. The optional compare argument may be any of the constants defined in the following table. If either of the string arguments are Null, the function returns a Null.

Constant	Value	Description
vbBinaryCompare	0	A case-sensitive comparison.
vbTextCompare	1	A case-insensitive comparison.
vbDatabaseCompare	2	Based on an Access database sort order.

```
lNum = InStr(1, "Johnny", "h", vbBinaryCompare)
```

Returns:

```
lNum = 3
```

Mid(string, start, [length])

The Mid function returns a string from within another string. The string argument may be any valid string. The start argument is a long data type indicating the position within string to start. The optional length argument indicates the total number of characters to return. If it is omitted, the remainder of the string is returned.

Note: Do not confuse this with the Mid statement. Although the names are the same, the syntax is different.

```
sString = Mid("Johnny", 3)
```

Returns:

```
sString = "hnny"
```

Left(string, length)

The Left function returns a string representing the specified number of characters taken from the left side of the string argument. The string argument may be any valid string and the length argument may be any valid long. If the length argument is longer than the string, the entire string is returned.

```
sFName = Left("Billy Bucknerd", 4)
```

Returns:

```
sFName = "Bill"
```

Right(string, length)

The Right function returns a string representing the specified number of characters taken from the right side of the string argument. The string argument may be any valid string and the length argument may be any valid long. If the length argument is longer than the string, the entire string is returned.

```
sLName = Right("Billy Bucknerd", 4)
```

Returns:

```
sLName = "nerd"
```

Trim(string)

The Trim function trims both the leading and trailing spaces from a string.

```
sName = Trim("  Peanut   ")
```

Returns:

```
sName = "Peanut"
```

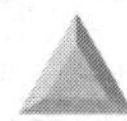

Tip: This is a helpful function when you are searching for a value that may contain spaces. For instance, suppose you want to perform some action if a user doesn't enter a value in a text box; you can use the Trim function to avoid logic errors if the user should enter a few blank spaces accidentally.

LTrim(string)

The LTrim function trims the leading spaces from a string.

```
sName = LTrim("  Peanut   ")
```

Returns:

```
sName = "Peanut   "
```

RTrim(string)

The RTrim function trims the trailing spaces from a string.

```
sName = RTrim("  Peanut   ")
```

Returns:

```
sName = "  Peanut"
```

Chr(charcode)

The Chr function returns the character associated with the specified character code. The charcode argument is a number that corresponds to a character. This function is often useful when programmatically inserting text that is difficult or confusing to represent in VBA.

The following two examples are identical:

```
MsgBox Chr(34) & "Washington" & Chr(34)
MsgBox """Washington"""
```

Note: Some of VBA's intrinsic functions have two versions, one that returns a variant and one that returns a string. Unless a "$" character is the last character of the function, a variant will be returned. Variants are easier to work with because incongruent data types are automatically converted. However, you may want to use the string versions if: 1) you want to minimize memory requirements, as strings are smaller than variants; 2) you want to detect when data of one type is converted to another; or 3) you write data directly to random access files.

String Statements

The following statements are often useful for manipulating strings. Unlike functions, statements do not return a value and are used to manipulate data directly. Pay close attention to the syntax of the following statements.

Option Compare {Binary | Text | Database}

When this statement is used it must appear in a module before any variable or constant declarations.

Option Compare Binary

All strings will be compared on a sort order derived from the machine's internal binary representations. This is the default setting. It results in a case-sensitive comparison of all strings.

Option Compare Text

All strings will be compared without regard to case. This option is often helpful when trying to match user input to fixed data. Oftentimes, users will spell data correctly, but they may not capitalize appropriately.

Option Compare Database

This setting results in string comparisons based on the sort order determined by the database. It can only be used with Microsoft Access.

Mid(stringvar, start, [length]) = string

The Mid statement replaces a portion of a string with another string. The stringvar argument may be any valid string. The start argument is a long indicating where in the string to start. The optional length argument is a long indicating the number of characters to replace (if omitted, the entire string is replaced). The number of characters replaced is always equal to or less than the number of characters in the stringvar argument.

This example incorporates the Option Compare statement:

```
Option Compare Text 'should appear before variable declaration
sName = "sgt. Bill J. Smith"
If Left(sName, 4) = "SGT." Then
Mid(sName, 1, 4)"Cpt."
End if
```

Returns:

```
sName = "Cpt. Bill J. Smith"
```

RSet

The RSet statement right aligns a string and replaces the characters of the existing string. The string will contain the same number of characters as the original.

```
sName = "sgt. Bill J. Smith"
RSet sName = "Puppy"
```

Returns:

```
sName = "             Puppy"
```

LSet

The LSet is statement left aligns a string and replaces the characters of the existing string. This statement operates the same as the RSet statement above except that the string is left aligned.

```
sName = "sgt. Bill J. Smith"
LSet sName = "Puppy"
```

Returns:

```
sName = "Puppy             "
```

Conclusion

This chapter served as an introduction to VBA variables and variable declaration. Variables are an integral part of programming in any language. We also looked at constants and their use. Of course, in most programming you need to interact with the user in some fashion; on this topic we discussed the MsgBox function and the InputBox function. Although both of these functions are very basic, you will probably find yourself working with them at some point. Finally, because your Word programming will undoubtedly involve working with string variables, we discussed numerous functions that can be used to work with them.

Chapter 6

Controlling VBA Code

Introduction

Once you understand the basic elements of the VBA programming language, you can create fairly rudimentary macros. When most people think of macros, they think of one completely linear task that executes lines of code sequentially before finishing. The programming involved in complex document automation requires a greater understanding of how to control the execution of the VBA code. VBA provides several conditional statements and loop functions to greatly enhance the efficiency and complexity of your code. This chapter introduces the various ways you can control program flow using VBA.

Conditional Statements

Inevitably, you will encounter a situation that requires you to code around two or more possible situations. In other words, you will need your code to make decisions for you. This is the first step away from linear macro programming. Perhaps you need to execute different subroutines depending on whether a Boolean variable is True or False, or maybe you have numerous situations to account for. Using conditional statements enables you to implement code that will handle these situations ahead of time. Following are VBA's conditional statements and functions.

If Statements

If...Then

```
If expression Then statements
```

The simplest If statement is the use of one line of code implemented midstream to check something. When an If statement is only one line, an End If is not needed. For example:

```
If x = 10 Then MsgBox "You have reached the maximum amount."
```

The preceding example demonstrates a simple If statement that displays a message box. The message box indicates that the user has reached the maximum amount of whatever the x variable is tracking. In most instances, however, you will probably handle such a situation in a more complex manner. You may want to display the message box to the user and then take a different course of action. For example:

```
If x = 10 Then
    MsgBox "You have reached the maximum amount."
    Exit Sub
End If
```

In the preceding example, the message box is only displayed to the user if x = 10. If x = 10, the program automatically exits the subroutine without executing any of the code following the Exit Sub statement. This type of statement is normally used within a loop. The loop incrementally increases the variable x, but when x reaches 10, the code returns to the calling procedure in the call stack.

If...Then...Else...End If

```
If expression Then
statements
Else
[elsestatements]]
End If
```

This type of If statement is very similar to the last, except for the ability to have a catchall that handles any situation or value other than the original If statement. Using our previous example, suppose that we want to handle x = 10 in the same manner — by displaying the message box and exiting the subroutine. The only difference is that now we want to increment x by 1 and call an external function (xManipulator) if x does not equal 10. Now, the If statement will evaluate x and if x does not equal 10, the Else branch of the statement will execute.

```
If x = 10 Then
    MsgBox "You have reached the maximum amount."
    Exit Sub
Else
    x=x+1
    Call xManipulator
End If
```

If...Then...ElseIf...End If

```
If expression Then
statements
ElseIf expression Then
[elseifstatements]]
Else
[elsestatements]]
End If
```

This structure is very similar to the If...Then...Else...End If structure, but it involves evaluating more than one criterion before kicking into the Else branch of the logic. The following example is a subroutine that you can copy directly to the VBE to see exactly how these statements work.

```
Sub If_ElseIf_Else_EndIf()
Dim x As Integer
For x = 1 To 5
If x = 1 Then
    MsgBox x
ElseIf x = 2 Then
    MsgBox "elseif"
Else
    MsgBox "else"
End If
Next x
End Sub
```

Once you understand the basic structure of the If statement, it becomes apparent how useful it can be in programming. It is worth mentioning that there is no limitation to the number of ElseIf statements that you can use in your code. You can also embed multiple If statements within an If statement.

IIf Function

```
IIf(expr, truepart, falsepart)
```

This is a close cousin to the regular If statement. IIf is actually a function because you pass it two sets of data, and it evaluates both and returns a value. The IIf function evaluates both truepart and falsepart, even though it returns only one of them.

Caution: Beware of undesirable results when using IIf. Because it evaluates both sets of data, when evaluating the falsepart you may incur an error, such as a division by zero, even if expr is True.

Select Case

```
Select Case testexpression
[Case expressionlist-n
[statements-n]] ...
[Case Else
[elsestatements]]
End Select
```

Frequently, a programmer learns the If statement and figures that it can handle all of his decision logic needs. The result is that the code is filled with If...ElseIf statements that have numerous ElseIf branches, all evaluating the same variable. A far more efficient way of controlling this code is to use the Select Case statement. While If...Then...Else statements can evaluate a different expression for each ElseIf statement, the Select Case statement evaluates an expression only once, at the top of the control structure.

```
Select Case Number
Case 1 to 40
    MsgBox "40 or under"
Case 41, 42, 43, 44
    MsgBox "Mid 40s"
Case 45 to 100
    MsgBox "Old Geezer"
Case Else
    MsgBox "Error, greater than 100"
End Select
```

The previous example evaluates the value of the variable Number and matches it against the Case expressions. When it evaluates to the correct Case clause, the code following the Case clause is executed. After the code has completed, the code resumes running at the next line immediately following End Select.

Note: If Number were to match more than one Case clause, only the code following the first Case clause executes.

The Case Else clause indicates the catchall code to be executed if no match is found in the above Case clauses. Case Else is not required, but using it to pop up a message box can be useful to alert the user of an unforeseen value being evaluated. In the event that there is not a match in any of the Case clauses, execution continues at the statement following End Select. Select Case statements can be nested. Each nested Select Case statement must have a matching End Select statement.

Loops

Although there are many different types of loops, their basic function is to determine how many times a block of code should be executed. The main consideration is to understand the differences in the way each looping convention acts. This enables the programmer to use the correct loop for every convention. Even though you may have a favorite loop procedure, it is still important to understand each convention. Sometimes, trying to fit a problem into a particular loop is like trying to fit a round peg into a square hole.

The For...Next Loop

This loop repeats a block of code a specified number of times based on a counter. The counter will be incremented (or decremented) each time the loop is executed. You can also define the number by which to increment the loop. Its syntax is as follows:

```
For counter = start To end [Step step]
[statements]
[Exit For]
[statements]
Next [counter]
```

The For...Next statement syntax has these parts:

counter: The counter is required. It is a numeric variable that will be used as a loop counter. The variable can't be a Boolean or an array element (see the For Each...Next loop below).

start: This required value is the initial value of the counter.

end: This required value is the final value of the counter.

step: This is the optional part of the loop that is the amount counter is changed each time through the loop. If not specified, step defaults to one.

statements: These are the statements between For and Next that are executed the number of times the loop runs.

After the code in the loop has executed, the counter is incrementally increased by step. The value of step can be any valid incremental amount. The loop must then evaluate whether it should run the code again, or if the loop should be exited with program execution beginning immediately following the Next statement.

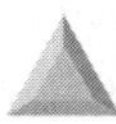

Tip: Do not change the value of the counter in the code that's inside the loop. This can lead to logic errors that are very difficult to debug.

You can also place Exit For statements inside the loop to trigger an exit from the loop. Obviously, you will want to place them in some sort of conditional statement, otherwise the Exit For will trigger every time and the code will not loop properly. Like all of the conditionals, you can also embed For...Next loops in other For...Next loops.

Caution: Remember the exponential growth you will encounter when embedding loops within other loops. Two loops that run 50 times each run 100 times total when placed in series, but when one loop is run within the other, the code effectively runs 2,500 times. This is because the second loop will run 50 times through based on each execution of the first loop.

Note: You can omit counter in a Next statement, and execution continues as if counter is included.

The For Each...Next Loop

This loop repeats a block of code by looping through each element in an array or collection. This is the correct loop to use when trying to loop through a collection of object type variables. Keep in mind that unlike For...Next loops, you can't use For Each...Next to modify the element value. The syntax is as follows:

```
For Each element In group
[statements]
[Exit For]
[statements]
Next [element]
```

The For Each...Next statement syntax has these parts:

element: This required value is the variable that will be used to iterate through the collection or array. Collections use variant variables. Arrays use either variant variables or object variables.

group: This required value is the name of an object collection or array (except an array of user-defined types).

statements: This is an optional part of the loop. These can be one or more statements that are executed on each item in group.

The code enters the For Each block for every element in the group. When the loop has cycled through every element in the group, the loop is exited and program execution continues immediately after the Next statement. You may also include Exit For statements in a For Each loop as another means of exiting the loop. Finally, just like For...Next loops, you can embed For Each...Next loops within other For Each...Next loops.

Tip: The For Each...Next loop isn't available when using an array of user-defined types. (See the section on arrays in Chapter 5.)

The Do...Loop Statement

The Do...Loop repeats a block of code while a condition is True or until a condition becomes True. It has two alternative syntaxes. In one instance of the Do...Loop, the condition is evaluated at the top of the loop (attached to the Do part). In the other instance, the condition is evaluated at the bottom of the loop (attached to the Loop part). Keep in mind that if the condition is evaluated at the bottom of the loop, the loop will always be run at least one time. The syntax is as follows:

```
Do [{While|Until} condition]
[statements]
[Exit Do]
[statements]
Loop
```

Or, you can use this syntax:

```
Do
[statements]
[Exit Do]
[statements]
Loop [{While|Until} condition]
```

The Do...Loop statement syntax has these parts:

condition: This is a numeric expression or string expression that is either True or False. If condition is Null, condition is treated as False.

statements: One or more statements that are repeated while, or until, condition is True.

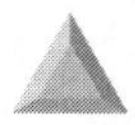

Tip: You can use Exit Do statements anywhere within the Do...Loop as a means of exiting the loop.

The While...Wend Loop

The While...Wend loop executes a series of statements while a condition is True. When the condition is True, all the statements within the loop are executed until the Wend statement is encountered. Once the statements are executed, control returns to the While statement and condition is checked again. If condition is still True, the statements are executed again; if condition is no longer True, the program's execution will resume at the line immediately following the Wend statement. Like most loops, you nest While...Wend loops within themselves, with each Wend matching the most recent While. The syntax is as follows:

```
While condition
[statements]
Wend
```

The While...Wend statement syntax has these parts:

condition: This is a numeric expression or string expression that evaluates to True or False. When condition is Null, it is treated as False.

statements: These are the statements that will be executed while condition is True.

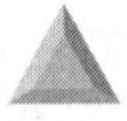

Tip: The Do...Loop statement provides a more structured and flexible way to perform looping.

Alternative Flow Control

Besides conditional statements and loops, VBA has other ways to control program flow. These are discussed here.

On...GoTo and On...GoSub

These are less frequently used ways to control the flow of program execution. Most programmers think only of On Error GoTo, but you can use these statements to evaluate many different expressions. Programmatically, they cause execution to branch to a specified line, depending on the value of an expression. The syntax is as follows:

```
On expression GoSub destinationlist
On expression GoTo destinationlist
```

The On…GoSub and On…GoTo statement syntax has these parts:

expression: This can be any numeric expression that evaluates to a whole number from 0 to 255, inclusive. If expression is any number other than a whole number, it is rounded before it is evaluated.

destinationlist: This is a list of line numbers or line labels separated by commas.

The value of expression determines which line is branched to in destinationlist. If the value of expression is less than 1 or greater than the number of items in the list, one of the following results occurs:

If expression is	Then
Equal to 0	Control drops to the statement following On...GoSub or On...GoTo.
Greater than number of items in list	Control drops to the statement following On...GoSub or On...GoTo.
Negative	An error occurs.
Greater than 255	An error occurs.

You can mix line numbers and line labels in the same list. You can use as many line labels and line numbers as you like with On...GoSub and On...GoTo; however, if you use more labels or numbers than fit on a single line, you must use the line continuation character to continue the logical line onto the next physical line.

Tip: Select Case provides a more structured and flexible way to perform multiple branching.

GoSub...Return

This branches to and returns from a subroutine within a procedure. You can use any line label or line number for the line argument. GoSub and Return can be used to bounce anywhere within a procedure, but both GoSub and Return must be in the same procedure. You can run into some logic errors if you use multiple GoSubs in a single subroutine because the first Return statement that the execution comes across will cause the flow to branch back to the line after the most recent GoSub statement. The syntax is as follows:

```
GoSub line
line
Return
```

Note: You can't enter or exit Sub procedures with GoSub...Return.

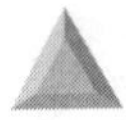

Tip: In most cases, your code will be much easier to follow if you create separate procedures. This is a more structured alternative to using GoSub...Return.

Stop

This stops execution of the code and forces the program into break mode. Stop statements can be placed anywhere in procedures to suspend execution. If you need to resume execution of the program, you can simply press F5 or press the Run button on the Standard toolbar. Stop statements work exactly like setting a breakpoint in the code, but have the added advantage that they are not lost when you close out of the program. The syntax is:

```
Stop
```

Note: Make sure you know the difference between the Stop statement and the End statement: Stop doesn't clear any variables while End does.

Choose

The Choose function selects and returns a value from a list of arguments. The Choose function's return value is determined by the index number and the possible list of choices in the function; i.e., if index is 1, Choose returns the first choice in the list; if index is 2, it returns the second choice, and so on. The Choose function returns a Null if the index is less than 1 or greater than the number of choices listed. The index value will be rounded to the nearest whole number before being evaluated if it is not an integer when passed. The syntax is:

```
Choose(index, choice-1[, choice-2, ... [, choice-n]])
```

The Choose function syntax has these parts:

index: This required numeric expression should contain a value from 1 to the number of available choices.

choice: There must be at least one of these. It is a variant expression that contains one of the possible choices.

Choose is most often used to look up a value in a list of possibilities. For example, if index evaluates to 3 and the list evaluates to choice-1 = "Shani," choice-2 = "Peanut," and choice-3 = "Debra," Choose returns "Debra." This makes the Choose function very useful if there is some correlation between the index value and the option within the choice list. There are some potential problems when using the Choose function. Keep in mind that like the IIf function, every choice in the list will be evaluated even though only one will be returned. You can check this using the MsgBox function in each of the choices. Every time one of the choices is evaluated, a message box will be displayed even though Choose will return only one of them.

Partition

The Partition function returns a string that indicates where a number falls within a series. If any of the parts is Null, the Partition function will return a Null. Partition will return a range with enough leading spaces so that there are the same number of characters to the left and right of the colon as there are characters in stop, plus one. This ensures that if you use Partition with other numbers, the resulting text will be handled properly during any subsequent sort operation. If interval is 1, the range is number:number, regardless of the start and stop arguments. The syntax is:

```
Partition(number, start, stop, interval)
```

The Partition function has these required arguments:

number: This is a whole number that you want to evaluate against the ranges.

start: This is a whole number that is the start of the overall range of numbers. The number can't be less than 0.

stop: This is a whole number that is the end of the overall range of numbers. The number can't be equal to or less than start.

interval: This is a whole number that is the interval spanned by each range in the series from start to stop. The number can't be less than 1.

End

The End statement ends a procedure or block of code. When the End statement is executed, all variables lose their values. If you need to preserve these variables, use the Stop statement instead; you can then resume execution while preserving the value of those variables. The End statement provides a way to force your program to halt. For normal termination of a Visual Basic program, you should unload all forms. Objects created from class modules are destroyed, files opened using the Open statement are closed, and memory used by your program is freed. The syntax is:

```
End
End Function
End If
End Property
End Select
End Sub
End Type
End With
```

The End statement has these forms:

End: This is never required but may be placed anywhere in a procedure to end code execution and clear all variables.

End Function: This is required to end a Function statement.

End If: This is required to end a block If…Then…Else statement.

End Property: This is required to end a Property Let, Property Get, or Property Set procedure.

End Select: This is required to end a Select Case statement.

End Sub: This is required to end a Sub statement.

End Type: This is required to end a user-defined type definition (Type statement).

End With: This is required to end a With statement.

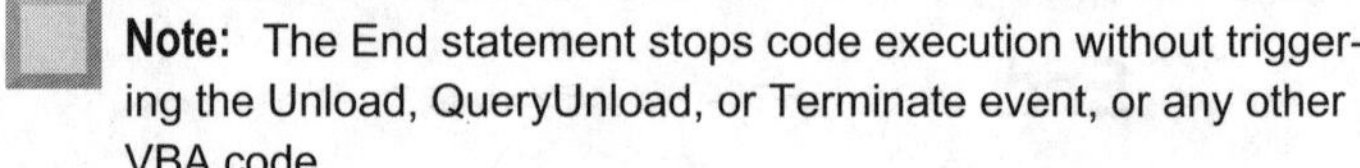

Note: The End statement stops code execution without triggering the Unload, QueryUnload, or Terminate event, or any other VBA code.

Arithmetic Operators

Add

The Add operator can be used to add numbers (expressions) together. If one or both expressions are Null expressions, the result will be Null. If both expressions are Empty, the result is an integer. However, if only one expression is Empty, the other expression is returned unchanged as *result*. When used for simple arithmetic addition using only numeric data types, the data type of *result* is usually the same as that of the most precise expression. The order of precision, from least to most precise, is byte, integer, long, single, double, currency, and decimal. For further information, please see the table below. The syntax is:

```
result = expression1+expression2
```

The + (Add) operator has these parts:

result: Any numeric variable

expression1: Any valid expression

expression2: Any valid expression

If at least one expression is not a variant, the following rules apply:

If	Then
Both expressions are numeric data types (byte, Boolean, integer, long, single, double, date, currency, or decimal)	Add
Both expressions are string	Concatenate
One expression is a numeric data type and the other is any variant except Null	Add
One expression is a string and the other is any variant except Null	Concatenate
One expression is an Empty variant	Return the remaining expression unchanged as *result*
One expression is a numeric data type and the other is a string	A type mismatch error occurs
Either expression is Null	*result* is Null
Both variant expressions are numeric	Add
Both variant expressions are strings	Concatenate
One variant expression is numeric and the other is a string	Add

The following are exceptions to the order of precision described above.

If	Then *result* is
A single and a long are added	A double
The data type of *result* is a long, single, or date variant that overflows its legal range	Converted to a double variant
The data type of *result* is a byte variant that overflows its legal range	Converted to an integer variant
The data type of *result* is an integer variant that overflows its legal range	Converted to a long variant
A date is added to any data type	A date

Note: The order of precision used by addition and subtraction is not the same as the order of precision used by multiplication.

Subtract

The Subtract operator can be used in two different ways: to find the difference between two numbers, or to indicate the negative value of a numeric expression. The first syntax example below shows the Subtract operator being used to find the difference between two numbers. The second syntax example shows the Subtract operator being used to indicate the negative value of an expression.

```
result = number1–number2
–number
```

The – (Subtract) operator has these required parts:

result: Any numeric variable

number: Any numeric expression

number1: Any numeric expression

number2: Any numeric expression

Again, *result* is usually the same as that of the most precise expression with the order of precision being byte, integer, long, single, double, and currency. The following table shows the exceptions to this order:

If	Then *result* is
Subtraction involves a single and a long	Converted to a double
The data type of *result* is a long, single, or date variant that overflows its legal range	Converted to a variant containing a double
The data type of *result* is a byte variant that overflows its legal range	Converted to an integer variant
The data type of *result* is an integer variant that overflows its legal range	Converted to a long variant
Subtraction involves a date and any other data type	A date
Subtraction involves two date expressions	A double

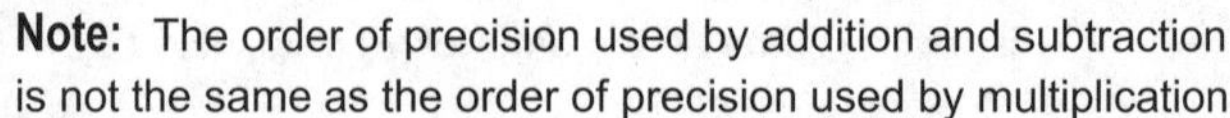

Note: The order of precision used by addition and subtraction is not the same as the order of precision used by multiplication.

Multiply

The Multiply operator is used to multiply two numbers together. The syntax is:

```
result = number1*number2
```

The * (Multiply) operator has these required parts:

result: Any numeric variable

number1: Any numeric expression

number2: Any numeric expression

As with the previous mathematical functions, the data type of *result* is usually the same as that of the most precise expression. The order of precision, from least to most precise, is byte, integer, long, single, currency, double, and decimal. The following table shows the exceptions to this order:

If	Then *result* is
Multiplication involves a single and a long	Converted to a double
The data type of *result* is a long, single, or date variant that overflows its legal range	Converted to a variant containing a double
The data type of *result* is a byte variant that overflows its legal range	Converted to an integer variant
The data type of *result* is an integer variant that overflows its legal range	Converted to a long variant
If one or both expressions are Null expressions	Null
If an expression is Empty	Treated as 0

Divide Integer

The Divide Integer operator is used to divide two numbers and return an integer result. The syntax is:

```
result = number1\number2
```

The \ (Divide Integer) operator has these required parts:

result: Any numeric variable

number1: Any numeric expression

number2: Any numeric expression

Numeric expressions are rounded to byte, integer, or long expressions before the division is actually performed. Usually, the data type of *result* is a byte, byte variant, integer, integer variant, long, or long variant, regardless of whether *result* is a whole number. Any fractional portion is truncated. However, if any expression is Null, *result* is Null. Any expression that is Empty is treated as 0.

Divide Floating Point

The Divide Floating Point operator is used to divide two numbers and return a floating-point result. The syntax is:

```
result = number1/number2
```

The / (Divide Floating Point) operator has these required parts:

result: Any numeric variable

number1: Any numeric expression

number2: Any numeric expression

Any expression that is Empty is treated as 0. The data type of *result* is usually a double or a double variant. The following are exceptions to this rule:

If	Then *result* is
Both expressions are byte, integer, or single expressions	A single unless it overflows its legal range, in which case, an error occurs
Both expressions are byte, integer, or single variants	A single variant unless it overflows its legal range, in which case, *result* is a variant containing a double
Division involves a decimal and any other data type	A decimal data type
One or both expressions are Null expressions	Null

Logical Operators

AND

The AND operator is used to perform a logical conjunction on two expressions. The syntax is:

```
result = expression1 AND expression2
```

The AND operator has these required parts:

result: Any numeric variable

expression1: Any expression

expression2: Any expression

If both expressions evaluate to True, *result* is True. If either expression evaluates to False, *result* is False. The following table illustrates how *result* is determined:

Expression1	Expression2	Result
True	True	True
True	False	False
True	Null	Null
False	True	False
False	False	False
False	Null	False
Null	True	Null
Null	False	False
Null	Null	Null

The AND operator also performs a bitwise comparison of identically positioned bits in two numeric expressions and sets the corresponding bit in *result* according to the following table:

Expression1	Expression2	Result
0	0	0
0	1	0
1	0	0
1	1	1

NOT

The NOT operator is used to perform the logical negation on an expression. The syntax is:

```
result = NOT expression
```

The NOT operator has these required parts:

result: Any numeric variable

expression: Any expression

The following table illustrates how *result* is determined:

Expression	Result
True	False
False	True
Null	Null

In addition, the NOT operator inverts the bit values of any variable and sets the corresponding bit in *result* according to the following table:

Expression	Result
0	1
1	0

OR

The OR operator is used to perform a logical disjunction on two expressions. The syntax is:

```
result = expression1 OR expression2
```

The OR operator has these required parts:

result: Any numeric variable

expression1: Any expression

expression2: Any expression

If either or both expressions evaluate to True, *result* is True. The following table illustrates how *result* is determined:

Expression1	Expression2	Result
True	True	True
True	False	True
True	Null	True
False	True	True
False	False	False
False	Null	Null
Null	True	True
Null	False	Null
Null	Null	Null

The OR operator also performs a bitwise comparison of identically positioned bits in two numeric expressions and sets the corresponding bit in *result* according to the following table:

Expression1	Expression2	Result
0	0	0
0	1	1
1	0	1
1	1	1

Comparison Operators

Following is a table that briefly describes the comparison operators you will frequently be working with in VBA. Keep in mind exactly how these operators work if you are using them in If statements — you can encounter nasty logic problems simply by having a "greater than or equal to" when what you really want is a "greater than." You will notice that the table contains a list of the comparison operators and the conditions that determine whether *result* is True, False, or Null.

Operator	True if	False if	Null if
< (Less than)	expression1 < expression2	expression1 >= expression2	expression1 or expression2 = Null
<= (Less than or equal to)	expression1 <= expression2	expression1 > expression2	expression1 or expression2 = Null
> (Greater than)	expression1 > expression2	expression1 <= expression2	expression1 or expression2 = Null
>= (Greater than or equal to)	expression1 >= expression2	expression1 < expression2	expression1 or expression2 = Null
= (Equal to)	expression1 = expression2	expression1 <> expression2	expression1 or expression2 = Null
<> (Not equal to)	expression1 <> expression2	expression1 = expression2	expression1 or expression2 = Null

When comparing two expressions, you may not be able to easily determine whether the expressions are being compared as numbers or as strings. The following table shows how the expressions are compared:

If	Then
Both expressions are numeric data types (byte, Boolean, integer, long, single, double, date, or currency)	Perform a numeric comparison
Both expressions are strings	Perform a string comparison
One expression is a numeric data type and the other is a variant that is, or can be, a number	Perform a numeric comparison
One expression is a numeric data type and the other is a string variant that can't be converted to a number	A type mismatch error occurs
One expression is a string and the other is any variant except a Null	Perform a string comparison
One expression is Empty and the other is a numeric data type	Perform a numeric comparison, using 0 as the Empty expression

If	Then
One expression is Empty and the other is a string	Perform a string comparison, using a zero-length string ("") as the Empty expression

If *expression1* and *expression2* are both variant expressions, their underlying type determines how they are compared. The following table shows how the expressions are compared or the result from the comparison, depending on the underlying type of the variant:

If	Then
Both variant expressions are numeric	Perform a numeric comparison
Both variant expressions are strings	Perform a string comparison
One variant expression is numeric and the other is a string	The numeric expression is less than the string expression
One variant expression is Empty and the other is numeric	Perform a numeric comparison, using 0 as the Empty expression
One variant expression is Empty and the other is a string	Perform a string comparison, using a zero-length string ("") as the Empty expression
Both variant expressions are Empty	The expressions are equal

When a single is compared to a double, the double is rounded to the precision of the single. If currency is compared with a single or double, the single or double is converted to currency. Similarly, when a decimal is compared with a single or double, the single or double is converted to a decimal. For currency, any fractional value less than .0001 may be lost; for decimal, any fractional value less than 1E–28 may be lost, or an overflow error can occur. Such fractional value loss may cause two values to compare as equal when they are not.

IS/LIKE

IS and LIKE are used to compare expressions. If you are familiar with database queries, you are probably familiar with the way these operators work. The IS and LIKE operators have specific comparison functionality that differs from the operators in the previous table. The behavior of the LIKE operator depends on the Option Compare statement. Briefly, Option Compare Binary results in context-sensitive string comparisons, while Option Compare Text results in string comparisons that are case insensitive.

You can use LIKE in conjunction with built-in pattern matching for string comparisons. The pattern-matching features allow you to use wildcard characters, character lists, or character ranges, in any combination, to match strings. The question mark (?) is used to represent any single character, the asterisk (*) is used to represent zero or more characters, and the (#) character is used to represent any single digit (0 to 9). The syntax is:

```
result = expression1 comparisonoperator expression2
result = object1 IS object2
result = string LIKE pattern
```

Comparison operators have these required parts:

result: Any numeric variable

expression: Any expression

comparisonoperator: Any comparison operator

object: Any object name

string: Any string expression

pattern: Any string expression or range of characters

Concatenation

& Operator

The & operator is used to force string concatenation of two expressions. The syntax is:

```
result = expression1 & expression2
```

The & operator has these required parts:

result: Any string or variant variable

expression1: Any expression

expression2: Any expression

If an expression is not a string, it is converted to a string variant. The data type of *result* is string if both expressions are string expressions; otherwise, *result* is a string variant. If both expressions are Null, *result* is Null. However, if only one expression is Null, that expression is treated as a zero-length string ("") when concatenated with the other expression. Any expression that is Empty is also treated as a zero-length string.

+ Operator

The + operator is used to sum two numbers. The syntax is:

```
result = expression1+expression2
```

The + operator has these required parts:

result: Any numeric variable

expression1: Any expression

expression2: Any expression

Because this operator is also used to concatenate strings, you may not be able to determine whether addition or string concatenation will occur when you use the + operator. Use the & operator for concatenation to eliminate ambiguity and provide self-documenting code.

If at least one expression is not a variant, the following rules apply:

If	Then
Both expressions are numeric data types (byte, Boolean, integer, long, single, double, date, currency, or decimal)	Add
Both expressions are string	Concatenate
One expression is a numeric data type and the other is any variant except Null	Add
One expression is a string and the other is any variant except Null	Concatenate
One expression is an Empty variant	Return the remaining expression unchanged as *result*
One expression is a numeric data type and the other is a string	A type mismatch error occurs
Either expression is Null	*result* is Null

If both expressions are variant expressions, the following rules apply:

If	Then
Both variant expressions are numeric	Add
Both variant expressions are strings	Concatenate
One variant expression is numeric and the other is a string	Add

Call

This statement transfers control to a sub procedure, function procedure, or dynamic link library procedure (*.dll files). You are not required to use the Call keyword when calling a procedure; however, if you use the Call keyword to call a procedure that requires arguments, *argumentlist* must be enclosed in parentheses. If you omit the Call keyword, you also must omit the parentheses around *argumentlist*. If you use either Call syntax to call any intrinsic or user-defined function, the function's return value is discarded. To pass a whole array to a procedure, use the array name followed by empty parentheses.

```
[Call] name [argumentlist]
```

The Call statement syntax has these parts:

Call: This is an optional keyword that may help future programmers understand that you were calling another procedure.

name: This is the required name of the procedure to call.

argumentlist: This is an optional list that includes a comma-delimited list of variables, arrays, or expressions to pass to the procedure. Components of *argumentlist* may include the keywords ByVal or ByRef to describe how the arguments are treated by the called procedure. However, ByVal and ByRef can be used with Call only when calling a DLL procedure. On the Macintosh, ByVal and ByRef can be used with Call when making a call to a Macintosh code resource.

Conclusion

This chapter explored some ways of controlling execution of the VBA code. VBA provides several conditional statements and loop functions to greatly enhance the efficiency of your code, although they also add complexity. It covered conditional statements that help you control the way your code will branch and branching techniques that allow you to avoid initializing variables and performing procedures that may be unnecessary. This chapter also introduced several different ways of creating loops. Another important element of advanced programming is a good understanding of what operators are available and how they work. These operators allow you to use conditional statements and loops properly.

Chapter 7

VBA Projects

Introduction

This chapter focuses on two individual VBA projects. The first project demonstrates the use of dynamically created controls. Dynamically created controls are frequently necessary in document automation programming. The Index property is available for most VB controls. VBA, however, doesn't provide an Index property for controls and thus doesn't provide for dynamic control creation in the same manner as VB. The second project demonstrates how Word can be used to create what is essentially a document assembly system that customizes itself for each user.

Dynamic Control Creation with VBA

Programmers familiar with Visual Basic may be surprised to find that Microsoft neglected to include control arrays in VBA 6.0. Control arrays allow the creation of run-time controls, as long as a control of the same type already exists and the existing control has an index of 0.

The Index property is available for most VB controls. VBA, however, doesn't provide an Index property for controls and thus doesn't provide for dynamic control creation in the same manner as VB. But with a little creativity, you can accomplish practically the same thing.

The Conventional Method

The main thing to remember about controls is that they are objects. As objects, they have properties and methods you can manipulate at design time or run time to achieve the desired results. This chapter presents two common ways to create controls at run time in VBA. Virtually any run-time control creation will use a variation of one of these two methods. The most common way — the conventional way — is to create a control object variable to contain the run-time control, as shown in Listing 7-1 below. This example uses a multi-page control with three text boxes.

Listing 7-1: Conventional method — please note the additional code specified in the code blocks below.

```
Option Explicit
' Dimension a variable as a new instance of Form1.
Dim frmNew As New UserForm1
' Dimension specific object arrays.
Dim pg(1 To 5) As New Page
Dim txtFName(1 To 5) As New Control
Dim txtLName(1 To 5) As New Control
Dim cboTle(1 To 5) As New Control
' Dimension a counter variable so that it keeps its value.
' Note: This could also be done locally with a static
' variable that would exist for the life of the module.
Dim x As Integer, y As Integer
Private Sub cmdNewForm_Click()
' Display a dynamically created version of the UserForm.
frmNew.Show
End Sub
Public Sub cmdNewPage_Click()
' Used to keep track of how many pages are created and
' sets the array index accordingly.
x = x + 1
' Prevent user from getting error.
If x = 6 Then
MsgBox "You can only create 6 total pages!", vbCritical
Exit Sub
```

```
End If
' Set member of page array to the newly created page.
Set pg(x) = Me.MultiPage1.Pages.Add
' Set members of the control arrays to the
' newly created controls.
Set txtFName(x) = pg(x).Controls.Add("Forms.TextBox.1")
txtFName(x).Left = 36
txtFName(x).Top = 12
txtFName(x).Width = 132
Set txtLName(x) = pg(x).Controls.Add("Forms.TextBox.1")
txtLName(x).Left = 36
txtLName(x).Top = 36
txtLName(x).Width = 132
Set cboTle(x) = pg(x).Controls.Add("Forms.ComboBox.1")
cboTle(x).Left = 36
cboTle(x).Top = 60
cboTle(x).Width = 132
End Sub
Public Sub cmdValue_Click()
Me.Hide
' Run a loop that displays the value of the textboxes.
For y = 1 To Me.MultiPage1.Pages.Count
If y = 1 Then
MsgBox "The value of the text is " & _
Me.txtFirstName.Value
Else
MsgBox "The value of the text is " & txtFName(y - 1)
End If
Next
End Sub
```

Before we get to the first example of adding run-time controls, let's take a look at the creation of a run-time form. Sometimes, all the functionality you require can be accomplished by creating another instance of the form at run time. The following lines of code (also found in UserForm1) will create a run-time instance of the form:

```
Dim frmNew As New UserForm1
Private Sub cmdNewForm_Click()
frmNew.Show
End Sub
```

Notice that in this case, the new form contains all the controls and functionality of the original form. (You can move the forms to different areas and hit the button to see that it's creating new forms.) However, there will be times when you want to see all of the additional sets of controls at once. This is where the multi-page control becomes quite useful. UserForm1 (see Figure 7-1) uses the following code to create an additional page every time the New Page command button's Click event is fired:

```
Private Sub cmdNewPage_Click()
Me.MultiPage1.Pages.Add
End Sub
```

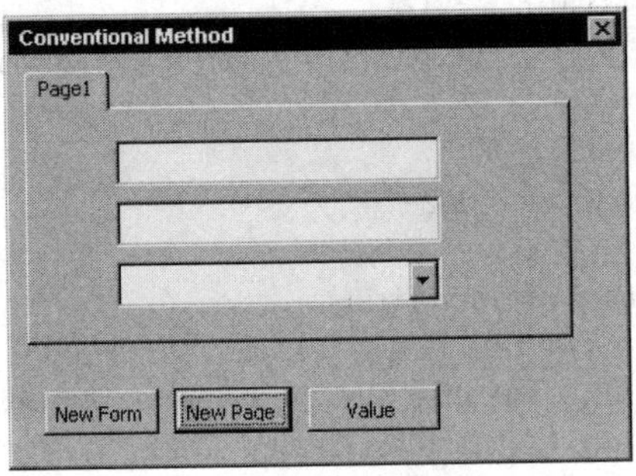

Figure 7-1

This code creates a new page, but it's not assigning another object variable to the page, and thus the new page's properties are difficult to work with. If, however, we set the page equal to an object variable, we gain access to some added functionality. (Note that the Set keyword is always used with object variables.) The most complete way of adding pages is to create an array of pages using the following code:

```
Dim pg(1 To 5) As New Page
Private Sub cmdNewPage_Click()
Static x As Integer
x = x + 1
Set pg(x) = Me.MultiPage1.Pages.Add
End Sub
```

This code uses pg(1 To 5) to capture each of the newly created pages. Each of these pages can be individually accessed using the appropriate member of the array.

However, we're still only creating blank pages — and blank pages aren't very helpful. To add functionality, we need to add controls to the new pages.

Again, we can accomplish this through the use of arrays and the appropriate object variables. One of the parameters of the Control.Add method is Name. The Name argument can become confusing. In most cases, it's easier to refer to the index value of the array. The following code, when added to the New Page command button, will create additional controls and the corresponding object variables.

```
Set txtFName(x) = pg(x).Controls.Add("Forms.TextBox.1")
txtFName(x).Left = 36
txtFName(x).Top = 12
txtFName(x).Width = 132
Set txtLName(x) = pg(x).Controls.Add("Forms.TextBox.1")
txtLName(x).Left = 36
txtLName(x).Top = 36
txtLName(x).Width = 132
Set cboTle(x) = pg(x).Controls.Add("Forms.ComboBox.1")
cboTle(x).Left = 36
cboTle(x).Top = 60
cboTle(x).Width = 132
```

Note that we used slightly different names for each of these controls. VBA forces you to do this because control arrays are not intrinsically allowed. If you try to set a control array with the same name as an existing control, the dialog box shown in Figure 7-2 will be displayed.

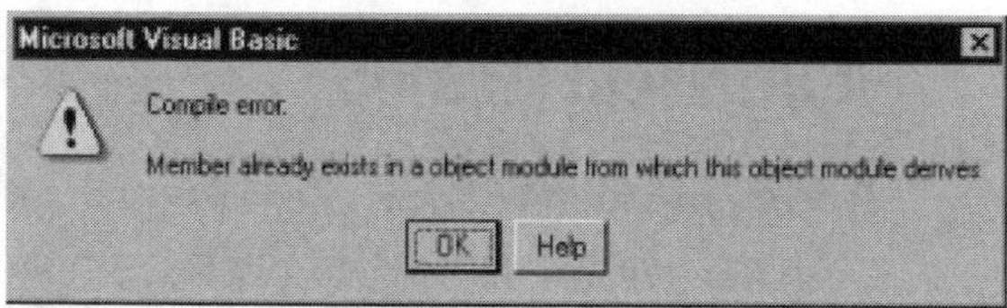

Figure 7-2

The value command button runs a simple message box procedure that demonstrates how you can use the values of the dynamically created controls. In short, you can use the values of dynamically created controls in any of the ways in which you could use design-time controls and their values.

At this point we should carefully analyze the controls we're creating. We're dimensioning the variables as "controls" but not as actual text boxes or combo boxes. The result is that some of the properties and methods of the controls will *not* show up with the IntelliSense feature, but this doesn't mean they're not available. IntelliSense recognizes only that the variable is a control, but it doesn't know the actual type of control. Therefore, IntelliSense lists the properties common to all controls.

For example, IntelliSense won't display the BackColor property, but assigning a value to the BackColor property is still syntactically correct. When assigned to the Click event of a command button, the following code will change the background color of the text box. Note that we cannot use the New keyword when dimensioning variables to be text boxes; we get a type mismatch error if we try to create an array of specific controls. Thus, we must use the Control type for our dynamically created controls.

```
txtFName(x).BackColor = vbRed
```

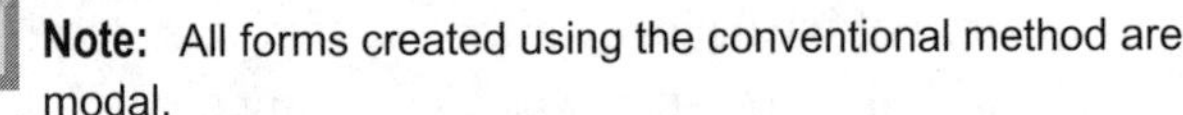

Note: All forms created using the conventional method are modal.

A Shortcut Method

Every programmer knows there is often more than one "correct" way of accomplishing a given task. The previous section walked through what is, essentially, an alternative means of creating dynamic control arrays. Obviously, this requires the explicit declaration of object variables to contain the run-time controls. This provides you with full access to the control's properties.

There is a quicker way that provides basically the same control over the dynamically created controls. The shortcut method is shown in Listing 7-2 on the following page. The following code demonstrates a copy-and-paste method of adding a collection of controls to another multi-page:

```
Private Sub cmdNewPage_Click()
Static x As Integer
x = x + 1
Me.MultiPage1.Pages(0).Controls.Copy
Me.MultiPage1.Pages.Add
Me.MultiPage1.Pages(x).Paste
End Sub
```

This code copies the controls from the first page and pastes them to the newly created pages. All this is done without creating object variables to represent either the pages or the controls. At first glimpse, adherents of the traditional way of creating controls will most likely scoff at such a method. However, the programmer still has full control over all the properties of the control — except now none of them will show up through the IntelliSense feature.

Again, a simple loop runs through the pages of the multi-page control and displays a message box with the value of the control indexed at 0. This is somewhat trickier than setting an object variable equal to the new control. In this method, we must know the index of the control as it exists on the page. If worse comes to worse, you can set values to the controls and distinguish them by displaying message boxes corresponding to each index on the page.

Notice that we're using the SelectedItem property to identify which page is active. The Color button changes the back color of the text box on the selected page. This is useful to demonstrate that the controls are actually being copied and pasted every time the Click event fires. If you add a page while the first page's text box is white, the newly created page contains a white text box. If you change the first page's text box to red and add another page, its text box will be red and the second page's text box will remain white. This demonstrates that you're really creating new objects with every Click event (see Figure 7-3).

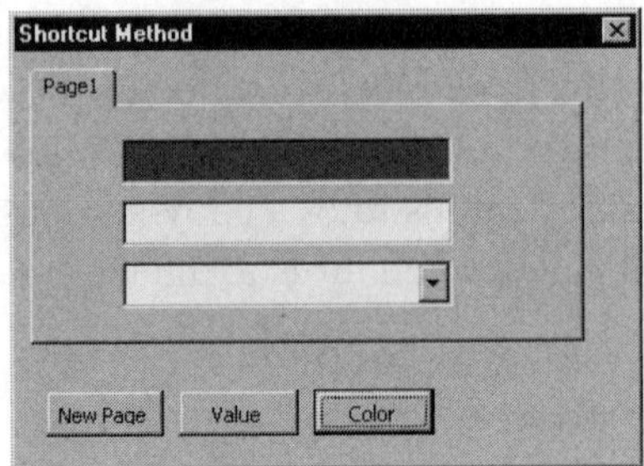

Figure 7-3

Listing 7-2: Shortcut method

```
Option Explicit
Private Sub cmdColor_Click()
' If statement to change the color of the textbox.
With Me.MultiPage1.SelectedItem.Controls(0)
If .BackColor = vbRed Then
.BackColor = vbWhite
Else
.BackColor = vbRed
End If
End With
End Sub
Private Sub cmdNewPage_Click()
' Counter variable used to keep track of the index.
Static x As Integer
' Adds 1 to x every time the procedure is run.
x = x + 1
' The following three lines copy the controls from the
' design time page, add one page to the multipage
' control, and finally paste the controls to the newly
' created page.
Me.MultiPage1.Pages(0).Controls.Copy
Me.MultiPage1.Pages.Add
Me.MultiPage1.Pages(x).Paste
End Sub
Private Sub cmdValue_Click()
Dim y As Integer
' A loop to display the values of the run-time controls.
For y = 1 To Me.MultiPage1.Pages.Count
Me.MultiPage1.Value = y - 1
```

```
MsgBox Me.MultiPage1.SelectedItem.Controls(0).Value
Next y
End Sub
```

A Final Note

Remember that these run-time controls are "passive" controls. In other words, you cannot trap for their events. While there are ways of creating active run-time controls, they are beyond the scope of this chapter. The preceding examples offer most of the functionality necessary when using dynamically created controls.

Automating Document Creation with Word Templates

With a little creativity, Word can easily be programmed to dramatically save time in document production, data gathering, and inter-office application automation. You can use Word templates to create what is essentially a document assembly system that customizes itself for each user. Such templates can totally eliminate the weekly or, in some cases, daily cutting and pasting, and provide uniform documentation throughout any organization. Imagine the benefit if remote users need to submit information in a consistent manner, e.g., a national sales force submitting written proposals.

This section describes such a document "assembly line" — a template system you can easily customize and augment to fit your needs. Following is the code behind the frmInfo UserForm setup.

Listing 7-3: Code for the frmInfo UserForm

```
Option Explicit
Dim sDesigPath As String
Dim sIniFile As String
Private Sub UserForm_Initialize()
' "Me" is always the active UserForm.
```

```
With Me
' Initialize textboxes with Word's option settings.
' Note that these can still be changed.
.txtYourname = Application.UserName
.txtInitials = Application.UserInitials
' This adds each label to the list at run time.
With cboYourtitl
.AddItem "President"
.AddItem "Vice President"
.AddItem "Assistant Vice President"
.AddItem "Senior Vice President"
.AddItem "First Vice President"
.AddItem "Administrative Assistant"
.AddItem "Secretary"
.AddItem "Treasurer"
.AddItem "Lowly Cube Grunt"
End With
With cboClosing
.AddItem "Very truly yours,"
.AddItem "Sincerely,"
.AddItem "Sincerely yours,"
.AddItem "Respectfully,"
.AddItem "Respectfully yours,"
End With
End With
End Sub
' Ends the running procedure and unloads the form.
Private Sub cmdCancel_Click()
End
End Sub
Private Sub cmdFinish_Click()
' Checks the second address textbox for a null value.
' If it contains a null value, sets it equal to "x".
If Me.txtAdd2.Value = "" Then
Me.txtAdd2.Value = "x"
End If
' Create subfolder in the UserTemplates path. When
' populated with templates it will appear in the
' New dialog box.
sDesigPath = _
Options.DefaultFilePath(Path:=wdUserTemplatesPath)
MkDir (sDesigPath & "\Basic Templates")
' Save this template to the new directory under 3 names.
```

```
ActiveDocument.SaveAs FileName:=sDesigPath & _
"\Basic Templates\" & "Fax.dot"
ActiveDocument.SaveAs FileName:=sDesigPath & _
"\Basic Templates\" & "Letter.dot"
ActiveDocument.SaveAs FileName:=sDesigPath & _
"\Basic Templates\" & "Memo.dot"
' Create the initialization file and set the keys
' equal to the textbox values.
sIniFile = sDesigPath & "\Basic Templates\Personal.ini"
System.PrivateProfileString( _
sIniFile, "Personal", "Name") = Me.txtYourname
System.PrivateProfileString( _
sIniFile, "Personal", "Fax") = Me.txtFax
System.PrivateProfileString( _
sIniFile, "Personal", "Phone") = Me.txtPhone
System.PrivateProfileString( _
sIniFile, "Personal", "Title") = Me.cboYourtitl
System.PrivateProfileString( _
sIniFile, "Company", "Add1") = Me.txtAdd1
System.PrivateProfileString( _
sIniFile, "Company", "Add2") = Me.txtAdd2
System.PrivateProfileString( _
sIniFile, "Company", "City") = Me.txtCity
System.PrivateProfileString( _
sIniFile, "Company", "State") = Me.txtState
System.PrivateProfileString( _
sIniFile, "Company", "Zip") = Me.txtZip
System.PrivateProfileString( _
sIniFile, "Personal", "Closing") = Me.cboClosing
System.PrivateProfileString( _
sIniFile, "Company", "Company") = Me.txtCompName
' This closes the template, unloads the form,
' and displays a MsgBox.
ActiveDocument.Close SaveChanges:=wdDoNotSaveChanges
Unload Me
MsgBox "Select File | New and click Basic Templates.", _
, "Basic Template Setup"
End
End Sub
```

What It Does

The setup template creates three other templates and stores information needed to complete them in an initialization (.ini) file. This is done simply by opening the file, which displays a UserForm requiring the user to enter basic information such as name, address, and phone and fax numbers (we'll discuss it more in a bit; it's shown in Figure 7-5). This information is saved in an initialization file for the new templates.

Next, a folder named \Basic Templates is created under \Program Files\Microsoft Office\Templates. This causes the folder to appear as a page on the New dialog box, which is displayed by selecting File | New from the Word menu. This folder will be populated with three templates: Fax.dot, Letter.dot, and Memo.dot, as shown in Figure 7-4.

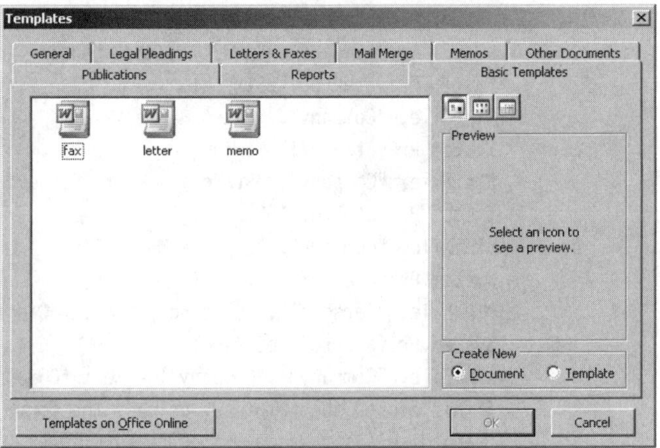

Figure 7-4

At this point the original template is no longer necessary. The three new templates will run their own UserForms so the user can input relevant information and use a "link" to the initialization file to finish creating the resulting documents. The finished documents will contain both the user's default information (stored in the initialization file) and the specific information entered by the user.

How It Works

Word contains auto macros that run when certain events occur. The AutoOpen macro, for example, runs when a document or template is opened. The AutoNew macro runs whenever "New" is used to run a template. This file stores both of these macros in a VBA module, but note that the ThisDocument section can contain them as well.

```
Sub AutoOpen()
' Ensure the three new templates aren't opened (only File |
      New).
If ActiveDocument.AttachedTemplate = "Letter.dot" Then
MsgBox "You must use these as File | New"
ActiveDocument.Close SaveChanges:=wdDoNotSaveChanges
End
ElseIf ActiveDocument.AttachedTemplate = "Fax.dot" Then
MsgBox "You must use these as File | New"
ActiveDocument.Close SaveChanges:=wdDoNotSaveChanges
End
ElseIf ActiveDocument.AttachedTemplate = "Memo.dot" Then
MsgBox "You must use these as File | New"
ActiveDocument.Close SaveChanges:=wdDoNotSaveChanges
End
End If
' Display Information form in the original template.
frmInfo.Show
End Sub
```

You do not want someone opening a template and overwriting fields by accident. The If...Then...ElseIf structure ensures the resulting fax, memo, and letter templates cannot be opened by mistake. Attempting to open one of these templates displays a message box. When the user clicks OK, the template will close. Setting the Close method's SaveChanges parameter to wdDoNotSaveChanges prevents the save dialog box from being displayed when the template is closed. The final statement in the AutoOpen macro is:

```
frmInfo.Show
```

The setup UserForm, named frmInfo, is shown in Figure 7-5. The code associated with UserForm is shown in Listing 7-4. This UserForm is only displayed when the original template runs the AutoOpen macro. It contains labels, command buttons, combo boxes, and text boxes (all of which can be enhanced by setting the ControlTipText property to provide additional information when the user highlights them with his or her mouse). The combo boxes and text boxes are used to obtain information from the user that will be stored in the initialization file. As you can see, the AddItem method is used to set the list of each combo box at run time. You may also want to set the combo box's Enter event to fire its DropDown method so it will automatically display the list.

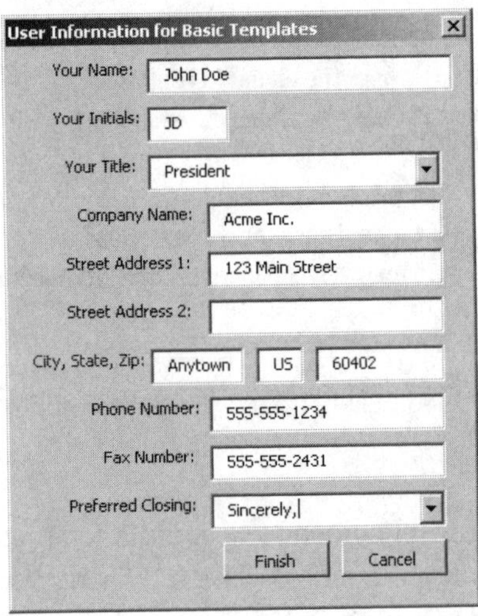

Figure 7-5

The event handler for the Cancel button simply contains the End command. A good precaution, however, would be to close the template to prevent tampering. Nevertheless, use Application.Quit with great care, as most users loathe a program shutting down without asking first.

The Finish button must accomplish three things: creating a subfolder that appears in the user's File | New menu, populating this folder with templates, and saving the user's basic information in an initialization file. The newly created templates will use these initialization settings as well as the UserForm results to update the Word fields and produce a document.

You can see in Listing 7-3 that a locally declared string variable, *sDesigPath*, is set equal to:

```
Options.DefaultFilePath(wdUserTemplatesPath)
```

This path corresponds to the settings in Word's Tools | Options | File Locations | User Templates section. The DOS MkDir command uses a concatenated filename consisting of the variable and a new folder name (including a backslash) to create the subfolder in the default UserTemplates path. The subfolder has been created, but it won't show up as a page in the New dialog box until it contains templates. Note that the page has the same name as the folder.

The next step is to save the template under the new template names in this folder (or to FileCopy other templates). Here, the SaveAs method of the ActiveDocument is used. The *Filename* argument is set equal to *sDesigPath*, representing the default UserTemplates folder, the name of the new folder, and the names of the three new templates.

The final step is creating the initialization file to store the user information so the other templates can later retrieve it. This is done using the System.PrivateProfileString property. This property takes three arguments: *Filename*, *Section*, and *Key*. The initialization file is given the standard .ini extension.

The *Filename* argument specifies the location of the initialization file. The file can be stored anywhere, but the new template subfolder is the most convenient place because the *sDesigPath* variable already exists, specifying its location. Further, keeping files in a central location is a good practice and saves future programmers from unnecessary hunting.

The *Section* argument indicates the heading within the initialization file where the information is stored. The file may be broken into sections for easier reference. The code in Listing 7-3 uses personal and company sections. Notice that the values are stored in the correct section independent of the sequence in which they are created.

The last part of the System.PrivateProfileString is the *Key* argument. It specifies the precise location in the INI file where the information resides. Listing 7-3 shows these keys are set equal to the value of the form's text boxes and combo boxes. The Value property for a TextBox or ComboBox is always identical to its Text property. Value is the default property of both controls, and therefore doesn't require specific identification.

Figure 7-6 shows how the *Key* values are stored in the initialization file. Keep in mind that if a user enters incorrect information in the basic setup, the initialization values are easily changed using any ASCII editor, such as Notepad.

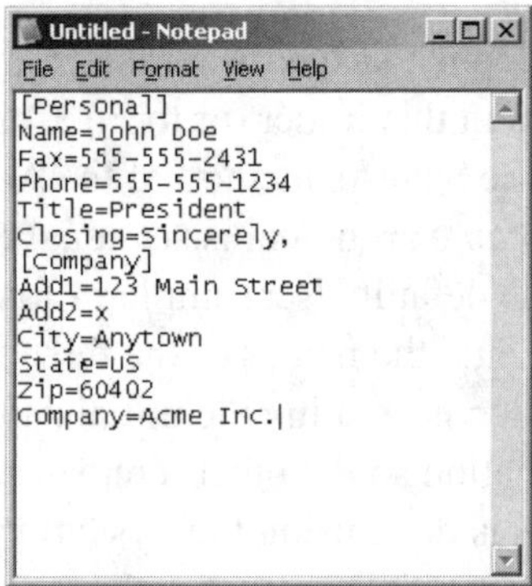

Figure 7-6

Attending to the housecleaning items is the last order of business. The active document is closed without the user being prompted to save changes. Then, the UserForm is unloaded and a message box is displayed instructing the user to view the newly created templates. When the user clicks OK, End is used to finish the setup.

The Newly Created Templates

Each new template produces a different document, even though they are exactly the same except for their names. The AutoNew macro runs every time the user goes to File | New | Basic Templates and chooses one of them. Remember that the AutoOpen macro prohibited these new templates from being opened. The original template, however, contained an AutoNew macro that has been copied to each of the three new templates. This macro controls which UserForm will be displayed. The work of creating the document is left to the UserForm.

```
Sub AutoNew()
' Turned off ScreenUpdating to save time and prevent user
' from seeing background work.
Application.ScreenUpdating = False
' Display correct UserForm depending on AttachedTemplate
' property.
If ActiveDocument.AttachedTemplate = "Letter.dot" Then
frmLetter.Show
ElseIf ActiveDocument.AttachedTemplate = "Fax.dot" Then
frmFax.Show
ElseIf ActiveDocument.AttachedTemplate = "Memo.dot" Then
frmMemo.Show
End If
End Sub
```

The first thing the AutoNew macro does is turn ScreenUpdating off. This prevents users from seeing the document's fields being updated and the sections being deleted. In larger templates this can provide a marked speed improvement as well.

The next If structure uses the AttachedTemplate property to check which template is being used. The Name property of the ActiveDocument will not work. Remember that a template is only the basis for a document. The name of the ActiveDocument would be Document*n*, with *n* being the number of the newly created document. The If statement displays the appropriate UserForm.

The three UserForms are shown in Figures 7-7 through 7-9. The code behind each new template's UserForm is generally the same, as shown in the code listings below. So rather than discuss each UserForm individually, we'll discuss the basic approach. If there are lists or default values, those are set in the form's initialization event. All variables are explicitly declared and the Cancel button fires the End command.

Figure 7-7

Listing 7-4: Code for the frmFax UserForm

```
Option Explicit
Dim sIniFile As String
Private Sub cmdCancel_Click()
' End running procedure and unload the form.
End
End Sub
Private Sub cmdFinish_Click()
With ActiveDocument
' Set Docvariables equal to UserForm values.
.Variables("sTowho").Value = Me.txtTowho.Value
.Variables("sRe").Value = Me.txtRe.Value
.Variables("iNopages").Value = Me.txtNopages.Value
' Set Docvariables equal to ini file keys.
sIniFile = Options.DefaultFilePath( _
Path:=wdUserTemplatesPath) & _
"\Basic Templates\Personal.ini"
.Variables("sCompName") = _
System.PrivateProfileString( _
sIniFile, "Company", "Company")
.Variables("sYourname") = _
System.PrivateProfileString( _
sIniFile, "Personal", "Name")
```

```
.Variables("sFaxno") = System.PrivateProfileString( _
sIniFile, "Personal", "Fax")
.Variables("sPhoneno") = System.PrivateProfileString( _
sIniFile, "Personal", "Phone")
.Variables("sAdd1") = System.PrivateProfileString( _
sIniFile, "Company", "Add1")
.Variables("sAdd2") = System.PrivateProfileString( _
sIniFile, "Company", "Add2")
.Variables("sCity") = System.PrivateProfileString( _
sIniFile, "Company", "City")
.Variables("sState") = System.PrivateProfileString( _
sIniFile, "Company", "State")
.Variables("sZip") = System.PrivateProfileString( _
sIniFile, "Company", "Zip")
' Set empty textboxes to empty strings to avoid errors
' appearing in the documents.
If Me.txtCompany.Value  "" Then
.Variables("sCompany").Value = Me.txtCompany.Value
Else
.Variables("sCompany").Value = " "
End If
If Me.txtFaxno.Value  "" Then
.Variables("sFax").Value = Me.txtFaxno.Value
Else
.Variables("sFax").Value = " "
End If
If Me.txtPhoneno.Value  "" Then
.Variables("sPhone").Value = Me.txtPhoneno.Value
Else
.Variables("sPhone").Value = " "
End If
End With
' Unload the running UserForm.
Unload Me
' Update Docvariable fields and unlink them.
With ActiveDocument
.Fields.Update
.Fields.Unlink
End With
' Delete sections of template that won't be used.
ActiveDocument.Sections(1).Range.Delete
ActiveDocument.Sections(2).Range.Delete
ActiveDocument.Sections(2).Range.Delete
```

```
' Turn ScreenUpdating back on.
Application.ScreenUpdating = True
End Sub
```

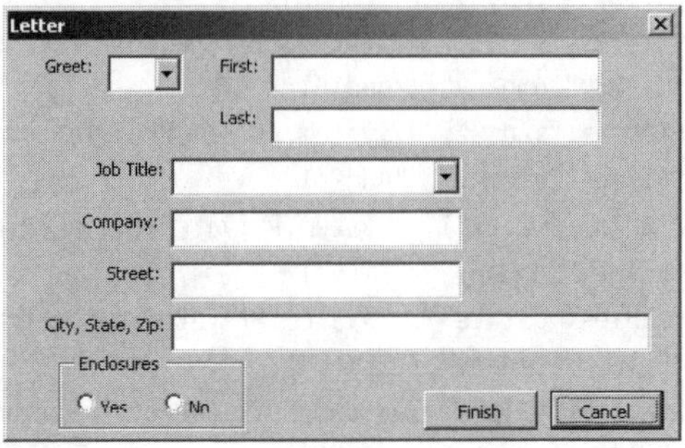

Figure 7-8

Listing 7-5: Code for the frmLetter UserForm

```
Option Explicit
Dim sIniFile As String
' Set lists for the comboboxes.
Private Sub UserForm_Initialize()
With Me
With cmbGreet
.AddItem "Mr."
.AddItem "Mrs."
.AddItem "Ms."
.AddItem "Dr."
.AddItem "Mr. & Mrs."
.AddItem "Mr. & Ms."
.AddItem "Dr. & Mrs."
.ListIndex = 0
End With
With cmbJob
.AddItem "President"
.AddItem "Vice President"
.AddItem "Executive Vice President"
.AddItem "Senior Vice President"
.AddItem "Assistant Vice President"
.AddItem "Chairman"
.AddItem "Treasurer"
.AddItem "Secretary"
.AddItem "Chief Financial Officer"
.AddItem "Attorney At Law"
.AddItem "General Counsel"
```

```
End With
' Set initialization for option buttons.
Me.optEnclosureNo = True
End With
End Sub
Private Sub cmdCancel_Click()
' End running procedure and unload form.
End
End Sub
Private Sub cmdFinish_Click()
With ActiveDocument
' Set Docvariables equal to UserForm values.
.Variables("sGreet").Value = Me.cmbGreet.Value
.Variables("sFirst").Value = Me.txtFirst.Value
.Variables("sLast").Value = Me.txtLast.Value
.Variables("sStreet").Value = Me.txtStreet.Value
.Variables("sCtyst").Value = Me.txtCtyst.Value
.Variables("sToComp").Value = Me.txtCompany.Value
.Variables("sTitle").Value = Me.cmbJob
' Set up the enclosure option.
If Me.optEnclosureYes = True Then
.Variables("bEnc").Value = "x"
End If
' Set Docvariables equal to ini file keys.
sIniFile = Options.DefaultFilePath( _
Path:=wdUserTemplatesPath) & _
"\Basic Templates\Personal.ini"
.Variables("sCompName") = _
System.PrivateProfileString( _
sIniFile, "Company", "Company")
.Variables("sYourname") = _
System.PrivateProfileString( _
sIniFile, "Personal", "Name")
.Variables("sYourfax") = System.PrivateProfileString( _
sIniFile, "Personal", "Fax")
.Variables("sYourphone") = _
System.PrivateProfileString( _
sIniFile, "Personal", "Phone")
.Variables("sAdd1") = System.PrivateProfileString( _
sIniFile, "Company", "Add1")
.Variables("sAdd2") = System.PrivateProfileString( _
sIniFile, "Company", "Add2")
.Variables("sYourtitl") = _
System.PrivateProfileString( _
sIniFile, "Personal", "Title")
```

```
.Variables("sCity") = System.PrivateProfileString( _
sIniFile, "Company", "City")
.Variables("sState") = System.PrivateProfileString( _
sIniFile, "Company", "State")
.Variables("sZip") = System.PrivateProfileString( _
sIniFile, "Company", "Zip")
.Variables("sClosing").Value = _
System.PrivateProfileString( _
sIniFile, "Personal", "Closing")
End With
' Unload the running UserForm.
Unload Me
' Update the Docvariable fields and unlink them.
With ActiveDocument
.Fields.Update
.Fields.Unlink
End With
' Delete sections of the template that won't be used.
ActiveDocument.Sections(1).Range.Delete
ActiveDocument.Sections(1).Range.Delete
ActiveDocument.Sections(2).Range.Delete
' Turn ScreenUpdating back on.
Application.ScreenUpdating = True
End Sub
```

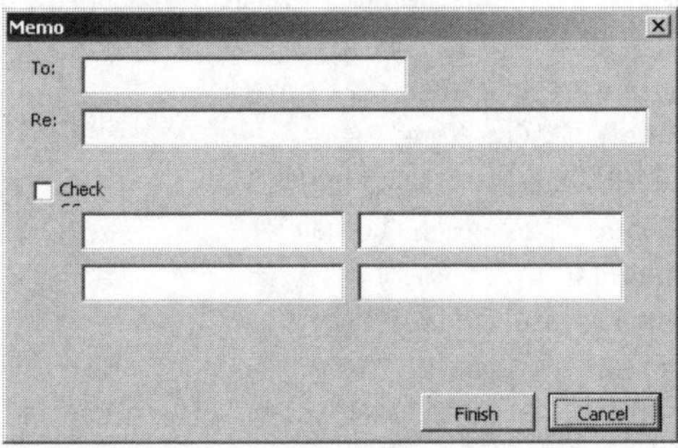

Figure 7-9

Listing 7-6: Code for the frmMemo UserForm

```
Option Explicit
Dim sIniFile As String
' Keep the user from seeing the textboxes unless the user
' clicks the CC control.
Private Sub UserForm_Initialize()
With Me
.txtCc1.Visible = False
.txtCc2.Visible = False
.txtCC3.Visible = False
.txtCc4.Visible = False
End With
End Sub
' If the CC checkbox is checked make the four textboxes for
' CC's visible; otherwise invisible.
Private Sub chkCcs_Click()
If Me.chkCcs = True Then
With Me
.txtCc1.Visible = True
.txtCc2.Visible = True
.txtCC3.Visible = True
.txtCc4.Visible = True
End With
Else
With Me
.txtCc1.Visible = False
.txtCc2.Visible = False
.txtCC3.Visible = False
.txtCc4.Visible = False
End With
End If
End Sub
Private Sub cmdCancel_Click()
' End the running procedure and unload the form.
End
End Sub
Private Sub cmdFinish_Click()
With ActiveDocument
' Set the Docvariables equal to the UserForm values.
.Variables("sTowho").Value = Me.txtTowho.Value
.Variables("sRe").Value = Me.txtRe.Value
' Set Docvariables equal to .ini file keys.
sIniFile = Options.DefaultFilePath( _
Path:=wdUserTemplatesPath) & _
```

```
"\Basic Templates\Personal.ini"
.Variables("sCompName") = _
System.PrivateProfileString( _
sIniFile, "Company", "Company")
.Variables("sYourname") = _
System.PrivateProfileString( _
sIniFile, "Personal", "Name")
.Variables("sYourphone") = _
System.PrivateProfileString( _
sIniFile, "Personal", "Phone")
' Set empty textboxes to empty strings to avoid having
' errors appear in the documents.
If Me.txtCc1.Value  "" Then
.Variables("sCc1").Value = Me.txtCc1.Value
Else
.Variables("sCc1").Value = "x"
End If
If Me.txtCc2.Value  "" Then
.Variables("sCc2").Value = Me.txtCc2.Value
Else
.Variables("sCc2").Value = "x"
End If
If Me.txtCC3.Value  "" Then
.Variables("sCc3").Value = Me.txtCC3.Value
Else
.Variables("sCc3").Value = "x"
End If
If Me.txtCc4.Value  "" Then
.Variables("sCc4").Value = Me.txtCc4.Value
Else
.Variables("sCc4").Value = "x"
End If
End With
' Unload running UserForm.
Unload Me
' Update the Docvariable fields and unlink them.
With ActiveDocument
.Fields.Update
.Fields.Unlink
End With
' Delete sections of the template that won't be used.
ActiveDocument.Sections(1).Range.Delete
ActiveDocument.Sections(1).Range.Delete
```

```
ActiveDocument.Sections(1).Range.Delete
' Turn screen updating back on.
Application.ScreenUpdating = True
End Sub
```

The Finish button handles the creation of the document. Each form's Finish button does primarily the same thing. The first part of the code is a large With block that uses the ActiveDocument object. The ActiveDocument.Variables(Index) property corresponds to each DocVariable field in the template, with the index being the name of each DocVariable field (DocVariable fields are discussed in the next section). The syntax requires the DocVariable name to be enclosed in quotation marks.

The first part of the With block sets the Value property of each DocVariable equal to its corresponding text box value. The second set of variables is set equal to the corresponding key of the initialization file. Note the *Filename* argument of the System.PrivateProfileString that is again declared to the newly created subfolder. A variable could have been set to this path earlier. However, this code would be very important if this were actually a separate template being copied to that folder by the template setup UserForm. While copying one file three times is convenient, many programmers (myself included) don't like a file to contain forms and code that will never be used.

The next part of the With block is a set of If statements that check the value of certain TextBoxes. If the TextBox contains a value, then that value is set equal to the corresponding DocVariable field. If the TextBox is blank, the code automatically sets it equal to a space. Note that a space is a one-character string and is different from a null value. If a null value is passed to a DocVariable, the resulting document will contain the message "Error, Variable not defined" in place of the DocVariable field. Inserting a blank avoids these errors.

The next step is to update the fields in the document using the ActiveDocument.Fields.Update method. This goes through every DocVariable field in the document and sets the values defined in the code preceding it. After the fields are updated, they must be unlinked.

Finally, the sections of each template that won't be used are deleted, e.g., the fax template deletes the memo and letter section. This is accomplished by using the Delete method of each section's Range property. Note that the index value of each ActiveDocument.Section is decremented by one as they are deleted, i.e., if you delete the first section, the second section will become the first, the third will become the second, etc.

After the superfluous sections are deleted, the form is unloaded and ScreenUpdating is set to True so the user can see the finished document.

The Template

We've been focusing on the VBA aspect of this technique. However, the template itself must enable the variable values to be transferred. To create a blank template, select File | New | Template | Blank Document in Word. The text is divided into three sections using the Insert | Break | Next Page command. Breaking the text into three sections allows the manipulation of one section without affecting the others.

There are several ways to transfer text from a VBA UserForm to the resultant document. This chapter uses DocVariable fields. DocVariable fields have several advantages over the alternatives. One is that the DocVariable field may be formatted in the template at design time. The resulting text will appear in the same format as the DocVariable field. For example, the DocVariable *sCompname* is formatted using bold text, a shadow, and 14-point font. The corresponding text in the finished document will be formatted the same.

Another advantage is that the same DocVariable field may appear many times in the template. This is a distinct advantage over inserting text at bookmarks. Further, in very large documents it's faster to update and unlink

DocVariable fields than to include Merge fields or Ref fields.

Another advantage is that DocVariable fields can be embedded in If fields. This opens the possibility for multiple language dependencies. An example would be an If field looking at a Boolean value and setting gender-specific pronouns throughout an entire document.

A very simple If field is used in the address portion of the Fax and Letter section. VBA code could delete a line, but the simpler alternative is to create an If field that checks for an "x" value. If the second line of the address is omitted in the original setup template, the initialization *Key* is set to "x". That value is passed to the If field. If it is anything other than an "x", it is inserted in the document. If the *Key*'s value is "x", it responds by moving the line below it up to compensate. If fields can even be embedded within other If fields.

As you can see, the setup template produces the illusion that it creates three different, customized templates. With minor changes, this provides a way to set up your own templates on individual computers by distributing a single file. You may need to include some brief instructions since many users have Word set to prompt them when a document contains macros.

Keep in mind that future templates can reference the same initialization file, modify it, or create an entirely new one. Furthermore, variable values can be stored in the Windows registry, in the document properties, or in tables, or by using sequential file access or re-initializing DocVariable fields. For more information on the topics addressed by this chapter, see the corresponding topics in Microsoft Word and Visual Basic for Applications Help. And don't forget to set the tab order of the controls in your forms!

Conclusion

This chapter has focused on two individual VBA projects. The first project demonstrated the use of dynamically created controls. Dynamically created controls are frequently necessary in document automation programming. The Index property is available for most VB controls. VBA, however, doesn't provide an Index property for controls and thus doesn't provide for dynamic control creation in the same manner as VB. The second project demonstrated how Word can be used to create what is essentially a document assembly system that customizes itself for each user. The following chapters will begin introducing some of the new concepts behind Word 2003 XML.

Chapter 8

Word's XML Functionality

Introduction

This chapter introduces the new features of Word 2003 to create and edit XML documents. Word has always had the ability to create customized solutions to walk users through the creation of documents. First there was WordBasic, then VBA, and now Microsoft has introduced a new tool — smart documents. In order to understand how smart documents work, we first need to examine the new XML components that Word has introduced. This chapter will allow you to work through some very basic examples, which are designed to give a quick but thorough introduction to these new features. Smart documents are solutions that utilize XSD, XML, and a Code Behind (via Visual Studio) custom task pane to interact with the user. Code Behind is Microsoft's new terminology to describe writing Visual Studio solutions that exist "behind" the document — as opposed to VBA solutions that reside as part of the document. As you'll see, the new Code Behind features are made possible via an XML manifest that describes the different components of your XML solution.

Creating and Using Schemas

The real power of XML lies in using a vocabulary that describes the meaning of the document, not just the appearance. This XML document identifies the meaning of the data elements, not just their location in the document.

The following figure shows what the raw XML looks like without any of the associated word formatting (WordprocessingML) in it.

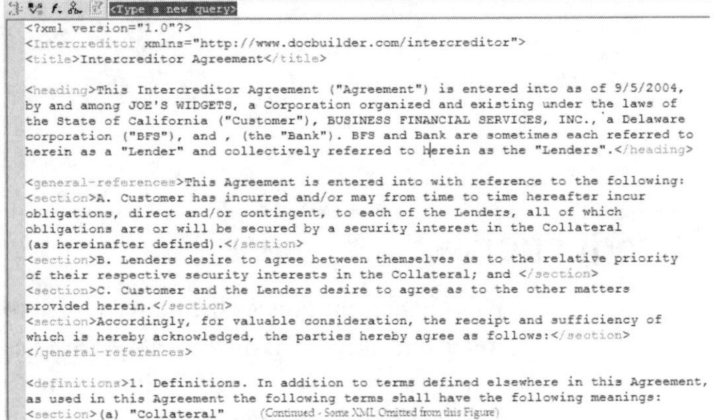

```
<Type a new query>
<?xml version="1.0"?>
<Intercreditor xmlns="http://www.docbuilder.com/intercreditor">
<title>Intercreditor Agreement</title>

<heading>This Intercreditor Agreement ("Agreement") is entered into as of 9/5/2004,
by and among JOE'S WIDGETS, a Corporation organized and existing under the laws of
the State of California ("Customer"), BUSINESS FINANCIAL SERVICES, INC., a Delaware
corporation ("BFS"), and , (the "Bank"). BFS and Bank are sometimes each referred to
herein as a "Lender" and collectively referred to herein as the "Lenders".</heading>

<general-references>This Agreement is entered into with reference to the following:
<section>A. Customer has incurred and/or may from time to time hereafter incur
obligations, direct and/or contingent, to each of the Lenders, all of which
obligations are or will be secured by a security interest in the Collateral
(as hereinafter defined).</section>
<section>B. Lenders desire to agree between themselves as to the relative priority
of their respective security interests in the Collateral; and </section>
<section>C. Customer and the Lenders desire to agree as to the other matters
provided herein.</section>
<section>Accordingly, for valuable consideration, the receipt and sufficiency of
which is hereby acknowledged, the parties hereby agree as follows:</section>
</general-references>

<definitions>1. Definitions. In addition to terms defined elsewhere in this Agreement,
as used in this Agreement the following terms shall have the following meanings:
<section>(a) "Collateral"     (Continued - Some XML Omitted from this Figure)
```

Figure 8-1

The same raw XML displayed in Figure 8-1 can also be opened in Microsoft Word 2003 as you can see in Figure 8-2.

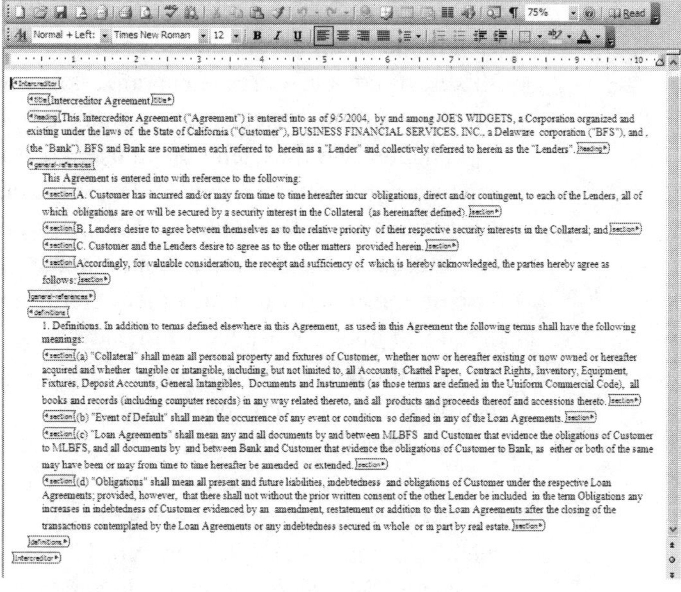

Figure 8-2

Introduction to the XML Toolbox

Microsoft Office Word 2003 can incorporate a free, downloadable toolbox from www.microsoft.com (search "Word XML toolbox download"). Word 2003 allows you to work with the XML representation of a document just as you would work with a regular Word document, allowing you to save, edit, and even create well-formed XML documents from scratch. This section introduces the Microsoft Office Word 2003 XML Toolbox and explains how you can use it in your document automation projects.

Word 2003 XML support allows you to create meaningful tags so that you can structure and organize the text (data) within your Word document. This allows you to view your traditional Word document not only as a document but also as a repository of structured data. For example, the sample document used in this chapter is an Intercreditor Agreement. This is a common form document among lenders who are loaning money to a specific business entity. This document specifically describes what each lender is entitled to in the event the borrower defaults (this is, of course, a gross generalization, but the legal meaning isn't important in this context). In this introductory chapter, we'll pretend that a user creates this document from scratch and then wants to define the elements within the document via Word 2003 XML markup. This way, the information in the document could then be sent to a database or consumed via some other external system. One of the most important aspects of the new XML features of Word is the ability to view a traditional Word document as having both a printable document aspect and a data repository aspect contained within XML. This allows previously unusable data (or, at least, unusable by conventional means) to be repurposed in ways that are meaningful to a specific organization. Further, Word 2003 allows you to associate XML schemas with a document so that its contents are clearly organized and defined. XML schemas even allow the XML document to be validated according to the data definition contained in the schema.

Note: Many of the XML features discussed in this chapter, except for saving documents as XML with the Word XML schema, are available only in Microsoft Office Professional Edition 2003 and standalone Microsoft Office Word 2003.

Microsoft designed Word 2003 to be as easy to use for as many people as possible. This means that some functionality was intentionally left out because it could be confusing to end users. The fact that you're reading this book means you are obviously a little more involved with Word than the typical business user and thus fall into the category Microsoft refers to as a "developer" of Word solutions. As a developer, you would be well advised to download and install the XML Toolbox for Microsoft Office Word 2003. It's available completely free of charge, and its sole purpose is to make it easier to work with the complex features of Word XML solutions development.

Once you've installed the toolbox, the Word XML Toolbox toolbar appears in your standard Word configuration (see Figure 8-3). You can hide or show the toolbar by selecting the View menu, clicking on Toolbars, and then selecting the Word XML Toolbox item from the list.

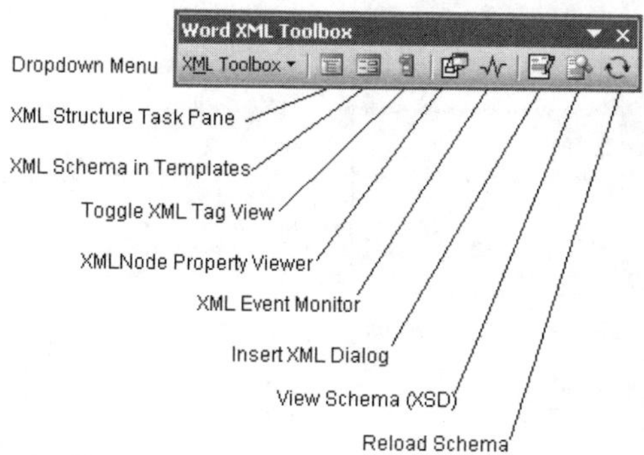

Figure 8-3

Caution: The toolbox only works with Microsoft Office Word 2003 and requires that .NET Programmability Support is enabled on your development computer prior to attempting to install or run the toolbox.

Derived XML Schemas

As you've seen above, assigning XML markup to different pieces of the document is relatively straightforward. However, this alone does not associate the document with an XML schema. Before we associate our XML document with a schema, we need to create a schema. Fortunately, the XML Toolbox includes a neat feature that does exactly that. In Figure 8-4 you'll notice that the XML Toolbox has an item for generating inferred schemas.

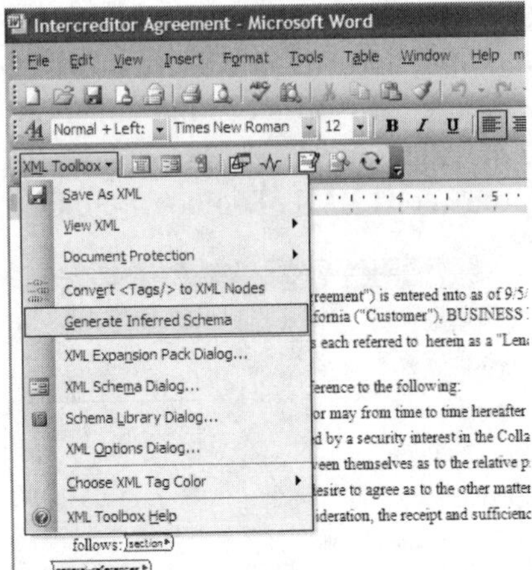

Figure 8-4

Before you generate your schema, you should make sure the most recent version of the document you are working on is saved. Then, on the Word XML Toolbox toolbar, click Generate Inferred Schema. The toolbox presents you with a dialog box as shown in Figure 8-5, in which you provide the root for the schema, its namespace, and a final file path.

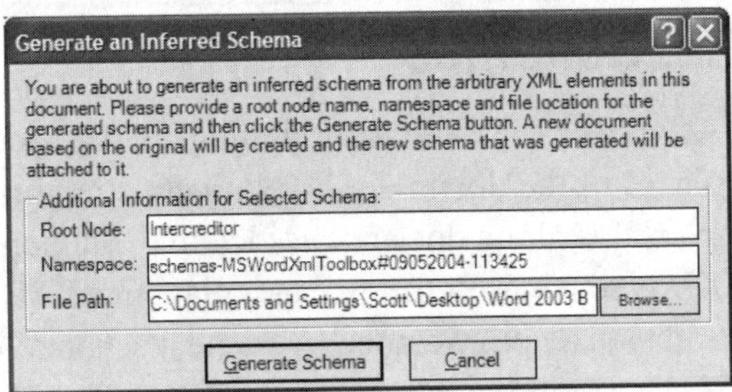

Figure 8-5: The toolbox lets you infer a schema and save it as a separate file.

Once you create the file, the Microsoft XML Toolbox displays a message box informing you that the schema has been generated. This dialog also informs you that a new document has been created. This new document already has the schema associated with it.

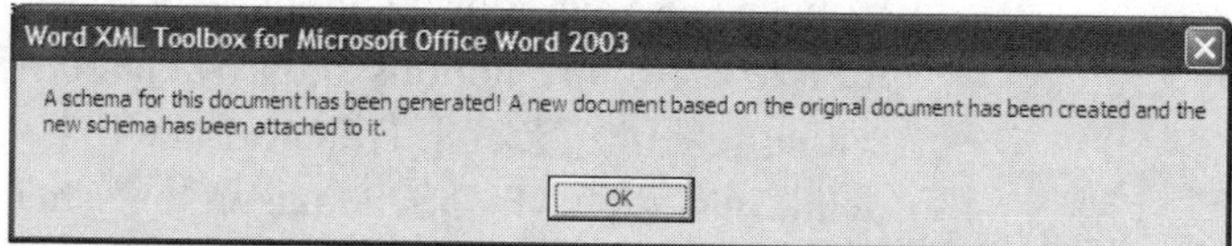

Figure 8-6

The Toolbox also generates a new document with the schema already associated. Don't worry if the schema looks exceedingly complex at this point. You can open the schema in the editor of your choice, but Internet Explorer and Notepad are just fine. We will dive into XML schemas in more detail in Chapter 9. For our current purposes, we just want to walk through the steps so that the following chapters will make more sense to you. Our example file schema is shown in Figure 8-7.

```
<?xml version="1.0" encoding="utf-16"?>
<!--Schema generated by the Word XML Toolbox for Microsoft Office Word 2003-->
<xs:schema xmlns:tns="schemas-MSWordXmlToolbox#09052004-113425"
attributeFormDefault="unqualified" elementFormDefault="qualified"
targetNamespace="schemas-MSWordXmlToolbox#09052004-113425"
xmlns:xs="http://www.w3.org/2001/XMLSchema">
  <xs:element name="Intercreditor">
    <xs:complexType mixed="true">
      <xs:sequence>
        <xs:element name="Intercreditor">
          <xs:complexType mixed="true">
            <xs:sequence>
              <xs:element name="title" type="xs:string" />
              <xs:element name="heading" type="xs:string" />
              <xs:element name="general-references">
                <xs:complexType mixed="true">
                  <xs:sequence>
                    <xs:element maxOccurs="unbounded" name="section" type="xs:string"/>
                  </xs:sequence>
                </xs:complexType>
              </xs:element>
              <xs:element name="definitions">
                <xs:complexType mixed="true">
                  <xs:sequence>
                    <xs:element maxOccurs="unbounded" name="section" type="xs:string"/>
                  </xs:sequence>
                </xs:complexType>
              </xs:element>
            </xs:sequence>
          </xs:complexType>
        </xs:element>
      </xs:sequence>
    </xs:complexType>
  </xs:element>
</xs:schema>
```

Figure 8-7

You may notice some other things that the Word XML Toolbox does by default. If you check the Word 2003 schema library, you'll see that the associated schema has been added. The Word schema library is used to specify the namespaces that your document can access. It can also be used to configure options and associated XSLT Transforms with a schema. (XSLT Transforms will be covered in more detail in Chapter 11.) Schemas in the schema library are available to attach to a document and are listed on the XML Schema tab of the Templates and Add-ins dialog box.

If a schema appears in the schema library, it is available for the template solution you are working on. In our example, make sure the Intercreditor Agreement document is active and choose Templates and Add-ins to see the list of schemas currently available. In this example, we'll be saving everything to the local drive on your machine. For enterprise solutions, you'd probably be creating and testing them locally and then working through your managed deployment solution to make them available to the enterprise users. This usually involves placing them on a publicly available file share or, perhaps, a Microsoft SharePoint site.

Now, we want to associate the document with the schema and make sure that it validates against the schema. (Of course, intuitively we know that it will because it is all being created based on the same source information, but working through this section is worth the effort.) Next, select the box next to the schema we just created and in the Schema validation options section, check the box next to Validate document against attached schemas. Save the changes to the Intercreditor Agreement document.

Adding XML Markup to a Document

Now that we have an XML schema in our schema library, we can begin marking up an existing Word document to make it conform to the schema. This is actually the process of defining sections of the document according to the rules laid out in the schema. For purposes of this section, we'll take a simplified version of the Intercreditor Agreement and mark it up. You can find this in the downloads in the Chapter 8 examples section as Simple Intercreditor. The text of the Simple Intercreditor document is shown in Figure 8-8.

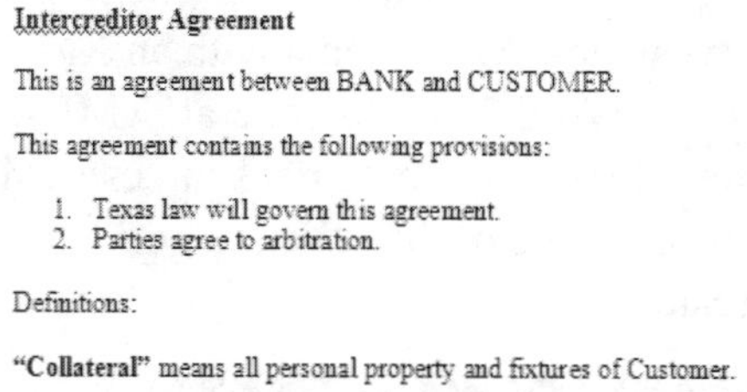

Intercreditor Agreement

This is an agreement between BANK and CUSTOMER.

This agreement contains the following provisions:

1. Texas law will govern this agreement.
2. Parties agree to arbitration.

Definitions:

"Collateral" means all personal property and fixtures of Customer.

Figure 8-8

Now, let's suppose we have an existing document that we want to attach to an XSD schema. We already have a schema in our schema library thanks to the work we did at the beginning of the chapter. Open the Simple Intercreditor document if you haven't already done so. As you'll see, the document is simply a trimmed-down version of the document we have been working with through this entire chapter. Now that you have the document open, choose Tools | Templates and Add-Ins. This will display the dialog box shown in Figure 8-10.

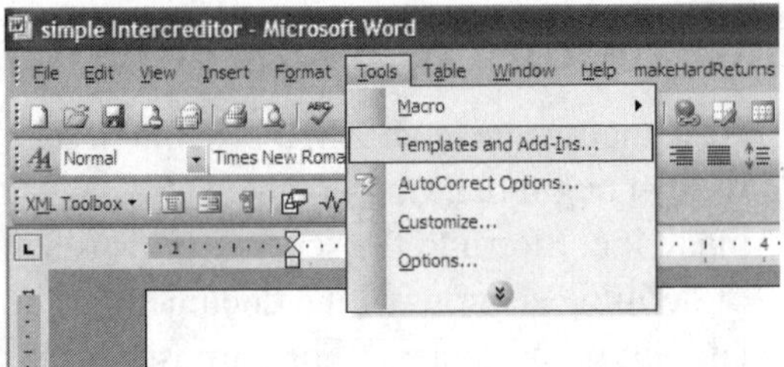

Figure 8-9

Once you have the Templates and Add-Ins dialog open, select the XML Schema tab. As you've already seen, this tab displays the available XML schemas. The process of associating an XML schema with an XML document is not specific to Word 2003. In general, XML documents can contain references to external sources. XML schemas are just one example of this. We are going to select the schema we created above.

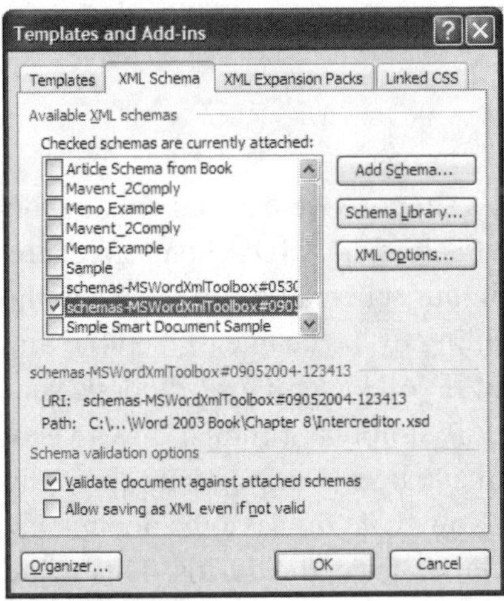

Figure 8-10

You'll notice that the URI lists the information that was generated by the XML Toolbox. This information is informative, but it is important to note that it is arbitrarily assigned by the XML Toolbox. There was nothing intrinsic to the document that caused the XML Toolbox to assign the associated identifier to this namespace. The important thing, of course, is that the reference to the schema is correct. Word takes care of this for you, but you could just as easily edit the WordprocessingML in Notepad and add the reference yourself. (From a practical standpoint, you will almost never be in a position where you need to do this, but it is important to realize that you are just working with text that happens to conform to the rules of XML.)

The Schema validation options allow you to define how you want Word to validate the document according to the schema. As you can see in Figure 8-10, we've checked the Validate document against attached schemas option because we want to make sure that our document is valid according to the schema we've chosen. We'll cover validity and well-formedness in the following chapters. You'll also notice that the option Allow saving as XML even if not valid is purposely not checked. This will force the user to make the document conform to the validity rules ascribed within the XML schema; otherwise, he or she will not be able to save changes to the document.

Once you've selected OK on the Templates and Add-ins dialog, you'll be prompted as to whether you want to apply the root element to the entire document or just the selected portion of text. For our purposes, we want to apply the schema against the entire document. This is because we are basically using a one-to-one approach, utilizing one document and one schema. It's important to note that you have the option of applying many different schemas against many different selections in the document. You also have the option of making a document conform to more than one schema if you so choose (thus, the check boxes instead of option buttons).

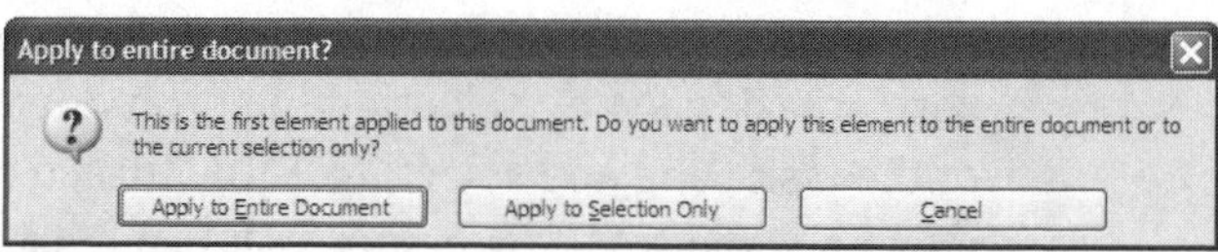

Figure 8-11

After applying the schema to the current document (Simple Intercreditor) you'll notice that the entire document is encapsulated between two tags. These correspond to the XML opening tag of <Intercreditor> and the XML closing tag of </Intercreditor> but Word neatly interprets them for you and displays them to you in a user-friendly, colorful way. These colors are also modifiable via the XML Toolbox by selecting the appropriate color under Choose XML Tag Color.

Consistent with the entire Word interface, squiggly lines are displayed to indicate that there may be a problem. In this case, the maroon squiggly lines running down the left side of the screen indicate that the document does not conform to the associated XML schema. Even though we've added the root element (Intercreditor) to the document, there are still other elements defined in the XML schema that are not defined within our document. Fortunately, Word 2003 provides an easy-to-use interface to define such elements right within the Word application.

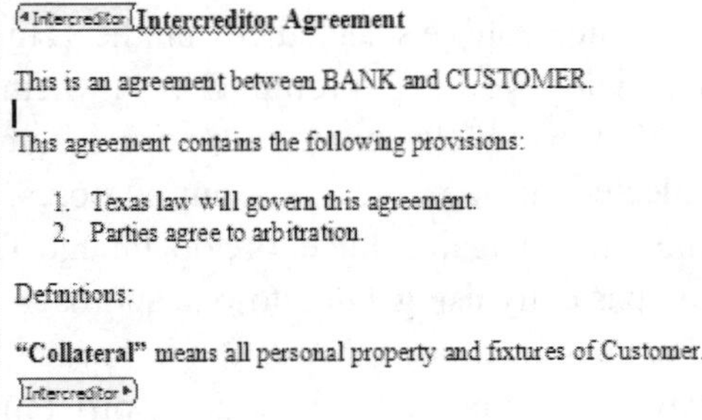

Figure 8-12

If your task pane is not visible, please make it visible by selecting View | Task Pane. You can then navigate to the correct task pane by selecting the drop-down at the very top of the task pane and selecting XML Structure. You should now have the XML Structure task pane visible within your Word application. At this point, your task pane should look identical to the one shown in Figure 8-13. The main portion of the task pane is dedicated to a tree-view control that shows the elements as they have been currently defined in the existing document. This task pane is "intelligent" in that it also displays problems with your markup via question marks and check box prompts.

Note: The Show XML tags in the document check box merely toggles the visibility of the maroon placeholders on and off within the user interface. This is a convenient feature to use when simultaneously editing and marking up a document. Many times you may inadvertently move or delete text. It may be difficult to see exactly what it will look like when the tags are displayed, so Microsoft has provided an easy mechanism to toggle the visibility back and forth.

At the bottom of the task pane you can see the elements that you can apply to the current selection. Some people find the process of assigning element names to "chunks" of text (selections) counterintuitive. Once you get the hang of it, you'll find that assigning markup is actually fun! The bottom list box displays only the available elements for the context you are currently working in. For instance, Figure 8-14 shows all of the child elements of the root node. This is because we currently have the cursor positioned within the beginning and ending tags for Intercreditor. If you have the List only child elements of current element check box selected (as shown in Figure 8-13), once you begin adding markup, the window will only display elements relevant to where your cursor position resides. This assistance does not mean the interface is entirely foolproof. You can still add elements that break the rules of the schema. These will be displayed in

Figure 8-13

the top tree-view window in a yellow caution marker with a black "X" inside.

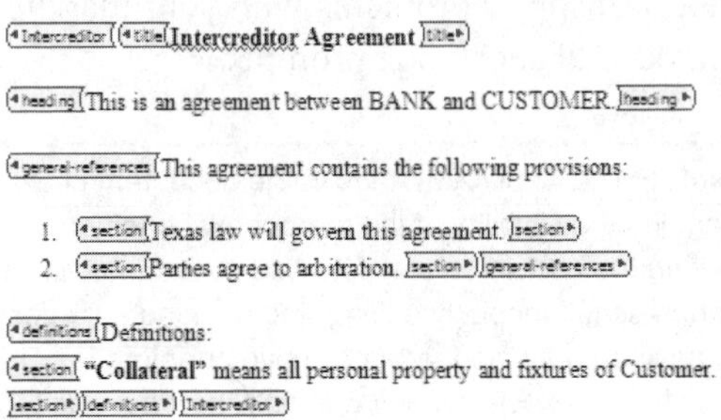

Figure 8-14

Continue marking up your text until it resembles the text shown in Figure 8-14. Keep in mind the hierarchical nature of the XML schema we are working with when assigning your markup. This means that all of the elements need to be properly nested. Intercreditor is the root element that should surround every other element in the document. The following elements should appear within the Intercreditor brackets in this order with no overlap: title, heading, general-references, definitions. In addition, general-references can have multiple section elements.

Once your text is properly marked up, you'll notice that the view in the task pane has changed dramatically. If you've done everything correctly, your task pane should resemble the one displayed in Figure 8-15. If you take a closer look you will be able to see that XML documents are always hierarchical in nature, which means they always have a top-level or root element and then child elements. This is displayed

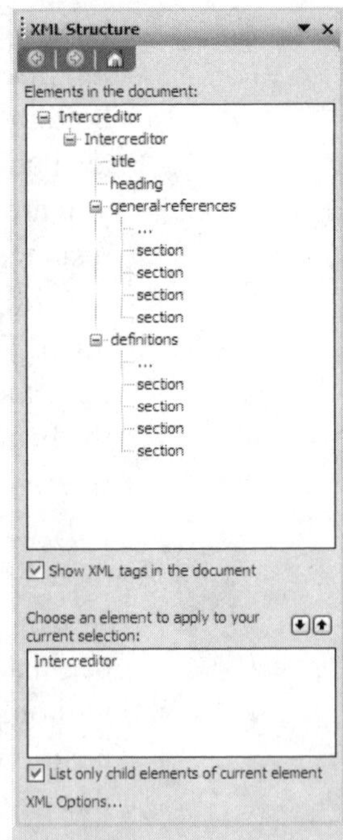

Figure 8-15

in the task pane via the collapsible plus (+) and minus (–) signs. If you're familiar with Windows, then you're familiar with how these options work. You can navigate through long documents using these features as well. You can see how the XML task pane serves not only as a view to the structure of the data but also as a shortcut to the various areas within the XML file as well.

The next thing we want to do is to save out the data from our example. This may sound easy, but there are big implications involved with what we are actually doing. First, normally we would just save the document and you'd be done with it. We can do exactly the same thing here, but we can save it as an XML document. What we're really doing when we save as XML is saving it as WordprocessingML, which contains all of the pertinent Word information (and, as you'll see, there is a lot of information outside of just "text" in a Word document) as well as our given text.

Secondly, by assigning XML tags to a document you've defined those selections as actual data elements. From an IT perspective, there is a big difference having a DOC file that has a customer's name in it and having an XML file that has a CustomerName element. Word documents have been notoriously hard to work with from a data perspective.

Lastly, we have the ability to eliminate all of the proprietary WordprocessingML information from the XML file and save it strictly as XML. For now, choose File | Save As to display the Save As dialog box shown in Figure 8-16. In the bottom right-hand corner you'll notice that the Save data only check box is selected. This option tells Word to exclude all of the WordprocessingML elements from the resultant XML file. As you'll see, this means that all of the formatting, styles, document properties, etc., will not be stored with the XML. Word is saving the document as a raw XML file. This doesn't mean Word can't open it right back up; it just means that the other information contained within the document is eliminated.

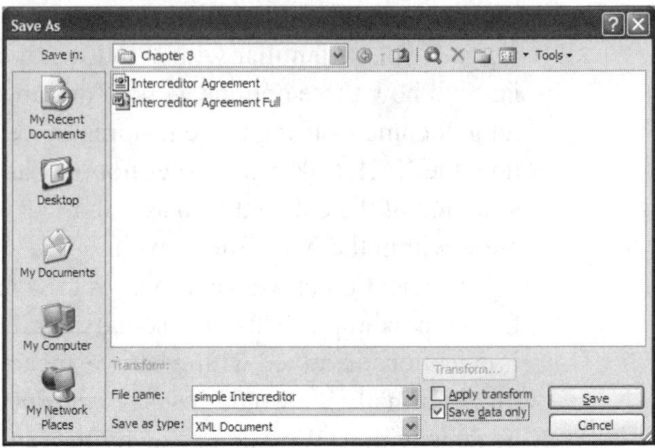

Figure 8-16

After we save the document as data only we can open it up via Internet Explorer. Figure 8-17 shows what the XML representation of the file looks like when displayed in IE. You'll notice that the top of the file is an XML declaration and appears in blue. The color blue indicates that the line is informational only and does not affect the structure of the XML. This is important because, as you'll see, every XML document needs one — and only one — root element. If, for instance, the declaration at the top was not interpreted as XML, the document would not adhere to the well-formedness structure set out for XML documents.

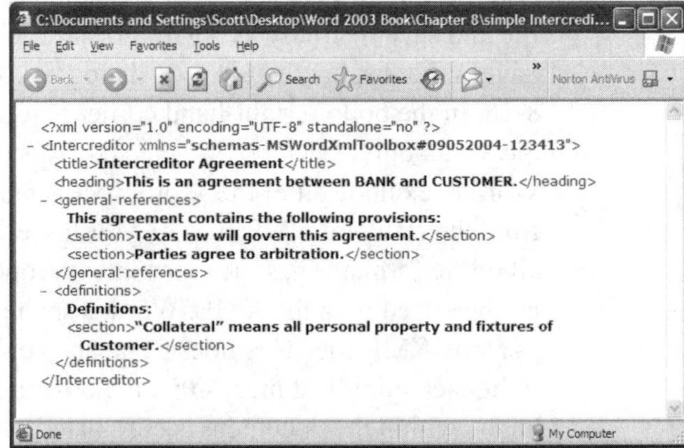

Figure 8-17

Next, you'll notice that the root element Intercreditor appears on the second line much as you'd expect. In addition, there is an XML *attribute* (covered in detail in subsequent chapters) that defines the associated schema. This section appears in bright red. This is the same schema that was associated with the document via the Word interface. At the time, we noted that we could add the same association via text simply by typing it in correctly via Notepad. You can now see exactly how that association would be accomplished. Further, the fact that this attribute appears within the Intercreditor opening bracket means that the attribute applies to the Intercreditor element — which, in turn, means it applies to this entire document. Attributes, by definition, can contain metadata about the element they appear within. Attributes cannot exist apart from an element. Finally, you'll notice that there are no other attributes in our XML file.

In the rest of the XML file, you'll notice that the elements appear in normal weight and in blue and maroon text. The data is represented in bold, black text. This does not mean that the text would appear as bold within Word. Quite the contrary; all formatting is gone in this data-only representation of our Simple Intercreditor document. You'll also notice that the tags appear in the exact sequence that was laid out in the Word interface. Internet Explorer only displays well-formed XML. Because of the XML standards, IE doesn't know how to display malformed XML and will not display it at all but will instead display a descriptive user message.

If we switch back to Word, we can open up the data-only XML file we saved and see how the result appears (shown in Figure 8-18). Figure 8-17 shows exactly what you'll see when the data-only version is opened back up in Internet Explorer. The first thing you'll notice is that all of the formatting has disappeared. Next, you will see that all of the elements appear nested with no semblance of the indentation applied to the earlier document. This information is also not stored in data-only mode. The most important thing to recognize about data-only mode is that you are defining exactly what appears in the face of the document as the data.

It's a good exercise as well to toggle between viewing the XML markup and not viewing the XML markup. You can do this via the XML Structure task pane as described above. Figure 8-18 shows how Word displays the XML document when View Markup is turned on, while Figure 8-19 shows how the XML is displayed without the markup visible.

```
[Intercreditor
    [title Intercreditor Agreement title]
    [heading This is an agreement between BANK and CUSTOMER. heading]
    [general-references
        This agreement contains the following provisions:
        [section Texas law will govern this agreement. section]
        [section Parties agree to arbitration. section]
    general-references]
    [definitions
        Definitions:
        [section "Collateral" means all personal property and fixtures of Customer. section]
    definitions]
Intercreditor]
```

Figure 8-18

Intercreditor Agreement
This is an agreement between BANK and CUSTOMER.

This agreement contains the following provisions:
Texas law will govern this agreement.
Parties agree to arbitration.

Definitions:
"Collateral" means all personal property and fixtures of Customer.

Figure 8-19

Transforming the XML Back into Something Meaningful via XSLT

So now we have this XML data and we know that it is valid according to our XSD schema. We also know that XML provides powerful ways to repurpose data so that it can do different things or be displayed in different ways. The mechanism for controlling the display of this data is called an Extensible Stylesheet Language Transformation (XSLT), or simply a transform. Transforms can be amazingly complex or incredibly simple. For example, after you validate an XML data file against a schema, you can apply a transform that turns the data into a very complex report for management purposes. This same data file can be transformed into an HTML page on the corporate web site. The data file could even be transformed into a PowerPoint presentation.

This same XML data file could be transformed to facilitate the exchange of data between back-end systems such as databases. The combination of an XML data file, an XSD schema, and an XSLT Transform constitutes a basic XML system. Word 2003 provides all of the tools that are needed to create such a system. In fact, we are in the process of doing just that right now.

Figure 8-20 shows the shell of a typical transform. Again, this is merely text that conforms to XML's rules. You can create XSLT Transforms via something as simple as Notepad. The top line is a declaration that the document conforms to XML. The root element is xsl:stylesheet with two attributes: the version number corresponding to the version of stylesheet and a namespace declaration that declares the stylesheet as an XSLT Transform.

```
<?xml version='1.0'?>
<xsl:stylesheet version="1.0"
xmlns:xsl="http://www.w3.org/1999/XSL/Transform">

<xsl:template match="/">

</xsl:template>

</xsl:stylesheet>
```

Figure 8-20

Now that we've introduced the bare minimum of how an XSLT Transform works, let's take a look at a couple of quick, meaningful examples. Figure 8-21 shows a complete XSLT Transform based on the XML data we've saved out in the simple Intercreditor.xml file. The first thing you will notice is the namespace declaration section near the top of the file. In addition to the standard namespace declaration referencing the w3 standard Transform namespace, there is a declaration associating the WordprocessingML namespace with the "w" prefix. There is also an "ns6" declaration referencing the schema we created earlier in the chapter.

```
<?xml version='1.0'?>
<xsl:stylesheet version="1.0"
xmlns:xsl="http://www.w3.org/1999/XSL/Transform"
xmlns:w="http://schemas.microsoft.com/office/word/2003/wordml"
xmlns:ns6="schemas-MSWordXmlToolbox#09052004-123413" >

<xsl:template match="/">
<w:wordDocument xml:space="preserve">
    <w:body>
        <w:p>
      <w:r>
       <w:t>this is an
        <xsl:value-of select="ns6:Intercreditor/ns6:title"/>
       </w:t>
      </w:r>
     </w:p>
    </w:body>
</w:wordDocument>
</xsl:template>

</xsl:stylesheet>
```

Figure 8-21

The XSLT processing begins with the xsl:template match tag found on the sixth line from the top. This is simply telling the XSL interpreter to match against the root node of the XML file it is attempting to transform. After this tag, the direct use of WordprocessingML begins. The first tag declares that we are working with the "w" (WordprocessingML) namespace and it is a Word document. The xml:space attribute simply declares that the spacing will be preserved. This will affect the look of the resultant Word document. The body section is where the text will be displayed. You will see that the text is nested beneath <w:p>, <w:r>, and <w:t> tags. As you'll see in Chapter 10, this is the fundamental structure for a text run in WordprocessingML. Within this structure is the predefined text "this is an," which will simply appear in the resultant Word document. Finally, you'll see the xsl:value-of tag, which is a processing instruction that tells the XSL processor to go out and grab a piece of data and insert it at a specific place.

Before we show what the resultant Word document looks like when the XLST transform is applied, let's see what the XML file actually looks like in Internet Explorer. Figure 8-22 displays the file as it appears in Internet Explorer. Again, you can see all the sections in XML exactly as they are interpreted by IE. Notice how the same file is displayed differently than it appears in Word, despite it having the same underlying data. In addition, you'll see the attribute declaration referencing the XML schema we created earlier.

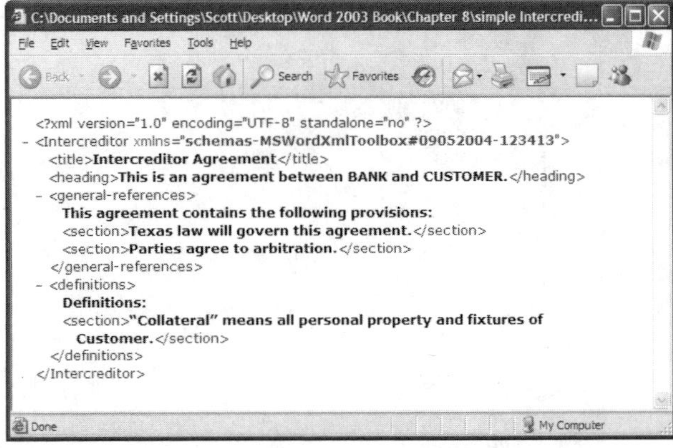

Figure 8-22

Now, let's step through the process of associating the transform with the XSD file created above and then viewing the transformed XML we just saw in Internet Explorer.

1. First we need to open the XML file in Microsoft Word. Stylesheets are associated with schemas in Word's schema library. In Microsoft terminology, these are "solutions." In order to associate the XSL file with the XSD file via Word, select **Tools | Templates and Add-ins** and click on the **XML Schema** tab.
2. Once you are in the Schema tab, click on the schema library and select the schema created by the XML Toolbox above.
3. Now, it's just a matter of clicking **Add Solution** and browsing to the location of the XSLT Transform. In this instance, you will use the default type, which is **XSLT transformation**. You can enter an alias in the Alias box so that there is a more meaningful name associated with the solution. In this case, I've merely used the name **Intercreditor 01** to reference the first XSLT Transform we will look at.

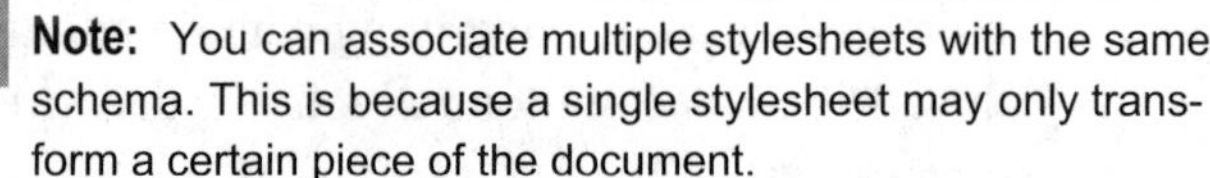

Note: You can associate multiple stylesheets with the same schema. This is because a single stylesheet may only transform a certain piece of the document.

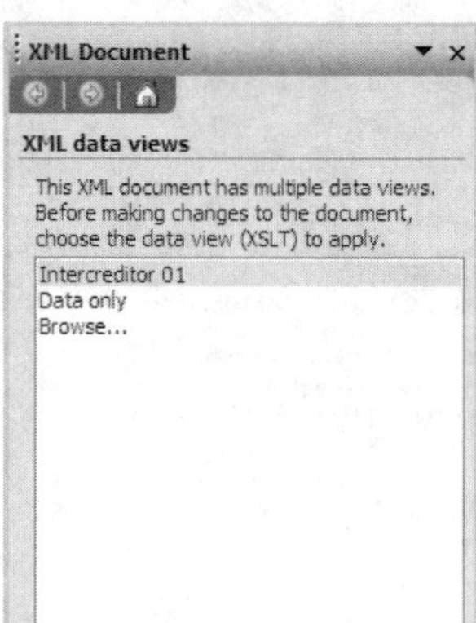

Figure 8-23

The task pane should appear similar to Figure 8-23. This displays the different data views available to a particular XML document. In this case there are two views currently available. The first view is the "Intercreditor 01" solution view, which applies the XSLT Transform to our XML file (as long as the XML file is valid according to the associated schema as well). Selecting this choice in the list box displays a simple Word document as shown in Figure 8-24.

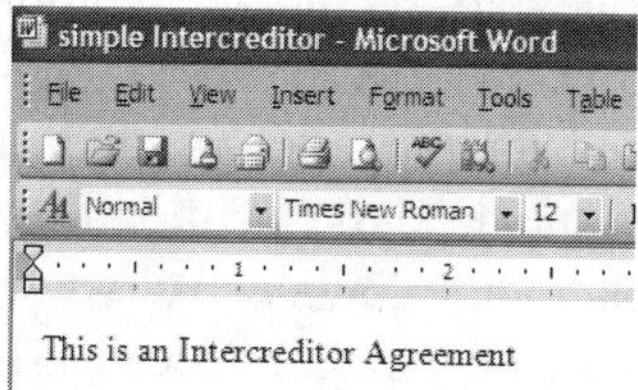

Figure 8-24

You can also select the Data only view to display the XML file as it appears in Figure 8-25. This shows the XML tags according to Word's XML representation. Word allows you to toggle back and forth between the two views and also allows you to choose a different XSLT solution with the Browse option. Selecting the Browse option opens the FileOpen dialog and allows you to associate a different XSLT Transform altogether.

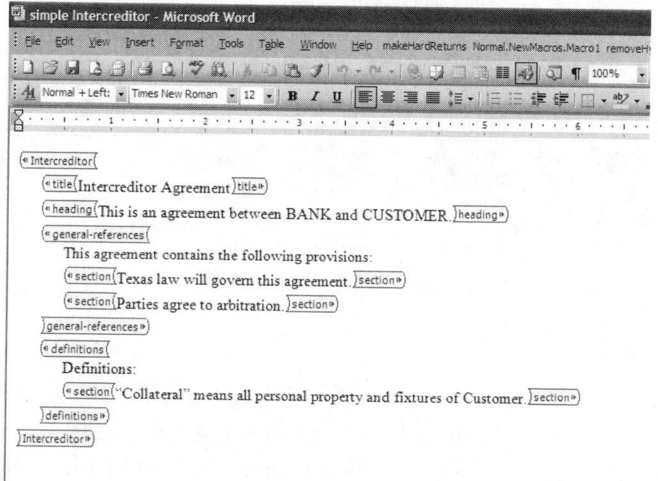

Figure 8-25

We're almost finished with the introduction to the new XML features of Word 2003. As you can see, things have gotten very complex behind a seemingly normal Word document. There is one more XSLT solution (Intercreditor02) that we will briefly examine to cover a specific point. In the Intercreditor 01 solution, we simply grabbed one piece of data (the "title" tagged data) from the XML file and displayed it via WordprocessingML with some associated text. As you'll see in Chapters 10 and 11, WordprocessingML and XSLT are very powerful.

Select Browse from the task pane and navigate to the directory where you placed the solution files accompanying this chapter (available for download at www.docbuilder.com and www.wordware.com/files/wordvba2). Once you've found the Chapter 8 directory, choose Intercreditor02.xsl. This dynamically applies the transform to the XML data so that Word will display the result in the standard Word document window. After selecting the Intercreditor02 solution, the Word task pane should look similar to Figure 8-26 and the resulting document should look like Figure 8-27.

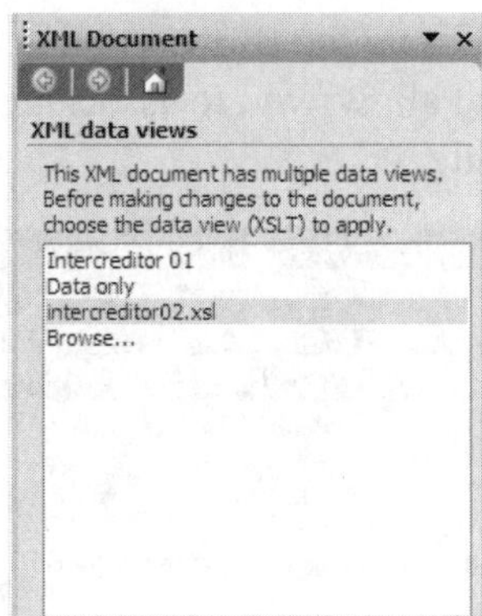

Figure 8-26

As you can see in Figure 8-27, the XSLT solution "looped" through the nested <section> elements in the <general-references> section to create a Word table containing a row for each entry. This is simply to show a slightly more complex use of XSLT and WordprocessingML. The accompanying XSLT file is shown in Figure 8-28 as it appears when opened via Internet Explorer.

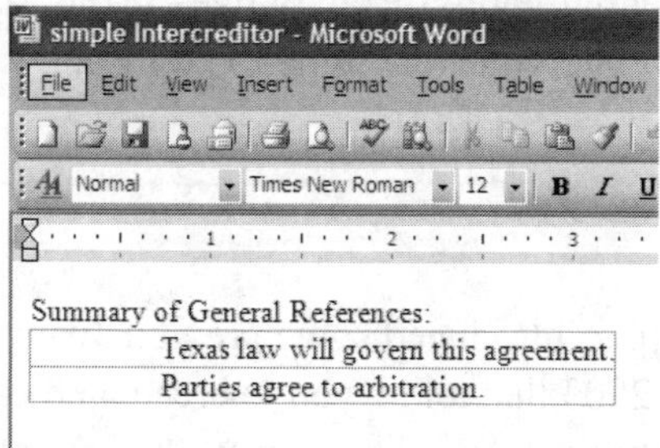

Figure 8-27

The XSLT Transform shown in Figure 8-28 is only the relevant WordprocessingML piece of the file. In all other respects, the file is identical to the solution displayed above in Intercreditor 01. This section shows a normal text run (static text) for the line, "Summary of General References:" and then introduces the xsl:for-each processing command. This command is what allows Word to loop through the sections and display them appropriately in the table. The table is created by the <w:tbl>, <w:tblPr>, <w:tr>, and <w:tc> WordprocessingML tags. It isn't important at this

```
<w:wordDocument xml:space="preserve">
  <w:body>
      <w:p>
        <w:r>
          <w:t>Summary of General References:</w:t>
        </w:r>
      </w:p>
    <xsl:for-each select="ns6:general-references/ns6:section">
      <w:tbl>
       <w:tblPr>
        <w:tr>
         <w:tc>
          <w:p>
           <w:r>
            <w:t>
             <xsl:value-of select="."/>
            </w:t>
          </w:r>
         </w:p>
        </w:tc>
       </w:tr>
      </w:tblPr>
     </w:tbl>
   </xsl:for-each>
  </w:body>
</w:wordDocument>
```

Figure 8-28

stage to know exactly how to use the tags or what the tags mean, but it is important to grasp the tremendous power available when using XSLT to transform XML data into what essentially looks exactly like the old-fashioned Word document everyone has come to know and love.

Conclusion

This chapter introduced some previously unseen features of Word 2003 that allow you to create and edit XML documents. Although Word has always had the ability to create customized document solutions, smart documents now offer a way to walk users through the creation of documents. Smart documents are dependent upon all of the new XML features in Word 2003; understanding the new XML components introduced in Word 2003 is vital to utilizing smart documents. This chapter allowed you to work through some very basic examples designed to give a quick but thorough introduction to these new features. Smart documents are solutions that utilize XSD, XML, and a Code Behind (via Visual Studio) custom task pane to interact with the user.

Chapter 9

XML Introduction

Introduction

The last chapter was an introduction by fire to the new XML features of Word 2003. This chapter is meant to slow things down a bit and introduce some XML fundamentals along with some of the things that the introduction of XML has made possible to Word 2003. If you are unfamiliar with XML, it is highly recommended that you read through this chapter in its entirety. If you are comfortable with your knowledge of XML, you may wish to read it purely for its supplemental value. A good understanding of XML is necessary to utilize the new XML-related functionality provided in Word 2003. In general, the reader should be able to grasp most of what is necessary by working through the projects in this chapter.

A Brief Look at Word 2003 and XML

The DOC file has been Word's faithful companion since its inception and the DOC file format has obviously served users well. The problem with the doc format is that it is a proprietary binary format and it isn't easy to access data from within these files. (Although I've seen numerous instances of a large directory housing Word documents that acted as database, this is not good architecture.) Fortunately, Word 2003 offers several new options, including the use of XML as a native Word format. By saving documents in the new XML format, information can be retrieved easily via standard XML tools (XPath queries).

There are several intriguing uses of XML with Word 2003. One possibility is to transform XML documents into other types of documents with Word 2003. Microsoft has released an XSLT processor that takes a Word 2003 XML document and transforms it into an HTML document. The resultant document can be viewed via a web browser. The implication is not merely that a document can be saved as HTML; we've been able to do that since Word 2000. The real power lies in the ability to transform the data within the Word document and make it available via the web.

Word 2003 also includes features to force the entry of data into an XML document. All of this is done behind the scenes, transparent to the user. One particular frustration of IT departments everywhere has been the inability to use data housed within Word documents. Word 2003 changes all of that. It will obviously take some time for the IT community to embrace this functionality, but Microsoft has made it available nonetheless. Essentially, a document can be annotated via an XML schema and then protected. This will allow users to only add or edit information in specific locations throughout the document. When the user saves the document, the data is written directly to an XML document. This allows the data specific to the XML document to be easily consumed by another application or a database.

What Is XML?

XML is a markup language for documents containing structured information. Structured information contains both content (words, pictures, etc.) and metadata. Metadata provides some indication of what role that content plays (for example, content in a section heading has a different meaning from content in a footnote, which means something different from content in a figure caption or content in a database table, etc.). A markup language is a mechanism to identify structure within a document. The XML specification defines a standard way to add markup to plain text documents via opening and closing tags.

In order to fully understand XML, it is important to understand the needs that gave rise to it and the reason why it was created. XML was created primarily so that richly structured data could be exchanged over the Internet. The readily available alternatives were HTML and SGML, neither of which were ideal for this purpose. HTML does not provide for a completely arbitrary structure. SGML provides arbitrary structure, but is too complex to implement for the vast majority of purposes that gave rise to XML.

A Note on the Word "Document"

XML has emerged as a standard mechanism for transferring data between applications. For the purpose of this book, the word "document" refers not only to traditional Word documents but also to the more specific Word XML document. An attempt will be made to differentiate the types, but keep in mind that the terminology is the same.

How XML Compares with HTML

Initially, many people are apt to lump XML and HTML together conceptually. This is most likely because of the similarity of this syntax, as they both use opening and closing tags. However, in HTML, both the tag semantics and the tag set are fixed because they must be interpreted by a browser. An <h1> is always a first-level heading, and the tag <BorrowerFirstName> is meaningless. A browser interprets HTML tags to determine how to format what is in between the opening and closing tags. With XML, a browser such as Internet Explorer makes sure the XML document adheres to the rules of XML.

The W3C (World Wide Web Consortium), in conjunction with browser vendors and the WWW community, is constantly working to extend the definition of HTML to allow new tags to keep pace with changing technology and to bring variations in presentation (stylesheets) to the web.

In contrast to HTML, XML does not have a prescribed tag set or semantics of its use. XML is really a metalanguage for describing markup languages in general. XML facilitates the definition of structural relationships between data and allows for those relationships to be represented via the use of tags. The metadata concerning the structural relationship of the data can be accomplished via the use of attributes, which are also defined by the XML specification.

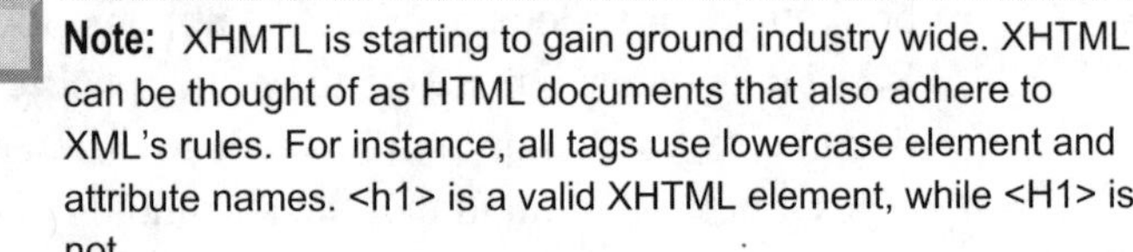

Note: XHMTL is starting to gain ground industry wide. XHTML can be thought of as HTML documents that also adhere to XML's rules. For instance, all tags use lowercase element and attribute names. <h1> is a valid XHTML element, while <H1> is not.

XML Compared with SGML

Roughly speaking, XML is a restricted form of SGML. SGML stands for Standard Generalized Markup Language defined by ISO 8879. SGML has been the standard, vendor-independent way to maintain repositories of structured documentation for a long, long time. One of the downfalls of SGML is that it is not well suited to serving documents over the web. SGML is too unstructured to be of much use in the lightweight world of the web. Defining XML as a restricted form of SGML does not mean that one needs to understand SGML, but rather implies that a completely SGML-compatible system would inherently be able to utilize XML. However, such a discussion is largely theoretical in the context of this book.

XML Development Goals

The XML specification sets out specific goals for XML. If you are interested in more technical detail about a particular topic, please consult the specification. Following is a brief overview of the goals XML hopes to address. For more information, please consult the World Wide Web Consortium web site at www.w3.org.

XML should be Internet friendly. XML documents must be as accessible as HTML documents, and users should be able to view XML documents as easily as they can view HTML documents.

XML needs to support a wide variety of applications. XML should be flexible enough to be beneficial to a wide variety of diverse applications: authoring, browsing, content analysis, etc. Although the initial focus is on serving structured documents over the web, it is not meant to narrowly define XML.

Every effort should be made to keep XML a clean and "tight" specification — free from superfluous options. This translates into keeping the number of optional features in XML to an absolute minimum. Neat-to-have features inevitably create compatibility problems when users want to share documents.

XML documents need to be human-legible and reasonably clear of confusion. The idea here is that if you don't have an XML browser and you are attempting to decipher a block of XML, you should be able to look at it in the text editor of your choice and be able to ascertain what the data is, what the elements are, and how it is structured.

There has been a conscious effort throughout the development of XML that the XML design should be prepared quickly. From a historical standpoint, information technology standards efforts are notoriously slow. The original need for XML was immediate, and XML as a concept was to progress as quickly as possible.

There has always been a focus toward accessibility. The standard promulgated a vision that XML documents shall be easy to create. Obviously, there are some extremely complicated XML documents in existence. However, it is still relatively easy to whip up a valid XML document with Notepad.

XML Basics

The following sections discuss some of the concepts necessary for understanding XML.

Well-Formedness Rules

XML elements and attributes must follow certain rules in order for the document to qualify as being "well formed." If a document is not well formed, the document is technically not XML — even if it has an .xml extension. Most programs that deal with XML will not work if a document is not well formed.

The XML specification prohibits XML parsers from trying to fix or even understand malformed documents. If the parser or browser conforms to the XML specification, all it can do is issue a message that substantively reports the error. In other words, the industry standard when encountering malformed XML is to report the error and abort the program. There are more than 100 different rules an XML document must follow in order to be considered "well formed." Don't let that statistic scare you; most of these rules prohibit things that are counterintuitive anyway.

XML Declaration

XML declarations are used to describe the various types of XML authoring. The Standalone Document Declaration allows the document author to specify whether external markup declarations may exist. This attribute can be equal to yes or no and is always the former in well-formed documents. The encoding declaration allows authors to specify the character encoding that they are using. This declaration only needs to be used by authors who are using a character encoding other than US-ASCII, the most common, or UTF-8.

There are three basic XML declarations listed below. The first two declarations can be used to describe well-formed and valid XML documents, respectively. The third declaration can be considered the default XML declaration, stating that it is an XML version 1.0 document, that it cannot stand alone from external markup declarations, and that it is encoded in UTF-8, an 8-bit Unicode character encoding. Use the first XML declaration when creating your own well-formed XML documents.

```
<?xml version="1.0" standalone="yes"?>
<?xml version="1.0" standalone="no"?>
<?xml version="1.0" standalone="no" encoding="UTF-8"?>
```

Naming Conventions

The following rules apply to names for elements, attributes, and entities within XML.

- Names should only use a colon if they use namespaces, which are a way of indicating the markup language that a particular element or attribute is utilizing. Namespaces will be discussed in more detail later.
- Names can contain letters (a-Z), periods (.), colons (:), underscores (_), and numbers (1-9). In all cases, the name *must* start with a letter, colon, or underscore.
- Names cannot start with the characters "XML" in either lowercase, uppercase, or mixed. These characters are considered to be reserved according to the standards from the W3C.

Valid	Invalid
<fourth> </fourth>	<4th > </4th>
<borrower.name>	<borrower:name> *
<member>	<xmlMember>

* If there is no "borrower" namespace

Caution: Remember that in all instances XML is case sensitive.

XML Elements

Every XML document has elements. Elements can simply be thought of as the tags in the XML document. In addition to the naming conventions described above, there are some basic rules that apply to elements. This section discusses those rules.

Top-Level Element (Document Element)

XML requires that there is a single top-level element that contains everything within the XML document. This is sometimes referred to as the "document element." In XHTML, the top-level element is <html> (lowercase, of course). This is one of the rules of well formedness of XML.

Well Formed	Not Well Formed
<?xml version="1.0" standalone="yes"?>	<?xml version="1.0" standalone="yes"?>
<borrower>	<borrower>
<first.name>Scott</first.name>	</borrower>
</borrower>	<first.name>
	</first.name>

End Tags

Well-formed XML must always have starting and ending tags unless they are considered "empty elements," which use a special syntax. The ending tag must always have the element name prefixed with the forward slash character (/). The data will appear between the beginning and ending tags.

Empty elements are elements that do not utilize two tags. In this case there is simply one tag that has a space and a forward slash before the closing angle bracket rather than having both starting and ending tags. Keep in mind that these elements are described as "empty" because they cannot contain data between the opening and closing bracket. However, some XML documents use a data attribute within the tag to identify the data.

Well Formed	Not Well Formed
<?xml version="1.0" standalone="yes"?> <borrower> <first.name>Scott</first.name> </borrower>	<?xml version="1.0" standalone="yes"?> <borrower> <first.name>Scott<first.name> <borrower>
<?xml version="1.0" standalone="yes"?> <borrower> <first.name data="Scott" /> </borrower>	<?xml version="1.0" standalone="yes"?> <borrower> <first.name data="Scott"> </borrower>

Nested Elements

Elements in XML must be properly nested. As we've seen with the top-level element, everything must reside appropriately within the element that houses it. Technically speaking, this is a requirement of HTML as well, but browsers have been very liberal when interpreting HTML. Properly nested elements will form a hierarchy within the document with the top-level element as the root of the hierarchy.

In HTML, many people become sloppy and do something like the following:

```
<b><p>Rob Mathews</b> is a good guy.</p>
```

This will appear properly in almost all browsers but is not technically correct. Instead, it should appear properly nested as:

```
<p><b>Rob Mathews</b> is a good guy.</p>
```

XML Attributes

There is no requirement that an XML document utilize attributes. Conceptually, attributes are used as metadata within the XML document to provide additional information regarding the element. In some cases, authors use attributes to contain data as seen in the above example of empty elements. In most instances, this is done merely to save space.

Attributes are name-value pairs that appear within the element's opening tag. The value can be enclosed in either single or double quotes. There must be an equal sign (assignment operator) between the name and value indicating that the value is assigned to that particular attribute.

Note: Single and double quotes cannot be used interchangeably within the same element.

Well Formed	Not Well Formed
<?xml version="1.0" standalone="yes"?>	<?xml version="1.0" standalone="yes"?>
<borrower>	<borrower>
<first.name data="Scott" />	<first.name data=Scott />
</borrower>	</borrower>

Entity References

You're probably familiar with a number of entity references from HTML. For example, © inserts the copyright symbol and ® inserts the registered trademark symbol. XML predefines the five entity references listed in Table 9-1. These predefined entity references are used in XML documents in place of specific characters that would otherwise be interpreted as part of markup. For instance, the entity reference < stands for the less than sign (<), which would otherwise be interpreted as beginning a tag.

Table 9-1

Entity Reference	Character
&	&
<	<
>	>
"	"
'	'

Caution: In XML, unlike HTML, entity references must end with a semicolon. > is a correct entity reference; > is not.

Standard less than signs and ampersands in normal XML text are always interpreted as starting tags and entity references respectively. Therefore, less than signs and ampersands that are text rather than markup must always be encoded as < and & respectively. Attribute values are text, too, and as you already saw, entity references may be used inside attribute values.

Other than the five entity references already discussed, you can only use an entity reference if you define it in a DTD first. In case you're unfamiliar with DTDs, if the ampersand character & appears anywhere in your document, it must be immediately followed by amp;, lt;, gt;, apos;, or quot;. All other uses violate well-formedness.

Comments

XML comments are almost exactly like HTML comments. They begin with `<!--` and end with `-->`. All data between the `<!--` and `-->` is ignored by the XML processor. It's as if it weren't there. This can be used to make notes to yourself or your coauthors, or to temporarily comment out sections of the document if needed.

Since comments aren't elements, they may be placed before or after the root element. However, comments may not come before the XML declaration, which must be the very first thing in the document. However, comments may surround and hide tags.

There is one final constraint on comments. The two-hyphen string (`--`) may not occur inside a comment except as part of its opening or closing tag.

It also means that you may run into trouble if you're commenting out a lot of C, Java, or JavaScript source code that's full of expressions such as `i--` or `numberLeft--`. Generally, it's not too hard to work around this problem once you recognize it.

Processing Instructions

Processing instructions are like comments that are intended for computer programs reading the document rather than people reading the document. However, XML parsers are required to pass along the contents of processing instructions to the application on whose behalf they're parsing, unlike comments, which a parser is allowed to silently discard. The application that receives the information is free to ignore any processing instruction it doesn't understand.

Processing instructions begin with `<?` and end with `?>`. The starting `<?` is followed by an XML name called the target, which identifies the program for which the instruction is intended, followed by data for that program. For instance, let's pretend that the following instruction occurs in a file:

```
<?xml-stylesheet type="text/xml" href="Intercreditor01.xsl"?>
```

The target of this processing instruction is `xml-stylesheet`, a standard name that means the data in this processing instruction is intended for any web browser that can apply a stylesheet to the document. `type="text/xml" href="Intercreditor01.xsl"` is the processing instruction data that will be passed to the application reading the document. If that application happens to be a web browser that understands XSLT, then it will apply the style sheet `Intercreditor01.xsl` to the document and render the result. If that application is anything other than a web browser, it will simply ignore the processing instruction.

Note: The XML declaration is technically not a processing instruction. The difference is academic unless you're writing a program to read an XML document using an XML parser. In that case, the parser's API will provide different methods to get the contents of processing instructions and the contents of the XML declaration.

Finally, `xml-stylesheet` processing instructions are always placed at the document's beginning between the XML declaration and the root element start tag. Other processing instructions may also be placed in this area (sometimes called the "prolog"), or at almost any other convenient location in the XML document, either before, after, or inside the root element. For example, PHP processing instructions generally appear wherever you want the PHP processor to place its output. The only place a processing instruction may not appear is inside a tag or before the XML declaration.

The target of a processing instruction may be the name of the program it is intended for or it may be a generic identifier such as `xml-stylesheet` that many different programs recognize. The target name `xml` (or `XML`, `Xml`, `xMl`, or any other variation) is reserved for use by the W3C. However, you're free to use any other convenient name for processing instruction targets. Different applications support different processing instructions. Most applications simply ignore any processing instruction whose target they don't recognize.

The `xml-stylesheet` processing instruction uses a very common format for processing instructions in which the data is divided into pseudo-attributes; that is, the data is passed as name-value pairs, and the values are delimited by quotes. However, as with the XML declaration, these are not true attributes because a processing instruction is not a tag. Furthermore, this format is optional. Some processing instructions will use this style; others won't. The only limit on the content of processing instruction data is that it may not contain the two-character sequence (`?>`) that signals the end of a processing instruction. Otherwise, it's free to contain any legal characters that may appear in XML documents.

Adding XML Tags in Word 2003

Okay, so you're probably asking yourself, "What does all of this have to do with Word 2003?" Let's take a baby step and add XML tags to a document in Word 2003. As in the previous chapter, please make sure you have the XML Toolbox downloaded and installed. If you need instructions, refer to the beginning of Chapter 8. To get started, just start typing some XML tags in a Word document (we can save it as a template later) and arrange them in the order that you want. Be sure to terminate them by using the forward slash character. Figure 9-1 shows the document and one way to order the XML tags.

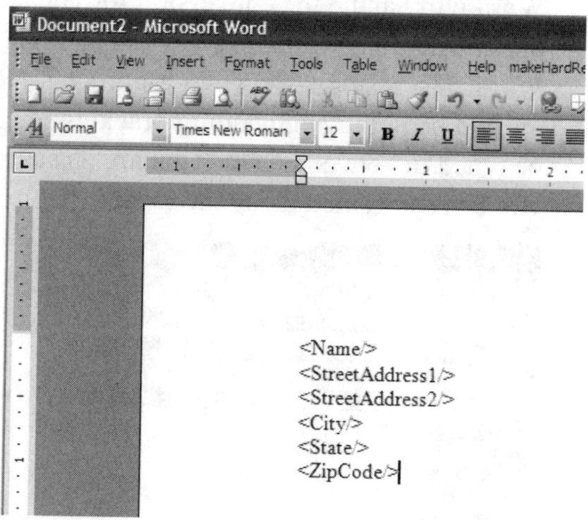

Figure 9-1: Typing XML tags directly in a document

Remember, we are still working simply. At this point, the XML tags may look like XML to you, but Word thinks of them as regular text. They are not yet identified as real XML tags so that Word responds to them as full-fledged XML in a structured document rather than just ad hoc textual input. To convert the text to true XML, on the XML Toolbox menu, click Convert <Tags/> to XML Nodes as shown in Figure 9-2.

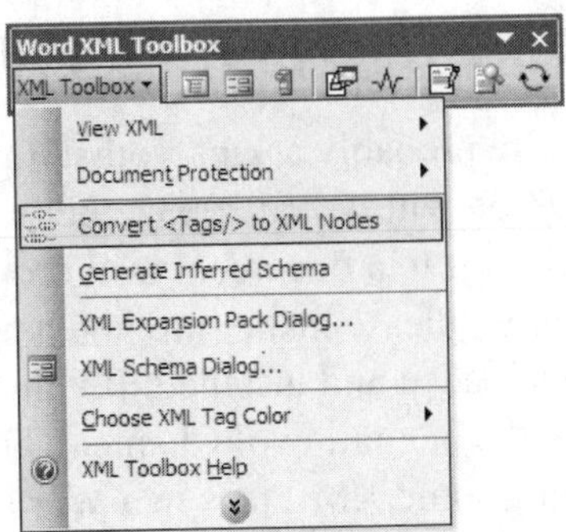

Figure 9-2: Converting ad hoc text into true XML nodes

Word will handle the conversion for you and display the previously marked-up text as valid XML interpreted by Word. The result is shown in Figure 9-3. Notice that Word created beginning and ending brackets so that the text can be typed in between them. This text is actually the data that will be represented in an XML file.

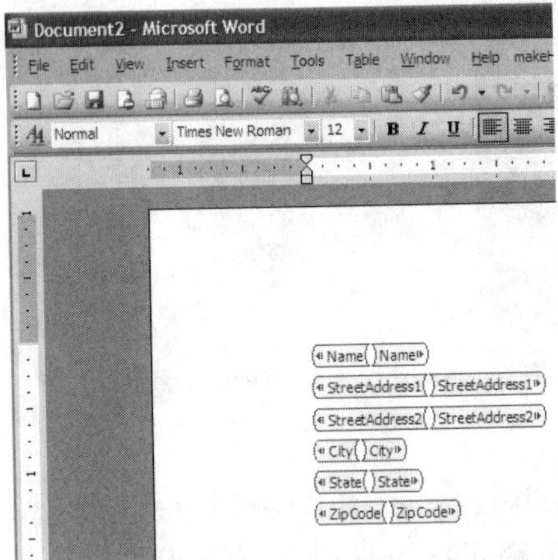

Figure 9-3: The result of converting to XML nodes

As you can see, Word 2003 is pretty smart when working with XML. The tags are named appropriately and arranged as previously defined. In addition, this document is already well formed, as Word will not create anything but a well-formed XML document when using the XML Toolbox.

Adding Placeholder Text

Our XML template now has some fundamental XML elements defined. However, as it stands, it is not very user-friendly or informative as to how it should be used. There are very few instances where an end user should actually see the XML tags in the document. Word 2003 provides a convenient mechanism for changing the way the user works with marked-up XML documents. This mechanism is the addition of designated placeholder text for each of the XML tags in the document. This allows you as the document author to define the appropriate placeholder text and set the precise location where you want the text to be displayed. The Word XML Toolbox includes a tool to change XML attributes for the tags in the document and add placeholder text quickly and easily. First, position your cursor inside the Name tags in the newly created document. Once you've positioned your cursor, select the Toolbox toolbar and click the XmlNode Property Viewer button (see Figure 9-4).

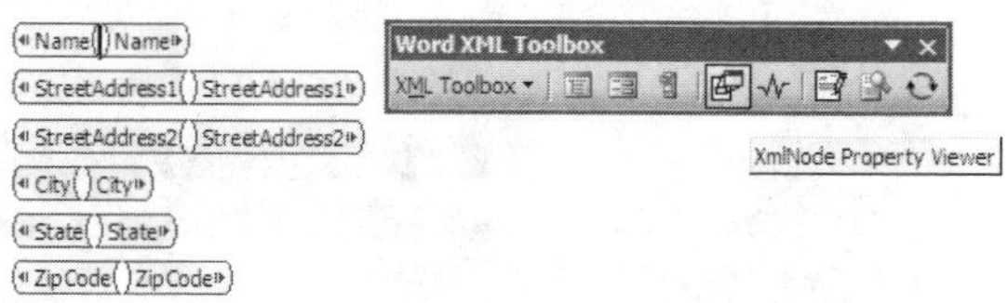

Figure 9-4: Accessing the XmlNode Property Viewer

The viewer allows you to move through the nodes in the document and view or change the attributes of the corresponding element. Figure 9-5 shows the highlighted Name XML element and its properties in the viewer. Type the placeholder text as shown and click Next Node >> in the viewer to move to the next node in the document. Work through each node and enter generic placeholder text as shown in Figure 9-5. After making changes to the nodes, close the viewer.

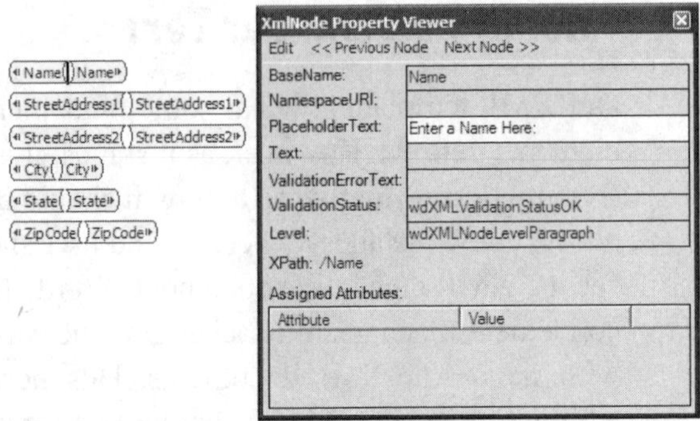

Figure 9-5

It's now possible to see what an end user would see when viewing the document without the XML tags showing. This is done by toggling the Tag View off so that the document will display the placeholder text. The most convenient mechanism to do this is via the Word XML Toolbox. After you access the Toolbox, you switch between viewing the document with the tags displayed and without them displayed by clicking the Toggle XML Tag View button as shown in Figure 9-6.

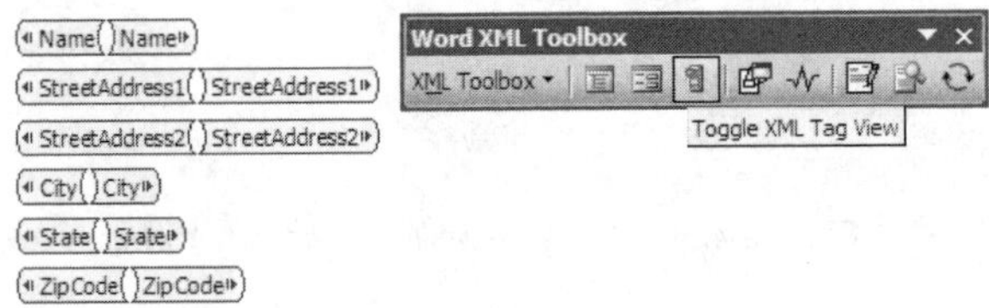

Figure 9-6

The document with placeholder text should appear as shown in Figure 9-7. If you've been around Word development for a while, this should look similar to a frequently used workaround in document templates. People have been using the MacroButton field for years as a placeholder in document templates because of its particular behavior. Microsoft intended for the MacroButton field to be an interactive tool for launching macros within the context of a document. However, more frequently, people chose to use the field simply as a placeholder for text because it displayed a user prompt that disappeared when someone began typing in the field.

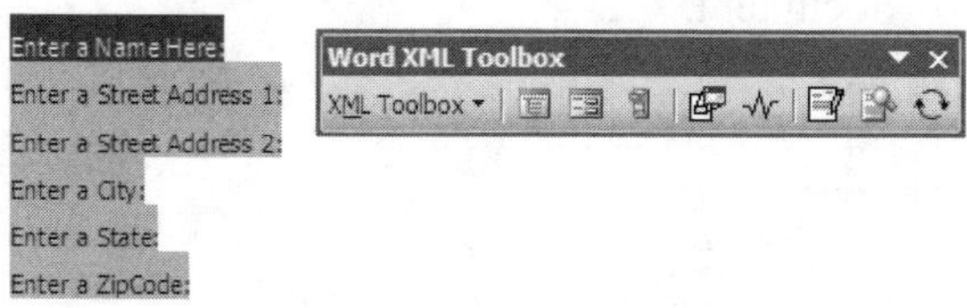

Figure 9-7

Inserting XML

The template is now ready to apply formatting and set up styles so that the user has an easier time working with the resultant document. One of the most important features for Word 2003 developers is the addition of XML support to the Range and Selection objects. As you saw in the chapters covering VBA, these objects (Range and Selection) are two of the most frequently used objects when working programmatically with a Word document or template. The Word 2003 object model allows you to create Range or Selection objects in the classical sense, but then also allows you to work with them as true XML. Programmatically, the enhanced Word 2003 Range object supports a method called InsertXML that lets you insert arbitrary XML directly into the document.

For example, let's open the VBA editor (Alt + F11) and enter the macro shown in Figure 9-8. This InsertSomeXML macro is meant to show a simple example of how we can insert XML programmatically into our document. First, we'll declare a line to select the entire ActiveDocument. This allows us to then use the HomeKey method of the Selection object to position the cursor (the active Selection object) directly at the beginning of the document. The next line then uses the Selection object (the selection is the first line of the ActiveDocument) to insert beginning and ending tags (example tags) with the associated “This is an Address example” text. Also, notice that we are using a Chr(13) value at the end of the line to force a hard return to keep everything looking pretty in the document.

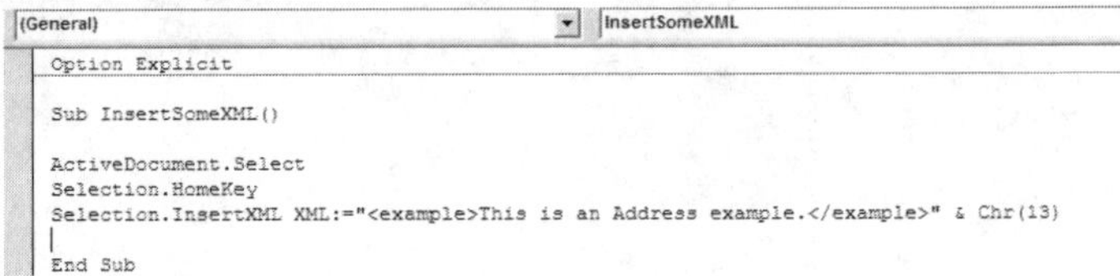
(General)
InsertSomeXML
Option Explicit
Sub InsertSomeXML()
ActiveDocument.Select
Selection.HomeKey
Selection.InsertXML XML:="<example>This is an Address example.</example>" & Chr(13)
End Sub

Figure 9-8

In order to run the macro, simply position the cursor between the beginning Sub and the End Sub lines and press F8. This will start the code execution at the first line as indicated by the yellow highlighting that will appear on the screen. You can then step through the code by continuing to press F8 until code execution stops. You will see which line is being executed as the yellow highlighting moves from line to line.

Figure 9-9 shows how the XML looks after the line has been programmatically inserted and the XML viewing has been toggled off.

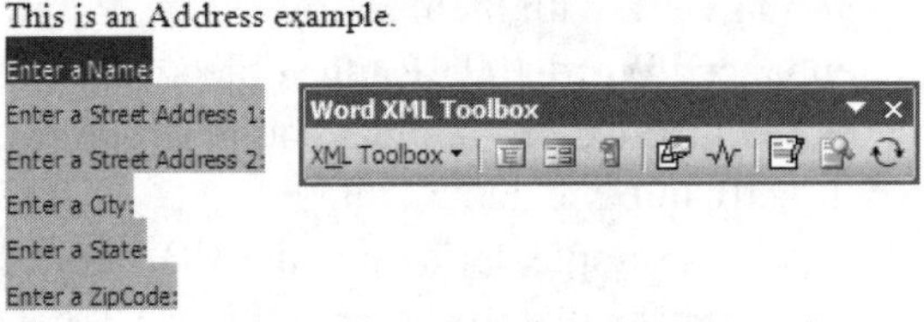
This is an Address example.
Enter a Name:
Enter a Street Address 1:
Enter a Street Address 2:
Enter a City:
Enter a State:
Enter a ZipCode:
Word XML Toolbox
XML Toolbox

Figure 9-9

Figure 9-10 shows how the XML looks after the line has been programmatically inserted and the XML viewing has been toggled on.

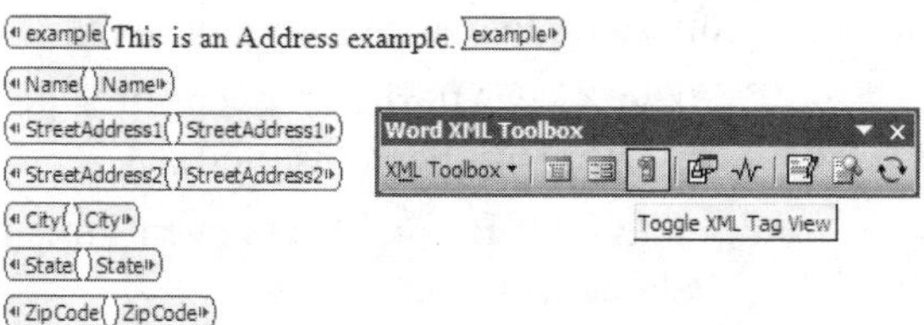

Figure 9-10

If the specified XML text cannot be inserted into the specified range or selection, an error message is displayed. Use the InsertXML method to insert text marked up with either arbitrary XML or Word XML. The XML must be well formed. If it uses Word XML, then it must also be valid according to the Word XML schema. For more information on the Word XML schema, please refer to the Word XML Content Development Kit, which you can find on the Microsoft Developer Network (MSDN) web site. If the specified XML text cannot be inserted into the specified range or selection, an error message is displayed.

Word 2003 XML Events

One of the most difficult aspects of working with Word-based solutions has been responding via the appropriate VBA code when a user is accessing a particular section of a template. Word 2003 has introduced a series of events that fire when XML-related things happen. For example, if an XML node is added that is in the wrong place, an event fires. When a user navigates among nodes, events fire as each node is entered and exited. When a user enters text into specific nodes of the XML document, events are also triggered. This has large implications because there is now the ability to trigger specific actions in exact relation to a user navigating through the document. This, in turn, also leads ultimately to a better user experience.

The following two events pertain to the Document object:

- The XMLAfterInsert event fires just after a new element has been inserted.
- The XMLBeforeDelete event fires just before an element is deleted.

These events pertain to the Application object:

- The XMLValidationError event fires when a validation error occurs in the document and receives a single parameter: a reference to the node with the error.
- The XMLSelectionChange event fires when you select a new node. This event receives parameters: the WordSelection object for the newly selected material, references to both the node that lost focus and the node that gained focus, and a reason code.

We can see how one of the preceding events is triggered programmatically by quickly adding a new subroutine to our existing example. Enter the subroutine shown in Figure 9-11 and begin stepping through the code. You'll see that the code execution jumps to the Document_XMLAfter-Insert subroutine following the insertion of the XML in the first subroutine.

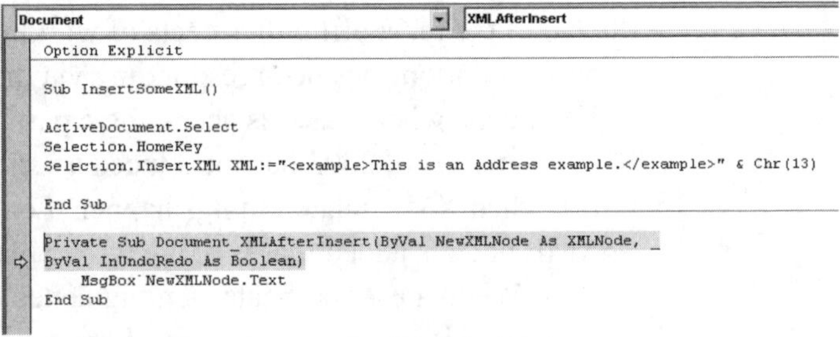

Document
XMLAfterInsert
Option Explicit
Sub InsertSomeXML()
ActiveDocument.Select
Selection.HomeKey
Selection.InsertXML XML:="<example>This is an Address example.</example>" & Chr(13)
End Sub
Private Sub Document_XMLAfterInsert(ByVal NewXMLNode As XMLNode, _
ByVal InUndoRedo As Boolean)
MsgBox NewXMLNode.Text
End Sub

Figure 9-11

A Quick Introduction to XSD Schemas

There is something about the term "schema" that intimidates some people. Don't be one of those people. For the purpose of this book a schema is just an ordinary XML file that lists the rules for what can and cannot appear in another XML file. Put more simply, schemas allow programs to validate data. You will see how XSD schemas work through a number of examples in this book.

Schemas provide the framework for structuring data and ensuring that it follows a certain format. Schemas can provide an additional check on the content and structure of an XML document. For many programs, it isn't enough that an XML file is well formed. In many cases, an XML file must be "valid" according to a given schema.

When the data in an XML file conforms to the rules provided by a schema, that data is said to be valid. The process of checking an XML data file against a schema is called (logically enough) validation. The big advantage to using schemas is that they can help prevent corrupted data. They also make it easy to find corrupted data because XML simply stops when it encounters a problem.

Office 2003 Generalizations

The first thing to note is that Word 2003 (and the Office 2003 suite in general) does not provide a schema editor. There are several outstanding editors now available, but you'll have to obtain them in addition to Office. Of course, you can always do it the old-fashioned way and use Notepad until it no longer suits your needs.

In general, an XML schema specifies the order of tags in the XML document, indicates mandatory and optional fields, specifies data types of fields, and so on. Perhaps most importantly, the schema ensures that data values in the XML file are valid as they pertain to the parent application. The XML Schema Definition Language (XSD) enables you to define the structure (elements and attributes) and data types for XML documents. It enables this in a way that conforms to the relevant W3C recommendations for XML schema. XSD is the primary schema definition language, although the DTD (Document Type Definition) standard is still in use.

Note: The XML Schema specification is much longer than the XML specification. This chapter will only serve as a general introduction.

Validity — Beyond Well Formed

The first threshold an XML document must meet is that it must be well formed. This simply means that the document meets the requirements to be an XML document. A well-formed XML document is one that satisfies the usual rules of XML. For example, in a well-formed document there is exactly one data root node, all opening tags have corresponding closing tags, tag names do not contain spaces, the names in opening and closing tags are spelled in exactly the same way, tags are properly nested, etc.

The next threshold is that of validity, which means that the document passes the tests set forth in the schema. It is important to note that a valid document is also one that is well formed. In this sense the schema acts as a contract, specifying exactly what one application or part of an application must write into an XML file and another program can expect to be there. The schema unambiguously states the correct format for the shared XML.

DTD and XDR — A Little History

The first schema standard, developed alongside XML v1.0, was the DTD (Document Type Definition) schema. This, many believed, was not an ideal solution as a schema definition language, which is why Microsoft came up with XSD as its own suggested replacement and submitted this to the W3C for consideration. One of the problems was, and is, that DTDs are not XML based, so you have yet another language to learn to go with the proliferation that comes with XML (XPath and XSL, for example). Further, developers also found that DTD lacked the power and flexibility they needed to completely define all of the data types they wanted to represent in XML. A schema that can't validate all of the data's requirements is of limited use.

Types and Elements

First off, let's take a look at the same schema we used in Chapter 8 for the Intercreditor Agreement. This schema is shown in Figure 9-12. There are several basic things to observe. The first is that the schema definition is represented as a well-formed XML document. You will also note that schemas have a strong interrelation with namespaces. This is common to schemas in general, so a good understanding of namespaces is vitally important to understanding how XSD schemas operate. Finally, there is a built-in syntax to declare data types within the schema. You will see the type attribute used throughout all XSD files.

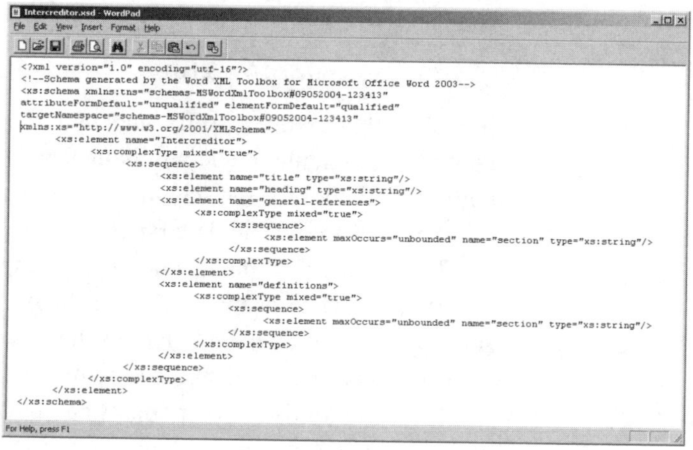

Intercreditor.xsd - WordPad

File Edit View Insert Format Help

```
<?xml version="1.0" encoding="utf-16"?>
<!--Schema generated by the Word XML Toolbox for Microsoft Office Word 2003-->
<xs:schema xmlns:tns="schemas-MSWordXmlToolbox#09052004-123413"
attributeFormDefault="unqualified" elementFormDefault="qualified"
targetNamespace="schemas-MSWordXmlToolbox#09052004-123413"
xmlns:xs="http://www.w3.org/2001/XMLSchema">
	<xs:element name="Intercreditor">
		<xs:complexType mixed="true">
			<xs:sequence>
				<xs:element name="title" type="xs:string"/>
				<xs:element name="heading" type="xs:string"/>
				<xs:element name="general-references">
					<xs:complexType mixed="true">
						<xs:sequence>
							<xs:element maxOccurs="unbounded" name="section" type="xs:string"/>
						</xs:sequence>
					</xs:complexType>
				</xs:element>
				<xs:element name="definitions">
					<xs:complexType mixed="true">
						<xs:sequence>
							<xs:element maxOccurs="unbounded" name="section" type="xs:string"/>
						</xs:sequence>
					</xs:complexType>
				</xs:element>
			</xs:sequence>
		</xs:complexType>
	</xs:element>
</xs:schema>
```

For Help, press F1

Figure 9-12

XSD schemas contain type definitions and elements. A type definition defines an allowed XML data type. An address might be an example of a type you might want to define. An element represents an item created in the XML file. If the XML file contains an Address tag, then the XSD file will contain a corresponding element named Address. The data type of the Address element indicates the type of data allowed in the XML file's Address tag.

Type definitions may be simple or complex. Simple and complex types allow definition of the new data types in addition to the 19 built-in primitive data types that include string, Boolean, decimal, date, etc.

- A simple type allows a type definition for a value that can be used as the content of an element or attribute. This data type cannot contain elements or have attributes.
- A complex type allows a type definition for elements that can contain attributes and elements.

Structure of an XSD

An XML schema is an XML document with the top-level schema element. The first requirement is that the schema element definition must include the following namespace:

```
http://www.w3.org/2001/XMLSchema
```

It could either assign a prefix such as *xsd* or *xs*, or it could make XMLSchema the default namespace. The prefix (if any) is used both for the schema component elements and in references to built-in data types.

To validate documents that use namespaces, you can specify a target namespace for the schema. Children of the schema element are called global schema components and are used to define items in the schema's target namespace.

Different kinds of components can have the same name within a given schema with one exception: Simple and complex types cannot share the same name (there would be no way to distinguish between them). Elements are not types, so element names may be the same as a complex or simple type. There is no logical relationship between them, so anything that interprets the schema can distinguish between them.

XSD schemas are self documenting and can be processed by more than the intended schema validator. This is accomplished via three mechanisms that all work together: unique identifiers, extension attributes, and annotation elements.

Unique Identifiers

Schema components (such as element and simpleType) are all defined with an optional "id" attribute. Every value that gets assigned to an "id" attribute must be unique from any other appearing anywhere within the schema document. This makes the use of tools such as XPath easier when trying to find the precise location of a given component. You can think of the "id" attribute as a key to each particular component.

Extension Attributes

Schema components can also contain arbitrary attributes (name them anything you want that is within the rules). This, of course, applies to anything other than the default (think "predefined") XMLschema namespace. These can be used for any number of things. They could contain metadata for use in describing the contents. They provide guideposts to describe how different elements should be processed. They could even be used to describe relationships between the various elements themselves.

Annotation Elements

XSD components can have annotation elements as their first sub-element. Annotation elements are just what they sound like: English-language annotations for ease of use. In fact, you can put in as many annotation elements as you want. This is what provides the ultimate flexibility in XSD.

You can essentially write notes as to the intended use within the XSD itself.

Each annotation element may contain as many "documentation" and "appinfo" children as you want. (You do not need to have any at all.) The documentation element is used to provide the type of user narrative descriptions we described above. They don't have to be used strictly to describe the schema. In fact, most times they are used as plain English instructions. In some cases, these values are extracted via programs and used to provide documentation about a given schema. The appinfo element adds some specific information for a particular application. These are supplemental elements and can provide further direction for processing a given XSD.

Types

In general, types are capable of being defined independent of the elements that use them. In addition, a given type may be utilized by one or more elements. You can think of types as reusable components within the schema that make up the base for an element. Types themselves do not contain any information about a given element. Rather, they provide the framework upon which elements will be built. In addition, the framework they provide can also be used by other types. Finally, if you only intend to use a certain type once within the schema, you could (but may not want to for future use) put the definition right into the given element.

Attributes

Just as you use an XSD schema's element entities to define the data that can be contained in the corresponding XML data elements, you can use attribute entities to define the attributes the XML element can have.

Why use attributes rather than elements (referred to as attribute-centric and element-centric XML)? Well, they are often interchangeable, so it is largely a matter of taste. Generally, however, elements should contain data, and attributes should contain information that describes the data.

Conclusion

In this chapter, you learned about XML's well-formedness rules. In particular, you learned that XML documents are sequences of characters that meet certain well-formedness criteria.

The text of an XML document is divided into character data and markup. An XML document is a tree structure made up of elements. Start tags and empty tags may contain attributes, which describe elements. Entity references allow you to include <, >, &, ", and ' in your document. Comments can document your code for other people who read it, but parsers may ignore them. Comments can also hide sections of the document that aren't ready for use. Processing instructions allow you to pass application-specific information to particular applications. In addition, you've seen some simple ways that Word 2003 uses XML and how VBA can be used to access the new XML objects.

Chapter 10

WordprocessingML Introduction

Introduction

In a nutshell, WordprocessingML is Microsoft's XML format for Word documents. When you choose to save a document, you can either save it in the traditional DOC format or you can choose "XML Document." The amazing thing is that the WordprocessingML version will contain exactly the same content — even metadata — that the traditional DOC document would. (Initially, I was very skeptical of this claim. I had some 10 MB templates loaded with UserForms, classes, and VBA code. Saving to the XML format didn't result in any loss of data.)

The only exception I've encountered is that WordprocessingML does not embed TrueType fonts, which is understandable given the distribution rights involved. Of course, this is only problemeatic if the user does not have the necessary font installed. All of this functionality does not come easily. The WordprocessingML schema file is almost 7,000 lines long. Fortunately, you do not need to be intimately familiar with it to be productive. This chapter should provide enough information for you to hit the ground running.

The only prerequisites to understanding WordprocessingML is that you have a solid understanding of Word and understand namespaces, XML, and how XSLT is able to transform XML. The examples in this chapter will progress from the seemingly simple to the relatively complex.

Basic WordprocessingML

Because WordprocessingML is essentially just a collection of text information, you can create a Word document in any text editor. This is exciting for several reasons. If you've ever tried to create server-side Word documents, you know that the overhead associated with instantiating Word made this exercise simply futile. Now, dynamically creating a feature-rich Word document is as easy as creating a text file. In fact, you don't even need to have Word to create Word documents. All you need is the ability to create text. Our first example will explore creating WordprocessingML the old-fashioned way — with Notepad.

```
<?xml version="1.0"?>
<?mso-application progid="Word.Document"?>
<w:wordDocument xmlns:w="http://schemas.microsoft.com/office/
word/2003/WordprocessingML">
  <w:body>
    <w:p>
      <w:r>
        <w:t>Hello, WordprocessingML</w:t>
      </w:r>
    </w:p>
  </w:body>
</w:wordDocument>
```

Obviously, the first line is the general XML declaration. This is required for all XML documents. The second line, "mso-application," includes a processing instruction that tells your computer to associate Word with this instance of the XML. Normally, your default XML editor (or Internet Explorer) will open the XML document if you were to double-click the document. This instruction tells your computer to open an instance of Microsoft Word to open the document. You are free to remove this line and test this out on your machine. You can still choose File | Open to open the XML document; it will just not open by default. (Notice also that Windows Explorer recognizes the instruction and presents the file using the Word XML icon.) Microsoft Word will include this line in all XML documents.

The next item to note is the namespace declaration (http://schemas.microsoft.com/office/word/2003/ WordprocessingML). If you browsed examples earlier out on the web, you might have noticed several different declarations. Unfortunately, there are still several beta version examples out there that include incorrect namespace declarations in their XSLT stylesheets. I've talked to several users who experienced extreme frustration trying to get "simple" examples to work, only to find that the namespace declaration was incorrect and Word was interpreting the resultant XML as simple XML and not WordprocessingML — thus displaying tags and not transforming it correctly.

The root element that declares this a Word document is the w:wordDocument element. Interestingly, the only required child element is the w:body element. Again, you can see the implication for creating documents outside of Word. Microsoft has chosen to make it very easy to create documents. This is an interesting strategy to further proliferate the use of Word as a standard document editor.

We'll discuss these in more detail later, but the <w:p> tag stands for "paragraph," <w:r> stands for "run," and <w:t> stands for "text." Generally, the document's text will appear in this descending order of elements:

```
<w:p>
  <w:r>
     <w:t>[text here]</w:t>
  </w:r>
</w:p>
```

The Word team made a fundamental decision to use attributes purely according to the XML specification. The result is that attributes are used only for metadata. None of the elements in the above example can have attributes. This decision affects the interaction with Word's XML features.

If you have a schema that is rich with attributes or uses attributes to contain actual data (for instance, <userName data="scott"/>), you'll be better off using XSLT to transform your XML document prior to working with it in Word. (Attributes will not even be displayed in the UI.) The impact of this for WordprocessingML is that child elements are the vehicle to add properties to the objects. Unless these properties are changed in the WordprocessingML, Word will display the document using the default styles and properties within the Normal template.

Tip. As you'll see in Chapter 11, you don't need to intimately understand every element of WordprocessingML. The general formula for creating your own stylesheets is to create a base document and cut and paste the relevant pieces into your stylesheet.

The w:wordDocument Element

The first element of note is the wordDocument element, which will house all other elements and usually have a slew of namespace declarations. You can think of this as the namespace warehouse for WordprocessingML. Let's take a look at some of the common declarations that will occur in your WordprocessingML documents.

```
<w:wordDocument xmlns:w="http://schemas.microsoft.com/office/
        word/2003/wordml"
xmlns:v="urn:schemas-microsoft-com:vml"
xmlns:w10="urn:schemas-microsoft-com:office:word"
xmlns:sl="http://schemas.microsoft.com/schemaLibrary/2003/core"
xmlns:aml="http://schemas.microsoft.com/aml/2001/core"
xmlns:wx="http://schemas.microsoft.com/office/word/2003/
        auxHint"
xmlns:o="urn:schemas-microsoft-com:office:office"
xmlns:dt="uuid:C2F41010-65B3-11d1-A29F-00AA00C14882"
xmlns:ns6="schemas-MSWordXmlToolbox#09052004-123413"
w:macrosPresent="no" w:embeddedObjPresent="no"
w:ocxPresent="no" xml:space="preserve">
```

We can work through these namespaces rather painlessly by referencing the abbreviated namespace. The “w” prefix namespace is where all of the core WordprocessingML elements and attributes are defined. The “v” prefix namespace is included so that elements in this namespace represent embedded Vector Markup Language (VML) images. The “w10” prefix namespace is used for legacy elements from Word X. It is used in HTML output. The “sl” prefix namespace is used with Word’s custom XML schema functionality. The “aml” prefix namespace is used to reference the Annotation Markup Language (AML) elements that are used to describe tracked changes, comments, and bookmarks. The “wx” prefix namespace provides “auxiliary hints” for applications other than Word that attempt to render documents containing WordprocessingML. The “o” prefix namespace is for “shared” document properties and custom document properties. They are shared in that they also apply to other Office applications, such as Excel. The “dt” prefix namespace is the XML Data Reduced (XDR) namespace, which qualifies the data type attributes of a document’s custom document property elements. The “ns6” prefix namespace references our customer XSD schema created in Chapter 8.

It’s also important to note the remaining attributes in the wordDocument element. The xml:space attribute is set to “preserve.” This is so that whitespace characters within the XML file are interpreted correctly. In general, the industry practice is to leave this set to “preserve” to make everyone’s life easier. Keep in mind that you should include xml:space="preserve" on the root element of any WordprocessingML document you create. The last three attributes of the w:wordDocument element are all optional and default to the value “no.”

The w:macrosPresent attribute must be set to “yes” when the document will contain VBA macros. Most likely, you will not be creating VBA macros with WordprocessingML, so this will probably not be an issue. The w:embeddedObjPresent attribute must be set to “yes” if the document has embedded OLE objects. Finally, the w:ocxPresent attribute must be set to "yes" when a control from Word's Control Toolbox is used within the document. These attributes are not required and you can safely leave them out without affecting the presentation of the finished document.

Adding Text to the Document

There are many great references available on WordprocessingML and what the available tags mean. This chapter will look at how to *use* WordprocessingML rather than explain what all of the various aspects mean. The text that is held within the document will always be contained in the **body** element. Text within the **body** element is always kept in a nested set of three elements: **t** (a piece of text), **r** (a run of text within a paragraph), and **p** (a paragraph). Figure 10-1 shows how our simple "Hello, WordprocessingML" example XML structure looks when viewed as XML within Word 2003.

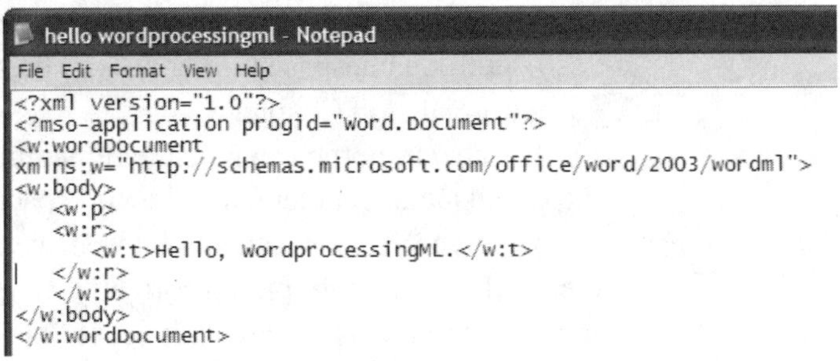

hello wordprocessingml - Notepad

File Edit Format View Help

```
<?xml version="1.0"?>
<?mso-application progid="Word.Document"?>
<w:wordDocument
xmlns:w="http://schemas.microsoft.com/office/word/2003/wordml">
<w:body>
   <w:p>
   <w:r>
      <w:t>Hello, WordprocessingML.</w:t>
   </w:r>
   </w:p>
</w:body>
</w:wordDocument>
```

Figure 10-1

The t (Text), r (Run), and p (Paragraph) Elements

As you can see, the lowest level of this hierarchy is the **t** element. This is the container for the text that makes up the document's content. This element will hold as much text as you need. As you'll see, it is impractical to think that you'll have a single **t** element because long runs of text will be broken up into paragraphs and strings with different formats. In addition, they may be interrupted by line breaks, graphics, tables, and other items in a Word document.

The **r** element is the top-level element for a run of text. This **r** element can contain multiple instances of **t** elements, with the **t** element representing the actual text to appear. Using the **r** element enables you to combine breaks, styles, and other formatting characteristics with the text contained within the root element of a particular text run. The <w:rPr> element is used to set the available properties for the text run and is always the first child of the **r** element.

The <w:rPr> element acts as a container for the property elements that will be applied to the rest of the children of the **r** element. The <w:rPr> container element provides a mechanism to control many options, including whether text in the following **t** elements is bold, underlined, or italicized. You can apply formatting via the <w:rPr> element, or you can apply individual styles to control the formatting of your resultant document.

Adding Sections

Sections are the mechanism WordprocessingML uses to control the layout of the page. The layout of the text that you insert will be subject to the properties that are applicable to that section of the document. The section element is defined by a section properties tag denoted by a <w:sectPr> element that appears at the *end* of each section. Word always inserts a <w:sectPr> element at the end of any new document that it creates.

New <w:sectPr> elements are created inside <w:pPr> elements every time new sections are added to a WordprocessingML document. The <w:sectPr> element indicates that one section has ended and a new one is beginning. The <w:sectPr> element will contain child elements that provide definition for the section immediately above where the elements show up. Figure 10-2 shows a <w:sectPr> element that indicates the end of a section. It defines the page width, page height, margins, and header/footer information.

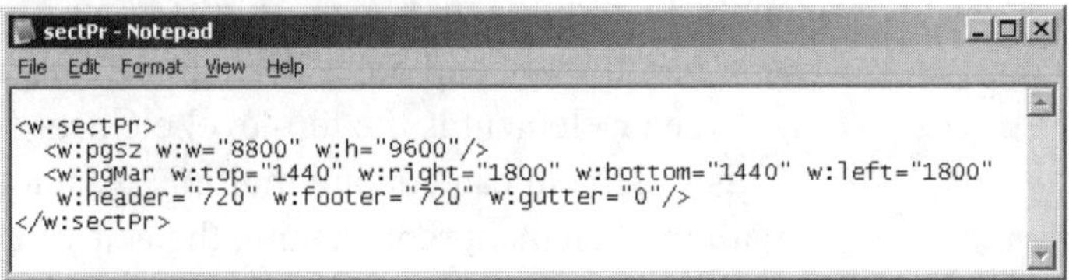

Figure 10-2

Note. The **sectPr** element isn't strictly required in a WordprocessingML document.

Inserting Breaks

If you're familiar with the <br> tag in HTML, you'll understand the section break in WordprocessingML. Typically, if you have multiple **t** elements in an **r** element, it's because you need to insert some other element in between the pieces of text. Figure 10-3 shows the WordprocessingML and the corresponding display when interpreted by Microsoft Word 2003. As you can see, the **br** element appears between the two **t** elements. This forces the second **t** element to a new line as displayed in Figure 10-4.

```
<?xml version="1.0"?>
<?mso-application progid="Word.Document"?>
<w:wordDocument
xmlns:w="http://schemas.microsoft.com/office/word/2003/wordml">
<w:body>
   <w:p>
   <w:r>
      <w:t>Hello, WordprocessingML.</w:t>
         <w:br w:type="text-wrapping"/>
      <w:t>Today is a great day.</w:t>
   </w:r>
   </w:p>
</w:body>
</w:wordDocument>
```

Figure 10-3

As you can see, the **br** element has a **type** attribute that allows you to specify the kind of break ("page," "column," "text-wrapping"). Because the default is "text-wrapping" (a new line), the **type** attribute in the previous example could have been omitted.

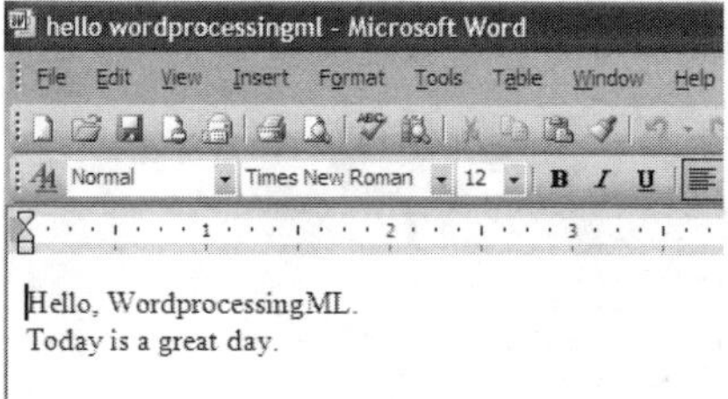

Figure 10-4

Creating Paragraphs

New paragraphs are defined in WordprocessingML using the **p** element. Keep in mind the difference between a break created with the **br** element with text-wrapping (equivalent to a "soft break" in Word — also created by pressing Shift + Enter) and a hard return that actually starts a new paragraph. Our existing WordprocessingML document with text in two separate paragraphs appears in Figure 10-5.

hello wordprocessingml - Notepad

File Edit Format View Help

```
<?xml version="1.0"?>
<?mso-application progid="Word.Document"?>
<w:wordDocument
xmlns:w="http://schemas.microsoft.com/office/word/2003/wordml">
<w:body>
 <w:p>
   <w:r>
      <w:t>Hello, WordprocessingML.</w:t>
   </w:r>
 </w:p>
 <w:p>
   <w:r>
      <w:t>Today is a great day.</w:t>
   </w:r>
 </w:p>
</w:body>
</w:wordDocument>
```

Figure 10-5

The resulting document is shown in Figure 10-6. As you can see in the formatting options in Figure 10-6, the paragraph marks are displayed at the end of each line. It's important to note the difference as the display of a

WordprocessingML document in Word may not reveal the actual structure of the document.

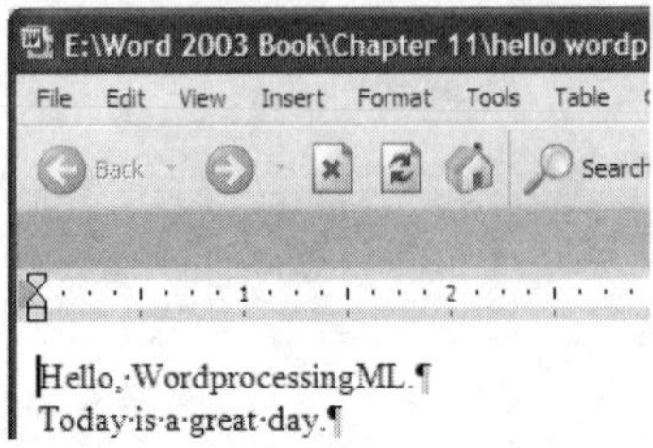

Figure 10-6

Inserting Tabs

Tab stops are defined in the <w:pPr> element, which is also a child of the **p** element. Within the <w:pPr> element, you can set the tab stops for the paragraph by using **tab** elements with the **tabs** element. The **tab** element allows you to position text horizontally on a line and move the following text to the next tab stop. Exactly where on the line that will be depends on how tab stops are defined in the document.

There are three attributes that you can use to set the parameters for an individual tab stop:

- **val**: This sets the type of tab to be used.
- **pos**: This sets the tab's position from the left edge of the document, in twips.
- **leader**: This defines the character used to fill the empty space between tab stops.

```
<w:pPr>
 <w:tabs>
  <w:tab  w:val ="center"     w:pos="1200"/>
  <w:tab  w:val="left"        w:pos="4200"/>
  <w:tab  w:val="decimal"     w:pos="7000"/>
 </w:tabs>
</w:pPr>
```

Figure 10-7

In Figure 10-7, you'll see that the paragraph has three tab stops at 0.8 of an inch (1200 twips), just shy of 3 inches (4200 twips), and another just shy of 5 inches (7000 twips), with each tab stop being a different type. There are 1440 twips to an inch. Figure 10-8 displays how Word 2003 interprets the XML and shows the tab stops in the document as well.

Caution. Tabs function only if the **xml:space** attribute is present on the **wordDocument** element and is set to "preserve."

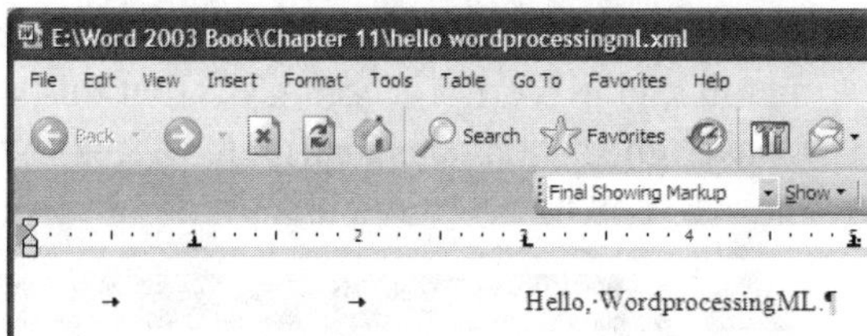

Figure 10-8

Formatting Text

Undoubtedly, the one area of WordprocessingML that you'll have the most frustration with is formatting (lists are discussed later in this book). The initial instinct is generally to apply formatting at the paragraph and run level. If you are a heavy Word user, you probably already know that the preferred mechanism of applying formatting is via Word's *styles*. If you're simply setting bold, underline, or italics for a single run, then you are probably okay. However, formatting via styles makes it easier to manage the appearance of your document.

No Mixed Content

There is one distinction to be cognizant of from the outset. WordprocessingML does things a little differently than HTML markup. In HTML, it is common to find formatting applied to individual words within a paragraph. For instance:

```
<p>Hello, <b>WordprocessingML.</b></p>
```

The above example simply applies bold formatting to the word "WordprocessingML," which is within paragraph tags. The natural instinct would be to attempt similar formatting with WordprocessingML, but this won't work. Instead, the sentence is distributed across two different text runs as shown in Figure 10-9.

hello wordprocessingml - Notepad

File Edit Format View Help

```
<?xml version="1.0"?>
<?mso-application progid="Word.Document"?>
<w:wordDocument
xmlns:w="http://schemas.microsoft.com/office/word/2003/wordml"
xml:space="preserve">
<w:body>
 <w:p>
  <w:pPr>
   <w:tabs>
    <w:tab  w:val ="center"     w:pos="1440"/>
    <w:tab  w:val="left"        w:pos="4320"/>
    <w:tab  w:val="decimal"     w:pos="7200"/>
   </w:tabs>
  </w:pPr>
  <w:r>
  <w:tab/>
   <w:tab/>
     <w:t>Hello, </w:t>
  </w:r>
  <w:r>
    <w:rPr>
     <w:b>
        <w:t>WordprocessingML.</w:t>
     </w:b>
    </w:rPr>
  </w:r>
 </w:p>
</w:body>
</w:wordDocument>
```

Figure 10-9

As you can see in Figure 10-9, the text is enclosed in two separate text runs. This produces the desired effect of having one word bolded within the sentence. The only difference is that it takes a little more text to produce than in HTML. Figure 10-10 shows how the above document looks when opened in Word 2003.

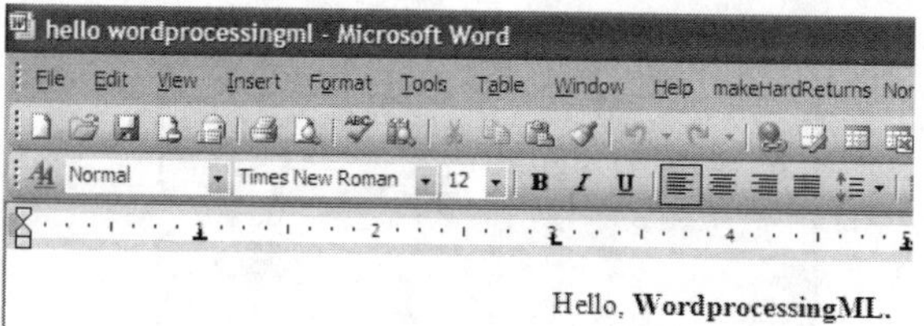

Figure 10-10

Formatting Runs of Text

You probably noticed in the above example that we made use of the <w:rPr> element. The property attributes for a particular run are defined via the <w:rPr> element. This element defines how a run is treated by Word by using property elements. Most of the children of the <w:rPr> element have a **val** attribute that is used to toggle the value on and off within the run. These are not strictly necessary as they default to "on" and can be terminated by an end tag if necessary. This means that the bolding element <w:b/> is equivalent to <w:b w:val=""on" />.

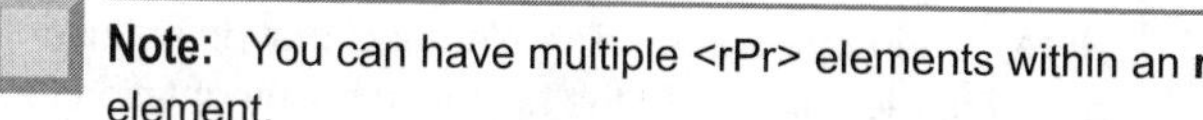

Note: You can have multiple <rPr> elements within an **r** element.

If the <w:rPr> element is present in a run, it must be the first element after the <w:r> tag. This is because the <w:rPr> element sets the properties for the entire run of text and controls how this text will be displayed. There are more than 40 possible children of the <w:rPr> element (including language-specific options), so we obviously won't be going into detail on each one of them. Table 10-1 displays the most commonly used options. In general, they correspond to the settings available on the Font dialog displayed in Figure 10-11.

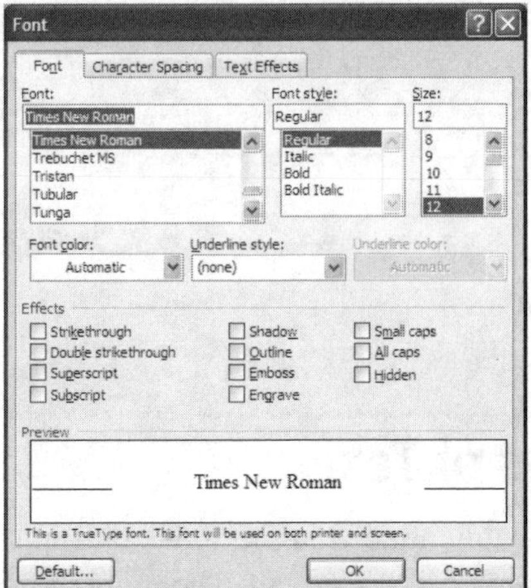

Figure 10-11

It's important to realize exactly what you are doing in relation to Word's styles when using the <w:rPr> element properties. You are essentially overriding the particular style that is applied to the run of text with <w:rPr> element properities.

Note: There are some <rPr> elements that do not use the **val** attribute. Please refer to the Microsoft documentation for more information. In other cases, some of the <rPr> children utilize the **val** attribute but have choices other than simply "on" and "off".

Figure 10-12 shows the XML structure for Word's Marching Red Ants text effect. In Table 10-1, you'll notice that several of the elements have the note "see Font dialog" for the values in the Definition column.

Tip. The best way to obtain the values you want is to create a document with the effect you are looking for and save it as XML. You can then open it up in the XML editor of your choice (Notepad is *not* good for this, so you'll want to arm yourself with something better) and search for the val attribute of the particular element you are looking to utilize.

```
hello wordprocessingml - Notepad
File Edit Format View Help
<?xml version="1.0"?>
<?mso-application progid="Word.Document"?>
<w:wordDocument
xmlns:w="http://schemas.microsoft.com/office/word/2003/wordml"
xml:space="preserve">
<w:body>
 <w:p>
  <w:pPr>
   <w:tabs>
    <w:tab  w:val ="center"    w:pos="1440"/>
    <w:tab  w:val="left"       w:pos="4320"/>
    <w:tab  w:val="decimal"    w:pos="7200"/>
   </w:tabs>
  </w:pPr>
  <w:r>
  <w:tab/>
   <w:tab/>
     <w:t>Hello, </w:t>
  </w:r>
  <w:r>
    <w:rPr>
     <w:effect w:val="ants-red">
         <w:t>WordprocessingML.</w:t>
         </w:effect>
    </w:rPr>
  </w:r>
 </w:p>
</w:body>
</w:wordDocument>
```

Figure 10-12

Figure 10-13 shows how Word interprets the **<w:effect w:val="ants-red">** tag in the XML document shown in Figure 10-12. This example could have also utilized a single, terminated **<w:effect w:val="ants-red" />** (note the " />" at the end) element within the <w:rPr> element. (In fact, this is the way Word 2003 would create the WordprocessingML representation.) This is because the effect property pertains to this individual run of text. It all goes back to the "No Mixed Content" topic described earlier.

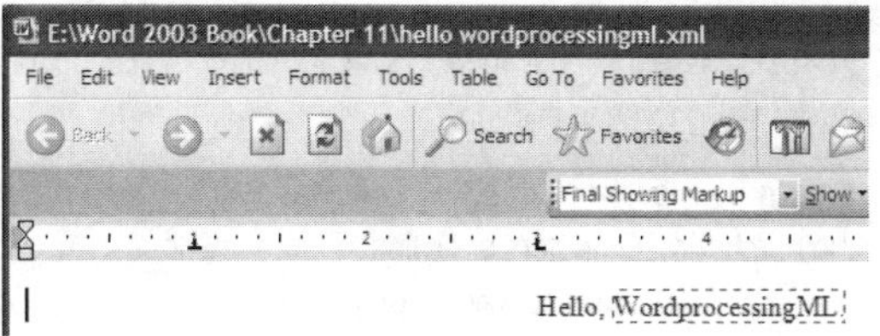

Figure 10-13

Table 10-1: Child elements of <w:rPr>

Element	Description	Definition
rStyle	This defines the character style for a run.	The character style is set in the styles section.
rFonts	Defines the fonts for a run.	A font named in the fonts section, or "default," "fareast," or "cs."
B	Sets Latin and Asian characters to bold.	"on" or "off"
b-cs	Sets complex script characters to bold.	"on" or "off"
I	Sets Latin and Asian characters to italic.	"on" or "off"
i-cs	Sets complex script characters to italic.	"on" or "off"
caps	Formats lowercase text as capital letters.	"on" or "off"
smallcaps	Formats lowercase text as capital letters and reduces their size.	"on" or "off"
strike	Draws a line through the text.	"on" or "off"
dstrike	Draws a double line through the text.	"on" or "off"
outline	Displays the inner and outer borders of each character.	"on" or "off"
shadow	Adds a shadow behind, beneath, and to the right of the text.	"on" or "off"
emboss	Makes text appear as if it is raised off the page in relief.	"on" or "off"
imprint	Makes selected text appear to be imprinted or pressed into page.	"on" or "off"
noproof	Formats the text so that spelling and grammar errors are ignored in this run.	"on" or "off"
snaptogrid	Sets the number of characters per line to match the number of characters specified in the docGrid element of the current section's properties.	"on" or "off"
vanish	Prevents the text in this run from being displayed or printed.	"on" or "off"
webHidden	Prevents the text in this run from being displayed when this document is saved as a web page.	"on" or "off"
color	Specifies either an automatic color or a hexadecimal color code for this run.	3-digit hexBinary or "auto"

Element	Description	Definition
spacing	The amount by which the spacing between characters is expanded or condensed.	Integer
W	Stretches or compresses text horizontally as a percentage of its current size.	Integer
kern	The smallest font size for which kerning should be automatically adjusted.	unsignedInt
position	The amount by which text should be raised or lowered in relation to the baseline.	Integer
Sz	Font size for the Asian and Latin fonts in this run.	Integer
sz-cs	Font size for complex script fonts in this run.	Integer
highlight	Highlights text so it stands out from the surrounding text.	"on" or "off"
U	Underline formatting for this run.	underlineValue (see Font dialog)
effect	Animated text effect for this run.	textEffectValues (see Font dialog)
bdr	Border for characters in this run.	borderValues (see Font dialog)
shd	Shading for characters in this run.	shdValues (see Font dialog)
fitText	Width of the space that this run fits into.	unsignedInt
vertAlign	Adjusts the vertical position of the text relative to the baseline and changes the font size if possible.	"baseline", "superscript", or "subscript"
Rtl	Sets the alignment and reading order for this run to right-to-left.	"on" or "off"
Cs	True if text in this run is complex script text.	"on" or "off"
Em	Sets the type of emphasis mark for this run.	"none", "dot", "comma", "circle", or "under-dot"
hyphen	Hyphenation style for this run.	String
lang	Languages for this run.	2-digit hexBinary or a string
asianLayout	Special Asian layout formatting properties.	See the schema.
specVanish	Property that makes text in this run always hidden.	"on" or "off"

Formatting Paragraphs

Nested within the **<w:p>** tag for paragraphs is a **<w:pPr>** element that defines the properties for a paragraph. We can take our existing Hello WordprocessingML example and remove the tabs in order to demonstrate how we can center the entire paragraph. The XML representation is shown in Figure 10-14.

```
hello wordprocessingml - Notepad
File Edit Format View Help
<?xml version="1.0"?>
<?mso-application progid="Word.Document"?>
<w:wordDocument
xmlns:w="http://schemas.microsoft.com/office/word/2003/wordml"
xml:space="preserve">
<w:body>
 <w:p>
  <w:pPr>
     <w:jc w:val="center"/>
  </w:pPr>
  <w:r>
     <w:t>Hello, </w:t>
  </w:r>
  <w:r>
    <w:rPr>
     <w:effect w:val="ants-red"/>
       <w:t>WordprocessingML.</w:t>
    </w:rPr>
  </w:r>
 </w:p>
</w:body>
</w:wordDocument>
```

Figure 10-14

The XML shown in Figure 10-14 displays the result shown in Figure 10-15. Notice that we are still using multiple **<w:r>** elements within the XML structure to achieve the desired effect. In addition, the above example uses the terminated tag structure that was discussed earlier.

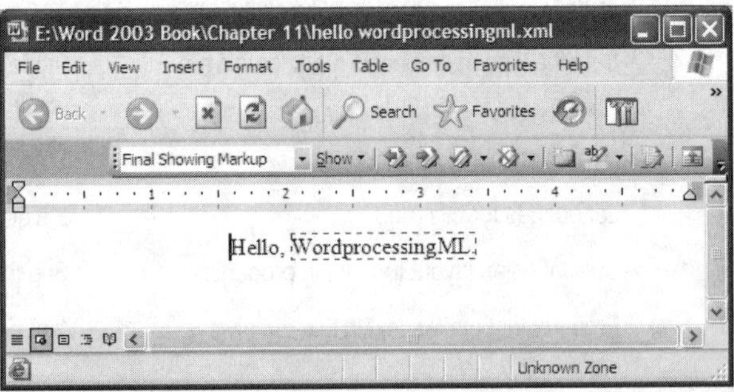

Figure 10-15

Table 10-2: Child elements of <w:pPr>

Element	Description	Definition
pStyle	This is used to set the Paragraph style.	String (a style defined in the styles element of the document)
keepNext	Prevents a page break between this paragraph and the next.	"on" or "off"
keepLines	Prevents a page break in this paragraph.	"on" or "off"
pageBreakBefore	Forces a page break before this paragraph.	"on" or "off"
framePr	Text frame and drop cap properties.	FramePrProperty
widowControl	Prevents Word from printing the last line of a paragraph by itself at the top of the page (widow) or the first line of a paragraph at the bottom of a page (orphan).	"on" or "off"
listPr	List properties.	listPrElt
supressLineNumbers	Prevents line numbers from appearing next to the paragraph. This setting has no effect in documents or sections with no line numbers.	"on" or "off"
pBdr	Borders for the paragraph.	pBdrElt
shd	Paragraph shading.	ShdValues
tabs	A container holding a list of tab elements.	tabsElt
suppressAutoHyphens	Prevents automatic hyphenation.	"on" or "off"
bidi	Sets the alignment and reading order for a paragraph to right-to-left.	"on" or "off"
adjustRightInd	Automatically adjusts the right indent when you are using the document grid.	"on" or "off"
snapToGrid	Aligns text to document grid (when defined).	"on" or "off"
spacing	Spacing between lines and paragraphs.	Two attributes: before, after. Each contains spacing distance in twips.
Ind	Paragraph indentation.	Integer (twips)
contextualSpacing	Don't add space between paragraphs of the same style.	"on" or "off"
suppressOverlap	Don't allow this frame to overlap.	"on" or "off"

Element	Description	Definition
Jc	Paragraph alignment.	"left", "right", "center", "both", "medium-kashida", "distribute", "list-tab", "high-kashida", "low-kashida", "thai-distribute"
textDirection	Orientation for the paragraph in the current cell, text box, or text frame.	"lr-tb", "tb-rl", "bt-lr", "lr-tb-v", "tb-rl-v"
outlineLvl	Outline level.	Integer
divId	ID of HTML DIV element this paragraph is currently in.	Integer
rPr	Run properties for the paragraph mark.	Properties for all r elements within this p element
sectPr	Section properties for the section that terminates at this paragraph mark.	Contains the properties for the section. Appears in the last paragraph in the section.

Utilizing Styles

Styles are a basic tool Word utilizes that allow you to create a group of style properties that can be applied as a unit either to individual paragraphs (within the <w:pPr> element) or runs (within the <w:rPr> element). You can use styles to streamline the formatting of the WordprocessingML text that you create. You can also minimize the amount of work required to change your document's appearance. The main advantage of using styles is that changing the appearance of a particular style cascades to all text that is subject to that style.

There are four possible style types in Word:

- Paragraph
- Character
- Table
- List

Every paragraph, run, table, and list in a Word document is associated with a style of the corresponding type. You've probably noticed that we haven't explicitly set any styles in our examples thus far. If a paragraph, run, table, or list in a WordprocessingML document doesn't explicitly specify an associated style, then it takes on the document's default style of the appropriate style type.

Note: If you are using Word, you are using styles — even if you aren't specifically aware of the particular style you are using.

When you create a new blank document in Word, you are creating a document attached to the Normal.dot document template. This means that all of the styles defined in your particular Normal.dot are available for use in the newly created document. These include, at minimum, a default style definition for each style type. If you don't include a <w:styles> element in your WordprocessingML, Word automatically creates the <w:fonts> element for you. In fact, if you save out your newly created WordprocessingML document as XML, Word will automatically insert four <w:style> elements, corresponding respectively to the four style types (paragraph, character, table, and list).

Defining Styles

The primary name of a style is denoted by the **w:val** attribute of the <w:name> element. This corresponds to the name shown in the Style drop-down menu in the Word 2003 Styles dialog. Also, for styles that came from a template, the primary name uniquely identifies the style in the attached template and is the basis by which styles are updated when the "Automatically update document styles" document option is turned on.

WordprocessingML uses the <w:styles> element to define the styles available to a particular document. This element is a top-level container directly beneath the

<w:wordDocument> element. There will be one <w:styles> element, and it will have one or more <w:style> elements underneath it. Each of these <w:style> elements defines a single style. All of the particular style information is kept in children of the <w:style> element.

There are three attributes that pertain to the <w:style> element:

- The **type** attribute specifies the type of style.
- The **styleId** attribute gives your style a name (used when invoking style in your WordprocessingML document).
- The **default** attribute indicates that this is the default style for a particular type of style.

For our example file, you should save out a Word document as XML. You can then navigate to the <w:styles> tag in the XML file using the XML editor of your choice. I've cut and pasted a portion of such a tag in Figure 10-16. You will probably have to work a little to get this section correct. There are a few things to keep in mind. You can cut a particular <w:style> XML section out of the WordprocessingML, but it still has to be nested within the <w:styles> </w:styles> elements — even if there is only one style.

hello wordprocessingml - Notepad

File Edit Format View Help

```
<?xml version="1.0"?>
<?mso-application progid="Word.Document"?>
<w:wordDocument
xmlns:w="http://schemas.microsoft.com/office/word/2003/wordml"
xml:space="preserve">
<w:styles>
<w:style w:type="paragraph" w:styleId="Heading1">
        <w:name w:val="heading 1"/>
        <w:basedOn w:val="Normal"/>
        <w:next w:val="Normal"/>
        <w:link w:val="Heading1Char"/>
        <w:rsid w:val="00FF3551"/>
        <w:pPr>
                <w:pStyle w:val="Heading1"/>
                <w:keepNext/>
                <w:spacing w:before="240" w:after="60"/>
                <w:outlineLvl w:val="0"/>
        </w:pPr>
        <w:rPr>
                <w:rFonts w:ascii="Arial" w:h-ansi="Arial" w:cs="Arial"/>
                <w:b/>
                <w:b-cs/>
                <w:kern w:val="32"/>
                <w:sz w:val="32"/>
                <w:sz-cs w:val="32"/>
        </w:rPr>

</w:style>
</w:styles>
<w:body>
 <w:p>
   <w:pPr>
        <w:pStyle w:val="Heading1"/>
   </w:pPr>
   <w:r>
     <w:t>Hello, WordprocessingML.</w:t>
   </w:r>
 </w:p>
</w:body>
</w:wordDocument>
```

Figure 10-16

Note that we have only declared the "**w**" namespace. By default, Word 2003 saves out information in a "**wx**" namespace as well. These elements are strictly informational and have all been deleted from the example below. You will want to do the same thing. When you remove or change the "**wx**" attributes' values, Word doesn't behave any differently when interpreting the file. Elements and attributes in the namespace designated by the "**wx**" prefix are for our benefit only and are of no internal use to Word. Figure 10-17 shows how our WordprocessingML is interpreted when viewed by Word 2003.

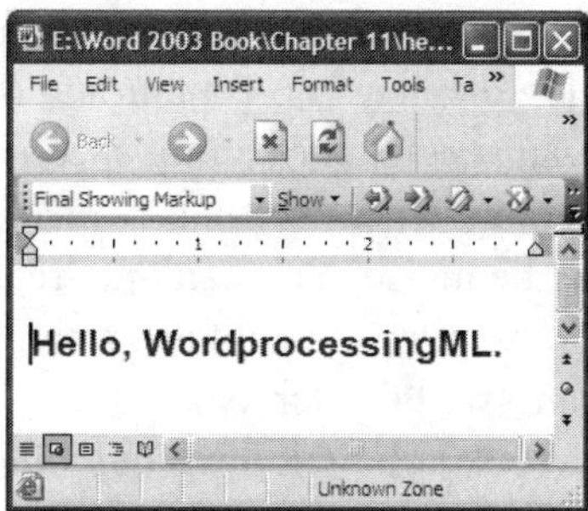

Figure 10-17

Extending Styles

The <w:basedOn> element is used to create a style based on another style. This element essentially allows you to extend an existing style. You can create variations on a style by altering or overriding the properties of the base style. As you can see in Figure 10-16, we've based this style on "Normal" to make use of the Normal style in the Normal.dot file. Keep in mind that the order of the <w:style> elements doesn't matter. You can use a **basedOn** style to extend <w:style> elements that occur either before or after it in the course of the document. The other child elements of the <w:style> element are:

- **name**: This is the name that will be displayed in the Style drop-down list.

- **locked**: This prevents end users from overriding the style.
- **hidden**: This prevents end users from seeing the style.
- **next**: This specifies the style to be used on new paragraphs.

Style Properties

As you can see in our examples, you create a style by adding the appropriate children to the <w:style> element. Every <w:style> element can contain <w:rPr> and <w:pPr> children that can specify formatting specific to the <w:r> and <w:p> sections. These settings override the character styles that may be in use. You can only refer to paragraph styles within a <w:pPr> element and only to character styles within an <w:rPr> element.

When you look at how it turns out all together, our WordprocessingML example defines a style that left-justifies the paragraph and combines the bold within the <w:rPr> tags and Arial font defined within <w:pPr> tags.

Property Conflicts

Word needs a predefined way to deal with conflicts because properties can be set at the **style**, **p**, and **r** element levels. Word defines three rules that are used to determine which properties will be in effect in a particular situation. These rules are as follows:

- Settings at the run level created via the <w:rPr> or <w:pPr> elements override any settings made in a style.
- If either of the <w:pStyle> or <w:rStyle> elements turns on a feature, then the feature is turned on regardless of other settings.
- The default style is only applicable if no explicit style is defined and no local setting is made.

Fonts

In general, there are two different things you can do when working with fonts in WordprocessingML: You can provide Word with information about the fonts being used in a document, and you can control the font used to display the text in the document.

Specifying Fonts

The <w:fonts> element specifies which fonts are used in your document. Every font that is in use in a particular document can take advantage of the default font properties that Word uses. In addition, you can use Word's font management system to specify default fonts when the requested font isn't available. The <w:fonts> element does not affect your document's appearance. It is simply a place to define information about the fonts used in a particular document.

Using Fonts

The <w:defaultFont> element specifies the default fonts for the document. This element controls the fonts to be used for displaying the text in the document. (Of course, as we've seen, this font can be overridden by a style or an <w:rPr> child element.) The <w:defaultFont> element uses attributes that allow you to specify the default fonts for four character sets: **ascii**, **fareast**, **h-ansi**, and **cs**. These character sets can be location specific, so be sure to check your local documentation.

Overriding the default font is accomplished by using the <w:rFonts> element in the <w:rPr> element. This is done either in the <w:rPr> element before the t element with the text or in an <w:rPr> element inside a <w:rPr> element. The <w:rFonts> element takes the same parameters (attributes) as the <w:defaultFonts> element. For example, the following element sets the font for a text run to the Tahoma font:

```
</w:style>
</w:styles>
<w:body>
 <w:p>
   <w:pPr>
        <w:pStyle w:val="Heading1"/>
   </w:pPr>
   <w:r>
     <w:t>Hello, WordprocessingML.</w:t>
   </w:r>
 </w:p>
 <w:p>
  <w:r>
   <w:rPr>
      <w:rFonts w:ascii="Tahoma" w:h-ansi="Tahoma" w:cs="Tahoma"/>
   </w:rPr>
   <w:t>Today is a great day to be alive.</w:t>
  </w:r>
 </w:p>
</w:body>
</w:wordDocument>
```

Figure 10-18

The font used to display your text doesn't have to be predefined in the <w:fonts> element at the start of the document. In this case, Word will attempt to choose an appropriate font from those available on the machine on which it is currently running. This may result in unforeseen results if Word chooses a poor substitute.

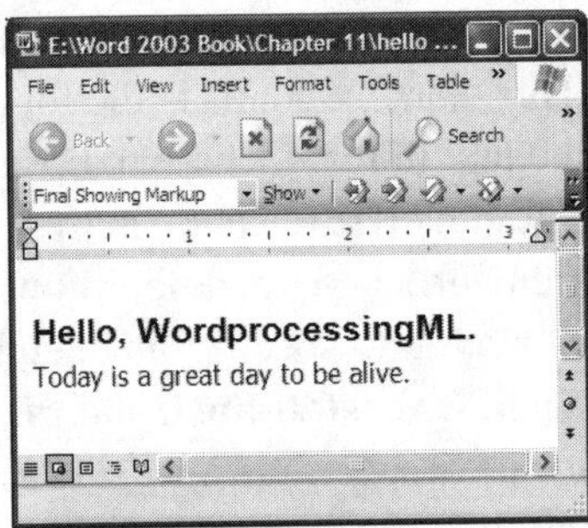

Figure 10-19

Conclusion

This chapter has served as an introduction to WordprocessingML. WordprocessingML is Microsoft's new XML format for Word documents. This format basically exposes the internal Word object model in an XML format. This allows you to create Word documents in an XML format in sources other than Word (even applications as simple as Notepad). Understanding WordprocessingML is important for server-side document creation and for the fundamental pieces of smart document solutions. As we continue working through future examples, you will continue to see examples of WordprocessingML in use. The next chapter expands on WordprocessingML and introduces XSLT as a solution to implement WordprocessingML as a document creation tool.

Chapter 11

XSLT Introduction

Introduction

XSL is an enormous topic in and of itself. This chapter attempts to provide a basic introduction to the way that XSLT stylesheets are used to process XML documents and give a little background on how this applies to Word 2003. XSLT is capable of performing very complex transformations. Essentially, it is a programming language itself that can shuffle, duplicate, suppress, order, delete, and add all of the XML objects available to it.

XSL is generally comprised of XSL-FO (formatting objects) and XSLT (transformation). XSLT was designed to transform an XML document into a different XML document by applying various transformation rules and utilizing a "processing engine" that takes both the source XML document and an XSLT stylesheet, which contains the transformation rules. This transformation occurs because of the XSLT stylesheet and the use of the XSL rules/transformation process. The XSL processor may then display the transformed document in a browser, print it, convert it to another format such as PDF, or email it to a predefined location.

A typical scenario involves several different companies that must communicate electronically. Consider several large banks working together to participate in a large loan. Due to the sheer size of the loan, the banks may want to spread the risk of the transaction among several different banks. Of course, they must be able to process each others' information. Each of their internal systems may use similar documents, but the systems will probably utilize different internal formats. To communicate they need to translate their various document types into a common one — XML. XSLT transformation is a good tool to transform the data so that it can be consumed by each of the different banks.

This chapter will introduce some basic concepts concerning the ability of XSLT to transform XML. You can think of Word 2003 as its own processing engine because it will take an XML source file and an XSLT stylesheet and transform the source file into WordprocessingML. WordprocessingML is the Word XML equivalent of the proprietary .doc format. It is even possible to use a WordprocessingML file as a source file and transform the contents into something else entirely using XSLT.

XSLT Stylesheets

Generally, XSLT looks remarkably similar to ordinary XML. In fact, XSLT stylesheets must adhere to all of the rules of XML. XSLT stylesheets are merely a specialized form of XML markup designed for specifying the transformation rules that will be applied to other XML documents. You can think of XSLT as just another document type. Figure 11-1 shows the shell configuration of a stylesheet. It starts with a general XML declaration followed by the specific stylesheet declaration.

```
<?xml version='1.0'?>
<xsl:stylesheet version="1.0" xmlns:xsl="http://www.w3.org/1999/XSL/Transform">

<xsl:template match="/">

</xsl:template>

</xsl:stylesheet>
```

Figure 11-1

This xsl:stylesheet declaration is also the root node of the XML document. Every stylesheet must have a namespace declaration for XSLT. This is what indicates that the XML document is in fact a stylesheet. The output file format can be specified using <xsl:output method="xml" /> to choose among producing XML, HTML, or plain text output.

The <xsl:stylesheet> element is where the various template rules will be specified. These template rules describe how the transformation will apply to each specific element within the source document. This should give you a glimpse into the complex nature of XSLT. You can specify different rules for every element type and attribute. Real-world XML files often contain hundreds or even thousands of different elements. Particular elements could even be processed differently if they share a type but have different attributes associated with them.

A Brief Look at HTML with XSLT

Most XSLT implementations provide the ability to transform XML into HTML. This is necessitated by the prevalence of web browsers and the ability to view data in a user-friendly graphical format. The most frequent scenario involves data being returned to a web application in an XML format. The web application must then present its traditional HTML display and transform the XML data into HTML for representation on the page. Thus, it is a combination of raw HTML and transformed XML being presented to the browser. This is very common when browsing table-driven data on web pages. Of course, there are a vast number of other concerns regarding persistence of data and updates to the data, but for the purposes of this chapter we are merely discussing the presentation of the XML being transformed.

It also takes advantage of many web designers' knowledge of HTML. If you format a document using element types from HTML, the page will look to a browser as if it had been created in HTML directly. You can think of this process as a conversion from XML markup to HTML markup. It is a useful way to publish XML documents to the web.

The shell of a stylesheet that generates HTML elements might look something similar to Figure 11-2.

```
<?xml version='1.0'?>
<xsl:stylesheet version="1.0" xmlns:xsl="http://www.w3.org/1999/XSL/Transform">
<xsl:output method="html" />

<xsl:template match="/">

</xsl:template>

</xsl:stylesheet>
```

Figure 11-2

Rules, Patterns, and Templates

XSLT Syntax

XSLT has a fairly straightforward syntax when you get used to working with it. It's important to note that any use of XSLT will adhere to XML's well-formedness rules. The following snippet displays the basic layout of an XSLT stylesheet. The "id" attribute is used to assign an identification number to the particular stylesheet. The "version" attribute can be used to track changes to the life cycle of the XSLT transform. The "xmlns" attribute represents the namespace for XSLT. The actual XSL stylesheet can be a collection of one or more templates.

```
<xsl:stylesheet
     id = id
     version = number
     xmlns = http://www.w3.org/1999/XSL/Transform>
     Style Rules here
     ......................
</xsl:stylesheet>
```

XSLT Template Details

The general syntax for a template rule is shown below. The "match" attribute specifies the XPath query that defines a node or set of nodes. These are the nodes that the processing instructions will manipulate. The XSLT processor takes all the instructions and literal elements and outputs them into a result tree.

```
<xsl:template match="node-set">
     .....instructions
     .....instructions
</xsl:template>
```

Processing Instructions

When an XSLT processor evaluates a template, it first generates a representation of the XML as a node tree. This tree is a representation of the hierarchical structure of the XML document that resides in memory for use by the XSLT processor. This representation includes the various relationships among the elements of the XML file. This includes whether they are children, parents, ancestors, descendants, or siblings relative to any other node inside the XML file.

Once this representation is created, the XSLT processor can begin working through the processing instructions that are defined in the template. The first step is to find the matching node according to the match attribute. Once the match is made, the XSLT processor will attempt to process the XML and generate a result. This result may be to create brand new elements and attributes depending upon the instruction. Following is a list of the commonly used processing instructions that make up an XSLT stylesheet. This list is by no means complete and is intended to expose you to the most commonly used features and functions of XSLT. Each of these will be discussed briefly below.

<xsl:apply-templates>
<xsl:value-of>
<xsl:output>
<xsl:element>
<xsl:attribute>
<xsl:text>
<xsl:when>
<xsl:if>
<xsl:for-each>
<xsl:comment>
<xsl:sort>
<xsl:copy>
<xsl:number>

<xsl:apply-templates>

<xsl:apply-templates> is the most basic XSLT instruction. It directs the XSLT processor to find the appropriate template to apply. This instruction is based on the type and the context of the selected node. This is generally used to incorporate other templates into the current processing instruction.

Syntax:

```
<xsl:apply-templates
     select="expression"
     mode="mode name">
</xsl:apply-templates>
```

<xsl:value-of>

The <xsl:value-of> instruction retrieves the value of a specified node and inserts the value as text. This is an instruction that you will work with frequently when creating WordprocessingML. You can think of this particular instruction as a brother of the SQL SELECT statement except that we are dealing directly with an XML document.

Syntax:

```
<xsl:value-of
    select = expression
    disable-output-escaping = "yes"|"no">
</xsl:value-of>
```

<xsl:output>

The <xsl:output> element specifies the option to use in creating the result tree. This applies to general XSLT transformations. For the purposes of this book we are actually creating XML — in the form of WordprocessingML. However, the XML we are creating can be interpreted and displayed as a Word document thanks to the new XML features of Word 2003.

The result tree output can be:

- XML
- HTML
- Text

Syntax:

```
<xsl:output
    method="xml"|"html"|"text"
    version="version"
    encoding=encoding
    omit-xml-declaration="yes"|"no"
    standalone="yes" | "no"
    cdata-section-elements=QNames
    indent="yes"|"no" />
```

<xsl:element>

The <xsl:element> instruction is used to create an XML element in the resultant output. This instruction creates an element and lets you specify the name with the "name" attribute. You can also use predefined attributes with the "use-attribute-sets" attribute.

Syntax:

```
<xsl:element
     name="element-name"
     use-attribute-sets=attribute set names>
</xsl:element>
```

<xsl:attribute>

If you need to create an attribute within an element you can do so by using the <xsl:attribute> instruction. It creates an attribute node and attaches it to the currently specified output element.

Syntax:

```
<xsl:attribute
     name = "attribute-name">
</xsl:attribute>
```

<xsl:text>

The <xsl:text> instruction is another mechanism to create text nodes within your output. This instruction is frequently used to create whitespace in the resulting output. Generally, XSLT processors will ignore whitespace in the other instructions but maintain the whitespace specified in this particular instruction. You may also use the <xsl:preserve-space> element to preserve whitespace in the resultant document. When "disable-output-escaping" is set to "yes," the element will be placed in the resultant document literally without the use of escape characters.

Syntax:

```
<xsl:text
     disable-output-escaping="yes"|"no">
</xsl:text>
```

<xsl:when>

The <xsl:when> element appears within an <xsl:choose> instruction and specifies a conditional set of instructions to execute if the when statement is true.

Syntax:

```
<xsl:when
     test=boolean-expression>
</xsl:when>
```

<xsl:if>

The <xsl:if> instruction is the main conditional operator within XSLT. The "test" attribute provides the condition in the source data to test. The instructions embedded within the if statement are only processed if the condition specified in the "test" attribute is evaluated to *true*.

Syntax:

```
<xsl:if
     test=boolean-expression>
</xsl:if>
```

<xsl:for-each>

<xsl:for-each> is the main looping structure used to process sets of nodes within XSLT. (This instruction will also evaluate a single node.) The nodes are selected by the expression contained in the "select" attribute. Each of these nodes is then processed according to the instructions below.

Syntax:

```
<xsl:for-each
     select=expression>
</xsl:for-each>
```

<xsl:comment>

<xsl-comment> generates a comment element in the output document. The text generated appears between the starting "<!--" characters and the ending "-->" characters. The nodes generated by this instruction will not be evaluated by any further processing.

Syntax:

```
<xsl:comment>
     Comment text
</xsl:comment>
```

<xsl:sort>

<xsl:sort> sets a sort criteria for node lists selected by <xsl:apply-templates>. For each of the nodes selected that the sort operator is working on (specified by either: <xsl:apply-templates> or <xsl:for-each>), the sort instruction creates a sort key by evaluating the expression held in the "select" attribute and creating a key for it. The nodes are then sorted according to this key. The "data-type" attribute determines whether the nodes are sorted by alphabetic or numeric order. The optional "order" attribute specifies whether the sort is in increasing or decreasing order. The default if this attribute is omitted is ascending. The optional "case-order" attribute specifies whether the sort will have upper- or lowercase letters listed first in the sort. The default if this attribute is omitted is to list uppercase letters first.

Syntax:

```
<xsl:sort
     select=expression
     lang="lang"
```

```
    data-type="text"|"number"
    order="ascending" | "descending"
    case-order="upper-first"|"lower-first"
/>
```

<xsl:copy>

The <xsl:copy> instruction copies the current node from the source to the output. If the current node is the root node, the children of the copy are the result of applying the <xsl:copy> instruction. If the current node is a child element, then any namespace nodes from the original element are actually copied over.

Syntax:

```
<xsl:copy
    use-attribute-sets="att set names">
</xsl:copy>
```

<xsl:number>

The <xsl:number> instruction inserts a formatted number into the result document. This is most often used in WordprocessingML when trying to keep an incremental counter to number table rows or list items. You control what number is generated by using the "level," "count," and "from" attributes. The number is formatted according to the format-number() function. The "format" attribute is a series of tokens that specifies the format to be used for each number in the list. If there are no format tokens, the default value of 1 is used, which generates a sequence 1 2 … 10 11 12…. Each number after the first is separated from the immediately preceding number by the separator token preceding the format token used to format that number. If there are no separator tokens, a period character is used (".").

The "value" attribute defines the expression that will be converted to a number and output to the result tree. If no "value" attribute is specified, the <xsl:number> element inserts a number based on the position of the current node in the source tree.

The “lang” attribute specifies which of the predefined language’s alphabet is used. If no lang value is specified, the language is determined from the system environment.

Syntax:

```
<xsl:number
    level="single" | "multiple" | "any"
    count=pattern
    from=pattern
    value=number-expression
    lang=nmtoken
    format=string
/>
```

The Microsoft Transform Inference Tool

As you’ve seen, creating a complete XSLT Transform from scratch could be a fairly daunting task. Fortunately, Microsoft has recently provided a free tool available as a download from their web site to help you with the process. The Transform Inference tool allows you to create XSLT transformations easily that can help you quickly transform similar XML files into documents with complex and rich formatting.

You begin using the tool with a raw XML file that is representative of the XML files you wish to transform. You then apply formatting to the XML file in Microsoft Word 2003 such that it becomes a template of how you want to format all other similar XML files. When completed, this document is called the seed document and is used by the Transform Inference tool to create the transform.

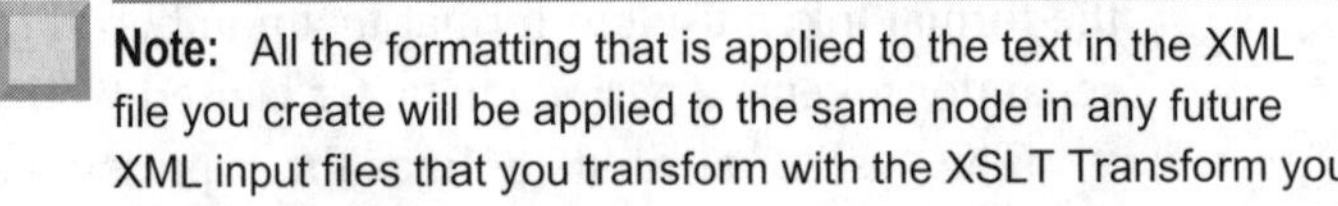

Note: All the formatting that is applied to the text in the XML file you create will be applied to the same node in any future XML input files that you transform with the XSLT Transform you create with the Inference tool.

The Transform Inference tool is purely a command-line tool. This means that there is no graphical user interface that you will use to interact with it. Instead, you’ll need to know where the files you are working with are and you'll need to use the Windows command line. (You can invoke it in WinXP by selecting **Start | Run** and then typing **cmd** into the resulting window as shown in Figure 11-3.)

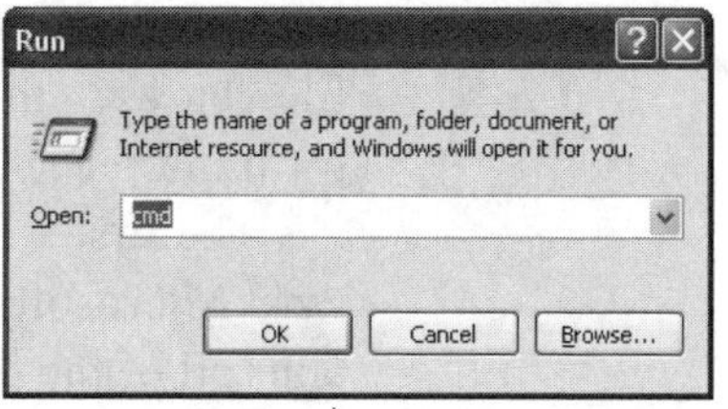

Figure 11-3

You can obtain the Transform Inference tool by visiting Microsoft's site and searching for "Transform Inference Tool." The installation procedure is very straightforward. Once you've installed the tool you may need to move some files around to make your life easier. After installing, try typing "wml2xslt" at the command line. If Windows does not recognize the command, you can either add the location of the files to your path or copy the appropriate files to the C:\windows\system32 directory. This allows you to work with the files from the command line in any directory. Otherwise, you'll have to manually navigate to the default installation directory from the command line. Figure 11-4 shows the highlighted files that should be copied.

Figure 11-4

For this quick example, we'll use the topstories.xml RSS from Yahoo!. These files are freely downloadable by navigating your web browser to http://rss.news.yahoo.com/rss/topstories. This file is an up-to-date compilation of all the Yahoo! News top story files. In this case, we'll be working with RSS 2.0 and will be able to create an XSLT

Transform that should work with any RSS 2.0 compliant file you want to use. The important thing is that the Transform Inference tool will actually be doing the work for us.

The first step in using the Inference tool is to create what Microsoft calls a seed document. This document contains all of the default formatting that you will want the Transform Inference tool to recognize. You can begin creating your seed document by opening an RSS file in Word 2003. In this case, you don't need to work with all of the repeating groups that appear in the RSS file, but you may want to keep at least two so that Word knows it is a repeating group. In addition, as you're working with your document it is always important to keep viewing it in Internet Explorer to make sure the document is well formed. In Word, delete all but two or three of the repeating groups, making sure to keep the document well formed. Figure 11-5 shows the general RSS structure with an Item node highlighted.

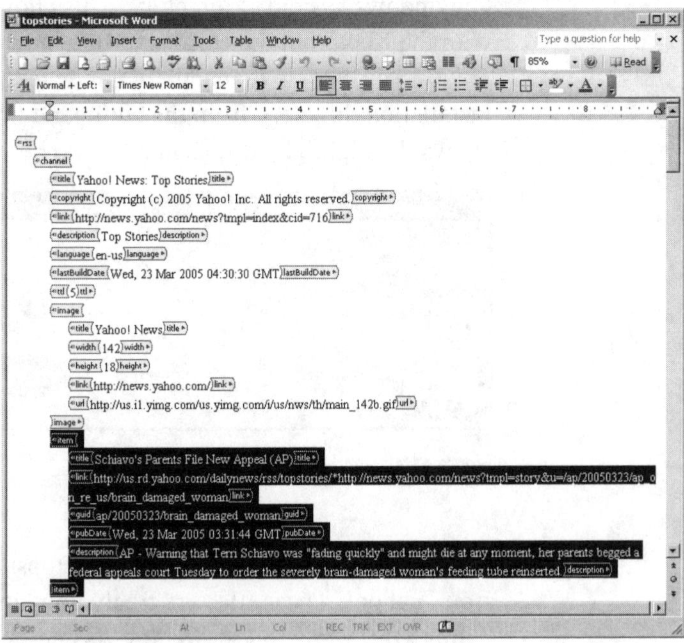

Figure 11-5

In order to use the Transform Inference tool you will need to have your seed document attached to an XSD schema. We've walked through creating and attaching schemas in previous chapters, but here is a quick reminder of how to accomplish this: (1) You need to download and install the Word XML Toolbox from www.microsoft.com, (2) choose Generate Inferred Schema from the XML Toolbox for your current XML file (in this case, the RSS file you are working with), and (3) follow the menu prompts and respond accordingly.

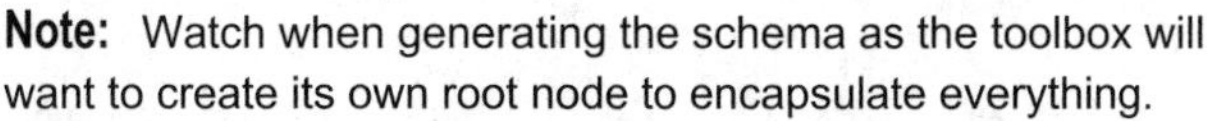

Note: Watch when generating the schema as the toolbox will want to create its own root node to encapsulate everything.

Once you have your schema created, mark up the XML document in any way you choose. Remember, you are only responsible for the Word formatting; the Transform Inference tool will take care of creating the resultant XSLT. The idea is to format each element in the file the way you want that element formatted in other similar files to which you will apply the transform. The files that receive the transform are called input files. Therefore, as a general rule, the seed document should contain at least one of every element that appears in the input files. You'll want to iterate through this process so that you can see the resultant XSLT and WordprocessingML for each of the changes that you make. Mark up the document as you'd like — alternating between toggling the XML tags on and off.

Once you've created your marked-up document, save it as WordprocessingML (don't save it as Data only) and invoke the command-line utility. Figure 11-6 shows the argument structure for the Transform Inference tool. It takes the qualified path of the XML document that you want to base the transform on as one of the arguments. Next, you can apply optional switches (described in the command utility) to pass parameters to the Inference tool. Figure 11-6 also shows these switches as they appear in Windows.

```
Command Prompt
Microsoft Windows XP [Version 5.1.2600]
(C) Copyright 1985-2001 Microsoft Corp.

C:\Documents and Settings\Scott>cd\

C:\>wml2xslt

wml2xslt.exe <seed document> [options]
 -o <outputfile> Outputs the generated XSLT to <outputfile>
 -ns <namespace> Process only <namespace> in the seed document
 -nsa            Processes all arbitrary XML namespaces in the seed document
 -os <node>      Orders the children of <node> according to the seed document
 -oi <node>      Orders the children of <node> according to inputs (default)
 -mx             Template mixed content as well as leaf nodes
 -db             Use databinding mode (see documentation) in the generated XSLT
 -v              Produce verbose error messages
 -nf             Produce XSLT, even if errors are encountered
 If two switches conflict, the rightmost is used.

The path is not of a legal form.
File load failed

C:\>_
```

Figure 11-6

Repeating Elements in Your Seed Document

When you format repeating elements in the seed document, the WML2XSLT tool recognizes them and includes them in the resulting transformation. In the seed document, the formatting of an element is considered any formatting that is applied both to its contents as well as some surrounding elements. You are not limited to just one type of formatting for each element. If you have three instances of the same element in your seed document, the input document gets exactly the same formatting as applied in the seed document, and any further elements get the formatting of the last instance specified. Therefore, an element takes the exact formatting of the text contained within it.

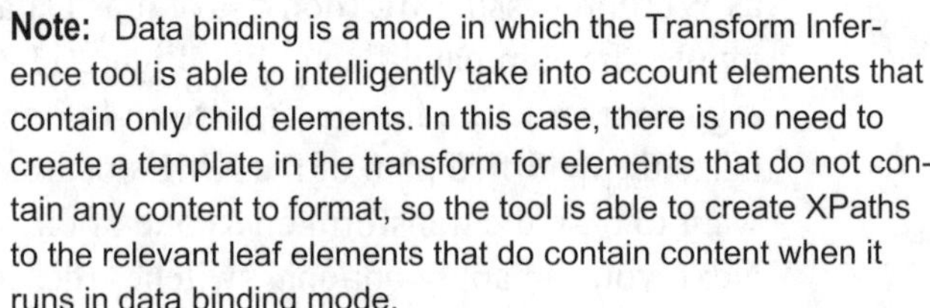

Note: Data binding is a mode in which the Transform Inference tool is able to intelligently take into account elements that contain only child elements. In this case, there is no need to create a template in the transform for elements that do not contain any content to format, so the tool is able to create XPaths to the relevant leaf elements that do contain content when it runs in data binding mode.

Once you have your seed document formatted exactly as you like it is time to save it to an appropriate location. You probably don't want to save it too "deep" in the Windows hierarchy, because you'll be navigating to the file from the Windows command line. In this case, I've saved a sample file called topstories.xml in the root of my e drive. Figure 11-7 shows what happens when the Transform Inference tool is invoked with the specified file passed through as an argument. The tool is invoked by typing **wml2xslt** and then issuing the appropriate parameters.

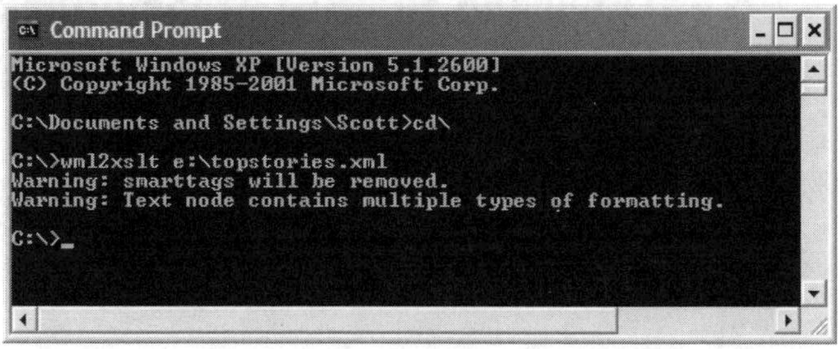

```
Command Prompt
Microsoft Windows XP [Version 5.1.2600]
(C) Copyright 1985-2001 Microsoft Corp.

C:\Documents and Settings\Scott>cd\

C:\>wml2xslt e:\topstories.xml
Warning: smarttags will be removed.
Warning: Text node contains multiple types of formatting.

C:\>_
```

Figure 11-7

The Transform Inference tool will create an XSLT file in the same directory as your seed document. In addition, the file will have the same name as your seed document but with an .xsl extension as opposed to the .xml extension of your seed document. Figure 11-8 shows the top portion of the XSLT file and all of the corresponding namespaces that were created.

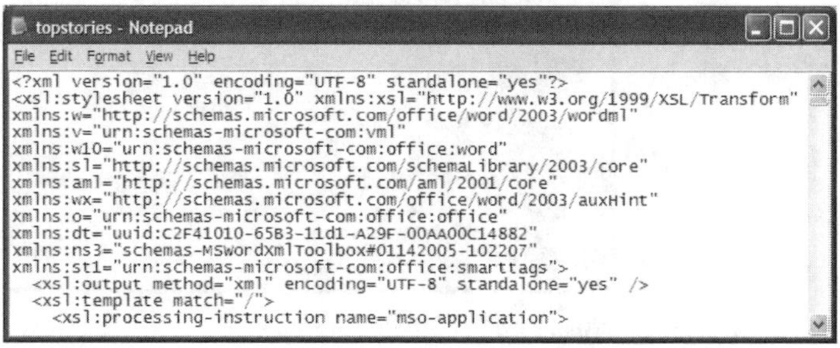

```
topstories - Notepad
File Edit Format View Help
<?xml version="1.0" encoding="UTF-8" standalone="yes"?>
<xsl:stylesheet version="1.0" xmlns:xsl="http://www.w3.org/1999/XSL/Transform"
xmlns:w="http://schemas.microsoft.com/office/word/2003/wordml"
xmlns:v="urn:schemas-microsoft-com:vml"
xmlns:w10="urn:schemas-microsoft-com:office:word"
xmlns:sl="http://schemas.microsoft.com/schemaLibrary/2003/core"
xmlns:aml="http://schemas.microsoft.com/aml/2001/core"
xmlns:wx="http://schemas.microsoft.com/office/word/2003/auxHint"
xmlns:o="urn:schemas-microsoft-com:office:office"
xmlns:dt="uuid:C2F41010-65B3-11d1-A29F-00AA00C14882"
xmlns:ns3="schemas-MSWordXmlToolbox#01142005-102207"
xmlns:st1="urn:schemas-microsoft-com:office:smarttags">
  <xsl:output method="xml" encoding="UTF-8" standalone="yes" />
  <xsl:template match="/">
    <xsl:processing-instruction name="mso-application">
```

Figure 11-8

You may recognize several namespaces in Figure 11-8, but most importantly you'll see the reference to the XSD schema that was created by XML Toolbox. You can then work with the resultant XSLT Transform by experimenting with other RSS XML documents. You can apply the transform either manually or automatically while opening a document or saving a document.

Applying an XSLT Transformation while Saving a Document

Caution: If you apply an Extensible Stylesheet Language Transformation (XSLT) when you save an Extensible Markup Language (XML) file, Word saves only data that is included in the output of the transformation.

You can manually apply the transform by navigating to the **File** menu and selecting **Save As**. In the Save as type box, click **XML Document**. In the File name box, type the document name. Select the **Apply transform** check box.

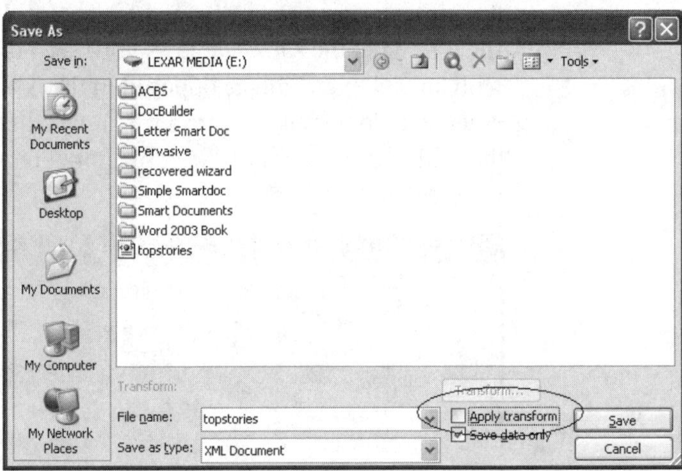

Figure 11-9

Conclusion

This chapter served as an introduction to XSLT and expanded upon WordprocessingML. The XML Toolbox is a great tool for creating XSD schemas, which are an integral part of working with XSLT Transforms in Word 2003. We've also looked at how the Microsoft Transform Inference tool can be used to create XSLT Transforms for use with all Word documents. XSLT is a large topic, but Microsoft has made it easy to create your transforms by creating the Inference tool. This tool allows developers to concentrate on the important tasks at hand and not worry about the technical details of XSLT.

Chapter 12

SmartDocs Introduction

Introduction

This chapter is designed to give a high-level introduction to smart documents and explain how you may be able to use them in your enterprise development. Smart documents raise the bar in terms of programming knowledge as you will now be required to use a tool outside of Word to develop a dynamic-link library file (DLL). In addition, you will be utilizing XML and XML schema to create other components associated with a smart document solution. Chapter 13 contains a more detailed example project of how to actually create a smart document. If you're unfamiliar with what a smart document actually is, then you should probably read this chapter in its entirety.

What Is a Smart Document?

Smart documents are designed to be intelligent solutions that are programmed to guide users through given tasks and offer assistance along the way. Smart documents are best utilized for structured processes that involve repetitive tasks. This could be anything from creating a simple, reusable memo to creating complex legal pleadings or loan documentation.

Microsoft intentionally made the smart documents technology flexible in terms of programming language support. Unlike working with simple VBA template solutions, to create smart documents you'll need to create dynamic-link library (DLL) files. These can be written in Microsoft Visual Basic version 6.0, Microsoft Visual Basic .NET, C#, Microsoft Visual C++ version 6.0, Microsoft Visual C++ .NET, or any programming language designed for the Microsoft .NET Framework.

Currently, smart documents are supported in Microsoft Office Word 2003 and Microsoft Office Excel 2003. This means that your solutions will not work with previous versions of Word. The advantage of that is that you can make full use of the new Word 2003 features without worrying about backward compatibility.

One of the most compelling aspects of smart documents is the possibility for interacting with a variety of databases. Traditionally, VBA had limited support for database access and it always involved creating references to DLLs that may not be present on other machines. This resulted in full-scale deployments for what appeared to be a simple document-based solution.

Overview of a Smart Document Solution

Before we start looking at the individual pieces of a smart document, it's important to understand (at a high level) how the pieces of a smart document interrelate. First, don't lose sight that this is a Word-based solution; when you think of a Word-hosted smart document, you need to think in terms of a Word document. Secondly, we've seen that XSD schemas define the layout for a particular XML file. A smart document has an associated schema that defines particular "sections" (*not* Word *sections*) of the Word document (it will actually be an XML file, but think of it in terms of a Word document for now). As you move among these schema defined sections, events are triggered and certain things can be programmed to happen in the task pane.

Smart Document Components

There are five main parts to a Word 2003 smart document solution. First, there is a Word or Excel document or template. This is the smart document that the user opens to perform a business function.

Note: In Office 2003, only Word and Excel support smart documents.

Second, there is an XML schema definition (XSD). The Word document is marked up with elements from the XML schema to overlay an XML data model on all or part of the document. "Marking up" the document is how the developer associates these specific areas with the XML schema elements.

Third, you have the action handler DLL, which can be developed in Visual Basic, Visual Basic .NET, Visual C++, or Visual C#. It is then deployed to a web or network server. This DLL implements the OLE interface ISmartDocument.

Fourth, there is an XML expansion pack manifest file that specifies the installation instructions for the solution. It provides the server location of the solution DLL and the solution's COM CLSID. It also mentions any other associated files needed for the solution and the solution ID. The solution ID uniquely identifies this smart document solution, but you are also free to use any unique identifier string as the solution ID.

Finally, there may be other files needed by the solution (such as GIFs or JPEGs, HTML, or document fragments) that you want to install on the local machine. These would be specified in the manifest and installed or updated automatically by Office when the smart document is opened.

They may then be used by your smart document solution code.

You can think of the XML elements, which factor the spreadsheet or document into logical structural components, as hooks to which your smart document solution can attach controls that assist the user in working with these various parts of the document. The behavior of these controls is defined by your action handler DLL at run time. The controls effectively become a sophisticated context-sensitive help system and are displayed in the new document actions task pane as the user moves into particular sections (corresponding to XML elements) of the document or spreadsheet. Because smart document controls can be much more than just help text, your context-sensitive help can actually act as a user assistant in completing the business task system for which the document is used.

Introduction to Developing Smart Documents

Before we discuss developing smart documents, we want to examine several things. First, we need to understand how smart documents work inside Microsoft Word 2003. Secondly, we need to see what controls we have at our disposal when creating smart documents. Thirdly, we need to decide whether we are going to use Component Object Model (COM) technologies or Microsoft .NET Framework technologies. Lastly, we need information regarding the security and privacy issues related to smart documents.

Smart Document Architecture

The smart document architecture for Word 2003 is fairly complex. It involves attaching an XML expansion pack to an XML document that uses an XSD schema and may even involve the use of an XSLT Transform. As you can see, there are a lot of considerations that go into creating a smart document solution. The typical VBA philosophy has been "open the VBA Editor and write some code."

Developing smart document solutions requires a bit more forethought to be successful.

Once you've created all the components that make up your smart document, you'll need to assemble all of these components together with the base document and get the solution ready for testing and deployment. This is done by attaching a schema and an XML expansion pack to a regular document. By definition, this is what turns a regular document into a smart document.

Once an XSD schema and an XML expansion pack are attached to a document, information about the schema and the XML expansion pack is compiled within the document. This information defines a particular location where the XML expansion pack and additional smart document components are stored. This allows the user to install or update the particular XML expansion pack that should be loaded when the smart document is opened.

Once you attach an XML expansion pack to your solution, any Word 2003 user who receives the document will be prompted to install the components needed to enable all smart document functionality. This is done through the XML expansion pack manifest file.

The Schema Library

One component of a smart document is that it has an entry in the Schema Library. If a Word 2003 document includes custom XML markup, Word checks the Schema Library registry subkey to determine which XML schema namespace is associated with the markup. If the XML expansion pack is not already attached to the document, Word checks several locations to determine whether an appropriate XML expansion pack exists. Figure 12-1 shows the Templates and Add-ins dialog with an XML expansion pack attached.

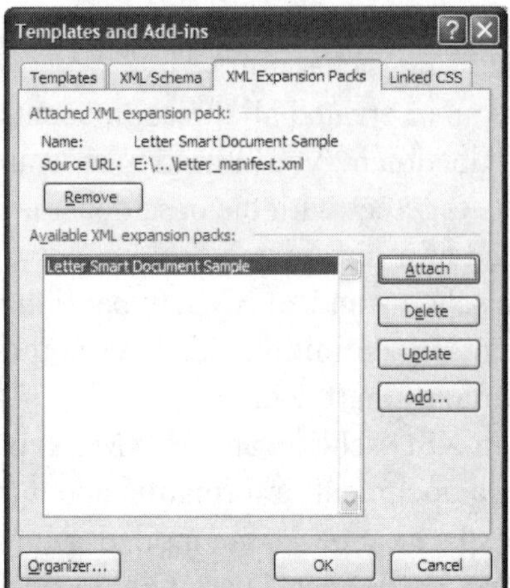

Figure 12-1

The Schema Library is a registry subkey that contains all known XML namespaces. It provides host applications with information about the location of components (for example, XML expansion packs, schemas, smart documents, and other files included with a smart document) that are associated with that particular namespace.

Implementing the ISmartDocument Interface

Now, let's drill down a little deeper into the components of a smart document. Another aspect of a smart document is that it will have a DLL file that is referenced in the manifest. This file is created in a development environment outside of Word. The most important thing to understand when you are programming a smart document solution is exactly how the ISmartDocument interface works. The blanket rule is that if you are creating a smart document, you will be implementing this interface. At first, it may seem somewhat counterintuitive, but once you get the hang of it, you will see that it is actually a quite elegant framework.

In most cases, you will be working with the Document Actions task pane as you have them defined in your smart document code. Although the methods in the API are executed in a specific order to render your actions in the Document Actions task pane, many of the properties in the API are dynamic. It's important to remember that this is entirely context sensitive. You are free to alter properties of the control at run time depending on the contents of a document or even depending on the value in another smart document control.

Note: You can use the Visual Basic for Applications object model for Word 2003 within the DLL as well.

Introduction to Working with Smart Document Controls

Now that you understand how the DLL you will be programming works, it's time to discuss how you will actually interact with the user. The Document Actions task pane is capable of holding controls just like a VBA form. When you are working with the controls on the task pane, you can adjust how they are displayed and how they function.

By using the ISmartDocProperties interface you can modify the display properties for all smart document controls. There are various built-in controls, but if these don't work for a particular scenario, you can always include custom ActiveX controls. These controls are represented by constants (you'll see these defined in the solution in the following chapter). These controls are briefly introduced below.

Regular Controls

You're probably already familiar with check boxes, combo boxes, list boxes, text boxes, and radio buttons. Smart documents contain the C_TYPE_CHECKBOX, C_TYPE_COMBO, C_TYPE_LISTBOX, C_TYPE_RADIOGROUP, and C_TYPE_TEXTBOX smart document controls. These controls function much like the corresponding controls on Windows Forms and Web Forms. The most important issue you'll encounter with these controls is determining which method you will use to maintain state information. These controls don't automatically maintain their state when they are used in smart documents.

Document Fragment Controls

There are two other smart document controls that allow you to create pieces of text, or boilerplate text, that your users can easily add to a new document. These controls are called the "document fragment controls" and are represented as C_TYPE_DOCUMENTFRAGMENT and C_TYPE_DOCUMENTFRAGMENTURL. The text for document fragments can be either hard-coded strings within your code or external documents that you reference from within your code.

Help Controls

There are two help controls available, C_TYPE_HELP and C_TYPE_HELPURL, but it's important to note that the Document Actions task pane doesn't support all HTML elements, attributes, and cascading style sheets (CSS) formatting. When you create help text for display in the Document Actions task pane, you create it by using Extensible Hypertext Markup Language (XHTML). You can either hard-code the help text into the smart document dynamic-link library (DLL) code or you can reference external XHTML files.

Hyperlink Controls

The C_TYPE_LINK smart document control allows you to create links within your smart document. These links can open web pages, open documents in other applications, or even execute an application. You can use hyperlinks as command buttons as well.

Image Controls

The C_TYPE_IMAGE smart document control displays images in the Document Actions task pane. These images can be manipulated via code using the InvokeControl method of the ISmartDocument interface. It's important to be cognizant of the image size you plan to use when working with images in the task pane since the task pane is relatively small.

Additional Controls

The C_TYPE_SEPARATOR and C_TYPE_LABEL smart document controls provide lines and labels, respectively. These controls have no special formatting issues.

ActiveX Controls

The C_TYPE_ACTIVEX control allows you to use ActiveX controls if one of the built-in controls doesn't work for your project. ActiveX controls provide an extensible framework in which to create your smart documents.

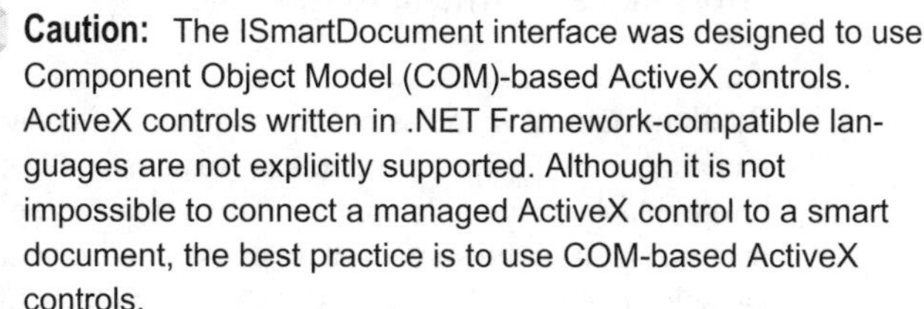

Caution: The ISmartDocument interface was designed to use Component Object Model (COM)-based ActiveX controls. ActiveX controls written in .NET Framework-compatible languages are not explicitly supported. Although it is not impossible to connect a managed ActiveX control to a smart document, the best practice is to use COM-based ActiveX controls.

Maintaining the State of Smart Document Controls

The standard smart document controls (text box, check box, radio button, combo box, and list box) don't automatically maintain state when you use them in a smart document. This means that every time the task pane is redrawn, these controls will revert to the value in the associated Populate method. Let's discuss some of the possible ways to maintain the state of smart document controls.

Information Stored within the Document

In some cases you will be able to control the state of a control based on information contained with the document. For instance, a particular text box may always initialize with the text stored in the title element of the XML file. In other cases, you could use the presence or absence of an element or attribute to determine the value of controls.

Global Variables

Another possibility is to use global variables to maintain the state of your controls. You might want to store a value in a global variable and initialize the control based on this variable every time. This approach may be useful for some simple scenarios, but using global variables can result in errors that are difficult to spot.

Caution: Global variables only work if you have only one document open that uses a specific XML expansion pack. If you have multiple documents open, and more than one of those documents uses the same XML expansion pack, your global variables are tied to the ISmartDocument interface, of which there is only one instance for the XML expansion pack, not for each individual instance of a smart document.

Using Custom Document Properties or Docvariables

The Word VBA object model allows you to create custom document properties or document variables that are stored within the document itself. You can use the Document-Properties object of the VBA object model or the Variables property of the Document object to create custom properties. This is a good method for "behind the scenes" values that may not be represented by something in the XML file. In addition, both of these methods persist between sessions of Word (the next time you open the document, these variables will still be present).

A Quick Look at a Very Simple Smart Document

Following is a cursory introduction to smart documents that will serve as a working example as to how smart documents work. As with all of the examples in this book, the code is downloadable from www.docbuilder.com and www.wordware.com/files/wordvba2. We'll start off by creating a very simple structure using Word 2003. As you can see in Figure 12-2, I've typed the text "<simpleSmart-Doc/>" into the body of the document. At this point, this isn't XML; this is just raw text entered into Word as a text editor. The real power of Word lies in some of the supplemental utilities that are downloadable free of charge from Microsoft.

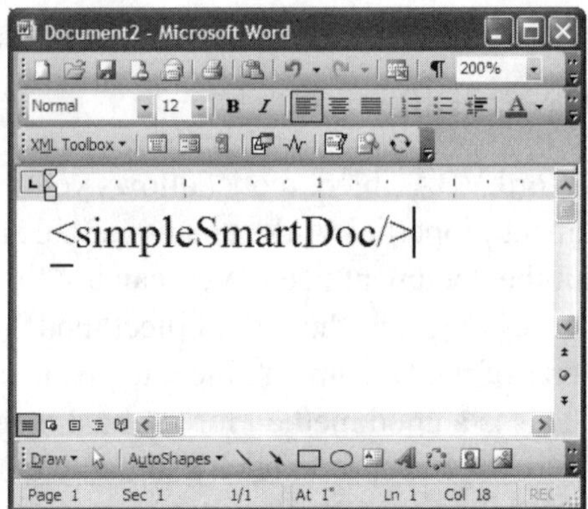

Figure 12-2

If you haven't already done so, please download the XML Toolbox from www.microsoft.com (see Chapter 8). This tool allows you to create well-formed XML from within the Word editor and also has a mechanism for turning normal text (that adheres to a specific convention) into XML. If you choose XML Toolbox | Convert <Tags/> to XML Nodes from the drop-down menu available on the toolbar, Word will convert the text shown in Figure 12-2 into the XML representation shown in Figure 12-3. As you can see, Word has taken the simple text and created both starting and ending XML tags within the Word document. This is the beginning of the markup process that was discussed in Chapter 9's introduction of the new XML features of Word 2003.

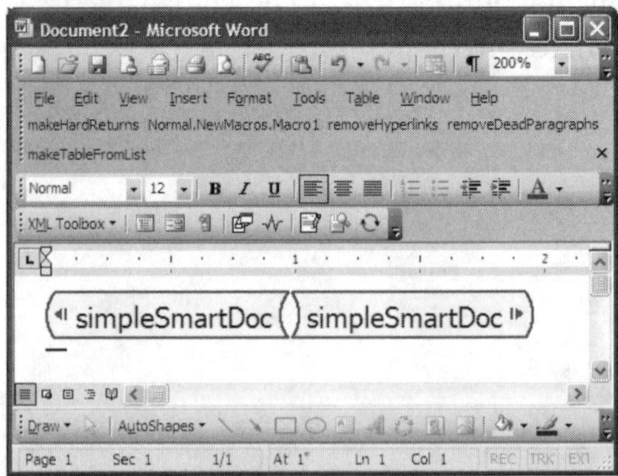

Figure 12-3

Obviously, this is an extremely simple example for introductory purposes. One requirement of a well-formed XML document is that it has a single root node. In this example, our root node is also the only node within the XML document ("simpleSmartDoc"). There is no requirement that any subsidiary nodes be added to the document to make it meet the well-formed requirements set forth for XML.

The XSD File

The next step to create our smart document is to create an XML schema (an XSD file) that will serve as the context-sensitive layout for the smart document solution. You can think of the structure the XSD lays out as the road map for how users will interact with your solution. Again, we will turn to the XML Toolbox to create our schema. In general, the XML Toolbox is a great mechanism to create valid schemas that you can use in your smart document solutions. This saves you from the intricacies of XSD (which, in many instances, is not necessary to reach your end goal).

Figure 12-4 displays the Generate an Inferred Schema dialog, which is accessed by selecting XML Toolbox | Generate Inferred Schema from the XML Toolbox drop-down. The prompt indicates that you need to type in the root node of the XML file you are basing the XSD upon. If you leave this blank, Word will insert an arbitrary root node around the XML that you have already created. For this example, you'll want to define "simpleSmartDoc" as the root node. The namespace element should already be filled out for you based upon an internal algorithm. The File Path text box simply allows you to name the file and specify the directory where you want the Toolbox to create the resultant XSD.

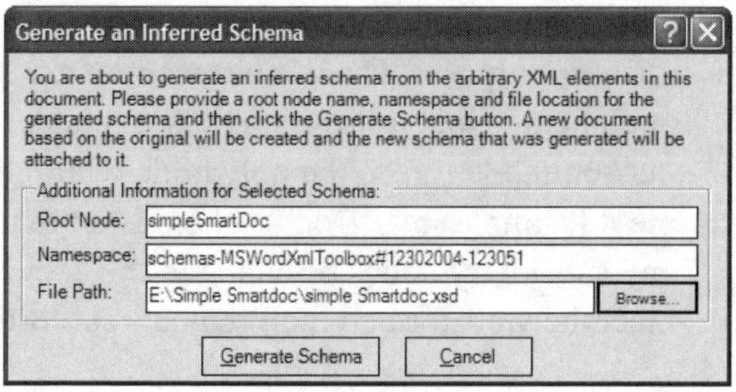

Generate an Inferred Schema

You are about to generate an inferred schema from the arbitrary XML elements in this document. Please provide a root node name, namespace and file location for the generated schema and then click the Generate Schema button. A new document based on the original will be created and the new schema that was generated will be attached to it.

Additional Information for Selected Schema:

Root Node: simpleSmartDoc

Namespace: schemas-MSWordXmlToolbox#12302004-123051

File Path: E:\Simple Smartdoc\simple Smartdoc.xsd [Browse...]

[Generate Schema] [Cancel]

Figure 12-4

Once you click Generate Schema, Word will generate a new document that you are free to save. We are not as interested in the document as we are with the schema attached to it. Remember the location of the file and use a uniform naming convention to make things easier on yourself as you are compiling the various components of your smart document solution later on.

Figure 12-5 shows the XSD file created by the above routine. As you can see, the first line includes the XML declaration. Line 2 is a comment generated by the Toolbox to inform you that the schema was generated by the XML Toolbox. The next couple of lines contain the namespace declarations. The rest of the XSD defines the simple structure of our XML file. This includes our root element, simpleSmartDoc, and the related information regarding the element type.

Note: Please keep in mind that the namespace declarations are used in multiple locations in your smart document solution.

simple_SmartDoc.xsd - Notepad

File Edit Format View Help

```
<?xml version="1.0" encoding="utf-16"?>
<!--Schema generated by the Word XML Toolbox for Microsoft Office Word 2003-->
<xs:schema xmlns:tns="schemas-MSWordXmlToolbox#12302004-123051"
attributeFormDefault="unqualified" elementFormDefault="qualified"
targetNamespace="schemas-MSWordXmlToolbox#12302004-123051"
xmlns:xs="http://www.w3.org/2001/XMLSchema">
  <xs:element name="simpleSmartDoc">
    <xs:complexType mixed="true">
      <xs:sequence>
        <xs:element name="simpleSmartDoc" type="xs:string" />
      </xs:sequence>
    </xs:complexType>
  </xs:element>
</xs:schema>
```

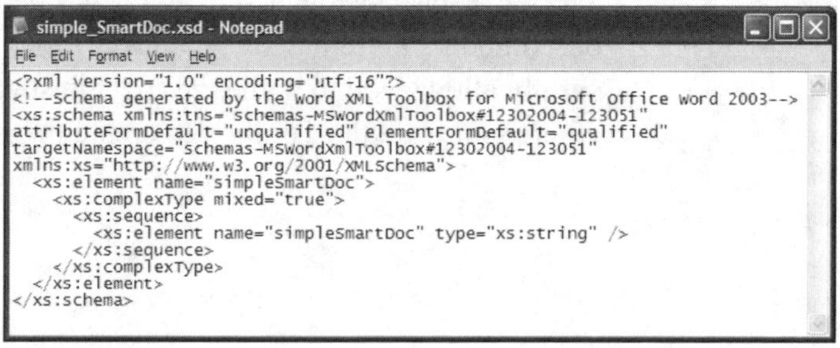

Figure 12-5

The DLL File

Now, that we have an XSD structure in place we are going to turn to another component of our solution — the VB 6.0 DLL that we must create. The following code section contains all of the code necessary to create the solution. This is contained in one class within a VB 6.0 DLL. The important thing to note is that the solution implements the ISmartDocument interface and thus must have a corresponding entry for every method and property exposed by this interface.

```
Option Explicit
Implements ISmartDocument

'Const cLETTER As String = cNAMESPACE & "#letter"
Const cSMARTDOCBODY As String = _
"schemas-MSWordXmlToolbox#12302004-123051#simpleSmartDoc"

Private strPath As String
Private xDoc As New MSXML2.DOMDocument30
Private xNodes As MSXML2.IXMLDOMNodeList
Private xNode As MSXML2.IXMLDOMNode
Private itemNode As MSXML2.IXMLDOMNode
Private x As Integer
Private sTitle() As String
Private sLink() As String
Private Declare Sub Sleep Lib "kernel32" (ByVal
        dwMilliseconds As Long)

Public Sub GoToSleep(ByVal lMilliseconds As Variant)
    On Error Resume Next
    If IsNumeric(lMilliseconds) Then
        If CLng(lMilliseconds) > 0 Then
            Call Sleep(CLng(lMilliseconds))
        End If
    End If
End Sub

Private Sub ISmartDocument_SmartDocInitialize(ByVal
        ApplicationName As String, ByVal Document As Object,
        ByVal SolutionPath As String, ByVal SolutionRegKeyRoot
        As String)
```

```
    xDoc.Load "e:\simple smartdoc\topstories.xml"
    'xDoc.Load "http://rss.news.yahoo.com/rss/topstories"

    'GoToSleep 10000

    xDoc.Validate
    Set itemNode = xDoc.SelectSingleNode("//rss/channel")

    For Each xNode In itemNode.ChildNodes
    If xNode.nodeName = "item" Then
        x = x + 1

        ReDim Preserve sTitle(x) As String
        sTitle(x) = xNode.ChildNodes(0).Text
        ReDim Preserve sLink(x) As String
        sLink(x) = xNode.ChildNodes(1).Text
    End If
Next xNode
End Sub

Private Property Get ISmartDocument_SmartDocXMLTypeCount()
        As Long
    ISmartDocument_SmartDocXMLTypeCount = 1
End Property

Private Property Get ISmartDocument_SmartDocXMLTypeName(ByVal
        smartDocID As Long) As String
    ISmartDocument_SmartDocXMLTypeName = cSMARTDOCBODY
End Property

Private Property Get ISmartDocument_SmartDocXMLTypeCaption
        (ByVal smartDocID As Long, ByVal LocaleID As Long)
        As String
    ISmartDocument_SmartDocXMLTypeCaption = "Yahoo News
              Stories"
End Property

Private Property Get ISmartDocument_ControlCount(ByVal
        SmartDocName As String) As Long
    ISmartDocument_ControlCount = x
End Property

Private Property Get ISmartDocument_ControlID(ByVal
        SmartDocName As String, ByVal ControlIndex As Long)
        As Long
```

```
    ISmartDocument_ControlID = ControlIndex
End Sub

Private Property Get ISmartDocument_ControlNameFromID(ByVal
        ControlID As Long) As String
    ISmartDocument_ControlNameFromID = cSMARTDOCBODY &
                   ControlID
End Property

Private Property Get ISmartDocument_ControlCaptionFromID(ByVal
        ControlID As Long, ByVal ApplicationName As String,
        ByVal LocaleID As Long, ByVal Text As String, ByVal
        Xml As String, ByVal Target As Object) As String
    ISmartDocument_ControlCaptionFromID = sTitle(ControlID)
End Property

Private Property Get ISmartDocument_ControlTypeFromID(ByVal
        ControlID As Long, ByVal ApplicationName As String,
        ByVal LocaleID As Long) As SmartTagLib.C_TYPE
    ISmartDocument_ControlTypeFromID = C_TYPE_LINK
End Property

Private Sub ISmartDocument_InvokeControl(ByVal ControlID As
        Long, ByVal ApplicationName As String, ByVal Target As
        Object, ByVal Text As String, ByVal Xml As String,
        ByVal LocaleID As Long)
Dim objNav As InternetExplorer
    Set objNav = New SHDocVw.InternetExplorer
        objNav.Navigate2 sLink(ControlID)
        objNav.Visible = True
    Set objNav = Nothing
End Sub

Private Sub ISmartDocument_PopulateTextboxContent(ByVal
        ControlID As Long, ByVal ApplicationName As String,
        ByVal LocaleID As Long, ByVal Text As String, ByVal
        Xml As String, ByVal Target As Object, ByVal Props As
        SmartTagLib.ISmartDocProperties, value As String)
End Sub

Private Sub ISmartDocument_OnTextboxContentChange(ByVal
        ControlID As Long, ByVal Target As Object, ByVal
        value As String)
End Sub
```

```
Private Sub ISmartDocument_ImageClick(ByVal ControlID As Long,
        ByVal ApplicationName As String, ByVal Target As
        Object, ByVal Text As String, ByVal Xml As String,
        ByVal LocaleID As Long, ByVal XCoordinate As Long,
        ByVal YCoordinate As Long)
End Sub

Private Sub ISmartDocument_OnCheckboxChange(ByVal ControlID As
        Long, ByVal Target As Object, ByVal Checked As Boolean)
End Sub

Private Sub ISmartDocument_OnListOrComboSelectChange(ByVal
        ControlID As Long, ByVal Target As Object, ByVal
        Selected As Long, ByVal value As String)
End Sub

Private Sub ISmartDocument_OnPaneUpdateComplete(ByVal Document
        As Object)
End Sub

Private Sub ISmartDocument_OnRadioGroupSelectChange(ByVal
        ControlID As Long, ByVal Target As Object, ByVal
        Selected As Long, ByVal value As String)
End Sub

Private Sub ISmartDocument_PopulateActiveXProps(ByVal ControlID
        As Long, ByVal ApplicationName As String, ByVal
        LocaleID As Long, ByVal Text As String, ByVal Xml As
        String, ByVal Target As Object, ByVal Props As
        SmartTagLib.ISmartDocProperties, ByVal ActiveXPropBag
        As SmartTagLib.ISmartDocProperties)
End Sub

Private Sub ISmartDocument_PopulateCheckbox(ByVal ControlID As
        Long, ByVal ApplicationName As String, ByVal LocaleID
        As Long, ByVal Text As String, ByVal Xml As String,
        ByVal Target As Object, ByVal Props As
        SmartTagLib.ISmartDocProperties, Checked As Boolean)
End Sub

Private Sub ISmartDocument_PopulateDocumentFragment(ByVal
        ControlID As Long, ByVal ApplicationName As String,
        ByVal LocaleID As Long, ByVal Text As String, ByVal
```

```
        Xml As String, ByVal Target As Object, ByVal Props As
        SmartTagLib.ISmartDocProperties, DocumentFragment As
        String)
End Sub

Private Sub ISmartDocument_PopulateHelpContent(ByVal ControlID
        As Long, ByVal ApplicationName As String, ByVal
        LocaleID As Long, ByVal Text As String, ByVal Xml As
        String, ByVal Target As Object, ByVal Props As
        SmartTagLib.ISmartDocProperties, Content As String)
End Sub

Private Sub ISmartDocument_PopulateImage(ByVal ControlID As
        Long, ByVal ApplicationName As String, ByVal LocaleID
        As Long, ByVal Text As String, ByVal Xml As String,
        ByVal Target As Object, ByVal Props As
        SmartTagLib.ISmartDocProperties, ImageSrc As String)
End Sub

Private Sub ISmartDocument_PopulateListOrComboContent(ByVal
        ControlID As Long, ByVal ApplicationName As String,
        ByVal LocaleID As Long, ByVal Text As String, ByVal
        Xml As String, ByVal Target As Object, ByVal Props As
        SmartTagLib.ISmartDocProperties, List() As String,
        Count As Long, InitialSelected As Long)
End Sub

Private Sub ISmartDocument_PopulateOther(ByVal ControlID As
        Long, ByVal ApplicationName As String, ByVal LocaleID
        As Long, ByVal Text As String, ByVal Xml As String,
        ByVal Target As Object, ByVal Props As
        SmartTagLib.ISmartDocProperties)
End Sub

Private Sub ISmartDocument_PopulateRadioGroup(ByVal ControlID
        As Long, ByVal ApplicationName As String, ByVal
        LocaleID As Long, ByVal Text As String, ByVal Xml As
        String, ByVal Target As Object, ByVal Props As
        SmartTagLib.ISmartDocProperties, List() As String,
        Count As Long, InitialSelected As Long)
End Sub
```

The Solution Manifest

The next step is to create an XML file called the Solution Manifest. This file contains all of the information necessary for Word to download the appropriate components necessary for your solution. One of the most important pieces of getting the Solution Manifest correct is to create a valid solution ID. (I just chose the number generated by the XML Toolbox. In a real solution, you will want to utilize a tool to generate a GUID.)

The other important part of the Solution Manifest is to make sure you define the proper CLSID for the DLL file you created. Obtaining the CLSID can be tricky. The best place to search for the CLSID is through the Windows registry. As you can see in Figure 12-6, the project name is "simple_SmartDoc" and the specific class we are searching for is "clsCodeBehind."

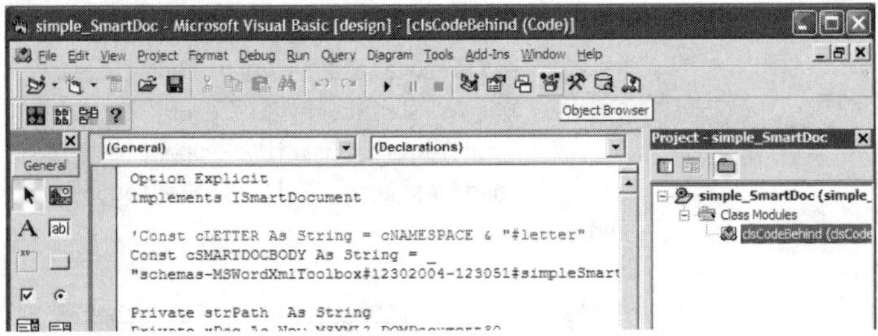

Figure 12-6

First, I'll invoke the Windows Registry Editor by typing **regedit** at the run command line (shown in Figure 12-7).

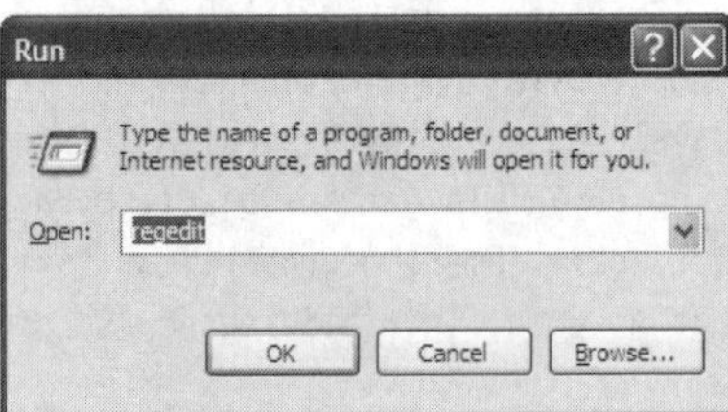

Figure 12-7

Once you've entered "regedit" in the Start | Run dialog, you should see a window similar to the one shown in Figure 12-8. Be very careful when working with the Windows registry. This is where the information necessary for your system to work properly resides. Even small changes in this area can have unforeseen, and sometimes catastrophic, results. We simply want to search the entire registry for an entry representing our VB project.

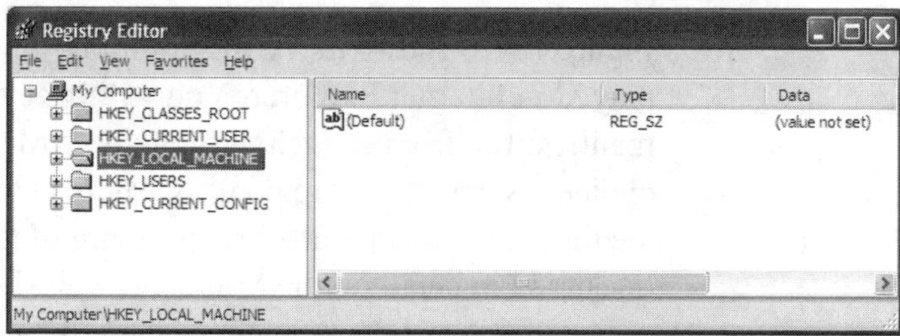

Figure 12-8

The general syntax of your search should be "projectname.classname," and you may have to sort through numerous entries until you find one that contains a "Clsid" entry for the particular solution you have created. You'll have to make sure you maintain binary compatibility as you continually compile your DLL; otherwise, your Clsid will be continually changing. As you can see in Figure 12-9, the CLSID for this particular solution on my machine is "EC3EBEF3-B7B4-4B62-B99D-C1AD1046E8D8" and is represented in the Data column. You can cut and paste the entry by simply double-clicking on the Name column in the appropriate entry. This will open an input box that allows you to cut and paste the number into your XML manifest. Pay special attention to make sure that you do not inadvertently alter the number.

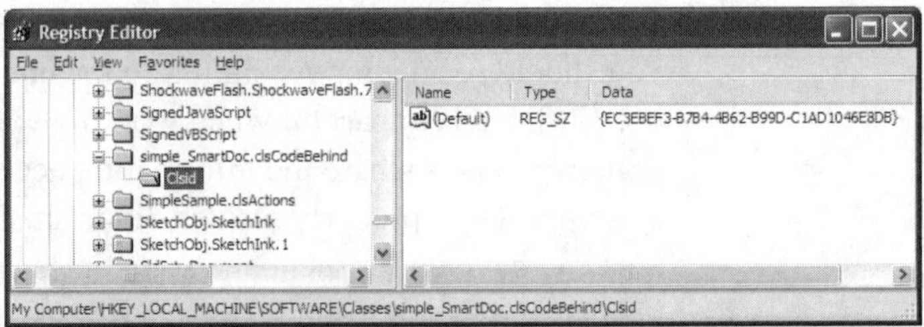

Figure 12-9

Figure 12-10 shows the XML Solution Manifest as displayed in Internet Explorer. You will have to create the manifest file from scratch through the XML editor of your choice. (Sorry, there are no nifty Microsoft solutions to create this file at this point.) The structure of this file is discussed in detail on the Microsoft web site, but you'll notice that the <uri> tag defines the same namespace that was created by the Word Toolbox when we created our XSD file above. You'll also notice that the solution's filepath corresponds to the DLL file that we created above.

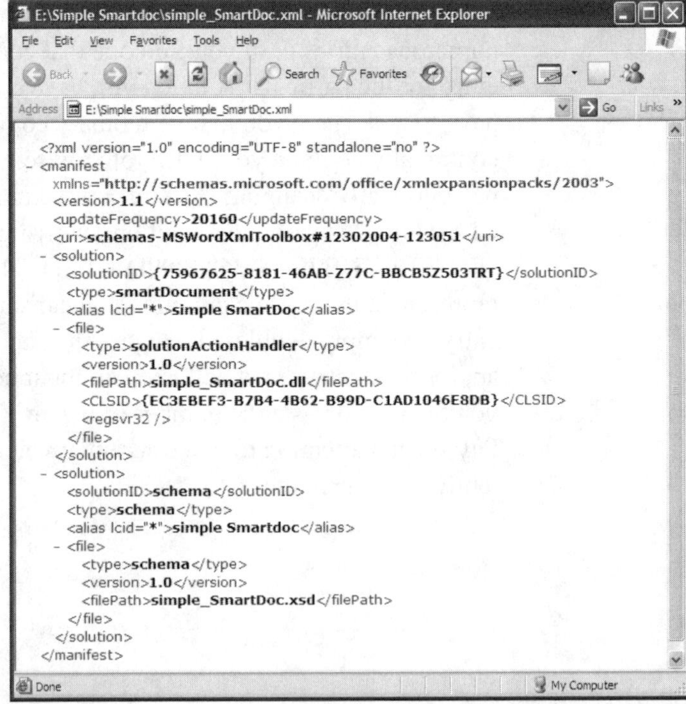

Figure 12-10

At this point, we have all of the components created that we will need in order to implement our smart document solution. We have an XSD that defines all of the "areas" of our XML document, a DLL that implements the ISmartDocument interface and triggers various actions in response to that interface, and an XML Solution Manifest that details these components and comprises the overall solution.

Now, we have to actually implement our solution in the context of Word 2003. The solution, of course, is dependent upon a Word document. Thus, the first step of implementing the solution is to create a Word document and attach the schema via the Templates and Add-ins dialog (select **Tools | Templates and Add-ins | XML Schema** tab) and choose the appropriate schema. See Figure 12-11.

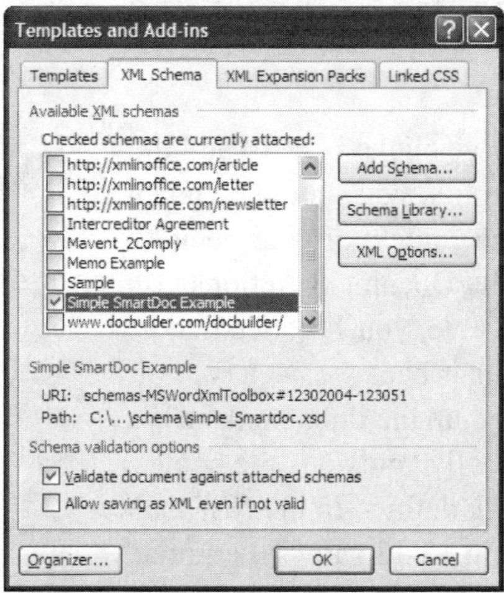

Figure 12-11

Once you have the appropriate schema selected, you will need to access the XML Expansion Packs tab (shown in Figure 12-12). This tab's options allow you to attach XML manifest files to a Word document. You can also delete, add, and update any of the existing expansion packs you may be utilizing on your machine. You can access the XML Expansion Packs tab by choosing **Tools | Templates and Add-ins | XML Expansion Packs**. As you can see in

Figure 12-12, I've navigated to my XML file and chosen the appropriate solution.

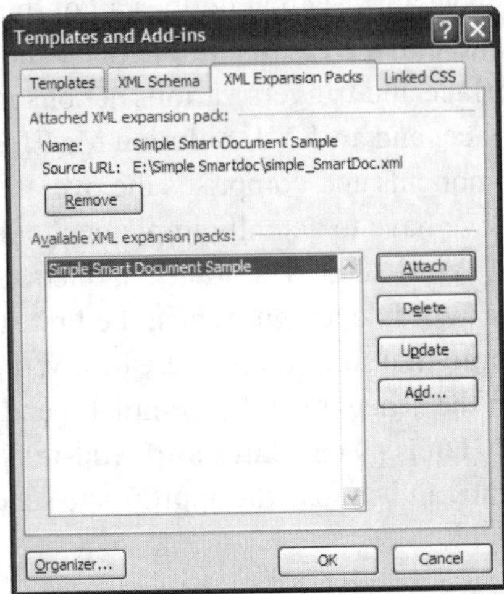

Figure 12-12

Once you've clicked OK to add the XML solution, you should be taken back to the context of your document. If the Document Actions task pane is visible, you'll notice that it is blank. This is because we have not yet marked up the document, so we are essentially "outside" the context of anything defined in the XSD solution. Figure 12-13 shows the initial state of the Document Actions task pane. This is prior to the addition of any of the XML markup to your document. The next step is to switch the task pane back to the XML Structure view.

Figure 12-13

Figure 12-14 shows the Word application with the XML Structure task pane showing. (The task pane has been moved so that both show up in the window.) As you can see, we've begun marking up the document according to the structure defined by the XSD defined in our solution. Fortunately, our solution is very simplistic and only requires us to add one element (node) to our XML document. The next step is to position the cursor within the opening and closing tags and to switch back to the Document Actions task pane.

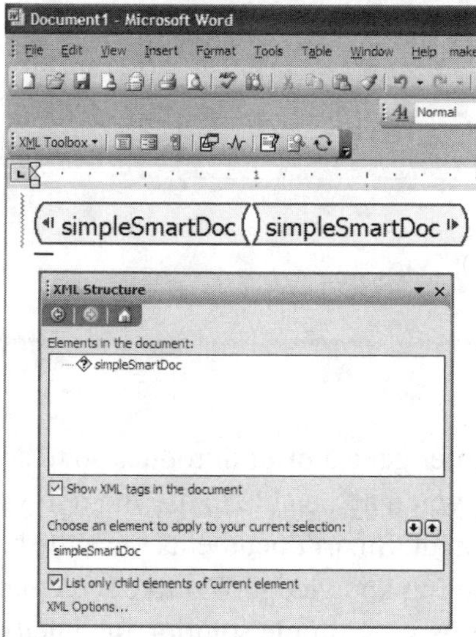

Figure 12-14

As you can see in Figure 12-15, positioning the cursor triggers our DLL to parse a Yahoo! RSS news file and display the corresponding links in the Document Actions task pane. Clicking on these links will launch an instance of Internet Explorer and cause the browser to navigate to the appropriate link. There is nothing complex in the code necessary to do this. In fact, the code behind the DLL is purposely simple to provide an easy introduction to how the process of working through a smart document solution actually works.

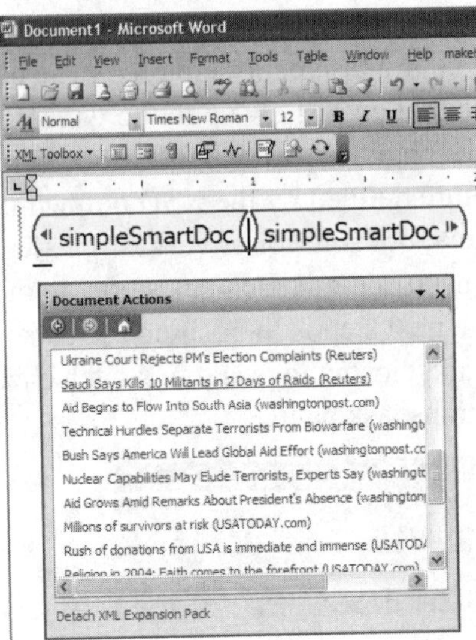

Figure 12-15

Conclusion

This chapter gave a brief introduction to smart documents and how you may be able to use them in your enterprise development. Smart documents raise the bar in terms of programming knowledge. You've seen that the components of even this very simple solution included an XSD schema, a DLL, and an XML manifest. This chapter was meant as a quick introduction so that the pieces discussed in the following chapter will make more sense. Please feel free to work through these examples from the sample code. The following chapter contains the technical details necessary to create a smart document.

Chapter 13

More on SmartDocs

Introduction

This chapter provides more information regarding the creation of smart documents as Word 2003 solutions. We will briefly discuss creating dynamic-link library files in more detail. We will then review all of the components of the Smart Document object model and how they can be used in your smart document solution. Smart documents are an integral part of the new Office development platform.

Creating a DLL with VB 6.0

The first step in creating your DLL is to start Visual Basic 6.0 Professional or Enterprise Edition. When the New Project dialog box appears, select the ActiveX DLL icon and then click OK. This will launch the normal VB Editor (which looks remarkably similar to the VBA editor).

Figure 13-1

Referencing the Smart Document Object Model

Next, you'll need to add a reference to the appropriate Smart Tags 2.0 Library, which is necessary for building smart documents. The References dialog is accessed from the Project menu instead of the Tools menu in VBA. Once you've navigated to the Project menu, click References, as shown in Figure 13-2.

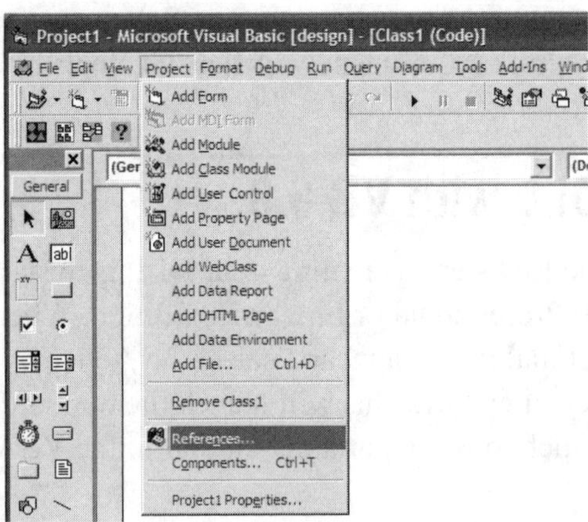

Figure 13-2

In the Available References list of the References dialog box, select the Microsoft Smart Tags 2.0 Type Library check box and then click OK. You will also need to add a reference to Word 11.0.

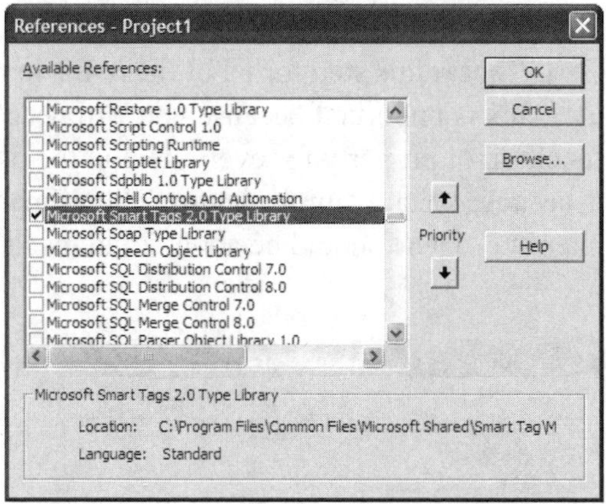

Figure 13-3

In a default installation of Office 2003, the type library is located at C:\Program Files\Common Files\Microsoft Shared\Smart Tag\MSTAG.TLB. The display name for this type library is the Microsoft Smart Tags 2.0 Type Library, and the type library's programmatic ID (progID) is SmartTagLib. The Smart Document object model is similar to the smart tag programmatic object model, so that's why the Smart Document object model lives inside of the smart tags type library.

Next, you'll need to add all of your smart document code to the DLL. In the Properties window rename your project to the appropriate name. You'll also want to rename the default Class1 class module. Finally, you will always need to implement the smart document interface so that you can implement the methods and properties necessary for your smart document. You will then want to type the following in the (General) (Declarations) section:

Implement SmartTagLib.ISmartDocument

This code instructs Visual Basic that you will be implementing the ISmartDocument interface in your DLL. In the Code window's Object list, select ISmartDocument. In the Procedure list, select ControlCaptionFromID [Property Get]. Repeat this step for all of the items in the Procedure list. This is important because you will need a subroutine, function, or property for every item in the drop-down. This is because we are "implementing" the ISmartDocument interface. There should be about 25 items in the Procedure list.

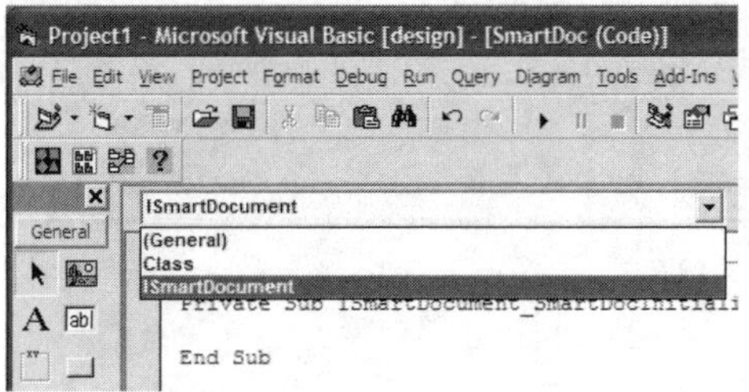

Figure 13-4

Debugging Information

In order to properly debug your smart document, you'll want to set some environment variables within the context of VB. Next, set debugging properties and make the DLL.

Once again, navigate to the Project menu and click Properties. Then click the Debugging tab. Select the Start program option. Type or browse to the WINWORD.EXE file.

Click OK. On the File menu, click Make DLL.

Now that you understand some of the basic smart document terms and you understand the smart document development cycle, it's time to explore the smart document programmatic object model that you can automate through code.

What Comprises a Smart Document

In order to create a smart document solution, you will need to write code to implement the 8 properties and 17 methods of the ISmartDocument interface. Figure 13-4 shows how the ISmartDocument interface appears once the proper reference is made. The following table lists the Smart Document object model's properties and methods in alphabetical order.

Table 13-1

Member Name	Description
ControlCaptionFromID property (String)	Assigns a unique ID number to a specific control.
ControlCount property (Long)	Assigns a unique namespace#element name and specifies the total number of controls assigned to the namespace#element name.
ControlID property (Long)	This returns an index number based on a unique namespace#element name. It is used to identify controls associated with the namespace#element name. As you programmatically add controls to a unique namespace#element name, the system defaults control ID numbering at one (1) and increments control ID numbers by one. Control index numbering is reset for each unique namespace#element name. You should add a "buffer" (such as ControlIndex + 100) to the default control index number to ensure that all controls have unique control IDs in the smart document solution.
ControlNameFromID property (String)	This specifies the control's unique name based on a specific control's unique ID number. This is the name that can be used from Word and Excel application object model code.
ControlTypeFromID property (C_TYPE)	This specifies the control's type (button, image, text box, and so on) as specified by a C_TYPE constant based on the specific control's unique ID number.
ImageClick method	Called when an image control is clicked.
InvokeControl method	Called when a hyperlink is clicked, a command button control is clicked, or, in Word only, a document fragment is clicked.
OnCheckboxChange method	Called when a specific check box control is selected or cleared.

Member Name	Description
OnListOrComboSelectChange method	Called when a selection is made in a specific list box or combo box control.
OnPaneUpdateComplete method	Called when the Document Actions task pane has been filled with controls and all of the controls in the task pane have been initialized.
OnRadioGroupSelectChange method	Called when a selection is made in a specific option button group.
OnTextboxContentChange method	Called when text changes in a specific text box.
PopulateActiveXProps method	Specifies the initial properties of an ActiveX control displayed in the Document Actions task pane.
PopulateCheckbox method	Specifies whether a specific check box control should be initially selected or cleared.
PopulateDocumentFragment method	Defines the initial contents of a document fragment.
PopulateHelpContent method	Defines the initial contents of XHMTL-formatted content.
PopulateImage method	Determines a specific image control's initial image.
PopulateListOrComboContent method	Defines the initial item list for a specific list box control or combo box control.
PopulateOther method	Defines the initial properties of a control that does not have a specific Populate method already available, such as buttons, labels, links, and separators.
PopulateRadioGroup method	Defines the initial option list for an option button group.
PopulateTextboxContent method	Defines the initial text for a specific text box control.
SmartDocInitialize method	Called when a smart document is attached to, or loaded by, a document or workbook.
SmartDocXMLTypeCaption property (String)	Given a namespace#element name, specifies the caption at the top of the Document Actions task pane when the corresponding XML element is selected in a document or workbook is clicked.
SmartDocXMLTypeCount property (Long)	Defines how many namespace#element names in the document or workbook have controls assigned to them. Each namespace#element name is assigned a unique ID number by the Smart Document object model. ID numbers start at 1 and are incremented by one by the object model.
SmartDocXMLTypeName property (String)	Associates a unique namespace#element name with a unique ordinal number assigned by the Smart Document object model.

Smart Document Type Names

Smart documents associate XML elements with smart document actions via context sensitivity implemented via an XSD schema. Understanding how smart document type names are created is critical in developing smart document solutions. XML namespaces guarantee that the elements in an XML file have unique names. It's important to know how to create smart document type names as they are referenced quite frequently in smart document solution code. You'll sometimes see smart document type names referred to as namespace#element names to enforce this relationship.

XML elements are identified in smart documents programmatically by their unique smart document type names. At the most basic level, a smart document type name consists of a namespace, followed by the "pound" character (#), followed by the unique XML element name.

As you create namespace#element names in smart document solution code, the Smart Document object model assigns a unique number to each namespace#element name. This number is known as the smart document type ID or namespace#element ID. Just remember for now that to automate the Smart Document object model, every XML element must have a unique namespace#element name and a unique namespace#element ID.

Control Indexes and Control IDs

The code that is used to actually automate the Smart Document object model usually works by creating controls in the Document Actions task pane and associating these controls with namespace#element names. These controls are dependent upon a unique control ID. When the smart document runs, it uses the combination of namespace#element names and unique control IDs to determine which controls to display in the Document Actions task pane, as well as what the initial state of the controls should be and what happens when users interact with the controls.

The Smart Document object model assigns a non-unique control index number to each control associated with a namespace#element name. This can be deceiving because while the control index number is unique for each control for each namespace#element name, the control index number is not unique across all of the controls in the smart document solution.

This means that even though the Smart Document object model assigned the control index numbers, it can't distinguish between two controls with the index number of 2 at run time. The answer is for you to programmatically assign every control in the smart document solution a unique control ID based on some increment of the control's index number.

Input Parameters

When you begin working with smart documents, you'll notice that most of the Smart Document object model's properties and methods accept one or more duplicate input parameters. Below is a table that lists all of the input parameters in alphabetical order.

Table 13-2

Input Parameter Name	Type
ActiveXPropBag	SmartDocProperties
ApplicationName	String
Checked	Boolean
Content	String
ControlID	Long
ControlIndex	Long
Count	Long
Document	Object
DocumentFragment	String

Input Parameter Name	Type
ImageSrc	String
InitialSelected	Long
List	Array of String
LocaleID	Long
Props	ISmartDocProperties
Selected	Long
SmartDocID	Long
SmartDocName	String
SolutionPath	String
SolutionRegKeyRoot	String
Target	Object
Text	String
Value	String
XCoordinate	Long
Xml	String
YCoordinate	Long

Control Type Constants

Control IDs are associated with control types via the ControlTypeFromID property. The C_TYPE constant is used to define the various types of control types. These control types are defined in the table below in the order of their numeric values.

Table 13-3

C_TYPE Constant Name	Numeric Value	Description
C_TYPE_LINK	2	Hyperlink
C_TYPE_HELP	3	XHMTL-formatted content
C_TYPE_HELPURL	4	URL to XHMTL-formatted content
C_TYPE_SEPARATOR	5	Separator
C_TYPE_BUTTON	6	Command button
C_TYPE_LABEL	7	Label control
C_TYPE_IMAGE	8	Image control
C_TYPE_CHECKBOX	9	Check box control
C_TYPE_TEXTBOX	10	Text box control
C_TYPE_LISTBOX	11	List box control
C_TYPE_COMBO	12	Combo box control
C_TYPE_ACTIVEX	13	ActiveX control
C_TYPE_DOCUMENTFRAGMENT	14	Document fragment
C_TYPE_DOCUMENTFRAGMENTURL	15	URL to a document fragment
C_TYPE_RADIOGROUP	16	Option button

Built-In Control Properties

The methods that begin with the word "Populate" accept an argument named Props. The Props argument, as well as the ActiveXPropBag argument of the PopulateActiveXProps method, represent an ISmartDocProperties collection that contains one or more property values for a particular control. The control properties that can be set are listed in Table 13-4.

Table 13-4

Property Name	Description
Align	The value “center” causes the control to be centered, “left” places the control along the left side, and “right” places the control on the right side of the pane. The default is to be left aligned.
Border	True to display a border when the user rests the mouse pointer on the control.
ControlOnSameLine	True to display the control on the same line as the control’s caption. The default value is False.
Expand	True to expand the document fragment’s or help topic’s content in the task pane.
ExpandHelp	True to expand the help control or help URL control contents in the task pane.
ExpandToFill	A Boolean that specifies whether to expand the ActiveX control to fill the task pane.
FontFace	The font face in which to display text.
FontSize	The font size in which to display text.
FontStyle	The value “none” (the default) or one or more of “underline,” “italic,” or “strikeout.”
FontWeight	The value “normal” (the default) or “bold.”
H	The height of the control in pixels. Negative values are ignored.
IsEditable	True to edit content in combo boxes.
IsMultiLine	True to allow the text box to accept multiple lines of text, each line separated by a carriage return/line feed character.
KeepAlive	A Boolean that specifies whether the control remains active even if the context of the control changes. Although the control is kept active as long as possible, it is not guaranteed to be active when the task pane is redrawn.
Layout	The value “LTR” specifies left-to-right reading order layout, while the value “RTL” specifies right-to-left reading order layout.

Property Name	Description
NumberOfLines	The number of lines to display in a text box or the number of lines visible without scrolling in a list box or combo box.
PasswordCharacter	A single character that is used to obscure typing into the text box so that it can be used as a password field.
SectionCaptionDirection	The value "LTR" specifies left-to-right reading order section control, while the value "RTL" specifies right-to-left reading order section control.
W	The width of the control in pixels. Negative values are ignored.
X	How far from the left position, in pixels, the control should be indented. Negative values are ignored.
Y	How far below the previous control should the control, in pixels, be positioned. Negative values are ignored.

Order of Events

When a document with a smart document solution behind it is opened (or when the solution is first attached), the following events occur in the smart document DLL:

1. The SmartDocInitialize method fires. This is the area where the preliminary initialization code runs when the smart document first loads.
2. The SmartDocXMLTypeCount property determines the number of namespace#element names that have controls assigned to them.
3. The SmartDocXMLTypeName property assigns namespace#element names to namespace#element IDs.
4. The SmartDocXMLTypeCaption property sets the text header that shows up at the top of the Document Actions task pane when a specific XML element is clicked.
5. The ControlCount property indicates how many controls are available to each namespace#element name.

6. The ControlID property assigns a unique ID to each control in the smart document solution.
7. The ControlNameFromID property gives each control a unique name so that it can be referenced from the Office object model (either Excel or Word).
8. The ControlCaptionFromID property assigns a caption to each control.
9. The ControlTypeFromID property determines each control's type.
10. As the Smart Document object model adds controls to the Document Actions task pane, each respective control's specific initialization methods are fired.
11. The OnPaneUpdateComplete method is called after all controls have been added to the Document Actions task pane and all of the controls have been initialized.
12. As the user interacts with the controls in the Document Actions task pane, the Smart Document object model fires events for each of the control's specific action methods.

SmartDocInitialize Method

The SmartDocInitialize method specifies the initialization code that will run when the smart document first loads. This method takes an input parameter in the form of a document. This object allows the developer to programmatically access the active document. The SolutionPath input parameter specifies the path where the solution files were installed.

SmartDocXMLTypeCount Property

The SmartDocXMLTypeCount property specifies how many namespace#element names have controls assigned to them. The ISmartDocument interface begins assigning ID numbers at 1 and increments ID numbers by one for each namespace#element name.

SmartDocXMLTypeName Property

The SmartDocXMLTypeName property assigns namespace#element names to namespace#element IDs. This property matches each namespace#element name to an ID.

SmartDocXMLTypeCaption Property

The SmartDocXMLTypeCaption property specifies the text that will appear at the top of the Document Actions task pane when a specific XML element is clicked. This property matches up namespace#element name ID numbers with text-based captions.

ControlCount Property

The ControlCount property specifies how many controls are available to each namespace#element name. You assign numbers to namespace#element names with this property. For each respective number the ISmartDocument interface automatically creates a number.

ControlID Property

The ControlID property specifies a unique ID number for each control in the smart document solution. Each control in the smart document solution must be uniquely identifiable by a number.

ControlNameFromID Property

The ControlNameFromID property assigns a unique name to each control so that it can be referenced from the Word object model. This property allows you to match control IDs to programmatically create control alias names.

ControlCaptionFromID Property

The ControlCaptionFromID property specifies a caption for each control. The control IDs can be assigned to the control captions.

ControlTypeFromID Property

The ControlTypeFromID property specifies each control's type. The control IDs can be assigned to the various predetermined control type constants.

Creating and Using XML Expansion Pack Manifests

The XML expansion pack manifest file describes the locations and behaviors of a particular solution's component files. A solution can be composed of as little as one file up to a virtually unlimited number of files. XML expansion pack manifest files can be used to distribute virtually any type of file as part of a Word 2003 solution. Primarily, you'll be using the manifest for distributing smart document DLLs. The components of an XML manifest generally could include XSD schemas, XSLT Transforms, additional DLLs, COM add-ins, text files, and configuration files.

XML expansion pack manifest files are referenced in Word 2003 through the Templates and Add-Ins dialog box's XML Expansion Packs tab. XML expansion pack manifest files can be linked together to create XML expansion pack manifest file collections. These collections allow one XML expansion pack manifest file to reference another XML manifest. This allows for various manifest packs to be interrelated.

The basic structure of an XML expansion pack manifest file looks like this:

```
xmlns="http://schemas.microsoft.com/office/xmlexpansionpacks
/2003"
<manifest>
    <version>
    <updateFrequency>
    <uri>
    <manifestURL>
    <solution>
        <solutionID>
        <type>
        <alias>
        <documentSpecific>
        <context>
        <targetApplication>
        <file>
            <runFromServer>
            <type>
            <managed>
            <application>
            <version>
            <filePath>
            <installPath>
            <CLSID>
            <CLSNAME>
            <PROGID>
            <templateID>
            <regsvr32>
            <registry>
                <registryKey>
                    <keyName>
                    <keyValue>
                        <valueName>
                        <valueType>
                        <value>
```

The XML expansion pack manifest file elements, in the order presented, are as follows:

Table 13-5: Children of the <manifest> element

<version>	A required version number for the XML expansion pack manifest file. The version number is used during the update process to determine whether a new version should be downloaded. Version numbers must follow the format major.minor, for example, 1.0, 1.1, 2.0, and so on. Version numbers such as 1.0.0 or 1.1.4809.2003 are not allowed.
<updateFrequency>	An optional amount of time that should elapse (in minutes) between client checks to the server that look for updates.
<uri>	An optional XML namespace that is associated with the solution. By default, the predefined URI http://schemas.microsoft.com/office/otherSolution is used for XML expansion pack manifest files not tied to a particular namespace.
<manifestURL>	An optional string that specifies the location of an XML expansion pack manifest file that will be installed with the current XML expansion pack manifest file.
<solution>	The wrapper element for a single solution in the schema library. This element occurs once per solution.

Table 13-6: Children of the <solution> element

<solutionID>	A required string that uniquely identifies this solution in the schema library. It is essential that the string is unique. You must identify each solution with a globally unique identifier (GUID), which can be generated with a tool such as guidgen.exe that is included with Microsoft Visual Studio .NET.
<type>	A required string that defines the solution type. Valid values include smartDocument, schema, transform, and other (for the solution element).
<alias>	A required string that specifies the friendly name of the solution exposed to the user in the XML Expansion Packs dialog box.

<documentSpecific>	An optional Boolean value that specifies whether the solution will be available to documents with XML in the namespace (False), or only to those documents that explicitly reference it (True). The default is True for smart document solution types and False for all other solution types.
<context>	For solutions of type transform only, a required element that defines the URI of the application that can use the transform.
<targetApplication>	An optional string for solutions of type smartDocument. This element specifies the applications in which the solution is valid.
<file>	The wrapper element for information on a single file within a solution. This element can occur an unlimited number of times per solution.

Table 13-7: Children of the <file> element

<runFromServer>	This optional element tells the application to run the current file from a server location (specified in the filePath element) rather than download the file to the client.
<type>	A required string that defines the current file's type. Valid values include template (a document update file), smartTagList (a MOSTL file with smart tag elements), solutionList (a MOSTL file with smart document elements), schema (a schema file), primaryTransform (a primary transform file), secondaryTransform (a secondary transform file), actionHandler (a smart tag DLL or smart document DLL), solutionActionHandler (a smart tag DLL or smart document DLL that's only loaded when a particular solution is loaded), recognizer (a smart tag recognizer DLL or assembly), solutionRecognizer (a smart tag recognizer DLL or assembly that's only loaded when a particular solution is loaded), actionAndRecognizer (a DLL or assembly that implements both the ISmartTagAction (or ISmartTagAction2) and ISmartTagRecognizer (or ISmartTagRecognizer2) interfaces), solutionActionAnd-Recognizer (a DLL or assembly that implements both the ISmartTagAction (or ISmartTagAction2) and ISmartTagRecognizer (or ISmartTagRecognizer2) interfaces and is only loaded when a particular solution is

<type> (cont.)	loaded), COMAddIn (a COM add-in DLL), installPackage (an MSI file that will run after it's downloaded), and other (files such as images, text, and so on).
<managed>	This optional element instructs the application to use the Visual Studio Tools for Office loader to load the current file, as opposed to the traditional Office COM component loader.
<application>	This optional element, only valid for files of type COMAddIn, defines the applications in which the COM object is valid. Valid values are Word and Excel. This element can occur up to two times per file.
<version>	A required string analogous to the version for the manifest, this element determines whether the current file needs to be updated during the update procedure. Version numbers must follow the format major.minor, for example, 1.0, 1.1, 2.0, and so on.
<filePath>	A required string that indicates the location of the current file.
<installPath>	An optional string that allows you to specify a path (relative to the root path for the solution in the schema library) where the current file will be installed.
<CLSID>	For DLLs, this required element contains the class ID (CLSID). This element is used to set up the registry.
<CLSNAME>	For managed DLLs, a required string that contains the class name for managed action handlers loaded with the Visual Studio Tools for Office loader.
<PROGID>	An optional string that contains the programmatic ID (progID). This element is only valid for files of type COMAddIn.
<templateID>	A optional string for files of type template that is used to uniquely identify a template to allow it to be replaced when updating. If the XML expansion pack manifest file specifies an update frequency, this element is required, but it will only be used if the template points to an XML expansion pack manifest file that includes a file element for the template itself.
<regsvr32>	This optional element instructs the application to register the current file using revsvr32.exe. This procedure is automatic for files of type COMAddIn.

<registry>	The wrapper element for a single registry entry for either an entire solution or an individual file. This element is only required if you want to install registry entries as part of your solution.

Table 13-8: Children of the <registry> element

<registryKey>	The wrapper element for a single registry key to be written. This element can occur an unlimited number of times per registry element.
<keyName>	A required string containing the name of the registry entry to be written.
<keyValue>	An optional wrapper element for a single registry entry to be written the current key. You can use the value of $PATH to be dynamically replaced with the path to the file, or you can use the value $SolutionRoot to be dynamically replaced with the registry path to the solution root. This element can occur an unlimited number of times per registry key.
<valueName>	A required string containing the name for a registry entry.
<valueType>	A required string containing the data type for a registry entry. Valid values include REG_SZ, REG_EXPAND_SZ, and REG_DWORD.
<value>	A required string containing the actual data for a registry entry. For string values, this string is optional. An empty string (REG_SZ) or a zero (REG_DWORD) is used by default.

In addition, if an Office smart document solution is being run from a web server, both the Microsoft Internet Explorer and Office security settings will affect whether the solution will run. If an XML expansion pack manifest file is on a server that is neither on the Internet Explorer trusted sites list nor in the intranet zone, no attempt will be made to retrieve it nor will users be prompted to add the site to the Internet Explorer trusted sites list. If an XML expansion pack manifest file is on a server that is trusted or on an intranet, whether the manifest will be loaded depends on whether it is signed. If it is signed and allowed to run, it is still subject to the user's Office security settings.

During smart document solution development, you can enable or disable XML expansion pack manifest file security checking by editing the REG_DWORD value DisableManifestSecurityCheck under the registry key HKEY_LOCAL_MACHINE\Software\Microsoft\Office\Common\Smart Tag.

A value of 1 disables XML expansion pack manifest file security checking, while a value of 0 enables it. If the registry setting is set to 1 (security checking is disabled) when you try to reference an XML expansion pack manifest file, a dialog box appears, warning the user that disabling security is dangerous. It also gives you the option to reenable the XML expansion pack security checking immediately by clicking Yes. You should only set this registry value to 1 on a development machine during development of the solution (where it may be inconvenient to digitally sign each component after every build), but be sure to reenable it for the final testing of signed components. It is highly inadvisable to disable XML expansion pack manifest file security checking on user machines.

Conclusion

This chapter provided more information regarding the creation of smart documents as Word 2003 solutions. It discussed creating dynamic-link library files in a bit more detail. The chapter then reviewed all of the components of the Smart Document object model and how they can be used in your smart document solution. Smart documents are an integral part of the new Office development platform.

Appendix

Word Commands

The following table contains a complete list of the Word 2003 commands.

Note: Not every Word command is available as a menu option; some are hidden or pertain to application-level events (such as minimizing the application). The figures below are graphical depictions of the more obscure, nested menus referenced in the command table. The Standard toolbar contains the File, Edit, View, Insert, Format, Tools, Table, Window, and Help menus.

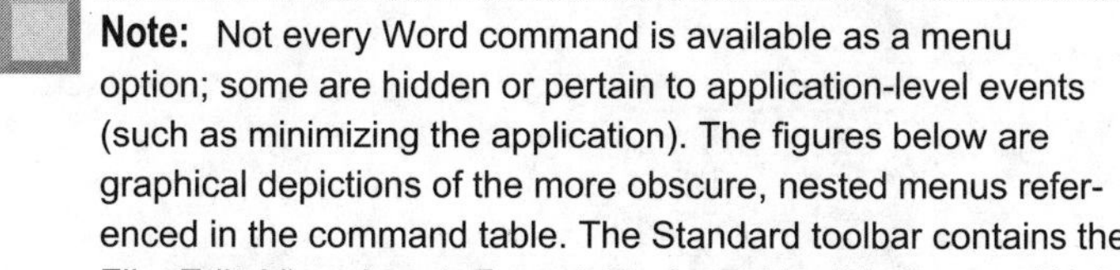

Figure 1: The Accept menu on the Reviewing toolbar

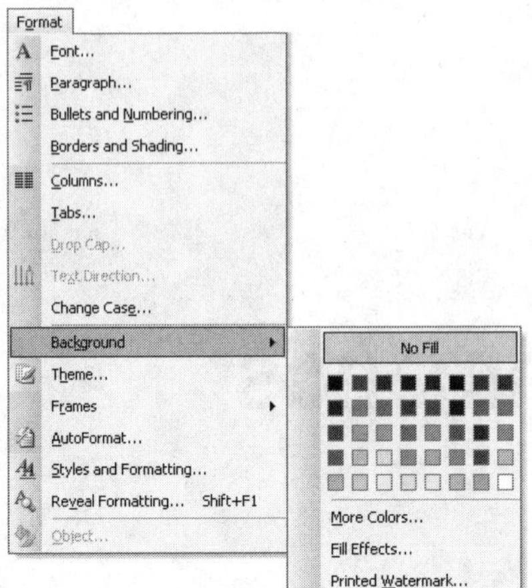

Figure 2: The Format Background submenu of the Format menu

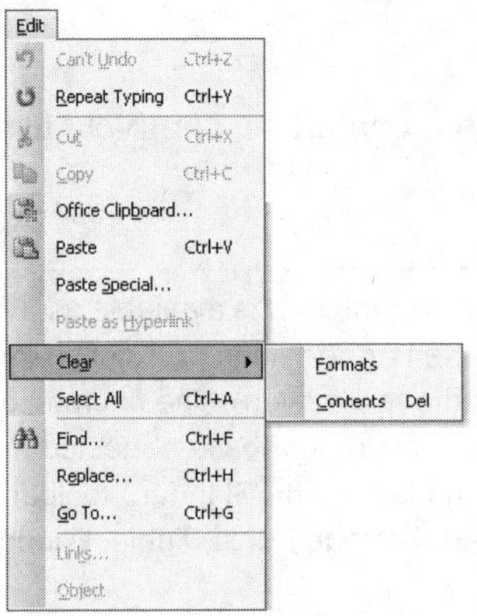

Figure 3: The Clear submenu of the Edit menu

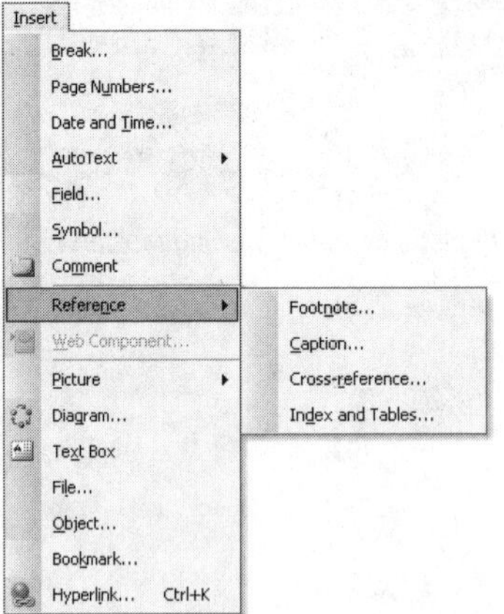

Figure 4: The Reference submenu of the Insert menu

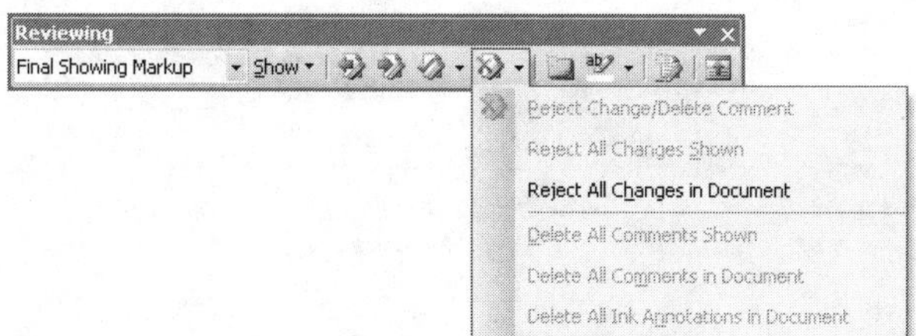

Figure 5: The Reject menu of the Reviewing toolbar

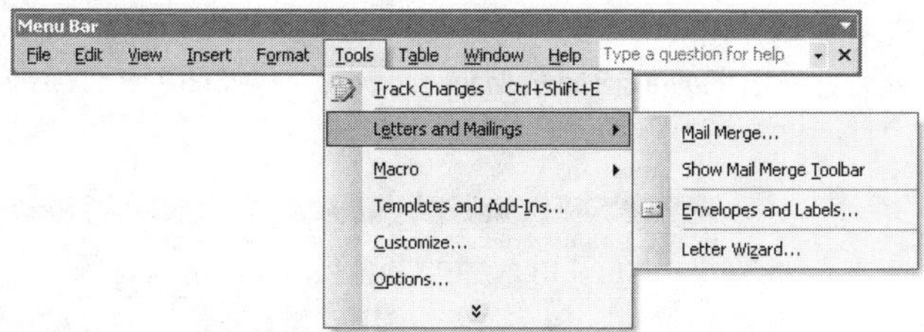

Figure 6: The Letters and Mailings submenu of the Tools menu

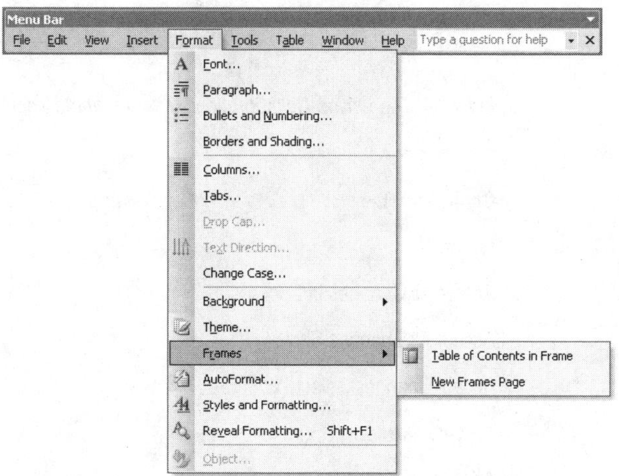

Figure 7: The Frames submenu of the Format menu

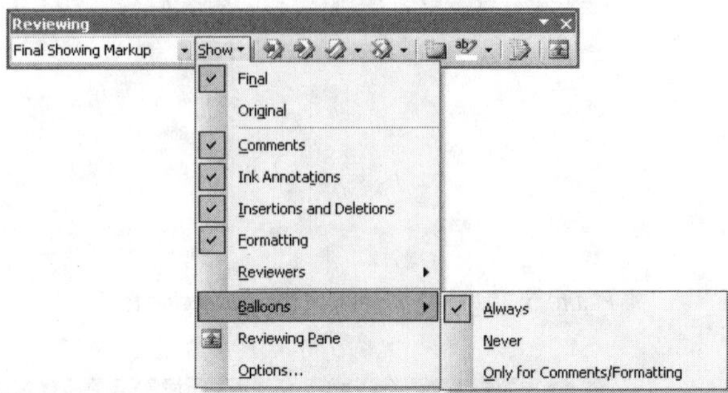

Figure 8: The Balloons submenu of the Show menu on the Reviewing toolbar

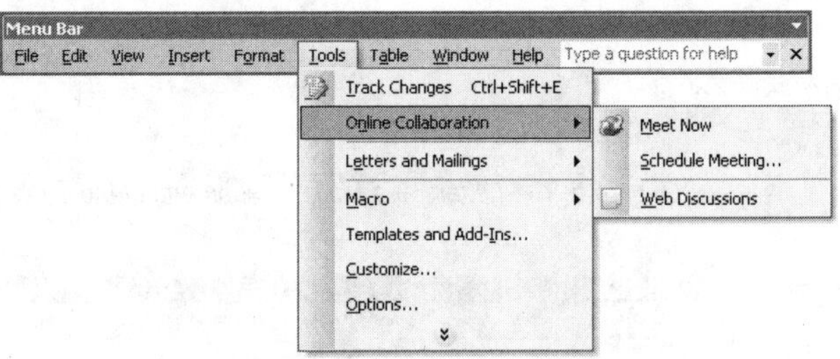

Figure 9: The Online Collaboration submenu of the Tools menu

Command Name	Key Sequence	Menu
About		Help
Accept All Changes in Doc		Accept
Accept All Changes Shown		Accept
Accept Changes Selected		
Activate Object		
Add Caption		
Add Record Default		
Add Fonts		
Address		
All Caps	Ctrl+Shift+A	
Annotation	Alt+Ctrl+M	
Annotation Edit		
Annotations		

Command Name	Key Sequence	Menu
App Maximize	Alt+F10	
App Minimize		
App Move		
App Restore	Alt+F5	
App Size		
Apply Heading1	Alt+Ctrl+1	
Apply Heading2	Alt+Ctrl+2	
Apply Heading3	Alt+Ctrl+3	
Apply List Bullet	Ctrl+Shift+L	
Arrange All		Window
Arrange Side By Side		
Auto Caption		
Auto Correct		Tools
Auto Correct Caps Lock Off		
Auto Correct Days		
Auto Correct Exceptions		
Auto Correct HECorrect		
Auto Correct Initial Caps		
Auto Correct Replace Text		
Auto Correct Sentence Caps		
Auto Correct Smart Quotes		
Auto Fit Content		
Auto Fit Fixed		
Auto Fit Window		
Auto Format	Alt+Ctrl+K	
Auto Format Begin		Format
Auto Format Style		
Auto Manager		
Auto Mark Index Entries		
Auto Scroll		

Command Name	Key Sequence	Menu
Auto Sum		
Auto Summarize		
Auto Summarize Begin		Tools
Auto Summarize Close		
Auto Summarize Percent of Original		
Auto Summarize Toggle View		
Auto Summarize Update File Properties		
Auto Text	F3	
Auto Text	Alt+Ctrl+V	
Automatic Change		
AW		
Background Fill Effect		Format Background
Background More Colors		Format Background
Background Watermark		Format Background
Bold	Ctrl+B	
Bold	Ctrl+Shift+B	
Bold Run		
Bookmark	Ctrl+Shift+F5	Insert
Bookshelf Define Reference		
Bookshelf Lookup Reference		Tools
Border All		
Border Bottom		
Border Horiz		
Border Inside		
Border Left		
Border Line Color		
Border Line Style		
Border Line Weight		
Border None		

Command Name	Key Sequence	Menu
Border Outside		
Border Right		
Border TL to BR		
Border Toolbar		
Border Top		
Border TR to BL		
Border Vert		
Borders		
Bottom Align		
Bottom Center Align		
Bottom Left Align		
Bottom Right Align		
Break		Insert
Browse Next	Ctrl+Page Down	
Browse Prev	Ctrl+Page Up	
Browse Sel	Alt+Ctrl+Home	
Bullet Default		
Bullet List Default		
Bullets and Numbering		
Bullets Numbers		
Busu		Language
Calculate		
Callout		
Cancel	Esc	
Caption		Reference
Caption Numbering		
Cell Options		
Center Align		
Center Para	Ctrl+E	
Change Byte		

Command Name	Key Sequence	Menu
Change Case		Format
Change Case	Shift+F3	
Change Case Fareast		
Change Kana		
Changes		
Char Left	Left	
Char Left Extend	Shift+Left	
Char Right	Right	
Char Right Extend	Shift+Right	
Char Scale		
Chart		
Check Box Form Field		
Check For Updates		Help
Checkin		File
Checkout		File
Clear	Del	Clear
Clear Form Field		
Clear Formatting		Clear
Close		
Close All		
Close or Close All		
Close or Exit	Alt+F4	
Close Pane	Alt+Shift+C	
Close Preview		
Close Reading Mode		
Close Up Para		
Close View Header Footer		
Code		
Color		
Column Break	Ctrl+Shift+Return	

Command Name	Key Sequence	Menu
Column Select	Ctrl+Shift+F8	
Column Width		
Columns		
Combine Characters		
Comma Accent		
Compare Versions		
Condensed		
Confirm Conversions		
Connect		
Consistency		
Consistency Check		
Contact Us		Help
Contents Arabic		
Context Help		
Continue Numbering		
Control Run		
Control Toolbox		
Convert All Endnotes		
Convert All Footnotes		
Convert Notes		
Convert Object		
Convert Text Box to Frame		
Copy	Ctrl+C	
Copy	Ctrl+Insert	
Copy As Picture		
Copy Format	Ctrl+Shift+C	
Copy Ink As Text		
Copy Text	Shift+F2	
Create Auto Text	Alt+F3	
Create Directory		

Command Name	Key Sequence	Menu
Create Envelope		
Create Labels		
Create Subdocument		
Create Table		
Create Task		
Cross Reference		Reference
Css Links		
Customize		Tools
Customize Add Menu Shortcut	Alt+Ctrl+=	
Customize Keyboard		
Customize Keyboard Shortcut	Alt+Ctrl+Num+	
Customize Menus		
Customize Remove Menu Shortcut	Alt+Ctrl+-	
Customize Toolbar		
Cut	Ctrl+X	
Cut	Shift+Del	
Database		
Date Field	Alt+Shift+D	
Date Time		Insert
Decrease Indent		
Decrease Paragraph Spacing		
Default Char Border		
Default Char Shading		
Delete All Comments in Doc		Reject
Delete All Comments Shown		Reject
Delete All Ink Annotations		Reject
Delete Annotation		
Delete Back Word	Ctrl+Backspace	

Command Name	Key Sequence	Menu
Delete Column		
Delete General		
Delete Hyperlink		
Delete Row		
Delete Style		
Delete Table		
Delete Word	Ctrl+Del	
Demote List		
Demote to Body Text		
Diacritic Color		
Dictionary		
Display Details		
Display Final Doc		Show Markup
Display For Review		
Display Original Doc		Show Markup
Display Shared Workspace Pane		Tools
Distribute Column		
Distribute General		
Distribute Para	Ctrl+Shift+J	
Distribute Row		
Do Field Click	Alt+Shift+F9	
Do Not Distribute		
Doc Close	Ctrl+W	
Doc Close	Ctrl+F4	
Doc Maximize	Ctrl+F10	
Doc Minimize		
Doc Move	Ctrl+F7	
Doc Restore	Ctrl+F5	
Doc Size	Ctrl+F8	
Doc Split	Alt+Ctrl+S	Window

Command Name	Key Sequence	Menu
Document Actions Pane		
Document Map		
Document Map Reading Mode		
Dot Accent		
Dotted Underline		
Double Strikethrough		
Double Underline	Ctrl+Shift+D	
Draft		
Draw Align		
Draw Callout		
Draw Disassemble Picture		
Draw Duplicate		
Draw Insert Word Picture		
Draw Menu Shadow Color		
Draw Menu 3D Color		
Draw Reset Word Picture		
Draw Reshape		
Draw Select Next		
Draw Select Previous		
Draw Snap to Grid		Draw
Draw Text Box		
Draw Toggle Layer		
Draw Unselect		
Draw Vertical Text Box		
Drawing		
Drawing Object		
Drawing Object Wrap Behind		
Drawing Object Wrap Front		
Drawing Object Wrap Inline		
Drawing Object Wrap None		

Command Name	Key Sequence	Menu
Drawing Object Wrap Square		
Drawing Object Wrap Through		
Drawing Object Wrap Tight		
Drawing Object Wrap Top Bottom		
Drawing Toolbar		
Drop Cap		
Drop Down Form Field		
Em Space		
Email Attachment Options		
Email Check Names		
Email Choose Account		
Email Envelope		
Email Flag		
Email Focus Introduction		
Email Focus Subject		
Email Message Options		
Email Options		
Email Save Attachment		
Email Select Bcc Names		
Email Select Cc Names		
Email Select Names		
Email Select to Names		
Email Send		
Email Signature Options		
En Space		
Enclose Characters		
End of Column	Alt+Page Down	
End of Column	Alt+Shift+Page Down	
End of Doc Extend	Ctrl+Shift+End	
End of Document	Ctrl+End	

Command Name	Key Sequence	Menu
End of Line	End	
End of Line Extend	Shift+End	
End of Row	Alt+End	
End of Row	Alt+Shift+End	
End of Window	Alt+Ctrl+Page Down	
End of Window Extend	Alt+Ctrl+Shift+Page Down	
End Review		
Endnote Area		
Endnote Cont Notice		
Endnote Cont Separator		
Endnote Now	Alt+Ctrl+D	
Endnote Separator		
Envelope Setup		
Envelope Wizard		Letters and Mailings
Envelopes and Labels		Letters and Mailings
Equation		
EServices		
Excel Table		
Exit		File
Expanded		
Extend Selection	F8	
Fax Service		Send To
Field		Insert
Field Chars	Ctrl+F9	
Field Codes	Alt+F9	
File		
Fill Color		
Find	Ctrl+F	
Find Reading Mode		
Fit Text		

Command Name	Key Sequence	Menu
Fix Broken Text		Tools
Fix Me		Help
Font	Ctrl+D	
Font	Ctrl+Shift+F	
Font Color		
Font Size		
Font Size Select	Ctrl+Shift+P	
Font Substitution		
Footer		
Footnote		Reference
Footnote Area		
Footnote Cont Notice		
Footnote Cont Separator		
Footnote Now	Alt+Ctrl+F	
Footnote Separator		
Footnotes		View
Form Field		
Form Field Options		
Form Shading		
Format Cell		
Format Ex Toolbar		
Formatting Pane		
Formatting Properties	Shift+F1	Format
Formatting Restrictions		
Formula		Table
Frame		
Frame or Frame Picture		
Frame Properties		
Frame Remove Split		
Frame Split Above		

Command Name	Key Sequence	Menu
Frame Split Below		
Frame Split Left		
Frame Split Right		
Frameset TOC		
Frameset Wizard		Frames
Getting Started Pane		
Go Back	Shift+F5	
Go Back	Alt+Ctrl+Z	
Go To	Ctrl+G	Edit
Go To	F5	Edit
Go to Header Footer		
Go to Next Comment		
Go to Next Endnote		
Go to Next Footnote		
Go to Next Page		
Go to Next Section		
Go to Previous Comment		
Go to Previous Endnote		
Go to Previous Footnote		
Go to Previous Page		
Go to Previous Section		
Goto Comment Scope		
Goto Next Linked Text Box		
Goto Prev Linked Text Box		
Goto Table of Contents		
Gram Settings		
Grammar		
Grammar Hide		
Graphical Horizontal Line		
Greeting Sentence		

Command Name	Key Sequence	Menu
Gridlines		
Grow Font	Ctrl+Shift+.	
Grow Font One Point	Ctrl+]	
Hanging Indent	Ctrl+T	
Hanja Dictionary		
Header		View
Header Footer Link	Alt+Shift+R	
Heading Numbering		
Headings		Table
Help	F1	
HHC	Alt+Ctrl+F7	Language
Hidden	Ctrl+Shift+H	
Highlight		
Horizontal in Vertical		
Horizontal Line		
HTMLBGSound		
HTMLCheck Box		
HTMLDropdown Box		
HTMLHidden		
HTMLImage Submit		
HTMLList Box		
HTMLMarquee		
HTMLMovie		
HTMLOption Button		
HTMLPassword		
HTMLReset		
HTMLSource		View
HTMLSource Do Not Refresh		
HTMLSource Refresh		
HTMLSubmit		

Command Name	Key Sequence	Menu
HTMLText Area		
HTMLText Box		
Hyperlink	Ctrl+K	
Hyperlink Open		
Hyphenation		Language
Hyphenation Manual		
Ichitaro Help		
Ignore All Consistence Error		
Ignore Consistence Error		
IMEControl		
IMEReconversion		
Increase Indent		
Increase Paragraph Spacing		
Indent	Ctrl+M	
Indent Char		
Indent First Char		
Indent First Line		
Indent Line		
Index		
Index and Tables		Reference
Ink Annotations		
Ink Comment		
Ink Split Menu		
Insert Column		
Insert Column Right		
Insert General		
Insert Row		
Insert Row Above		
Insert Row Below		
Insert Script		

Command Name	Key Sequence	Menu
Italic	Ctrl+I	
Italic	Ctrl+Shift+I	
Italic Run		
Japanese Greeting Closing Sentence		
Japanese Greeting Opening Sentence		
Japanese Greeting Previous Greeting		
Justify Para	Ctrl+J	
Label Options		
Language		Language
Learn Words		
Left Para	Ctrl+L	
Letter Properties		Letters and Mailings
Letter Wizard		Letters and Mailings
Letters Wizard JToolbar		
License Verification		
Line Color		
Line Down	Down	
Line Down Extend	Shift+Down	
Line Spacing		
Line Up	Up	
Line Up Extend	Shift+Up	
Links		Edit
List		
List Commands		
List Indent		
List Num Field	Alt+Ctrl+L	
List Outdent		
Lock Document		

Command Name	Key Sequence	Menu
Lock Fields	Ctrl+3	
Lock Fields	Ctrl+F11	
Lowered		
Ltr Para		
Ltr Run		
LTRMacro Dialogs		
Macro	Alt+F8	
Magnifier		
Mail As HTML		
Mail As Plain Text		
Mail As RTF		
Mail Check Names		
Mail Hide Message Header		
Mail Merge		
Mail Merge Address Block		
Mail Merge Ask to Convert Chevrons		
Mail Merge Check	Alt+Shift+K	
Mail Merge Convert Chevrons		
Mail Merge Create Data Source		
Mail Merge Create Header Source		
Mail Merge Create List		
Mail Merge Data Form		
Mail Merge Edit Address Block		
Mail Merge Edit Data Source	Alt+Shift+E	
Mail Merge Edit Greeting Line		
Mail Merge Edit Header Source		
Mail Merge Edit List		

Command Name	Key Sequence	Menu
Mail Merge Edit Main Document		
Mail Merge Field Mapping		
Mail Merge Find Entry		
Mail Merge Find Record		
Mail Merge First Record		
Mail Merge Go to Record		
Mail Merge Greeting Line		
Mail Merge Helper		
Mail Merge Insert Ask		
Mail Merge Insert Fields		
Mail Merge Insert Fill In		
Mail Merge Insert If		
Mail Merge Insert Merge Rec		
Mail Merge Insert Merge Seq		
Mail Merge Insert Next		
Mail Merge Insert Next If		
Mail Merge Insert Set		
Mail Merge Insert Skip If		
Mail Merge Last Record		
Mail Merge Next Record		
Mail Merge Open Data Source		
Mail Merge Open Header Source		
Mail Merge Prev Record		
Mail Merge Propagate Label		
Mail Merge Query Options		
Mail Merge Recipients		
Mail Merge Reset		

Command Name	Key Sequence	Menu
Mail Merge Set Document Type		
Mail Merge Shade Fields		
Mail Merge to Doc	Alt+Shift+N	
Mail Merge to EMail		
Mail Merge to Fax		
Mail Merge to Printer	Alt+Shift+M	
Mail Merge Toolbar		Letters and Mailings
Mail Merge Use Address Book		
Mail Merge View Data		
Mail Merge Wizard		Letters and Mailings
Mail Message Delete		
Mail Message Forward		
Mail Message Move		
Mail Message Next		
Mail Message Previous		
Mail Message Properties		
Mail Message Reply		
Mail Message Reply All		
Mail Select Names		
Manage Fields		
Mark Citation	Alt+Shift+I	
Mark Index Entry	Alt+Shift+X	
Mark Table of Contents Entry	Alt+Shift+O	
Master Document		
Menu Mode	F10	
Menu Org Chart Insert		
Merge Cells		
Merge Field	Alt+Shift+F	
Merge Revisions		Tools

Command Name	Key Sequence	Menu
Merge Split General		
Merge Subdocument		
Microsoft Access		
Microsoft Excel		
Microsoft Fox Pro		
Microsoft Mail		
Microsoft On The Web1		
Microsoft On The Web10		
Microsoft On The Web11		
Microsoft On The Web12		
Microsoft On The Web13		
Microsoft On The Web14		
Microsoft On The Web15		
Microsoft On The Web16		
Microsoft On The Web17		
Microsoft On The Web2		
Microsoft On The Web3		
Microsoft On The Web4		
Microsoft On The Web5		
Microsoft On The Web6		
Microsoft On The Web7		
Microsoft On The Web8		
Microsoft On The Web9		
Microsoft Power Point		
Microsoft Project		
Microsoft Publisher		
Microsoft Schedule		
Microsoft Script Editor	Alt+Shift+F11	
Microsoft System Info	Alt+Ctrl+F1	
Middle Center Align		

Command Name	Key Sequence	Menu
Middle Left Align		
Middle Right Align		
MMEmail Options		
MMFax Options		
MMNew Doc Options		
MMPrint Options		
Move Text	F2	
Multilevel Default		
Never Use Balloons		Balloons
New		File
New Comment		
New Context		
New Default	Ctrl+N	
New Dialog		
New Email		
New Print		
New Toolbar		
New Web		
New Window		Window
Next Cell	Tab	
Next Change or Comment		
Next Field	F11	
Next Field	Alt+F1	
Next Insert		
Next Misspelling	Alt+F7	
Next Object	Alt+Down	
Next Page		
Next Window	Ctrl+F6	
Next Window	Alt+F6	
No Insertion Deletion Balloons		Balloons

Command Name	Key Sequence	Menu
Normal	Alt+Ctrl+N	View
Normal Font Position		
Normal Font Spacing		
Normal Style	Ctrl+Shift+N	
Normal Style	Alt+Shift+Clear (Num 5)	
Normal View Header Area		
Normal.NewMacros.Macro1		
Normal.NewMacros.Macro2		
Normalize Text		
Note Options		
Number		Insert
Number Default		
Number List Default		
Number of Pages		
Object		Insert
OCX		
OCXButton		
OCXCheckbox		
OCXDropdown Combo		
OCXFrame		
OCXImage		
OCXLabel		
OCXList Box		
OCXOption Button		
OCXScrollbar		
OCXSpin		
OCXText Box		
OCXToggle Button		
Office Clipboard		Edit
Office Drawing		

Command Name	Key Sequence	Menu
Office On The Web		Help
OK		
Online		
Online Meeting		Online Collaboration
Open	Ctrl+O	
Open	Ctrl+F12	
Open	Alt+Ctrl+F2	
Open File		
Open or Close Up Para	Ctrl+0	
Open Subdocument		
Open Up Para		
Options		Tools
Options Auto Format		
Options Auto Format As You Type		
Options Bidi		
Options Compatibility		
Options Edit		
Options Edit Copy Paste		
Options File Locations		
Options Fuzzy		
Options General		
Options Grammar		
Options HHC		
Options Print		
Options Revisions		
Options Save		
Options Security		
Options Smart Tag		
Options Spelling		
Options Typography		

Command Name	Key Sequence	Menu
Options User Info		
Options View		
Organizer		
Other Pane	F6	
Other Pane	Shift+F6	
Outline	Alt+Ctrl+O	
Outline Collapse	Alt+Shift+-	
Outline Collapse	Alt+Shift+Num -	
Outline Demote	Alt+Shift+Right	
Outline Expand	Alt+Shift+=	
Outline Expand	Alt+Shift+Num +	
Outline Level		
Outline Master		View
Outline Move Down	Alt+Shift+Down	
Outline Move Up	Alt+Shift+Up	
Outline Promote	Alt+Shift+Left	
Outline Promote Heading1		
Outline Show First Line	Alt+Shift+L	
Outline Show Format		
Outline Split Toolbar		
Overtype	Insert	
Page	Alt+Ctrl+P	View
Page Break	Ctrl+Return	
Page Down	Page Down	
Page Down Extend	Shift+Page Down	
Page Field	Alt+Shift+P	
Page Number		
Page Numbers		Insert
Page Setup		
Page Up	Page Up	

Command Name	Key Sequence	Menu
Page Up Extend	Shift+Page Up	
Para Down	Ctrl+Down	
Para Down Extend	Ctrl+Shift+Down	
Para Keep Lines Together		
Para Keep With Next		
Para Page Break Before		
Para Up	Ctrl+Up	
Para Up Extend	Ctrl+Shift+Up	
Para Widow Orphan Control		
Paragraph		
Paste	Ctrl+V	
Paste	Shift+Insert	
Paste Append Table		
Paste As Hyperlink		Edit
Paste As Nested Table		
Paste Format	Ctrl+Shift+V	
Paste from Excel		
Paste Option		
Paste Special		Edit
Pause Recorder		
Permission		File
Phonetic Guide		
Picture		
Picture Bullet		
Picture Edit		
Post		Send To
Postcard Wizard		Letters and Mailings
Present It		Send To
Prev Cell	Shift+Tab	
Prev Field	Shift+F11	

Command Name	Key Sequence	Menu
Prev Field	Alt+Shift+F1	
Prev Object	Alt+Up	
Prev Page		
Prev Window	Ctrl+Shift+F6	
Prev Window	Alt+Shift+F6	
Previous Change or Comment		
Print	Ctrl+P	
Print	Ctrl+Shift+F12	
Print Default		
Print Preview	Ctrl+F2	
Print Preview	Alt+Ctrl+I	
Print Preview Full Screen		
Print Setup		
Promote List		
Proofing	F7	
Properties		File
Protect		Tools
Protect Form		
Protect Unprotect Document		
PSSHelp		
Raised		
Reading Mode		
Reading Mode Grow Font		
Reading Mode Ink Off		
Reading Mode Layout		View
Reading Mode Lookup		
Reading Mode Mini		
Reading Mode Pageview		
Reading Mode Shrink Font		
Record Macro Start		

Command Name	Key Sequence	Menu
Record Macro Stop		
Record Macro Toggle		Macro
Redefine Style		
Redo	Alt+Shift+Backspace	
Redo or Repeat	Ctrl+Y	
Redo or Repeat	F4	
Redo or Repeat	Alt+Return	
Redo or Repeat		Edit
Reject All Changes in Doc		Reject
Reject All Changes Shown		Reject
Reject Changes Selected		
Remove All Scripts		
Remove Bullets Numbers		
Remove Cell Partition		
Remove Frames		
Remove Record Default		
Remove Subdocument		
Rename Style		
Repaginate		
Repeat Find	Shift+F4	
Repeat Find	Alt+Ctrl+Y	
Replace	Ctrl+H	
Replace		Edit
Research		
Research Lookup	Ctrl+Shift+O	
Reset Char	Ctrl+Space	
Reset Char	Ctrl+Shift+Z	
Reset Form Field		
Reset Note Sep or Notice		
Reset Para	Ctrl+Q	

Command Name	Key Sequence	Menu
Reset Side By Side		
Restart Numbering		
Ret Addr Fonts		
Return Review		
Review Revisions		
Reviewing Pane		
Revision Marks Accept		
Revision Marks Next		
Revision Marks Prev		
Revision Marks Reject		
Revision Marks Toggle	Ctrl+Shift+E	
Revisions		
Right Para	Ctrl+R	
Routing Slip		Send To
Row Height		
Rtl Para		
Rtl Run		
RTLMacro Dialogs		
Ruler		
Run Print Manager		
Run Toggle		
Save	Ctrl+S	
Save	Shift+F12	
Save	Alt+Shift+F2	
Save All		
Save As	F12	
Save As		File
Save As Web Page		File
Save Frame As		
Save Html		

Command Name	Key Sequence	Menu
Save Template		
Save Version		
Schedule Meeting		Online Collaboration
Screen Refresh		
SCTCTranslate		
Search		File
Section Break		
Section Layout		
Security		
Select All	Ctrl+A	
Select All	Ctrl+Clear (Num 5)	
Select All		Edit
Select Cell		Edit
Select Column		
Select Cur Alignment		
Select Cur Color		
Select Cur Font		
Select Cur Indent		
Select Cur Spacing		
Select Cur Tabs		
Select Drawing Objects		
Select Number		
Select Row		
Select Similar Formatting		
Select Table	Alt+Clear (Num 5)	
Send For Review		Send To
Send Mail		
Send to Fax		Send To
Send to Online Meeting Participants		Send To
Sent Left		

Command Name	Key Sequence	Menu
Sent Left Extend		
Sent Right		
Sent Right Extend		
Set Drawing Defaults		
Shading		
Shading Color		
Shading Pattern		
Show Add Ins XDialog		
Show All	Ctrl+Shift+8	
Show All Consistency		
Show All Headings	Alt+Shift+A	
Show Changes and Comments		
Show Comments		Show Markup
Show Consistency		
Show Formatting		Show Markup
Show Heading1	Alt+Shift+1	
Show Heading2	Alt+Shift+2	
Show Heading3	Alt+Shift+3	
Show Heading4	Alt+Shift+4	
Show Heading5	Alt+Shift+5	
Show Heading6	Alt+Shift+6	
Show Heading7	Alt+Shift+7	
Show Heading8	Alt+Shift+8	
Show Heading9	Alt+Shift+9	
Show Hide		Help
Show Ink Annotations		Show Markup
Show Insertions and Deletions		Show Markup
Show Level		
Show Me		

Command Name	Key Sequence	Menu
Show Next Header Footer		
Show Para		
Show Prev Header Footer		
Show Property Browser		
Show Repairs		
Show Script Anchor		
Show Signatures		Tools
Show Sm Pane		
Shrink Font	Ctrl+Shift+,	
Shrink Font One Point	Ctrl+[	
Shrink Selection	Shift+F8	
Shrink to Fit		
Sign Out of Passport		File
Simple Number Default		
Skip Numbering		
Small Caps	Ctrl+Shift+K	
Sort		Table
Sort A To Z		
Sort Z To A		
Sound		
Sound Comment		
Space Para1	Ctrl+1	
Space Para15	Ctrl+5	
Space Para2	Ctrl+2	
Speech		Tools
Spell Selection		
Spelling		
Spelling Hide		
Spelling Recheck Document		
Spike	Ctrl+Shift+F3	

Command Name	Key Sequence	Menu
Spike	Ctrl+F3	
Split		Table
Split Cells		
Split Subdocument		
Sqm Dialog		Help
Start of Column	Alt+Page Up	
Start of Column	Alt+Shift+Page Up	
Start of Doc Extend	Ctrl+Shift+Home	
Start of Document	Ctrl+Home	
Start of Line	Home	
Start of Line Extend	Shift+Home	
Start of Row	Alt+Home	
Start of Row	Alt+Shift+Home	
Start of Window	Alt+Ctrl+Page Up	
Start of Window Extend	Alt+Ctrl+Shift+Page Up	
Status Bar		
Strikethrough		
Style	Ctrl+Shift+S	
Style By Example		
Style Gallery		
Style Modify		
Style Separator	Alt+Ctrl+Return	
Style Visibility		
Subdocument		
Subscript	Ctrl+=	
Summary Info		
Superscript	Ctrl+Shift+=	
Swap All Notes		
Symbol		Insert
Symbol Font	Ctrl+Shift+Q	

Command Name	Key Sequence	Menu
Sync Scroll Side By Side		
Table of Authorities		
Table of Contents		
Table of Figures		
Tabs		Format
Task Pane	Ctrl+F1	
TCSCTranslate		
TCSCTranslation		
Templates		Tools
Text Box Linking		
Text Box Unlinking		
Text Flow		
Text Form Field		
Theme		Format
Thesaurus		
Thesaurus RR	Shift+F7	Language
Time Field	Alt+Shift+T	
Tip of The Day		
To or from Text		
TOACategory		
Toggle Character Code	Alt+X	
Toggle Field Display	Shift+F9	
Toggle Forms Design		
Toggle Full		
Toggle Header Footer Link		
Toggle Main Text Layer		
Toggle Master Document		
Toggle Master Subdocs	Ctrl+\	
Toggle Page Boundaries		
Toggle Portrait		

Command Name	Key Sequence	Menu
Toggle Reading Mode Help		
Toggle Reading Mode Ink		
Toggle Reading Mode2 Pages		
Toggle Scribble Mode		
Toggle Text Flow		
Toggle Thumbnail		
Toggle Web Design		
Toggle XMLTag View	Ctrl+Shift+X	
Tool		
Toolbars		View
Top Align		
Top Center Align		
Top Left Align		
Top Right Align		
Translate		
Translate Chinese		
Translate Pane	Alt+Shift+F7	
Translate Pane		Language
Two Lines in One		
Txbx Autosize		
Un Hang	Ctrl+Shift+T	
Un Indent	Ctrl+Shift+M	
Un Indent Char		
Un Indent First Char		
Un Indent First Line		
Un Indent Line		
Underline	Ctrl+U	
Underline	Ctrl+Shift+U	
Underline Color		
Underline Style		

Command Name	Key Sequence	Menu
Undo	Ctrl+Z	
Undo	Alt+Backspace	
Unlink Fields	Ctrl+6	
Unlink Fields	Ctrl+Shift+F9	
Unlock Fields	Ctrl+4	
Unlock Fields	Ctrl+Shift+F11	
Update Auto Format	Alt+Ctrl+U	
Update Fields	F9	
Update Fields	Alt+Shift+U	
Update IMEDic		
Update Source	Ctrl+Shift+F7	
Update Table of Contents		
Update Toc		
Update Toc Full		
Use Balloons		Balloons
Using Help		
VBCode	Alt+F11	
Versions		File
Versions Server		Version History
Vertical Frame		
Web		View
Web Add Hyperlnk to Favorites		
Web Add to Favorites		
Web Address		
Web Component		Insert
Web Copy Hyperlink		
Web Go Back	Alt+Left	
Web Go Forward	Alt+Right	
Web Hide Toolbars		
Web Open Favorites		

Command Name	Key Sequence	Menu
Web Open Hyperlink		
Web Open in New Window		
Web Open Search Page		
Web Open Start Page		
Web Options		
Web Page Preview		File
Web Refresh		
Web Select Hyperlink		
Web Stop Loading		
Web Toolbar		
Web Toolbox		
Wizard		Table
Word Count		Tools
Word Count List	Ctrl+Shift+G	
Word Count Recount	Ctrl+Shift+R	
Word Left	Ctrl+Left	
Word Left Extend	Ctrl+Shift+Left	
Word Perfect Help		Help
Word Perfect Help Options		
Word Right	Ctrl+Right	
Word Right Extend	Ctrl+Shift+Right	
Word Underline	Ctrl+Shift+W	
Wrap Boundary		
Wrapping		
WW7_ Decrease Indent		
WW7_ Draw Text Box		
WW7_ Draw Vertical Text Box		
WW7_ Format Drawing Object		
WW7_ Increase Indent		
WW7_ Tools Options		

Command Name	Key Sequence	Menu
XMLDocument		
XMLOptions		
XMLStructure		
Zoom		
Zoom Page Width		
Zoom Whole Page		
Zoom100		
Zoom200		
Zoom75		

Index

T

Z